# *DECISION SUPPORT SYSTEMS:*

## CURRENT PRACTICE AND
## CONTINUING CHALLENGES

*TO CAROL*

# SERIES FOREWORD

This is the third book in the Addison-Wesley Series on Decision Support. The series aims at establishing a concept of the application of interactive technologies to management decision making through the development of tools that

    address nonstructured rather than structured tasks;

    support rather than replace judgment;

    focus on effectiveness rather than efficiency in decision processes.

The label "decision support" was chosen for the series to emphasize the end to which a decision support system (DSS) is a potential means. The term serves to highlight the need for concepts and methodologies to exploit any available technology. Decision support is therefore to a large extent the discipline of studying individual and organizational decision processes in order to

    identify design criteria for tools that can help improve their effectiveness;

    develop techniques and approaches for evolving a DSS as the user with the designer learns through system development and system use;

    observe the use and impact of a DSS in order to define better strategies for decision support;

    assess the opportunities and constraints for Decision Support in available and emerging management and information processing technologies.

Alter's book complements the earlier books in the series through its broad mapping of the use of computer systems in managerial tasks, across a range of organizations, types of decision situations and system architectures. He provides a rich exploration of "key issues related to the success" of systems efforts. As with the other two books in the series—*Decision Support Systems: An Organizational Perspective*, by Keen and Scott Morton, and *Electronic Meetings: Technical Alternatives and Social Choices*, by Johansen, Vallee, and Spangler—Alter's analysis does not isolate technical issues from behavioral ones, or vice versa. Some of the systems he describes are not decision support systems as defined by most workers in the field. His survey, however, is explicitly designed to help sharpen definitions, challenge assumptions, and draw attention to the diversity of factors that need to be considered when we attempt to define a DSS.

In the course of the last two to three years, the term "decision support systems" has moved rapidly toward becoming a cliché, and DSS may be one of the fads of the next few years. This phenomenon reflects in part a groping and a sense of frustration among both researchers and practitioners in the applied areas of Management Information Systems, Management Science, and Operations Research. We have far more technology than we can use; the current state of the art in modeling techniques, software methods, and analytic approaches to decision making is far in advance of organizations' ability to translate them into tools that are useful, useable, and used. Practitioners and managers complain about the lack of realism among researchers in these fields; the latter in turn find alarming the gap between what can be and what is. To a certain extent both practitioners and researchers therefore are all too willing to embrace a new label that might give them a fresh start and help erase the memory of past failures. However, there is at the same time an increasing recognition that the concept of decision support may help bridge the gap between theory and practice. The notion of support itself redefines criteria for design, methods for implementation, and system development objectives in a way that should make more sense to managers. It also suggests more effective strategies for applying the potentially valuable tools and skills of technical specialists in a fashion that they find both challenging and meaningful.

The new interest in DSS naturally focuses on systems rather than support. That said, there is a new momentum in research as well as practice. Jean-Claude Courbon and his colleagues at the University of Grenoble have defined "evolutive" design techniques for DSS that have been tested out in a variety of settings. David Ness at Wharton has similarly developed "middle-out" strategies for DSS development. He has also used a decision support approach for office automation. Ness's work thus illustrates a central theme in this series: the relevance of decision support as a framework for exploiting new technologies.

As Alter's survey implies, it is not at all easy to define a DSS or to provide a precise conceptual base. Like many rallying cries, decision support systems are intuitively clear as a concept but elusive to pin down and to evaluate. "Distributed processing" and "office automation" similarly lack clear definitions. Although this does not impede their practical application, it hinders the development of a set of clear, precise, and reliable principles and methods that can guide their application. Computer technology all too often creates a mismatch between claims and outcome when rallying cry is not based on sound frameworks. One aim of this series is to provide such a base for DSS, and Alter's book is one means toward this end.

*June 1979*                                                                 Peter G. W. Keen
                                                                            Charles B. Stabell

Ever since "management information system" replaced "electronic data processing system" as the popular term denoting computer applications in business, computer-aided decision making in organizations has been the object of high hopes, much speculation, and a great deal of frustration. Although the computer industry has enjoyed remarkable success in transforming the way business transactions and data are processed, MIS and management science professionals have been disappointed by the relatively limited use of these systems for managerial decision making.

In the 1970s, "decision support systems" emerged as a new, practical approach for applying computers and information to the decision problems faced by management. Although the term "decision support system" bears many additional connotations, the principal tenets of this approach are

- that these systems can be designed specifically to facilitate decision processes (as opposed to making clerical transaction processing more efficient),
- that these systems should support rather than automate decision making, and
- that these systems should be able to respond quickly to the changing needs of decision makers.

The recent surge of interest in decision support systems underscores the fact that much progress has been made, but that the search continues for better ways to address the real needs of decision makers.

This book is based on a large-scale study concerning the development and operation of decision support systems in organizations. The purpose of the study was to map out key issues related to the success of the systems. The study revealed a diversity of types of decision support systems and a wide range of usage and development patterns. Accordingly, instead of taking a dogmatic position on "how to guarantee successful decision support systems," this book emphasizes the choices that are available to developers and users of these systems. Although it cites related research, the book is primarily empirical, and it is strongly oriented toward implementation in organizations rather than toward technology. It balances eight case studies with eight survey-oriented chapters. The case studies provide the reader with a context and intuitive feeling for how decision support systems operate in organizations. The chapters provide overviews from particular viewpoints, such as types of systems, types of implementation patterns, types of difficulties encountered, and so on.

The book can be used for a wide range of purposes. MIS and management science professionals can use it as a source of ideas concerning design choices and implementation strategies. The chapters on types of systems and implementation risk analysis have proved especially valuable for this purpose. Business schools can use the book in a number of ways as a text for courses ranging from introductions to information systems through seminars in management science. In an introductory course, it can provide the students with a solid appreciation of how computer systems are being used to aid in decision making in business. Such use in an introductory course allows business students to learn about computer applications and their implementation without being deluged by details of technology that often lack interest for generalists. In a course on decision support systems, it can be used as the primary text and can be supplemented by research-related articles. It can also be used in conjunction with Keen and Scott Morton's *Decision Support Systems: An Organizational Perspective,* which takes a more conceptual approach. Finally, it can be used to provide an implementation-oriented component within the largely technical curriculum for computer system and management science specialists. In this form, the book can be used to help balance the often noted one-sidedness of strictly technical curricula for technical specialists.

## ACKNOWLEDGMENTS

Many individuals have generously contributed to this book. Most of these people—well over 100 of them—will remain anonymous in these acknowledgments. They are the system implementers and users who were interviewed in the course of the research on which the book is based. Without their help and willingness to share and explain their experiences, the book could not have been written.

Since this book is an outgrowth of my Ph.D. thesis, warm personal thanks must go to my thesis committee for their assistance and patience throughout that effort. Michael Scott Morton introduced me to the general area of decision support systems. His help and enthusiasm throughout and especially his willingness to endure a great deal of thrashing during the early stages of this research are certainly appreciated. John Little played an important role in the period during which the research took shape. His well-focused skepticism and methodological suggestions helped me decide how to proceed and helped me understand what I was and was not doing. Peter Keen served admirably as thesis chairman. In addition to providing detailed and thoughtful comments and criticism concerning each stage of the research and each draft of the thesis, he was a friend, advisor, and source of encouragement throughout.

I would like to thank M.I.T.'s Center for Information Systems Research and Sloan School of Management for financial support, without which the research could not have been undertaken.

I also want to thank Peter Keen and Charles Stabell, contributing editors of Addison Wesley's series in Decision Support, for their guidance and comments on early drafts of the manuscript. They played a vital role in helping to shape the final product.

Although many secretaries helped in typing parts of the manuscript, which was developed through what will later be called an "evolutionary process," special thanks must go to Chris Kutchinski, who typed the bulk of it, and also to Ann Morzov. Both Chris and Ann displayed a highly appreciated ability and willingness to get it right the first time.

Finally, I would like to thank my wife, Carol. Fortunately for our marriage, she did not have to endure most of the initial effort in the writing and therefore missed the opportunity to play the clichéd role of the long-suffering, martyred wife. Wait till next time.

*San Francisco*                                              S. A.
*June 1979*

# CONTENTS

CHAPTER **ONE**

Over the last several decades, there has been much speculation about the role of computers in management. Predictions that computers would take over many management functions encouraged counterclaims that computers could have only minimal impact since most management functions cannot be automated. The experience to date has fallen between these two extremes. Although very few management functions have been automated, advances in information retrieval, processing, and display technologies have certainly led to significant computer applications that help *people* perform management functions. Since the purpose of these systems is to *support* managers responsible for making and implementing decisions rather than to *replace* them, these applications are often called decision support systems (DSS).

It is possible to support managerial activities in many ways. Some DSSs help managers by expediting access to information that would otherwise be unavailable; others contain explicit models that provide structure for particular decisions. Some DSSs are primarily tools for individuals working more or less in isolation; others serve primarily to facilitate communication among people or organizational units whose work must be coordinated.

This is a book about decision support systems. It is based on two premises: (1) Decision support systems differ in many ways from the computerized data processing systems that have become commonplace in business and government. (2) Decision support systems constitute a significant current frontier in the application of computers. This book does not presume to answer all possible questions about an application area that is only now emerging from its infancy. Instead, its purpose is to teach and inform by providing a sampling and interpretation of the state of the art. This will be accomplished through a series of case studies plus discussions of some of the significant issues in current practice.

Figure 1 attempts to summarize some of the main distinctions between DSSs and the electronic data processing (EDP) systems that have become essential for the efficient operation of large-scale business and government enterprises. The main difference between DSS and EDP systems is in their basic purposes. EDP systems are designed to expedite and/or automate transaction processing, record keeping, and business reporting; DSSs are designed to aid in decision making and decision implementation. Note, however, that as Fig. 1 indicates, EDP systems and DSSs are by no means mutually exclusive. In fact, decision-oriented reporting systems often grow out of standard EDP systems that were initially developed mainly to improve efficiency in transaction processing and/or record keeping. Instead of belaboring the

1

degree of overlap or nonoverlap between DSSs and EDP systems, we will simply concentrate on systems designed primarily to help people make decisions.

The types of systems to be emphasized here also differ from standard EDP systems in the manner in which they are used and the types of benefits that are sought through their use. Unlike the EDP user, who receives standard reports on a periodic basis, the DSS user typically initiates each instance of system use, either directly or through a staff intermediary. Although most DSSs are used to facilitate line management, planning, or staff activities, EDP systems emphasize intrinsically clerical activities. Whereas the general orientation of EDP systems is toward mechanical efficiency, that of DSSs is more toward the overall effectiveness of individuals and organizations. EDP systems usually consolidate and report information about the past; many DSSs focus on the present and the future. Consistency is surely significant in any computerized system, but DSSs also place major emphasis on flexibility and ad hoc utilization.

The differences between DSSs and EDP systems are encapsulated in their underlying philosophies. Oversimplifying a bit, we can say that the basic philosophy of most EDP systems is to automate the storage and retrieval of data, thereby reducing costs, improving accuracy, and allowing quicker access to data concerning day-to-day operations. The philosophy underlying DSSs is that it is every bit as legit-

FIGURE 1   *Electronic Data Processing Systems versus Decision Support Systems*

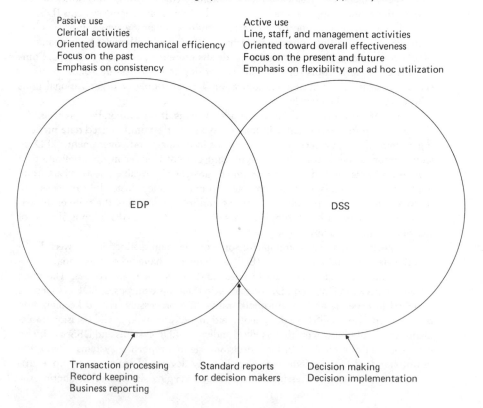

| Passive use | Active use |
| Clerical activities | Line, staff, and management activities |
| Oriented toward mechanical efficiency | Oriented toward overall effectiveness |
| Focus on the past | Focus on the present and future |
| Emphasis on consistency | Emphasis on flexibility and ad hoc utilization |

EDP

DSS

Transaction processing
Record keeping
Business reporting

Standard reports
for decision makers

Decision making
Decision implementation

imate to use computers to improve or expedite the processes by which people make and communicate decisions. Thus the emphasis of DSSs is on increased individual and organizational effectiveness rather than on increased efficiency in processing masses of data.

In many ways, decision support systems are a significant current frontier in the use of computers in business organizations. In performing the research study on which this book is based, I was rather surprised by the comparatively small number of systems that were thought of as being used for decision making, even in large companies. In part, I think this is a result of common unfamiliarity with the wide range of DSS possibilities that have been exploited successfully. In part, diffusion of innovation is the issue since the potential users of DSSs are often not the ones who conceive of the systems initially. In addition, there is simply the question of what one expects the computer to do. Wherever managers and designers think of the computer as a tool for automation and replacement rather than as a tool for support and facilitation, the prospects for decision support systems are dim. One of the purposes of this book is to indicate that although automation and replacement may be worthwhile computer system goals in some situations, they are not the only possible goals. Many of the organizations that have reaped major benefits from EDP applications have hardly scratched the surface of what can be done to support and facilitate decision making. I hope this book will provide ideas and impetus in that direction.

## SOURCES AND CONTENT

Most of the material presented here is drawn from a two-year research project concerning the development and use of decision support systems in organizations.[1] That study was motivated by the fact that surprisingly little empirical data was available in this area. For example, despite all the claims and counterclaims about computers' replacing managers or changing the nature of managerial work,[2] there was a dearth of information about how DSSs are actually used, who benefits from them, what the key issues leading to their success are, etc. In fact, this lack of data made it difficult even to get started because it wasn't obvious what to look for. Consequently, a largely exploratory approach was used. First, a series of major case studies were written in order to help identify some of the key issues. Next came a survey involving structured interviews of implementers and/or users of 50 additional systems. The case studies and much of the data in this book come from that exploratory research project.

The process of performing the interviews was a remarkable experience, largely because of the vast differences in the experiences and opinions that were encountered. If Monday's interview revealed the eternal truth that no manager would ever use a computer terminal directly, Tuesday's interview involved a manager with a terminal in his office. If Tuesday's interview demonstrated that no DSS could be developed successfully without strong involvement of the user, Wednesday's concerned a successful system that had been forced on a user who resisted it initially but

---

[1]The project was the basis of the author's Ph.D. thesis at M.I.T.'s Sloan School of Management.

[2]The debate along these lines began in the late 1950s and was reflected by such authors as Leavitt and Whisler (1958), Simon (1960), Burlingame (1961), and Myers (1967). Full references appear at the end of the book.

was eventually won over. If Wednesday's interview showed conclusively that a particular DSS could not be used effectively unless it was on-line, Thursday's was devoted to a successful system that was thought to be much more effective in batch mode. If Thursday's interviews revealed that a particular system was loved and revered by all users, Friday's return interviews at the same site typically found at least one individual who thought the system was a waste of time, effort, and money.

Although the study did not find universal truths that all DSS practitioners and users hold to be self-evident, it did reveal a great deal about the choices that are available in terms of what DSSs can do, how they can be used, and how they can be implemented successfully. In order to communicate what decision support systems are all about and what these choices really mean, this book will use a combination of case studies of individual systems and chapters that describe some of the patterns observed in the research study.

Part One contains a series of three case studies exemplifying the development and use of innovative decision support systems. These should provide the reader with a holistic impression of the types of systems that are grouped under the DSS heading and the types of issues that arise in the development and use of these systems.

Part Two consists of three chapters that summarize the descriptive findings of the research study. The basic theme of these chapters is the great variety in the choices that are available for DSS implementers and users. The first chapter in Part Two discusses a taxonomy of DSSs and presents illustrative examples of each of seven types of DSSs. The next chapter describes some of the many ways DSSs are used to improve the effectiveness of individuals. Once again, examples are used to illustrate each of the approaches presented. The final chapter in Part Two describes the advantages and disadvantages of each of the four common usage patterns for DSSs.

Part Three contains three chapters that summarize the study's findings concerning the successful implementation of decision support systems and a fourth chapter that discusses significant trends for the future. The first of these, Chapter 5, describes the different types of difficulties that were encountered by the systems in the sample. Chapter 6 discusses implementation patterns and their significance. Chapter 7 presents an approach for analyzing potential implementation problems. It begins by describing a series of implementation risk factors, i.e., early warning signs whose presence tends to reduce the likelihood of successful implementation unless appropriate implementation strategies are devised and used effectively. Examples of these implementation strategies and some of the determinants of their success are presented. Chapter 8 discusses some of the key trends that will affect the success of decision support systems in the next decade.

Part Four completes the book by presenting case studies whose purpose is to extend and solidify the reader's understanding of decision support systems. Each case study should be thought through and analyzed in terms of the ideas in the preceding chapters.

## AUDIENCES

This book is aimed at two audiences. The first audience consists of people in organizations whose responsibilities include the creation and/or use of decision support systems. For these readers, the book should serve as a source of ideas concerning systems that may be developed, patterns of use that may be employed, warning signals that should be monitored, and development strategies that may be used. In approaching each case study or descriptive chapter, these readers should keep a number of questions in the backs of their minds: Is this situation consistent with my own experience? Could this kind of situation arise in my organization? Could this kind of system or usage pattern meet a need in my organization? Why have we never attempted to do this sort of thing? If we have attempted it, what determined whether the results were similar to those described by the author?

This book can also be used as a text in several different graduate-level courses. It was written to be used in a course on management information systems or decision support systems, preferably as a companion volume to *Decision Support Systems: An Organizational Perspective* by Peter Keen and Michael Scott Morton. In this pairing, the earlier volume is used for much of the broad conceptual overview concerning managerial decision processes, and the current volume will provide case studies and detailed information about usage and implementation patterns. The current volume can also be used in several other types of courses. For instance, it has been used to complement a computer-oriented text in an introduction to computer-based systems, thereby addressing the generalist student's need to understand not only how computers work but also how they can be applied successfully in decision-making situations. It can also complement a technique-oriented text used in an introduction to management science, again acquainting the students with applications of the technical concepts. Finally, it can be used to provide case studies and data for a course on implementation concepts and methods.

To the degree possible, this book does not rehash technical material that is available from many other sources. Instead, it proceeds at a relatively nontechnical level and assumes that the interested reader will use the references provided to obtain additional information about such topics as computer hardware and software, statistical methods, optimization methods, project management, systems analysis, etc. Although most of this book can be understood by readers with little computer background, it is preferable that readers have a basic understanding of what computers can do and a general familiarity with quantitative methods.

# THREE CASE STUDIES
# OF DECISION
# SUPPORT SYSTEMS

# PART ONE

The term *decision support system* was defined in a rather general way in Chapter 1. Although it would be possible at this point to continue to expand that introduction and overview, doing so will be deferred in favor of a series of three case studies. The main reason for inserting the case studies at this point is to provide some interesting examples, thereby creating a context for the more general, survey-oriented chapters that follow. The three cases were chosen with an additional objective, namely, to demonstrate that decision support systems are not simply technical solutions to technical problems. Instead, finding a tentative technical solution is often only a first step. In the implementation process that follows, significant personal and organizational learning may take place, and in addition, the original solution may change to meet the needs and abilities of the potential users. Thus, in order to understand a DSS, it is necessary to appreciate not only what the computer code accomplishes but also how the system was developed and how people use it.

In accordance with this viewpoint, readers are encouraged to approach each case with the following seven types of questions in the backs of their minds.

1. *The system:* What does the system do? What is its technical configuration?

2. *The problem:* What problem does the DSS address? How does it help the user?

3. *The user:* Who uses the system and in what manner?

4. *The implementation:* How was the system conceived, developed, and installed? What problems arose in the implementation, and how were these problems addressed?

5. *The impact:* What impact has the system had? How was the impact measured?

6. *The evaluation:* Why is or isn't the system a success?

7. *20-20 hindsight:* What lessons were learned? What might have been done to make the system more successful?

After reading each case, it will also be worthwhile to compare it with the other cases and with other familiar situations. Things to think about include the following.

How are the cases similar or different, especially with regard to the seven questions above?

Are there instances in which the experience from one case might have been useful to users and/or implementers in another case?

Do there seem to be any general principles concerning the implementation and use of decision-support systems?

Although these questions are not easy to answer, thinking about them seriously will provide a useful introduction to the more general, overview-oriented chapters that follow.

# CONNOISSEUR FOODS: THE INTRODUCTION OF MODELING AND DATA RETRIEVAL CAPABILITIES

## CASE ONE

## I. INTRODUCTION

Connoisseur Foods is a large, multidivisional food company. In 1969, its top management decided that it would be worthwhile to encourage the development of organizational expertise in the general areas of computer models and systems. This case study was written in 1974 to describe the results of some of these efforts that are related to on-line computer applications.

### A. The Setting

In order to understand these developments, it is necessary to begin with the (simplified) organization chart of Connoisseur Foods in Fig. 2. Originally, Connoisseur Foods did not have a divisional structure. As its business grew, however, it split into separate divisions for farm products (canned goods) and beverages. In the 1950s, the division for frozen foods was created in response to the special opportunities and needs of that market. More recently, in an attempt to diversify, Connoisseur Foods has entered the toiletries market in addition to acquiring a number of subsidiaries. Each of the divisions has between three and ten major brands, a

FIGURE 2   Organization Chart of Connoisseur Foods

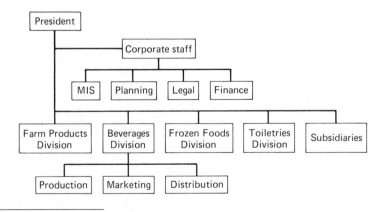

This case was written by Steven Alter and abridged by Peter Keen.

number of minor brands, and other potential products in the prototype stage. Usually, a brand manager is assigned to one or two major brands or to a number of minor brands. In addition, each division has production, marketing, and distribution departments, which cut across the brand manager structure.

Partially due to their dissimilar histories, the various divisions have different types of managerial personnel and different management styles. For instance, the Farm Products Division is an "old-line" division, whose top managers have worked their way up through the company from the bottom. In making major decisions, these old-line managers tend to rely on their lengthy experience in this market. Many decisions tend to be made by consensus, with responsibility defined rather vaguely. In this division, brand managers are responsible for many aspects of brand administration, but strategic decisions and advertising allocations are usually made by their superiors. In contrast, the Frozen Foods Division has younger personnel and tends to be somewhat more aggressive and more quantitatively oriented. Lines of responsibility are defined more clearly, with brand managers having a greater range of decision-making responsibilities.

## B. The Basis of This Case Study

This case study is based on interviews with the following individuals, who represent a range of viewpoints.

> James Carleton, Manager of Marketing Services under the Vice President for Marketing in the Farm Products Division.

> Albert Leland, Manager for Applications in the corporate Management Information Systems (MIS) group.

> Sam Mayer, Financial Analyst attached to the MIS group.

> Ed Donnelly, Vice President of Business Software Corporation (BSC), a programming and consulting company under contract with Connoisseur Foods.

The modeling and data retrieval systems discussed here are a combined effort of Connoisseur Foods and BSC personnel. This working relationship began when Albert Leland and Ed Donnelly met at a management seminar in 1969. At that time, Leland was becoming increasingly enthusiastic about the general possibility of applying sophisticated computer-based types of analysis to important marketing questions at Connoisseur Foods. He realized, however, that the level of expertise within Connoisseur Foods was probably insufficient for a major effort along those lines. After conversations with a number of top managers, Leland arranged for Donnelly to lead a series of seminars at Connoisseur Foods and to explore the possibility of extended consulting and programming help from BSC.

The first BSC efforts involved the development of aggregate market response models to aid in marketing decisions concerning advertising promotions, pricing, etc., in the Farm Products Division. Later a number of other models were introduced. Applications spread to other divisions. More recently, the main emphasis in the BSC involvement has shifted to a data retrieval system for sales information.

During the intervening five years, a great deal of organizational learning has taken place. Mr. Leland, though admitting to impatience with the slow process of change, feels that momentum has been attained, that these efforts have begun to play an important role in some decision making, and that they will certainly have an important role in the future. The next section will discuss the technical tools (i.e., market models and a data retrieval system) that were used in these efforts. The succeeding sections will discuss the manner in which the tools were used and the acceptance of these innovations.

## II. THE TECHNICAL TOOLS

### A. Aggregate Market Response Models

The aggregate market response models used by Connoisseur Foods apply to established products for which there exists a reasonable database (either intuitive or quantitative) of sales experience. The purpose of these models is to aid in decisions concerning advertising, pricing, promotion, etc., and then to help in tracking the effects of those decisions.

The first step in developing such a model is to decide on *reference conditions*. These are usually defined from sales and marketing activities in the recent past. Future sales and marketing decisions are viewed as having the purpose of creating some change in market conditions relative to conditions in the reference period.

The impact of marketing decisions on market conditions is expressed by means of response functions. A response function produces a response multiplier for any reasonable level of a controllable variable.

The response multiplier curve in Fig. 3 says that an advertising level of $x$ will produce a sales response multiplier of 0.8, and levels $y$ and $z$ will produce sales response multipliers of 1 and 1.2, respectively. (In other words, advertising at level $x$ will result in sales equal to 0.8 times sales in the reference period.) Note that advertising response is pictured as an "S-shaped" curve with upper and lower limits. This is a representation of the belief that past a certain point, additional expenditures for advertising will have no further impact on sales (in the short run, at any rate).

FIGURE 3    *A Sample Response Multiplier Curve*

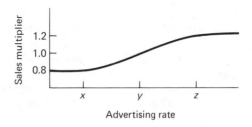

Advertising rate

After a response multiplier curve is developed for each controllable variable, the impact of any given marketing plan can be estimated. For instance, assume that a given marketing plan for Product A sets levels of advertising, promotion, and price, such that the multipliers read from the three appropriate response curves are 0.95, 1.2, and 1.1, respectively. The estimated sales for the period under consideration will be 0.95 • 1.1 • 1.2 times Product A sales during the reference period.

In addition to developing response curves for directly controllable variables, it is usually necessary to develop response curves for other variables, such as seasonality and trend. In some cases, it is also deemed appropriate to incorporate similar response curves for competitors' marketing strategies and the effects of those strategies on the sales of Connoisseur Foods' products.

The response curves are developed on the basis of a combination of hard data and intuition. Often the process involves the use of a Delphi method in reconciling the intuitions of a number of people who are familiar with the history of the brand being modeled. Wherever possible, actual sales data are used to augment judgment. Naturally, the credibility of these models increases with the quality of the available data and the consistency of historical relationships with people's intuitions.

When the market response model for a given product has been fully specified, it can be used to help in estimating the effect of various mixes of promotional activity. The key advantage in using an explicit mathematical model of this sort is that it forces the user to segment his problem into a number of manageable parts—in this case the individual response curves. Thus it allows him to bring his best judgment to bear on each part in turn without worrying about the interactions of these parts. The computer model will take care of the interactions later. This segmentation of effort minimizes a common problem, namely, that people tend to make decisions based on one or two key variables that are foremost in their minds at the time of the decision, neglecting other effects that may also be important. Thus the model forces the inclusion of more effects and helps the user perceive the consequences of the simultaneous application of his various subjective beliefs. This is an aid in his thinking and helps to rationalize the planning process.

The models are used interactively through a computer terminal. The decision maker or analyst enters a marketing plan and receives a printout of forecasted results. He can then evaluate variants on the plan as a way of developing a more satisfactory plan.

The process of developing and using such models is time-consuming and occasionally stressful because of the explicitness that is required. These models are normally developed by a team, not a single individual. Typically, an initial model is developed on the basis of only main factors, such as seasonality, trend, advertising, and promotions. Later, after tracking results have been obtained, the model can be expanded as is necessary.

Once again, it should be stressed that the models discussed here are appropriate for estimating and tracking the effects of marketing plans for established products that have shown reasonably stable or understandable sales behavior in the past. It should also be noted that the models are used in planning promotional strategies for frequently purchased food products. The approach described here may have to be modified if the products are consumer durables. It is likely that somewhat different models would be needed to aid in the marketing of industrial goods.

## B.  Data Retrieval

After one of the original seminars that Ed Donnelly presented for top managers of Connoisseur Foods, a strong feeling was expressed that the corporate EDP group tended to give poor service to marketing. The standard reports generated monthly by the computer were primarily detailed breakdowns of historical sales and accounting data. In order to convert these massive printouts into performance reports that were useful in marketing decisions, clerks were performing hours of hand calculation and retabulation. Furthermore, requests for special computerized reports usually involved delays of three weeks or more. Donnelly proposed that BSC develop a data retrieval system that would allow the generation of desired reports from a large sales database on either a standard or an ad hoc basis. He proposed an evolutionary approach. His programmers would start by bringing up an experimental system with a limited database for the Farm Products Division. Later it would be expanded.

At present this data retrieval system is partially implemented. Ideally, it will provide fast and flexible access to basic sales information. At the most disaggregated level, this information consists of sales in dollars and numbers of cases (or other sales units) for 13 periods per year for all item codes at each of the sales branches of Connoisseur Foods. The data retrieval system will produce certain standard reports periodically, will aid in the ad hoc generation of other standard types of reports, and will permit ad hoc retrieval and manipulation of any information in the database.

In order to facilitate the ad hoc type of usage, several levels of user language have been developed. They are called Programmer, Expert, and User modes. The most detailed is Programmer mode, which is directly involved with technical features of the computer system that are invisible to users at the simpler levels. Expert mode is intended for use by managers and analysts who want more flexibility than is offered by User mode and are willing to expend more effort in learning how to specify desired reports without automatic prompting.

The easiest level is the User mode. In this mode, the user initiates a report specification by naming the type of report he needs. The system responds with a series of questions that prompt the user through a logical specification of the report. In User mode, therefore, all the user must know is the type of report he wants and the data to be included. The system is responsible for ensuring the logical completeness of the specification and for finding the data and performing the printing. The following are examples of reports that can be requested through User mode:

1. *Display:* The user can display sales of a product or product class in a given sales branch or sales region during a given period.

2. *Compare:* The user can make comparisons such as the following.
   Sales for a period versus sales during the same period last year.
   Cumulative sales versus cumulative sales for the same period last year.
   Sales for one sales region versus sales for other regions.

3. *Variance reports:* Forecasted versus actual sales broken down by forecasting units.

4. *Sorted listings:* e.g., products listed in order of percentage gains or losses in sales as compared with last year.

5. *Exception listings:* e.g., all products more than 10 percent above or below last year's level of sales.

6. *Area test:* Often a promotional activity is undertaken in sales region A but not in B, C, or D. The area test routine helps in one of the most common types of analysis in the Farm Products Division, namely, evaluation of the impact of such a promotional activity. In specifying this kind of report, the user must give the starting and ending periods of the test, the products involved, the type of comparison he wants (comparison with averages, base period figures, or data from a year ago), the performance measure he wants (e.g., percentages, averages, differences), etc.

The potential database for the Farm Products Division consists of dollar and unit sales for 400 item codes across 300 sales branches for 13 periods per year. Ultimately this will grow to 20 to 40 million numbers. Since the database is so large, only a small subset of the most recent data will be maintained permanently on a disk. Most of the database will reside on tape.

When the retrieval system is completed, it will work as follows: A user will specify the data he needs. The system control program will check whether this data currently exists on the disk. If the data is available, the report will be generated immediately. If the data is not available, the system will store a request that will be processed by a data-extracting program that will be run overnight. This program will read the whole sales tape, extracting and storing on disk all data that are required to service the various retrieval requests. The next day, the data will be available to the user, who will access it directly from the disk. Since this "extract" program will be expensive to run, it will not be run every night; rather, it will be run automatically whenever a specified condition is met, such as the existence of three or more requests that need servicing or of one request that is more than two days old.

The logic underlying this retrieval strategy is based on the fact that most users want to look at only a limited portion of the database. Although it is desirable to have on-line access, the whole database is too large to maintain on-line. As a compromise, therefore, the most commonly used portions will be maintained on disk, and other parts can become available on disk temporarily on request.

## III. MODELING AND DATA RETRIEVAL EFFORTS IN THE FARM PRODUCTS DIVISION

The technical tools have now been described. The following section will discuss the use and acceptance of these tools in the Farm Products Division.

### A. The Introduction of Modeling Efforts

Ed Donnelly's original seminars helped convince the top managers of Connoisseur Foods that it would be desirable to nurture organizational expertise in marketing science. After discussions with Donnelly and Leland, a decision was made to attempt to develop an aggregate response model for a major brand in order to gain experience with this technology and to enable a more valid assessment of its potential. The decision to proceed came from above. The marketing vice president of the Farm Products Division was persuaded to encourage one of his brand managers to get involved in the development and use of a model to aid in planning marketing strategies. One of the main brands of the Farm Products Division was chosen to be the first brand for which a model would be implemented. There were two reasons for the choice. First, since it was an important and highly visible brand, efforts involving it would not receive half-hearted attention. Second, its history indicated that the construction of reasonably good response curves would be feasible.

From the start, there was a serious problem. The brand manager was not a quantitatively oriented individual. He was a former salesman who had worked his way up to brand manager for a major brand. He had always done a good job of selling and was quite competent in dealing with people, but he couldn't really bring himself to think in terms of response curves. Furthermore, the first attempt at doing something of this sort usually involves much trial and tribulation, wasted effort, and frustration. When the brand manager had been dragged through that difficult time, he was so disenchanted about both the model and the computer that it was difficult to get him to use the model as an integral part of his planning process.

### B.  The Process of Developing Brand Models

A review of this initial effort led to a more effective implementation for another brand. Based on further experience with these models, a process for model development emerged. The first step is to form a team of knowledgeable individuals who will participate. One of these people must be the brand manager who will use the model. Another is a model specialist who can elicit judgments from people, gain a consensus concerning these judgments, and incorporate the consensus in a computerized model. The remainder of the team includes a marketing specialist and others who work with the brand manager.

In the first meetings, the model specialist tries to elicit subjective response curves from each of the individuals on the team. These response curves are compared and reconciled. Often the discussions undertaken in reaching a consensus on a given response curve turn out to be a valuable learning experience. Wherever possible, the analysis of historical data is used to validate subjective opinions.

Getting this kind of effort going takes roughly three days of time for each of the team members plus five or six days of data analysis and computer work from one or two other persons. In total, this is about 15 days of brand-group time and about 10 days of technical input and analysis.

Usually the initial computerized model contains trend, seasonality, and two or three key planning variables, such as advertising and promotion. The model is used in tracking for a number of periods. The next stage is the inclusion of other factors that are believed to be important determinants of sales. For instance, the actions of a competitor may be required as part of the model if that competitor's promotions have a strong impact on the sales of a product of Connoisseur Foods. If so, an analysis should be undertaken of the effects of these promotions in the past. The analysis is then incorporated into the model.

In reflecting on this development process, James Carleton, Manager of Marketing Services, stated that the fact that the methodology allows people to encode their own estimates whenever hard data are not available is certainly one of its major strengths. However, it also causes a serious problem in implementation. The mere fact that so many estimates must be stated and reconciled means that it is necessary to have quite detailed and lengthy planning sessions with the people involved.

The role of the model specialist is crucial. In the opinion of Mr. Carleton, the procedure for developing models must be shepherded through by a person with a number of special qualities. He or she must be a real expert in the modeling technology, with knowledge concerning the computer routines, the underlying mathematical representations (such as lags, decay phenomena, etc.), and theoretical and practical marketing issues (such as the effects of continuous versus pulsed advertising). The model specialist also must be someone who is capable of leading a model development session. This means having a strong mind and good communication capabilities, because these sessions involve the explicit numerical reconciliation of the occasionally divergent views of the members of the brand team. If the specialist can't get the team members to think and interact in the right way, progress will not occur. The ability to achieve harmonious consensus among the people at the meeting is all the more important when one considers the fact that much of the understanding gained through these models is a direct result of the exercise of developing them.

## C. The Use of Aggregate Response Models

To date, aggregate response models have been used primarily for planning and tracking. As planning tools, these models are used to generate estimates of sales and profit for alternative promotional plans for a given brand. These plans include such variables as level of prices, level of advertising, media expenditures, media type (child TV, family TV, network vs. spot), copy effectiveness, number, type, and timing of trade promotions, etc. When the brand manager has tried a number of alternatives and is satisfied with his brand plan, he submits it to his superiors for approval or modification.

The estimates of future performance that are produced are not used as input to divisional forecasts or anything of the sort. They are used, however, in monitoring and evaluating brand performance and the effectiveness of the marketing strategy. This use of models is quite important and should be emphasized. A considerable variance between actual and predicted results that continues for several consecutive periods is a strong warning that something is changing in the marketplace (or that something is fundamentally wrong with the beliefs that are encoded in the model). At this point, further work with the model helps to identify the nature of the change in the market and to quantify its impact on sales.[1] Naturally, an unreliable or noncredible model cannot be used in this way. One of the reasons for the eventual acceptance of several brand models was the fact that the forecasts were generally within 3 percent of actual sales.

The amount of time spent using the models in an ongoing sense depends to a large extent on the brand manager and on how much he likes to work with models. Once a brand plan has been developed, it is necessary to wait for results from the marketplace. Typically, the monitoring process involves tracking during every period and a brand group review session once every three periods. The main purpose of these review sessions is to decide whether things have gone astray, to isolate the kinds of analysis that should be done, and to consider recovery procedures.

## D. The Impact of the Modeling Effort

Mr. Carleton felt that the main impact of modeling efforts in the Farm Products Division had been in terms of knowledge. He stated that they know much more than they knew previously concerning the way their most important product works in the marketplace. He doubted that the best possible use was being made of this knowledge currently, but he expected things to improve along these lines as experience increased. He alluded to some disagreement about whether the models had had an

---

[1]Little (1975) cites an example along these lines that he encountered in his work. In the situation he describes, a manager realized that a product was in trouble, even though its sales were roughly equal to those of the previous year. Based on a marketing plan, a reliable planning model had predicted a higher level of sales than had occurred. As a result of the early recognition of the problem, the product marketing plan was changed to include an additional promotion later in the year.

important impact on decisions to date. He thought not, although he said that one of the people working for BSC claimed that model-related changes in decisions had had a substantial impact on profits.

Mr. Carleton's basic feeling was that the modeling efforts had support from top management and from advocates such as himself, but that they lacked support from middle management. He felt that the middle managers would have to insist on expanded use of models by brand managers if the models were to have greater impact. He said that if he were the marketing VP, he would try to make sure that brand managers were quantitatively oriented. He would require that no brand plan be produced or changed without explicit evaluation based on a brand model. Furthermore, brand managers would have to submit printouts annotated with their own comments and analysis. It would not be possible to analyze all brands in this way, but he would make sure that all brand managers used models for their major brands.

### E.  Data Retrieval Efforts in the Farm Products Division

As mentioned earlier, the initial impetus for the development of an on-line sales data system in the Farm Products Division came from the marketing VP. He felt that the standard reports coming from existing computer systems were either too limited or too voluminous to be useful. Furthermore, any sort of special computerized analysis required weeks—if it could be produced at all. When model building was beginning to attain momentum, he felt that what he really needed was basic sales information in a timely and usable form. Two years ago, an initial experimental prototype of this system was implemented in the Farm Products Division. The system has grown to include the data base and capabilities mentioned earlier. At the time of writing, the project is heading toward its final phase.

The system, which has been in use at its current stage for about a year, requires the assistance of technical intermediaries. Typically, a brand manager decides he needs something and discusses it with Mr. Carleton. After clarifying exactly what it is that the brand manager wants, Mr. Carleton decides whether it is feasible to service the request. He then checks whether the needed information is available on the disk. If not, he programs the required analysis. If the information is on the disk, he submits a data request for the next run of the program that extracts data from the sales tapes.

Mr. Carleton feels that the final system will be used somewhat differently. In particular, he wants to eliminate the technical intermediary insofar as possible. Ideally, the manager will type his own request at a terminal and will find out whether the necessary information is available on the disk. If so, he will be able to obtain the reports he wants in an on-line fashion. If the information is not available, he will submit a request to the extracting program and will have to return to do his analysis after the next run of that program. In either case, the instances when he will need assistance in using the system will be the exception rather than the rule.

In order to make this kind of use feasible, the User mode of the retrieval language has been developed. In this mode, the user initiates computer-prompting routines by entering only the name of the type of report needed. The computer keeps track of the logical completeness of the specification, checks for errors, explains options, performs retrieval, prints reports, etc. If several users ask Mr. Carleton to help them with some kind of analysis that is not available through User mode, he will consider writing a User mode routine for that new kind of analysis.

The obvious limitation of anything like User mode is that it is inflexible. The trade-off here is between ease of use and the greater power and flexibility of Expert and Programmer modes. The strategy being employed is to encourage brand managers to learn User mode and to help them advance to Expert mode if they want to do so. One of the advantages of User mode is that beginners are much less likely to make serious mistakes in User mode than in Expert or Programmer mode. In general, one of the great advantages of having an on-line system is that mistakes in report specification can be caught and corrected quickly.

In a sense, the nonstandardized use of the data retrieval system should be more difficult than the use of brand models, because the brand models structure the environment for the user. They help the user make decisions within a set framework of questions and answers. The ad hoc use of the data retrieval system by brand managers will require an ability to search for structure and to develop structure. How brand managers will succeed at this and whether it is they or their assistants who actually use the system remain to be seen.

Mr. Carleton feels that the system will have been successful if, within one year, four or five of the brand managers are using the system regularly and interactively without coming to him for help. Whether this is the ultimate form of use depends in part on the attitudes of middle managers in the division. The likelihood that this will be the form of use will increase if they insist on the use of the system by the brand managers. If the brand managers (or their assistants) begin to use it frequently, they will need less help from technical experts as the more common operations become second nature.

## IV. OVERVIEW

This section is based on an interview with Albert Leland, Manager for Applications in the corporate MIS group. Mr. Leland played a key role in initiating and guiding the work described here.

### A. Advocacy and Top Management Support

Over the last several years, work on the modeling and retrieval efforts has progressed at a relatively constant rate in spite of the fact that two of those years were quite difficult for Connoisseur Foods. In part, the progress has been a result of continuing support by several members of top management. Mr. Leland feels that one of the main lessons to be learned from the experience at Connoisseur Foods is that it is quite important to have advocates at a very high level in the organization. It is not essential that these persons be users of the systems or services involved. Rather, the key factor is that they must be in a position to influence the direction of resource allocation.

The development of modeling and data retrieval technologies is not inexpensive, and the immediate benefits are not always clear. The justification for much of the initial work is necessarily based on pure faith. It is difficult to quantify the benefits from such efforts, even after they have attained momentum: "What is a good decision worth? What is the monetary value of knowing that a product has a certain probability of success? How can you really say that you wouldn't have come to that same conclusion using the traditional manual or intuitive approaches in the analysis?"

Resource allocations based on sheer advocacy clearly do not go on forever. In Connoisseur Foods, enough favorable experience has accumulated to support the original contentions of several executive vice presidents that the development and application of models and data retrieval systems would be worthwhile. A shift has now occurred, and much of the impetus for these efforts is beginning to come up from the bottom rather than down from the top.

Mr. Leland expressed concern over the fact that much of the top management advocacy along these lines still reflected the relatively uneducated view that this was a direction the world was taking and that Connoisseur Foods should be on board. In a sense, he considered this a bit of an indictment of his group, in that they haven't been able to keep top management up to date about the things that are happening and the benefits that have been or will be realized. One reason for this situation is simply time pressure and logistics: The applications group has been extremely busy with day-to-day work. In addition, it is simply quite difficult to get the top managers together for a series of progress review meetings.

Mr. Leland felt a very real need to try to explain the latest developments to them. He was concerned that the users might become so sophisticated that they wouldn't be able to communicate effectively with their own management. When a user has to present to management a proposal based on a rigorous and sophisticated analysis, the impact of what he has done will be lost if the managers do not understand the underlying formal concepts.

## B.  Resistance to Change

One of the reasons for the small number of model implementations to date is that some potential users and their superiors have not been sold on models and their benefits. A lot of work is required in dealing with models. When staffing is also relatively tight, the nonenthusiasts become concerned that the models will force them to spend less time on other aspects of their jobs, particularly fire-fighting. They often feel that if they have to give up something, they would prefer that it be the models.

In addition, there is a question of motivation. The brand managers who are directed to use models simply do so. The ones who have an option respond according to the type of person they are. Jokingly, Mr. Leland said that the rationale of extremely unenthusiastic individuals might go as follows:

> I just don't understand this kind of stuff. It simply is not my bag. I'm an idea man. I'm intuitive. I don't understand equations and that kind of stuff. I just use them when I have to put them on reports. I look at ads and see if they turn me on. I look at promotions and see if they turn me on. I try to get a feel for the market. It's an intuitive thing. In summary, I'm an intuitive animal, so don't bother me with facts.

Another aspect of this problem is fear of the black box—or Blox disease, as it is called by people in the applications group.

Speaking more seriously, Mr. Leland felt that resistance was basically quite reasonable and should not be terribly serious in the long run. "The analytic techniques are relatively new. It takes time for people to get used to them and to begin to believe in them. Over the long haul, people do change. Furthermore, the MBAs and other younger people coming up through the organization have better backgrounds for using analytic approaches and more of a feeling for their significance." In addition, a current trend at Connoisseur Foods is toward a kind of cross pollination, in which people are moving out of EDP into line areas. This will encourage the dispersion of quantitative expertise. In order to contribute to this trend, Mr. Leland tries to staff the EDP applications group with persons who will want to move into line positions, namely MBAs and others with business orientation rather than with strictly technical interest.

## C.  The Diffusion and Acceptance of Analytic Approaches to Decision Making

Mr. Leland stated that the real goal of his efforts is not the implementation of isolated systems or models. Rather, it is the institution of new approaches in corporate decision making. Basically, this means that everyone in the organization should use the new approaches where appropriate and should be able to communicate effectively with either superiors or subordinates concerning recommendations based on these methods. It does not mean that everything should be up on models. Rather, it says that when a model-based analysis suggests a particular course of action in resource allocation, it should be possible to reconcile that suggestion with overall considerations in a much more rigid and disciplined way.

Movement in a number of directions is increasing the degree of diffusion and acceptance of these models. Visible successes have been attained, both through the efforts described here and in a separate work involving lease analysis and other financial applications. Quantitative expertise is being developed among Connoisseur Foods personnel, particularly with the hiring of MBAs. Managers are learning to approach situations in a more disciplined way.

To date, these efforts have had a definite impact on the way some brand managers think about their markets. They have a much more explicit understanding of the market process they are involved in. Previously they made decisions and monitored their strategies for time intervals of a year. Now they can monitor the quality of a brand's position on a month-to-month basis. For the first time, it is possible to see the explicit impact of marketing decisions on the progress of the brand. Furthermore, the organization has become much more aware of the value of information, because information can now have a much more direct impact on planning decisions, which are an important determinant of sales and profit.

Mr. Leland closed the interview with an example that demonstrated that progress toward his overall goals was occurring. This example concerned his participation in a recent modeling effort undertaken by the marketing staff of one of the subsidiaries. The people in the subsidiary had heard about the use of models at Connoisseur Foods and felt that this approach might be of value to them. Since the corporate MIS applications group had had three years of experience with modeling technologies by that time, they felt confident that their personnel could organize and lead the proposed model-building efforts. The result turned out to be one of the most sophisticated applications yet attempted at Connoisseur Foods.

The application involved a subsidiary that produced a specialized food item. The market for this item was split among five major producers, of which the subsidiary was one, and a number of minor producers. A great deal of information was available concerning pricing, advertising, and promotional levels for each of the major brands by month for the previous five years.

An intensive six-day session was devoted to the development of a brand model that would include competitive responses. The model builders began by estimating response curves for the effect on sales of such variables as pricing, advertising, promotion, seasonality, and so on. Next they estimated the rules that each of their competitors used in generating competitive responses. They estimated response curves for the actions of their competitors. Throughout these estimation sessions, they attempted to back up their subjective claims with historical data. When the first version of the total model was ready, they ran it for the five years for which they had data and compared the model's "forecasts" with the actual sales. After several rounds of examining the results and retrofitting, they found that their yearly estimated sales results were generally within 5 percent of actual. As a result of this exercise, they have a much clearer notion of the effects of their own marketing decisions and also understand the interactions between their competitors much more clearly.

Mr. Leland will certainly see to it that this effort achieves visibility in the organization. Although he considers it unlikely that the "old-line" managers will ever develop or use models directly, he does feel that sufficient momentum has been attained in the past four years to ensure that efforts of this sort will become more commonplace and will become an accepted part of ongoing decision making at Connoisseur Foods.

## V. RECENT DEVELOPMENTS

Expertise acquired in working with marketing systems has led to major developments in financial analysis and planning. Problems in the financial-analysis area had become quite evident in recent years, with many difficulties stemming from the fact that the divisions operate autonomously, even employing independent accounting and planning structures. As a result, it was difficult at the corporate level to get a good handle on where the dollars really were and how dollar and human resources should be allocated. With the expertise acquired from the marketing work that had been done, it was possible to bring up a financial planning system that could generate uniform financial statements and consolidations without modifying the accounting procedures of the divisions. This effort has received considerable exposure, and it is being supported with a substantial level of staffing.

Conceived and programmed over an elapsed period of two years, this system has provided a vastly expanded capability for types of financial analysis that are conceptually simple but that couldn't be done effectively without reasonably uniform data definitions. A number of needs have been answered or are in the process of being answered. The first was simply to provide enough uniformity to allow comparability across divisions and product areas. Having attained reasonable uniformity, the system permits much more detailed analysis than was formerly possible. Whereas the analysis of budget vs. actual, year vs. year, item vs. item, division vs. division, etc., was previously limited to 36-line items, 240 items are now available. The new system also provides a projection facility that helps in corporate financial planning by highlighting submissions of division or product plans that are seriously at variance with historic trends. There may be good reasons for the variances, but it is important for central planners to be aware of these situations and to study them carefully.

Currently this system is being developed by the MIS group in cooperation with the finance group, which is responsible for validating the data and generating the standard reports. The plan for the immediate future is to move into the finance group a full-time systems person with responsibility for the ongoing use and development of the system.

In addition to system-oriented developments, model-oriented work is becoming commonplace in the finance group. The most important models currently in use are a lease-buy model and a risk-analysis model used in analyzing capacity expansions and new ventures. Each model is used by an analyst who does an analysis and then presents the findings to a decision maker.

The lease-buy model provided entree for management science efforts in the finance group. It was an application whose significance people could understand quite easily because it could help them choose among complicated but relatively clear-cut alternatives offered to them. Management recognized that an initial application of this model to a computer-acquisition decision probably saved the company on the order of $100,000 by leading to the adoption of an alternative that had not been favored initially.

The risk-analysis model required more learning because it involved both probabilistic concepts and discounted-cash-flow concepts. Although these concepts have not yet been fully implemented across the company, the seed has been planted. The financial analysts who work up the numbers leading to decisions about capacity expansion and new ventures understand these concepts and embed them in the analyses they perform.

To date, risk analysis has had some visible impact. Recently it helped people in the finance group come to a decision concerning a proposed capacity expansion on the basis of a set of assumptions concerning a brand's market share, the growth of that market, the capital expenditures required to maintain or extend market share, etc. After analyzing such standard measures as return on investment, cash flow, and discounted cash flow, the decision makers weren't sure, but somehow they felt that the project should not be undertaken. After the project was subjected to a risk analysis, which took into account subjective probability distributions for many of the assumptions, the reason for their reluctance became clear. The project had an unacceptable down-side risk. In this case, the risk analysis convinced them that their intuitions were correct. Perhaps as important, it also provided a vehicle for explaining their decision.

### Questions for the Reader

1. In the case study, two approaches were used for supporting decisions. What are the fundamental differences between the data-oriented and model-oriented approaches? What are the advantages and disadvantages of each?

2. Under what circumstances is it possible to develop a market model of the type described? How accurate must such a model be in order to be useful?

3. Would it be possible to develop a model that could generate an optimal decision for a brand? If it was also important to allocate a fixed advertising budget across the brands in a division, could a model choose the optimum allocation? If so, how would it be done? If not, why couldn't it be done?

4. One of the goals of quantitative approaches to management is to be more "scientific" in the process of management. Is the process of developing brand models scientific?

5. Is there any relationship between managerial style and the successful application of decision support systems such as those described in the case?

6. Mr. Carleton said that if he were marketing VP, he would "require that no brand plan be produced or changed without explicit evaluation based on a brand model." Do you agree with him?

7. If you were a top manager of a firm similar to Connoisseur Foods, to what extent would you encourage or require the development and use of decision support systems such as those described in the case?

8. To date, has the modeling effort been a success? The data retrieval system?

# GREAT EASTERN BANK: A PORTFOLIO MANAGEMENT SYSTEM

## CASE TWO

### I. INTRODUCTION

This case study concerns an on-line portfolio management system (OPM) in the Trust Department of a large eastern bank. The purpose of this system is to aid portfolio managers in retrieving and analyzing information relevant to portfolio-related decisions. After a lengthy cost/benefit study, the system was developed in close cooperation with bank personnel by a software company that was in the process of installing a similar system in a bank elsewhere.

The case begins with a brief description of the setting, the Trust Department of the Great Eastern Bank. There follows a discussion of the job of a portfolio manager, emphasizing the fact that investment decision making constitutes only part of the job. The next section concerns the on-line system (OPM) that was developed and the ways in which it is used. The last section traces the history of the system, focusing on the human implementation issues that arose and the lessons that were learned.

### II. SETTING

The Great Eastern Bank is a large bank with a number of line divisions, one of which is the Trust Division. The main service rendered by the Trust Division is the management of security portfolios owned by customers ranging from wealthy individuals to large pension funds. As a fee for this service, the bank receives a fixed annual percentage of the total assets managed. This percentage varies with the type of service desired by the customer; it is greater for aggressive accounts, which require frequent review, than for trust accounts, which require less time and attention from bank personnel because of the conservative nature of their goals.

The portfolio managers themselves are salaried and do not receive commissions, although their overall performance and experience are reflected in their salaries. The Trust Division employs approximately 50 portfolio managers, whose major fields in college ranged from business, finance, or economics to engineering or mathematics. Most of these individuals held at least one other job prior to joining the Trust Department at an average starting age of about 26. What amounts to a two- or three-year apprenticeship at the bank is necessary in order to learn the business well enough to make decisions without review. Many of the portfolio managers have spent part of the training period working as analysts in the Investment Research

This case was written by Steven Alter. Much of the information contained in it is based on research done by Michael J. Ginzberg. His help is sincerely appreciated.

Department. In general, they have a strong commitment to a career in the investment management field. Consequently, turnover in the division is quite low.

Among the departments in the Trust Division, four are relevant for our purposes. They are the Investment Research, Trust and Estate, Pension, and Capital Management Departments (Fig. 4).

*FIGURE 4    The Trust Division of the Great Eastern Bank*

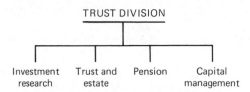

The Investment Research Department serves a staff function for the other three departments. Its 15 analysts are responsible for the maintenance of the "approved list," the list of stocks the portfolio managers may buy for their accounts. In addition, these analysts provide detailed analyses of the prospects for particular stocks or industries. The effectiveness of maintaining separate portfolio management and investment research functions depends in part on the ability of the investment research group to communicate effectively with the portfolio managers and to receive feedback from them.

Each of the portfolio managers is in one of the other three departments. Portfolio management responsibilities vary from department to department. Portfolio managers in the Trust and Estate Department usually manage a large number (average 160) of comparatively small accounts. For trust and investment management accounts, the main responsibility is to ensure that funds are invested in accordance with (1) the needs of the trust, (2) the investment policy of the bank, and (3) the economic outlook. For estate accounts, additional duties include collecting, conserving, and distributing the estate in accordance with the will of the testator. Within geographical regions, there is great competition for new trust or estate accounts. On the other hand, existing accounts tend not to show much movement, largely because of the personal relationship that develops between the portfolio manager and the client.

The Pension Department handles highly competitive, performance-oriented pension funds. A portfolio manager in this area usually manages only 10 to 15 funds and tracks their performance very closely. Compared with personally held accounts, pension funds are very large indeed. The direct clients are pension fund managers, who are quite willing to move their accounts to other trust departments if dissatisfied with performance. In fact, some of the larger pension funds have a policy of splitting their capital among four or five trust departments and replacing the worst performer each year with another trust department.

The Capital Management Department provides investment advisory and portfolio management services for the aggressive accounts of wealthy individuals who wish to accept comparatively high risk in order to attempt to obtain high growth or return. A portfolio manager in this area is responsible for approximately 30 accounts.

The goals of accounts in the various areas differ. Accounts in the Trust and Estate area tend to be relatively conservative in nature. Traditionally, a "prudent man" rule has applied here, whereby the preservation of capital rather than total return is a primary objective. In these accounts, the discretion of the portfolio manager is often limited by special provisions and requirements. These constraints range from special tax considerations to the client's idiosyncrasies and beliefs, e.g., that the account should never hold tobacco stocks or that 30 percent of its holdings should always be in plastics. Capital management accounts are also subject to special provisions and requirements, but they tend to be much more aggressive than Trust and Estate accounts and involve a much higher level of client involvement. Finally, there are the performance-sensitive Pension accounts, which are not subject to tax and which allow the portfolio manager greater overall discretion. In short, the goals and responsibilities of portfolio management are not homogeneous across accounts, and actions that are appropriate for one account may be totally inappropriate for others.

In general, competitiveness has become an important aspect of the whole portfolio management environment, both in attracting new accounts and in keeping large and potentially mobile pension accounts. Part of the competitive pressure on Trust Departments has come from the emergence of mutual funds, investment management services, and other new entries into the capital management field. With this heightened competition, the relatively conservative and even stodgy image of the banking industry has proved somewhat of a hindrance. Many banks have reacted with a conscious attempt to change their image by demonstrating that, while remaining prudent, they can also be progressive, aware, forward-looking, and so on. Although there were many reasons for undertaking the development of OPM, the competitive aspects of the business environment provided two important motivations since it was felt that advantages might be gained in terms of both actual performance and image.

## III. THE JOB OF A PORTFOLIO MANAGER

The purpose of OPM is to help portfolio managers in making investment decisions. In order to understand the impact of OPM, however, it is important to note that decision making is only one of the components of a portfolio manager's job. This section begins by discussing the other components in general, and it then focuses on investment decision making.

An obvious way to think about the aspects of any job is in terms of time allocation. On the basis of observations at a different bank, Gerrity (1970) says that a typical portfolio manager spent roughly comparable portions of time in customer contact, review and revision of portfolios, and scanning of the security market and related information. The time spent on a portfolio review varied from a few minutes to several hours. Without the aid of a system like OPM, most of these reviews involved a significant clerical effort on the part of the portfolio manager and his assistant in producing an adequate picture of current account status, updated from the latest computer-produced review. Pension fund managers typically tried to review their major accounts on a weekly basis, placing a high premium on easy access to current portfolio status and issue holdings across portfolios.

In a more detailed study at the same bank, Lavin (1972) generally agreed with Gerrity's findings. Portfolio managers spent most of their time reviewing and analyzing portfolios, taking care of administrative details, consulting with clients, and obtaining information. Those in different areas had different percentage allocations of their time. For instance, those in the personal trust area spent more time on client contact and administration than the others.

On the basis of several months of observation at the Great Eastern Bank, Ginzberg (1973) points out more strongly that different types of accounts require different types of attention. Obviously, someone with 10 pension funds will be able to spend more time on each of them than someone else with 160 trust or estate accounts. (In fact, some pension funds are reviewed on a daily basis.) Aside from time considerations, estate, trust, capital management, and pension portfolios tend to have different goals and require different levels of client interaction and administrative work.

For their investment decisions, most portfolio managers make either implicit or explicit use of some of the ideas underlying a growing and rather technical theory of portfolio decision making (e.g., Markowitz, 1959; Sharpe, 1970). This theory assumes that it is possible to quantify the level of risk and the expected level of return for any security. For two securities with equal levels of return, a rational investor should choose the one with lower risk. Therefore each additional unit of risk should be compensated by an additional unit of expected return. For a portfolio of securities, it should be possible to reduce risk by diversifying across securities whose movements are unrelated. Since it is impossible to diversify away all risk, a portfolio's objectives should include an explicit goal in terms of the trade-off between high risk and high return vs. low risk and low return. Furthermore, portfolios characterized as "growth funds" differ on the basis of risk from "income funds," with the former accepting a higher level of overall risk than the latter. Finally, taxation enters the picture, causing stocks with high dividend yields to be somewhat underpriced for nontaxable pension funds and overpriced for taxable personal portfolios; at the same time, high-risk stocks are overpriced for nontaxable portfolios and underpriced for taxable portfolios.

In no way does the limited statement above do justice to what has developed into a highly complex and rather elegant normative theory of portfolio decision making. The main point concerning this theory is that many of its underlying notions are included within the thought processes of portfolio managers, in spite of the fact that the theory has not developed far enough to permit automatic investment decision making. The basic shortcoming of the theory is that it is primarily concerned with the calculations of risk vs. return, whereas portfolio managers must take into account many other factors, such as liquidity, capital-gains taxes, personal idiosyncrasies of clients, and so on. In addition, neither the goals of most portfolios nor the available data on security market risk vs. return are sufficiently exact to determine portfolio decisions based on the theory alone, even if the theory encompassed all relevant considerations. Often, in fact, the clients' real goals are infeasible, e.g., high return and low risk, high dividends and low capital-gains taxes, etc. Thus the developing normative theory has helped clarify the nature of the trade-offs, but it has not progressed far enough to allow choices to be made solely on theoretically based calculations. This is particularly true for the majority of all portfolios that are taxable and subject to special arrangements and client needs.

Another very basic problem concerning the applicability of portfolio theory is that the traditional process of investment decision making has tended to be security-oriented rather than portfolio-oriented. (See Stabell, 1974, for a detailed discussion of this.) In a portfolio-oriented process, decisions are triggered by a perceived discrepancy between the goals and contents of a given portfolio. On the basis of this discrepancy, the decision maker searches for a new portfolio configuration more consistent with the portfolio's goals. In a security-oriented process, decisions are triggered by the general attractiveness of transactions in a given security. The decision maker then searches through the portfolios under his control, looking for those whose goals and special requirements would be served by either buying or selling that security. Traditionally, a security-oriented process has been used by large investment institutions, especially since they could execute block purchases at substantial brokerage discounts and could then distribute the purchases among their accounts. One of the initial concepts underlying the first version of OPM was that a computer-based system might permit a more portfolio-oriented decision process than was previously possible.

Given the current limitations of portfolio theory and the fact that many decisions are triggered by opportunities related to securities rather than portfolios, it is virtually impossible to rate a portfolio manager's decisions in any "objective" way. For this reason, the evaluation of portfolio managers is largely subjective. One department head gave the following criteria for the evaluation.

1.   Keeping customers happy; *getting along with* people.

2.   Keeping up-to-date on investment matters and adhering to the bank's and the division's investment policy and guidelines.

3.   Interpreting the economy in an appropriate fashion (e.g., avoiding cyclical issues as the economy peaks).

Thus the job of a portfolio manager consists of a number of components, of which investment decision making is only one. Doing the job well certainly requires an acceptable level of portfolio- and security-related performance, but it also involves client contact, administrative work, and other activities. The development and use of OPM should be considered within this framework.

## IV.  THE ON-LINE PORTFOLIO MANAGEMENT SYSTEM (OPM)

### A.  General Description

In order to help portfolio managers do a better job, the Trust Division of the Great Eastern Bank installed an on-line portfolio management system (OPM). This system was developed by an external software company that was in the process of implementing a similar system elsewhere. OPM was envisioned as a flexible, modular system, which could evolve over time as the users gained an understanding of the use of computers in the portfolio management process.

OPM is basically a data retrieval and display system. It is used by portfolio managers to help them examine portfolios and obtain information about particular securities. The data base of OPM consists of detailed information about particular securities, listings of the holdings within each account, and a cross-reference from each portfolio manager to his or her accounts. The thrust of OPM is to allow a portfolio manager to examine any account or security and to be able to scan across accounts in a large number of ways. This is done by means of a series of basic operators, which may be customized by the user to produce the reports needed. The customization is done by means of a menu selection process, although there exist default options in some cases.

Some of the currently available operators are summarized in Fig. 5 and illustrated in simplified "mock-up" form in an appendix to this case. These operators are intended to provide the users with data retrieval capabilities that will put at their fingertips much of the information they use in their decisions. The idea is to allow them to obtain this information quickly and in the form they want. The implicit model underlying the system is that the user can decide exactly what report is needed and can generate it by means of a single command customized for that purpose. The user thinks about the results obtained and then requests other reports if additional information is needed. Thus the main problem addressed by the system in its current form is that of data retrieval, i.e., helping the portfolio manager to do the job by providing current information in the desired form and without the necessity of extensive clerical work for each request. By performing these clerical functions, the system frees the user from these time-consuming duties and makes it possible to devote more time to portfolio analysis, customer relations, and other profitable enterprises.

FIGURE 5    Summary of Operators Available on OPM

| | |
|---|---|
| Directory: | Table; listed by account; aggregate figures |
| Scan: | Table; listed by account; holdings of one security |
| Groups: | Pictorial; within an account; breakdown by industry and security |
| Table: | Table; within an account; listing of all securities with detail |
| Histogram: | Pictorial; within an account; distribution of one data item over all securities |
| Scatter: | Pictorial; within an account; relationship between two data items over all securities |
| Summary: | Formatted full-page report; summary of an account |
| Issue: | Formatted full-page report; data about a security |

## B.  The Hardware

The first OPM terminal was installed in November 1972. At the time of this writing (October 1974) OPM is fully operational in a technical sense, although it is still undergoing a gradual process of change in terms of the precise information and operators that are available.

Technically, OPM is a system that is advanced in the "state of the art." Although the operators listed earlier appear to be reasonably straightforward, the sheer volume of data that the system would access resulted in highly sophisticated technical design requirements involving cathode ray tube (CRT) terminals, a minicomputer with its own disk, and a large computer that accesses the portfolio and security database.

The system is used through nine CRT terminals that are physically divided among the three departments of the Trust Division. There is also one hard-copy terminal, which is activated by pressing a "Print" button on a CRT terminal. The terminals are connected to a Super Nova minicomputer, which, together with a Diablo disk, provides an interface between the terminals and one of the bank's IBM 370/155 computers. The purpose of interposing the minicomputer at this point is to minimize any degradation of the bank's high-volume, production-oriented computing capabilities. The minicomputer monitors commands from the terminals. When it is satisfied that a command is complete, it transmits the command to the 370/155, in which a 400K-byte core partition is dedicated to the operation of OPM. When the appropriate report is generated, it is returned to the minicomputer and stored on the disk. The report that the user sees is then written from the minicomputer's disk under the control of the minicomputer. In this way, the 370/155 is used for the major computational tasks that the minicomputer cannot perform, and the minicomputer takes care of local input and output that would tie up the large computer unnecessarily.

Currently OPM is in operation only four hours each day in order to limit the high cost of maintaining a dedicated 400K core partition. It is not yet clear when the system will attain full-time use.

## C.  The Use of OPM

OPM has four purposes: investment decision making, account reviews, administration and client relations, and training.

### 1.  Investment Decision Making

The initial purpose of OPM was to aid portfolio managers in their decision making. It would do so by helping them in examining portfolios and in obtaining information about particular securities. Implicit in the initial concept was that the process of use would consist of "terminal sessions" in which the portfolio manager would request a series of reports that would help to move gradually toward a decision. At each stage in the session, the previously requested reports would provide the user with cues and information that would help to define the direction in which exploration of the overall situation should proceed.

In practice, this search-motivated process of use is employed only rarely. More typically, interaction is not a major factor in the use of OPM, even though it is on-line. Often users begin terminal sessions with very definite purposes in mind and try out several reports until they have generated the information they initially wanted. At this point, they often obtain hard copy, which they examine further at their desks. One user usually tries to generate all the hard copy to be needed for the day in a 10-minute session the first thing in the morning. Thus the value of the on-line nature of OPM is that it allows users to clarify and debug their own requests quickly and to obtain the information they want without delays and without requiring help from other individuals.

Note that OPM is not the only source of information for investment decision making. In fact, the primary data base for the Trust Department is the Trust Accounting System (TAS), a batch-oriented system that existed prior to OPM and that is used to update OPM on a daily basis. The information flow is as follows: A portfolio manager who decides to purchase or sell a security for a portfolio writes this information on a ticket that goes to the bank's stock trader. The stock trader executes the transaction if a counterpart buyer or seller is found. When the final transaction is booked, it enters TAS, which is used to update OPM later that same night. The lag between the commitment to perform a given transaction and the actual booking of that transaction is around five days (normal trading time for stocks).

Two observations should be made concerning this information flow: First, it is significant that the five-day lag motivates many portfolio managers to maintain their own manual accounting systems. These manual systems start with monthly prices for account holdings. The prices and holdings are updated during the month as the PM performs transactions. Since these manual systems are more up-to-date, the usage of OPM is reduced for portfolios with very recent transactions. One of the possible extensions of OPM would incorporate prospective transactions into a temporary database, which would allow OPM to represent a portfolio as it should look, provided that committed transactions are performed. The second observation is that OPM can be conceived of as an extension of TAS, which makes the TAS database accessible in a decision-related format. Before OPM existed, the only account information that was available without special clerical effort was a simple listing of the account as a series of securities. Such a listing was not at all conducive to thinking about the account in terms of risk vs. return, industry diversification, etc. One of the main reasons for developing OPM was to transform portfolio accounting information into portfolio decision information.

## 2.  Account Reviews

The second category of OPM use involves formal account reviews, which are required by law twice in three years although they are performed more frequently by the Great Eastern Bank. Recently the account-review procedure has been modified by means of a specific requirement that OPM hard copy be used as part of supporting documentation in the review. This standardization of review procedures has led to much more thorough account reviews and to better communication among portfolio managers and senior portfolio managers who review their work. It has also resulted in an increased degree of acceptance among some of the portfolio managers who had been reluctant to use OPM.

## 3.  Administration and Client Relations

The third type of OPM use involves client relations and account administration. Here the main contribution of OPM is that it provides a vehicle for demonstrating to clients that their accounts are under careful scrutiny and for explaining the rationale for the decisions that are taken. OPM is extremely effective in this regard since it generates much relevant information without additional clerical work and in formats that make sense and that relate directly to decisions.

## 4.  Training and Communication

The fourth use of OPM is as a training and communication device for portfolio managers. One of the interesting aspects of the portfolio management field is that there are many different ways of looking at any given portfolio and that portfolio managers sometimes develop interesting and original ways of approaching their decision problems. Therefore the manipulation capabilities of OPM provide an excellent way of facilitating the communication of these ideas. By starting with a hypothetical portfolio and allowing several portfolio managers to analyze it with the help of OPM, group training sessions can compare and explore the rationales that are used. This procedure is particularly helpful for training new or inexperienced portfolio managers. Another way OPM facilitates communication is through the *Issue* function, whose data is entered by the Investment Research Department for use by portfolio managers. This function has reduced the circulation of typed memoranda, which often became outdated without the portfolio manager's knowledge.

### 5. *Other Uses*

A potential use of OPM that comes up from time to time involves the possibility of building portfolio manager evaluation routines into OPM. Using such routines, a department manager might be able to compare the performance of portfolio managers in terms of return and also in terms of the way they maintained their portfolios. However, this use would pose a significant privacy question, since people resent being watched. Furthermore, many portfolio managers prefer to maintain the current subjective process of performance evaluation.

Even if it was determined that OPM should be adopted as a management control tool, it is not clear whether valid comparisons could be made because of the wide range of objectives among portfolios. A portfolio manager handling a large number of portfolios with conservative goals simply cannot get the kinds of return that are possible with more aggressive portfolios. And the problem goes still deeper. Particular portfolios often have unique characteristics. There may be special tax situations or special owner requirements, such as keeping a certain stock or staying out of certain industries. Thus any real performance evaluation scheme would have to encode the objectives and peculiarities of each portfolio and would then compare the actions that were taken with some model of what should have been done. Although some of the theory discussed earlier might be relevant to this task, the development of a truly meaningful performance measurement scheme for portfolio managers would be an extremely difficult task.

## V. THE IMPLEMENTATION AND ONGOING EVOLUTION OF OPM

This section traces some aspects of the history of OPM, emphasizing implementation issues related to the use of the system.

### A. The Decision to Develop OPM

In late 1969, the bank officer who is currently the implementation coordinator for OPM read an article in *Institutional Investor* that described a portfolio system then being developed for another bank. The system intrigued him. He invited the software company developing that system to visit the Great Eastern Bank and to present a demonstration.

In Spring 1970, an initial feasibility study was undertaken. Eventually it went through three phases, the first dealing with all the things such a system might accomplish, the second with the value of particular functions that seemed most appropriate, and the third with the monetary justification of the new proposed system. The Trust Division recommended that the system be developed. When a bank-wide priorities committee concurred, a contract was signed in February 1971.

The final cost-benefit analysis included a cost justification based primarily on the need for proportionately fewer portfolio managers as business grew, but also based on the effects of the system on developing new business, on improving profits from existing business, and on improving performance in general. As in many cost-benefit studies, there is some question of whether the numbers were the convincing factor or whether it was mostly a gut feeling on the part of top management that this would be a good thing. Certainly some people were more moved by estimated tangible benefits, and others were primarily interested in intangibles. Regardless of which aspect dominated, the feeling was that the system would help portfolio managers in major ways. In the words of the implementation coordinator:

> The intent was that the mechanics and the ability to examine alternative decisions by a portfolio manager would be facilitated by the system. He would be able to do things he might not ever have done before, plus things that he did do but which took a long time. He could do things with the system that support personnel were doing; therefore support personnel could be reduced. . . . We examined the portfolio manager's function and tried to provide him a tool to better perform those tasks that were programmable, not to make decisions as such, but to assist him in evaluating alternative courses of action so that he could make the right decision.

Developing OPM was not the only option considered. Several existing on-line portfolio systems marketed by time-sharing houses were looked at briefly. The conclusion was that these were inadequate for the task at hand. In particular, these systems had very bad response time and prohibitively high cost. For the kind of system that was desired, a customized development project was necessary.

When asked about the decision to go on-line rather than batch, the coordinator recalled a number of points. The system was to be a significant advance in the "state of the art" of running accounts. They were confident that the benefits of an on-line system would exceed its cost and honestly felt it was worth trying. An on-line system would be much more exciting in a lot of ways. It would give portfolio managers the flexibility to do things the way they wanted. It would also be a marketing aid. Certainly customers would be less likely to think this was just another traditional, stodgy bank when they saw that it had a system of this sort.

## B.  The Implementation Effort

### 1.  *Organization*

OPM was to be implemented by an external software company for use by up to 50 portfolio managers in three departments of the Trust Division. These were people with different types of experience, different levels of interests in computer-related innovations, and probably most important, different views of portfolio decision making.

Given the "state of the art" nature of the proposed system and the diversity of the people involved, it was essential to formalize the implementation process and to define specific responsibilities related to the project. Within the bank, the officer who had first introduced the concept of OPM was named implementation coordinator. He was to head an advisory committee of 10 portfolio managers who would be responsible for guiding the implementation process. Guided by experience in building a similar system in another bank, the technical implementation team in the software company included a team leader and several analysts and programmers. A phased implementation schedule was agreed upon, and work began.

## 2.  Technical Implementation Issues

Although this is a nontechnical discussion, the significance of technical problems must be mentioned. If the database had been small and could have been extracted easily from existing systems, implementing the kinds of operators mentioned earlier would not have been a great technical challenge. However, with the large portfolio data base that was needed, it was necessary to employ an advanced technical design that interfaced terminals with a large computer through a minicomputer. This kind of technology was new and unproven. Although it was clearly possible to develop software to accomplish this interfacing, such software was not available "off the shelf." Underestimation of the difficulty of producing and debugging this software resulted in an overoptimistic project schedule. In an attempt to recoup some of the lost time, OPM was made available to users in a fairly complete but not thoroughly debugged version. Although this did help move the user-training program closer to schedule, it resulted in a relatively long "shakedown" period, during which OPM went down frequently enough to cause serious user frustration. Thus, although the system was relatively simple in terms of the operators it provided to users, the fact that its internal details were quite sophisticated had a somewhat negative impact on users because of the initial malfunctions and resultant delays.

## 3.  Differences in Usage Patterns

The differences among portfolio managers in their use of OPM constitute one of the most interesting characteristics of this system. In terms of sheer volume, for example, some managers use it quite extensively, others use it occasionally, and some use it only in the mandatory account-review procedures. These differences can be attributed to a combination of factors, including commitment, training, convenience, patience with, and interest in the use of computers, and the actual operational requirements of departments and individuals. During the "technical shakedown" phase of system development, these differences were more striking than they are now. Prior to mandatory use of the system in account reviews, some portfolio managers used it quite extensively and others never used it.

The portfolio managers who made heaviest use of the system were 10 individuals in the advisory group responsible for helping guide the implementation process. These individuals had both commitment to the concept of OPM and training in its use. They also had terminals next to their desks. Even during the period of technical problems, the implementation coordinator felt that these individuals were using the system intelligently and imaginatively. In fact, he noticed the development of a bit of a clique among these heavy users of the system. To them it became a "common denominator" in expressing ways to manage accounts. At coffee breaks, members of this group were overheard discussing "what a weird *Groups* report that was" and asking, "What kind of *Groups* report do you like to see?"

Some of the other portfolio managers made little or no use of OPM during this period. Many cited the fact that they had no terminals at their desks and that they would have to disturb others in order to use the system. Unreliable system performance was certainly another primary reason for its minimal usage, since many individuals became discouraged when it went down and simply decided to wait until it became fully operational before trying to incorporate it into their work in major ways. This was partially a question of patience. Some managers were willing to tolerate the ambiguity of working with a computer that might go down before they obtained their results. Others were not. If the system was likely to crash, they simply wouldn't spend time working with it. The other side of this problem, of course, was that those who used OPM tended to feel frustrated when it didn't work. In addition, there was the matter of interest in computers. Some felt that OPM would be quite valuable to them when it became more consistent, even if they weren't using it temporarily. Others were not enthusiastic about computers and wished they could continue doing their jobs as they had in the past.

The following excerpts from Michael Ginzberg's (1973) notes on interviews during this shakedown period should help dramatize these differences.

### Mr. A of Trust and Estate

OPM is still viewed as somewhat of a toy. It hasn't reached the point of much usefulness. In any case, it is of no help until you have reached a decision about a stock. At that point you can use *Scan*.

I use *Scan* for finding where I hold a particular issue. *Table* is useful for reviewing accounts. *Groups* is a fascinating new way to look at an account and to see many new relationships. *Scatter* is intriguing but not of much use yet because the research data base is not yet on the system.

OPM is fantastic for impressing customers and communicating with them. Both sophisticated and unsophisticated customers are impressed with the command the bank has over its accounts. I expect that this will be one of its major advantages.

### Mr. B of Trust and Estate

To sum up the impact of the system in a word, it is *flexibility*. There is an important clerical time saving in keeping track of accounts and in finding which accounts do or don't hold any given issue. Further, it lets you know where you can act immediately and where you need approval (where you have to consult the owner). It gives you the latest information on fundamental numbers for an issue and an ability to look at an account in many different ways.

OPM will be a good marketing tool. Most customers are impressed, particularly the most knowledgeable ones. The customers have more confidence. On the telephone I can say, "We bought Disney last month, and you have a 7.2 percent gain," instead of just saying that I think there was some gain.

### Mr. C of Pension

I have attempted using the system twice. The system failed on both occasions. Also, the scope has bad lighting, and I have trouble reading it.

### Mr. D of Capital Management

I have made no use of the system beyond initial training. I will not experiment with it until I can do this without inconveniencing someone else.

### Mr. E of Capital Management

I have extremely active accounts where the customers want to make money and like to be involved in the investment process. The great advantage of this system is its speed. It gives me information I need to react quickly. It saves time and allows me to manage more money. It is an excellent selling tool which can be used to show the customers that I have a competitive edge. Hard copy is important because it is something I can give to customers.

*Mr. F of Trust and Estate*

As long as other information sources and standard paperwork is around, I will use this system mostly for special situations, such as giving hard-copy reports to customers.

During the period of technical difficulties, it was felt that the use of OPM would become more equalized as it became more reliable. However, as the system settled down, this opinion was not borne out particularly well. In spite of improved reliability, many portfolio managers remained reluctant to use the system.

There were a number of explanations for the continuing disparities in usage patterns. One was simply a question of personal change. Some portfolio managers felt that they had been doing an adequate job prior to OPM's existence and that they could continue doing an adequate job without it. Some noted that most of the information on OPM was already available through monthly TAS listings, and that they had to keep their own records anyway because of the five-day lag between making a buy or sell commitment and the entry of the completed transaction into the OPM database. There was some feeling that the reports available through OPM were useful in providing post hoc explanations, but they were limited in usefulness for active decision making because they didn't help as much as they might in evaluating or comparing decisions. This was partially due to the fact that the initial training demonstrated how to obtain information from the system but had not taught many of the portfolio managers how to use the system effectively for decision making. A remaining factor was the inconvenience and disturbance caused by using a terminal situated near someone else's desk.

### 4.  *Management Action to Increase Usage*

Trust Division management was somewhat disappointed by the relatively low level of usage as OPM was beginning to perform reliably. It was clear that some portfolio managers were quite enthusiastic about the system and were making imaginative use of it, but others seemed not to be interested or so motivated. The managers of the Trust Division felt that since this valuable tool was now available, an active effort should be undertaken to ensure that it was used effectively by all portfolio managers.

One of the main steps taken in promoting the use of the system was to require OPM outputs as a standard part of the periodic account reviews that are established by law. Instead of merely saying that some OPM reports must be included, the management carefully developed several specific account-review procedures. In addition to contributing to communication by providing a common frame of reference for account reviews, these procedures served the function of demonstrating to the reluctant users that the system was now available and could become accepted as a normal part of the process of portfolio management. Furthermore, this action served notice that management genuinely expected people to make good use of the tools that had been provided.

Another step taken in attempting to reach this goal was the scheduling of a series of training meetings. The purpose of the meetings was to transform people who knew how to obtain information from OPM into people who could use OPM effectively in analyzing a portfolio and coming to the appropriate conclusions for action. Typically, these sessions involved the several portfolio managers who were enthusiastic users of OPM and others who had not displayed as much interest. By demonstrating and discussing the use of OPM in analyzing hypothetical portfolios, the enthusiastic users not only provided ideas and hints for the others but also generated a form of peer pressure to get the others on board. The combination of teaching and peer pressure has proved successful in encouraging more uniform use of the system among the portfolio managers, although there remain those who are not yet heavy users. To facilitate further use of OPM as a vehicle for training and communication, a special terminal with a large screen display will be installed in a conference room. This will allow 10 to 20 portfolio managers to participate in the same discussion session.

In addition to building on the experience with peer teaching and mandatory use in account reviews, other steps toward increased usage are either in progress or in planning. The simplest of these is merely obtaining more CRT terminals in order to make system use more convenient.

Another way of encouraging expanded use is through the development of a number of extensions of the system, some of which are now being implemented. Earlier changes in OPM tended to involve adding new data fields or modifying the formats of some of the function outputs. The newer extensions are at a more conceptual level and involve an evolution toward the use of explicit models and toward more direct use of portfolio theory. When these initial extensions are completed, PMs will be able to set up and manipulate composite or hypothetical portfolio configurations by a trial-and-error process. This will allow them to think more easily about the impact of potential decisions. (*Postscript:* The usage of OPM doubled in the four months following the installation of a hypothetical portfolio function.)

Another possible extension would allow OPM to monitor portfolios by comparing their status with some normative model of what their status should be, given their objectives. When deviations occurred, the PM would be notified. This kind of function would require a system of encoding a portfolio's status, objectives, and special requirements. Such a system has not yet been developed. It would not entail shifting the responsibility for running portfolios to computers. Rather, the computer would simply warn the PM whenever certain simple deviations occurred. It would then be incumbent upon the PM to take any appropriate action.

People who are not familiar with the fiduciary trust business usually wonder why portfolio management is not being automated entirely. There are a number of answers. An obvious one is that total automation is contrary to the interests of the people in this field. Another is, as mentioned earlier, that the types of explicit models and knowledge that would be necessary for this type of automation simply are not yet available. Work is going on in these areas, but it is of a preliminary nature. It will probably be a long time before a really substantial part of the portfolio theory mentioned earlier is incorporated (by means of computers) into the process of portfolio management, and an even longer time before computers can be given any of the actual responsibility.

Another extension of OPM that is complicated, though conceptually feasible, is the incorporation of the tax considerations that are relevant to each portfolio. Primarily, this would entail a major expansion of the database, which currently contains only the book value of all holdings. The problem with book value is that capital-gains tax is based on the difference between selling price and buying price. A given portfolio may own two lots of stock X, one bought 20 years ago at $10 per share, the other bought one year ago at $200 per share. Under these circumstances, it may be advantageous to sell stock from one lot but not from the other. Thus the first step in incorporating tax considerations into OPM would be to expand its database and to decide what new operators would be appropriate in displaying and manipulating the additional data. The database expansion would be a major task since this information currently exists in the form of handwritten cards. Since it might be impractical to keep all of the data on-line, an alternative design would maintain this information on tape and would allow requests to be serviced on an overnight basis. Although contrary to the otherwise on-line nature of OPM, this procedure would be consistent with the basic philosophy of OPM, which is that the system can and should continue to grow as new potential uses arise.

Finally, it is possible that special OPM functions or usage procedures will be developed to help in managing particular types of accounts. For instance, a pension-fund manager with 10 accounts can keep track of them almost day to day and might be helped by very specific information concerning the effect of buying or selling particular securities on the total return of a pension-fund portfolio. At the same time, a trust-fund manager handling 200 accounts with a wide range of customer objectives might make extensive use of procedures (mentioned earlier) for keeping track of whether his accounts were meeting objectives and for triggering actions on his part.

## VI. SOME LESSONS THAT WERE LEARNED

This section is based on interviews with the head of the software company that implemented OPM and with the Trust Division's implementation coordinator. It states more or less directly a number of their conclusions concerning the key issues that arose in the development of OPM.

With regard to the implementation and use of OPM, it is important to note that the project was initially posed as an experiment with an uncertain outcome and that the results are not all in at the time of this writing. OPM differs in this respect from a standard MIS project, in which success typically hinges on the correctness and reliability of a series of programs in performing a sequence of data processing tasks that can be clearly specified in advance. When bank management gave the go-ahead for the project, they did have general mock-ups of the kinds of reports that would be generated by OPM, but they understood quite well that the exact form of use and the exact details of the system would necessarily evolve over time. In spite of these uncertainties, they felt that it was a worthwhile project and decided to proceed. In reviewing progress to date, they feel that they made the correct decision even though the impact of OPM on Trust Division performance is extremely difficult to quantify. Although they can point to some very clear benefits, such as better information in much better formats, less clerical work, better communication, improved image, etc., they cannot state with certainty that Trust Division performance has improved x percent as a result of having OPM.

A number of important lessons can be extracted from the experience of implementing OPM under these somewhat experimental circumstances. The first is that simply providing the technical tools does not necessarily result in use. Initially the system was viewed as one way of solving problems. In fact, it was no more than a series of tools that were available to be used as part of a behavior change process if people chose to use it in that way.

When only partial changes resulted from this *passive* implementation, management began to take an *active* role in ensuring that the behavioral changes would take place. It was necessary for the organization's leaders to state clearly that this was a useful system and that they were committed to its acceptance as part of the process of portfolio management. Furthermore, they found it necessary to take positive action in the form of establishing mandatory account-review procedures that involved the use of OPM.

Part of the lesson here is the importance of having users assume definite responsibility for the implementation of the system. This is to be distinguished from "participation," in which users inform the designers of what is needed but delegate final responsibility to the designers. The basic idea is simply that since users pay the money and since the system is for their use, they must manage the implementation if they want good results. Under this rationale, a user cannot claim that the system just isn't any good unless the problem stems totally from technical difficulties.

The head of the software company feels that the question of responsibility is extremely important because the systems person is basically an outsider and simply cannot know all the situational factors and idiosyncrasies that may have some effect on the ultimate outcome. The systems person, consequently, can create a technical product and can stimulate certain kinds of behavior but can't ensure an end product other than a technical end product.

In a situation where a system will ultimately have a large number of users, the acceptance of implementation responsibility can be very complicated. Consider the experience with OPM. Whereas the implementation coordinator and the 10-member advisory group were quite enthusiastic about it and used it heavily, other potential users didn't really get involved until their superiors decreed that the system must be used by everyone for certain purposes. In that situation, the user representative responsible for implementation had a dual role. On the one hand, he had to ensure that the right technical tools were being developed. This extended to very detailed questions of exactly what data fields should or would be available in any OPM function. In the words of the head of the software company, "a person in this position has to be tough in insisting that systems people not take shortcuts which may jeopardize the effectiveness of the final system." On the other hand, he had to monitor user acceptance as the system came up to be sure that all problems and questions were recognized and resolved in one way or another before they began to "fester," as sometimes happens when lines of communication are not open.

Another of the key issues in implementing a system of this sort is in the positioning of its introduction. There is great danger in being too autocratic and saying, "This is the system, and this is how it will work." In an evolving system like OPM, it is difficult to plan exactly how the system will turn out and exactly what benefits will accrue. The implementer who is too specific or autocratic about these things will surely miss the mark. It is especially important that all people involved with the developing system be aware of its goals and underlying premises and of the action that is expected from potential users.

The development of systems like OPM requires people who have a combination of abilities that is relatively rare. The systems people and project coordinators must have knowledge of the technology, a feeling for decision making, and an ability to communicate effectively concerning issues that sometimes have both factual and emotional content.

The fact that such people are rare exacerbates the problem of continuity in the management and execution of system implementation. The continuity problem is frequently encountered when one person takes over part of a project that was being handled by someone else. To avoid this problem, it is necessary either to insist that coordinating personnel remain in their positions until the system is complete or to avoid undertaking large projects.

As was demonstrated in this case, the technical challenges and inherent risks in producing a system that is advanced in the "state of the art" can lead to unfortunate consequences in user annoyance and skepticism. In this case, an underestimation of the potential difficulties in developing and debugging OPM resulted in delays and a serious cost overrun. This had a negative impact not only on the budget but also on the introduction process.

In an attempt to catch up, the system was made available to users in a partially debugged form. In this form, the individual functions were generally satisfactory, but the system itself went down frequently. As mentioned earlier, portfolio managers who were enthusiastic toward the development of OPM saw this as a temporary annoyance, whereas some of the others found the unreliability simply unacceptable and would not use the system at all. As these reactions lingered during a long shakedown period, the implementation team found that they were "digging themselves out of a hole instead of starting at ground zero." One lesson here is that it is extremely important to give people things when you say you will. One way of achieving this goal is for the technical implementers to operate with two separate delivery dates, i.e., an internal one, when the system should be ready, and a very conservative external one, when the user should expect the system to be in place.

Another lesson reinforced by the OPM experience is that any less than 95 percent reliability in a system of this sort can lead to serious dissatisfaction. At the same time, however, combining high-reliability requirements with time pressure has serious implications of higher cost. The balance between these factors is one of the issues that must be addressed by the managers of the implementation effort.

### Questions for the Reader

1. Assume that the bank has decided to attempt to automate portfolio decisions completely and has asked you to develop a method. Describe the approach you might try, with particular attention to the data that would be required.

2. Assume that the bank has asked you to develop a more objective way to evaluate portfolio managers. Describe the criteria you would propose, with particular attention to the data that would be required in applying your criteria.

3. Do you feel that the decision to develop the system was justified adequately?

4. Why did system usage differ so greatly among the portfolio managers? Is this a serious problem?

5. Did bank management take appropriate action in attempting to increase system usage? Did they go far enough? Should PMs be rewarded for using OPM or penalized for not using it?

6. Currently OPM is in operation only four hours each day. Could Trust Division management make a good case for keeping it in operation eight hours a day?

7. Has OPM been a success to date? Would it be possible to gather additional data that would allow one to make a stronger case as to the success or lack of success of the system? If so, how could that data be obtained?

APPENDIX

The following are sample mock-ups of eight OPM functions. In order to avoid divulging confidential details of the bank's portfolio management practices, some of these mock-ups differ from functions that are actually used.

FIGURE 6 The Directory Function

| | All amounts in thousands | | | | | Percent of total | | | | | | Account |
|---|---|---|---|---|---|---|---|---|---|---|---|---|
| Account name | Total value | Liquid assets | Common stocks | Bonds | Part equity | Liquid | Common | Bond | Part equity | Last trade | Last look | perfor-mance |
| A | 1,689 | 1,014 | 47,015 | 22,614 | 355 | 1.2 | 57.6 | 27.7 | .4 | 04/22 | 04/22 | 12.3 |
| B | 481 | 133 | 230 | 105 | 12 | 27.7 | 47.8 | 21.8 | 2.5 | 04/22 | 05/13 | 10.4 |
| C | 137,872 | 544 | 97,240 | 37,015 | 2,917 | .4 | 70.5 | 26.8 | 2.1 | 05/22 | 05/28 | 6.7 |
| D | 39,836 | 2,415 | 31,412 | 5,612 | 0 | 6.1 | 78.9 | 14.1 | .0 | 05/12 | 05/17 | 7.1 |
| E | 217,015 | 22,405 | 142,018 | 38,412 | 10,018 | 10.3 | 65.4 | 17.7 | 4.6 | 03/03 | 04/30 | 8.6 |
| F | 1,827 | 3 | 976 | 812 | 0 | .2 | 53.4 | 44.4 | .0 | 03/03 | 04/27 | 9.6 |

The Directory function gives a tabular overview of all accounts under the PM's jurisdiction. The table that is generated is sorted by any of a number of fields, including account identifier, market value, liquid assets, fixed income, performance, and so on. This sorting feature allows the PM to compare whole portfolios in a number of simple ways in addition to simply listing the portfolios under his or her jurisdiction.

FIGURE 7 The Scan Function

ACCOUNTS HOLDING COMPANY A

Jun 23 PRICE: 50

| | TOTAL | COMPANY A | | | OIL | | PETRCHM | | ACCOUNT | REORD |
|---|---|---|---|---|---|---|---|---|---|---|
| | ACCOUNT MKT VALUE | UNITS HELD | UNIT COST | PCT ACCT | # | PCT ACCT | # | PCT ACCT | CASH BALANCE | FOR 5.30% |
| Account A | 137,871,837 | 120,500 | 30 | 4.4 | 2 | 6.6 | 2 | 6.6 | 911,254 | 25,644 |
| Account B | 81,688,794 | 110,280 | 28 | 6.8 | 4 | 8.2 | 6 | 15.0 | 315,260 | 23,600− |
| Account C | 217,014,862 | 87,240 | 52 | 2.0 | 3 | 3.2 | 5 | 12.7 | 1,222,087 | 142,796 |
| Account D | 39,835,820 | 63,100 | 43 | 7.9 | 1 | 7.9 | 3 | 37.7 | 29,472 | 20,874− |
| Account E | 26,737,925 | 30,000 | 22 | 5.6 | 2 | 5.6 | 3 | 29.4 | 321,354 | 1,658− |
| Account F | 1,827,396 | 1,250 | 32 | 3.4 | 2 | 3.4 | 2 | 46.2 | 417,081 | 687 |
| Account G | 481,134 | 870 | 33 | 9.0 | 2 | 9.0 | 3 | 12.5 | 212,065 | 360− |
| Account H | 46,520 | 30 | 53 | 3.2 | 1 | 3.2 | 1 | 3.2 | 1,092 | 19 |

*FIGURE 8  The Groups Function*

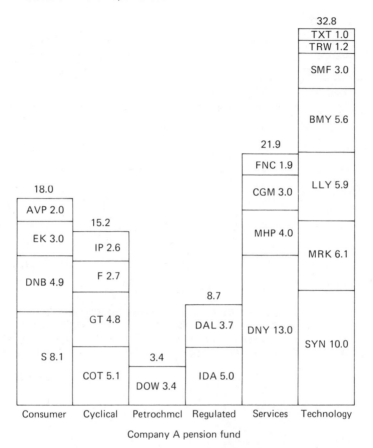

Company A pension fund

*The* Groups *function produces a picture of the distribution of the holdings in an account by broad industry groups. The six industry groups are consumer, cyclical, petrochemical, regulated, services, and technology. The display looks like a histogram and gives the percentage of the portfolio in each security and in each industry.*

◄ *The* Scan *function allows the PM to view the holdings of a particular security across a group of accounts. The PM selects the security, a sort key, and other information, such as whether percentages should be applied to the whole account or just the common-stock portion. The report that is produced includes (for each account) units of the security held, unit cost, percentage of that account devoted to this security, percentage of the account within this security's industry classification, the account's cash balance, and so on.*

*FIGURE 9   The Table Function*

JOHN DOE TRUST FUND

| P/E | SECURITY NAME | CUR MKT PRI | CUR EPS EST | 5 PE HI | 5 PE LO | PCT C/S ACT | PROJ ANNL DIVD | YLD ON DIVD |
|------|--------------|-----|------|----|----|----|------|------|
| 7.4 | Company A | 22 | 3.00 | 15 | 11 | 16 | 1.50 | 6.74 |
| 9.7 | Company B | 42 | 4.35 | 11 | 8 | 9 | 2.40 | 5.70 |
| 10.4 | Company C | 21 | 2.00 | 20 | 10 | 3 | .40 | 1.93 |
| 10.8 | Company D | 44 | 4.00 | 18 | 12 | 10 | .80 | 1.82 |
| 12.2 | Company E | 28 | 2.10 | 21 | 16 | 12 | .88 | 3.20 |
| 17.1 | Company F | 41 | 2.40 | 28 | 19 | 8 | 1.40 | 3.42 |
| 22.9 | Company G | 41 | 1.80 | 28 | 15 | 1 | .40 | 1.07 |
| 26.0 | Company H | 91 | 3.50 | 31 | 21 | 17 | .96 | 1.06 |
| 27.7 | Company I | 72 | 2.55 | 36 | 27 | 7 | 1.32 | 1.83 |
| 30.2 | Company J | 89 | 2.95 | 35 | 24 | 12 | 1.20 | 1.35 |
| 41.0 | Company K | 74 | 1.80 | 53 | 36 | 5 | 1.10 | 1.49 |

*The Table function provides a flexible way for the PM to design reports for reviewing the holdings of an account. The PM types the account name and a list of the data items wanted for each holding. Examples might be the current price/earnings ratio, the security name, its current market price, five-year high and low P/E ratios, value of the holding as a percentage of the account, projected dividends, and so on.*

*FIGURE 10   The Histogram Function*

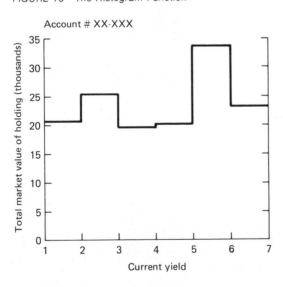

FIGURE 11    The Scatter Function

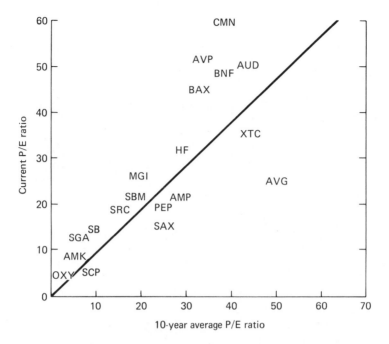

The Scatter *function allows the PM to examine the relationship between two data items associated with the securities held by an account. In order to obtain this two-dimensional plot, the PM specifies the account, together with the two data items to be displayed. An example of its use would be a scatterplot of current P/E ratio against 10-year average P/E ratio for the holdings in an account. OPM automatically selects the bounds on the horizontal and vertical axes so that all securities will fit on the display. The PM may also filter the data items so that the only securities that appear are of a certain type or fall within a specified range of data item values.*

◄ *The* Histogram *function allows the PM to view the distribution of any available data item for all the holdings within an account. For instance, a histogram of the total market value of accounts against their current yield can be assembled. The menu for* Histogram *asks the PM to type the data items needed on each of the axes and to indicate whether they should be given in percentage or dollar figures.*

FIGURE 12   *The Summary Function*

ACCOUNT #XX-XXX   JOHN DOE
ACCOUNT TYPE   IRREV PROBATE
DATE LAST TRAN 04/10/74

I.O. J. SMITH
T.O. J. JONES

| | | | BOND MATURITY BREAKDOWN | | |
|---|---|---|---|---|---|
| TOTAL MKT VALUE | 2,775,670 | 100.0 | | | |
| EQUITIES | 2,133,527 | 76.9 | ONE MONTH OR LESS | 50,000 | 7.0 |
| PFDS W/EQ | 0 | .0 | MONTH TO ONE YEAR | 0 | .0 |
| BONDS W/EQ | 0 | .0 | 1 to 5 YEARS | 0 | .0 |
| | | | 5 to 10 YEARS | 0 | .0 |
| PFDS | 19,700 | .7 | 10 to 20 YEARS | 0 | .0 |
| FIXED INCOME | 618,076 | 22.3 | OVER 20 YEARS | 655,000 | 93.0 |
| | | | TOTAL BONDS | 705,000 | 100.0 |
| MISC | 0 | | | | |
| LIQ ASSET (EX-CASH) | 4,000 | .1 | | | |
| PRIN CASH | 365 | .0 | | | |
| INC CASH | 21,132 | .7 | | | |
| ADJ LIQ ASSETS | 54,365 | 1.9 | | | |

DETAILED INVESTMENT PROVISIONS

_ _ _ _ _ _ _ _ _ _ _ _

_ _ _ _ _ _ _ _ _ _ _ _

The Summary *function displays various account-summary data, information descriptive of the account, notes on the investment provisions, investment authority, investment objectives, and so on. The summary report is divided into five general information groupings. (1) Report heading: people involved, type of account, etc. (2) Summarized holdings data: total market value, breakdown among categories, such as equities, preferreds, fixed income, liquid assets, etc. (3) Bond maturity breakdown. (4) Account description: investment provisions and authority, objectives, limitations, retention provisions, nature of investments, etc. (5) Account long title.*

*FIGURE 13*    *The Issue Function*

COMPANY A

| APPROVED CODE: A | FISCAL YR END: SEP |
|---|---|

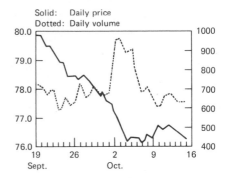

Solid:   Monthly prices
Dotted: Quarterly earnings

| PRICE | | PRICE RANGES | | |
|---|---|---|---|---|
| 10/17 | 74.375 | 1971 | | 57 - 78 |
| 9/18 | 68.500 | 1970 | | 48 - 90 |
| | | 1969 | | 72 - 136 |
| | | 1968 | | 48 - 130 |
| EARNINGS | | | | |
| LAST 12M JUN | 7.60 | 1972 HI | 9/12 | 134 |
| 1972 | 8.00 | 1972 LO | 2/25 | 76 |
| 1971 | 7.75 | | | |
| 1970 | 7.42 | DIVIDENDS | | |
| 1969 | 7.42 | PROJ 12 MOS | | 4.00 |
| 1968 | 6.82 | YIELD OF PROJ | | 5.39% |
| EST 1973 | 8.20 | | | |
| NEXT 12M SEP | 8.55 | EPS GROWTH RATE | | |
| | | PROJECTED | | 6.00% |
| P/E RANGES | | LAST 5 YEARS | | 1.28% |
| 1971 | 8.8 - 12.1 | SHRS OUTSTAND | | 23.361 |
| 1970 | 8.9 - 10.8 | TOT RET | | 32% |
| 1969 | 7.1 - 9.6 | | | |
| 1968 | 6.9 - 8.3 | | | |
| P/E (73 EPS) | 8.7 | | | |
| P/E PREF | 10.2 | | | |

Solid:   Daily price
Dotted: Daily volume

COMMENTS BY ANALYST

– – – – – – – – –
– – – – – – – – –

*The Issue function displays all the information pertaining to a specified issue on the approved list in a one-page display. This includes information concerning price, earnings, historical P/E ratios, dividends, number of shares outstanding, total return, and dated comments from investment analysis that might have bearing on decisions regarding this issue.*

# GOTAAS-LARSEN SHIPPING CORPORATION: A CORPORATE PLANNING SYSTEM

## CASE THREE

The Gotaas-Larsen Shipping Corporation is one of the larger subsidiaries of IU International (formerly International Utilities), a conglomerate operating in three major markets: energy; transportation and distribution; and environmental services. By the late 1960s, International Utilities had spent 10 years on a program of acquisition and diversification. To help manage its expanded activities, International Utilities set up a formal planning system. In 1970, Mr. Arthur Goldenberg, a member of the planning staff, was transferred to Gotaas-Larsen Shipping Corporation, initially as an internal consultant and subsequently as Vice President of Finance and Administration. Mr. Goldenberg viewed his assignment as being "to help Gotaas-Larsen in setting up a planning system. The output of the planning system was to be compatible with the system established at International Utilities."

This case study concerns the computerized systems developed under the leadership of Mr. Goldenberg between 1970 and 1974 to facilitate planning and control activities at Gotaas-Larsen. Throughout the case, there is a single underlying concern, namely, to identify the contribution of computerized systems to these planning and control activities. The case begins by providing some brief descriptive information about IU International and Gotaas-Larsen. The discussion then turns to the Gotaas-Larsen planning cycle and to specific activities related to strategic planning, capital expenditures, operational planning, and control. A summary reviews each type of activity and the role played by the corresponding computer applications.

## I. BACKGROUND

### A. The Parent Company

International Utilities (IU) was founded in 1924. As of 1973, IU was established in three major industry sectors with eight operating groups:

Energy markets, in which the Ocean Shipping (Gotaas-Larsen), Energy Systems, and Electric and Gas Services groups operated.

This case was written by Steven Alter and Sudeep Anand. The interest and encouragement of Mr. Arthur Goldenberg and Prof. Peter Lorange are sincerely appreciated.

Transportation and distribution markets, in which the Transportation Services and Distribution Services groups competed.

Environmental markets, where IU operated through its Waste Management Services, Water Management Service, and Land Management and Tourism groups.

Today (1974) the breadth of its geographical and market diversification has led IU to delegate all operating decisions to the management of each operating company. To manage its far-flung activities, IU has adopted strong centralized controls in finance and planning, however, with special emphasis on asset management and long-range strategic planning. The operating performance of management is then measured against objectives established through IU's planning system. Executive compensation is closely tied to the achievement of approved objectives. It is corporate policy to capitalize each operating group on the basis of its own debt capacity, in order that the capital structure of each operating group may reflect the characteristics of its own industry. Management views cash dividends as a form of corporate discipline, and each subsidiary is expected to pay an annual dividend to the parent company.

## B. Gotaas-Larsen Shipping Corporation

Gotaas-Larsen Shipping Corporation is the successor to a partnership formed in 1946 by the late Mr. Trygve Gotaas and Mr. Harry Irgens Larsen. Initially, Gotaas-Larsen managed ships for other owners, but later the company purchased vessels of its own. Gotaas-Larsen's first purchases were oil tankers, acquired in the early 1950s when the Korean War increased the need for U.S. shipping. Around 1961 the company entered its second major market area, bulk carriers. In August 1963 the company was acquired by IU for $13.2 million in common stock. Gotaas-Larsen's increasing need for capital was a major factor in its becoming part of IU. At the time of the acquisition, Gotaas-Larsen's fleet consisted of 12 ships totaling 350,000 dead weight tons (dwt). Over the next 10 years the company grew rapidly. As of 1973, the fleet consisted of 54 cargo ships totaling 4.1 million dwt and 6 passenger cruise ships. About 70–80 percent of Gotaas-Larsen's revenues come from its tankers, with the balance derived about equally from its bulk and cruise operations. Gotaas-Larsen owns (fully or partially) a large part of the fleet it operates. The remaining part is either chartered in from other owners or is operated by Gotaas-Larsen as agents. Figure 14 lists the Gotaas-Larsen fleet as of 1974 in terms of the type of shipping trade and the chartering arrangement for each ship at that time. Insert 1 explains the common types of chartering arrangements.

The legal corporate structure of the company is rather complicated. Typically, each vessel is owned by a separate company that is directly or indirectly a wholly owned subsidiary of Gotaas-Larsen Shipping Corporation. Most of the subsidiaries are incorporated in either Liberia or Panama to take advantage of favorable fiscal, tax, and operating conditions. U.S. income taxes must be paid on money remitted by these subsidiaries to the parent company. Gotaas-Larsen Inc., a wholly owned subsidiary of Gotaas-Larsen Shipping Corporation, provides centralized management services, including chartering arrangements for all the subsidiaries. For purposes of planning and operations, the organization chart may be viewed as one entity, as shown in Fig. 15.

---

**Insert 1: Types of Ships Charters**

The following five types of charters are used commonly in shipping.

*Time Charter.* This is the most common charter arrangement. The vessel is chartered for a specified period of time at a specified rate per deadweight ton of capacity per calendar month. Operating costs for crew, stores, maintenance, insurance, etc., are commonly paid by the owner; voyage costs, such as fuel, port and cargo charges, etc., are paid by the charterer.

*Bareboat Charter.* This is similar to a time charter, except that the shipper charters the boat "bare," provides his own crew, and pays all operating expenses. This is generally regarded as being analogous to leasing as a financing arrangement.

*Consecutive-Voyage Charter.* Under this arrangement, the ship is chartered for a specified number of consecutive voyages among specified ports over a specified time period. The charterer pays an agreed freight rate per ton of cargo lifted on each voyage. All expenses, including voyage costs, are paid by the owner.

*Single-Voyage Charter.* This is commonly known as a "spot market" charter. The vessel is chartered to lift a cargo from one or more leading ports to one or more discharging ports at a specified freight rate. Single-voyage charters are identical to consecutive-voyage charters in all respects except their one-time nature.

*Contract of Affreightment.* This type of contract provides for the shipment of a specified quantity and type of cargo from and to specified ports over a specified period of time at a certain freight payment per ton. It usually requires the owner to use vessels of certain minimum/maximum sizes. As with single-voyage charters, the owner pays all transportation costs.

---

### C.  The People Who Manage Gotaas-Larsen

In contrast to its complicated legal structure, Gotaas-Larsen is managed in a highly centralized manner by a small group of top managers who are international figures in the shipping industry. The style of strategic management at Gotaas-Larsen is largely set by the Chairman, Harry Irgens Larsen, and the President, Lewis Krall, whereas the day-to-day operations of the company are managed by the Executive Vice President, Finn Grape. All three receive staff assistance and financial advice from the Vice President of Finance and Administration, Arthur Goldenberg.

Mr. Larsen (aged 66) began his career with a ship brokerage in Norway and later, during World War II, worked for the Norwegian Government Shipping Agency in Montreal and New York. Mr. Larsen cofounded Gotaas-Larsen, Inc., in 1946 with Trygve Gotaas and served as a partner until 1956, when he became President and Chief Executive Officer. In 1963, when Gotaas-Larsen was merged in IU, he became a director and vice president of IU. Mr. Larsen also continued to be President of Gotaas-Larsen until 1971, when he became Vice Chairman of IU. Since 1972, he has also been Board Chairman and CEO of Gotaas-Larsen. Mr. Larsen has been an international figure in the shipping industry for many years.

*FIGURE 14   Charter Arrangements for Gotaas-Larsen Fleet (1974)*

## Gotaas-Larsen Fleet March, 1974

Bar indicates duration of charter

### TANKERS

| Ship | dwt | Ownership | Charter |
|---|---|---|---|
| Golar Betty | 216,629 dwt | 100% owned | Time charter expiring 1983 |
| Golar Kanto | 215,714 dwt | 100% owned | Consecutive voyages expiring 1975 |
| Golar Kansai | 215,824 dwt | 75% owned | Time charter expiring 1975 |
| Golar Nichu | 215,782 dwt | 100% owned | Consecutive voyages 6 months to 1974 — Time charter 1974-79 |
| Fernmount | 215,529 dwt | 40% owned | Consecutive voyages expiring 1975, consecutive voyages winter 1976 |
| Jalta | 156,188 dwt | 25% owned | Time charter expiring 1976 |
| Jalna | 156,188 dwt | 25% owned | Time charter expiring 1974 |
| Golar Nikko | 111,030 dwt | 100% owned | Bareboat expiring 1981 |
| Golar Liz | 107,023 dwt | 100% owned | Spot |
| Golar Ron | 106,239 dwt | 100% owned | Time charter expiring 1975 |
| Golar Toko | 86,792 dwt | 100% owned | Bareboat expiring 1981 |
| Golar Solveig | 60,861 dwt | 100% owned | Spot |
| Golar Siri | 55,960 dwt | 100% owned | Spot |
| Golar Martita | 42,210 dwt | 100% owned | Time charter expiring 1975 |
| Golar Bali | 15,540 dwt | 65% owned | Time charter expiring 1981 |
| Golar Bintan | 15,540 dwt | 65% owned | Time charter expiring 1981 |
| Golar Buatan | 15,540 dwt | 65% owned | Time charter expiring 1981 |
| Golar Surabaya | 15,540 dwt | 65% owned | Time charter expiring 1981 |
| Golar Bawean | 15,540 dwt | 65% owned | Time charter expiring 1981 |
| Golar Sabang | 15,540 dwt | 65% owned | Time charter expiring 1981 |
| Golar Sigli | 15,540 dwt | 65% owned | Time charter expiring 1981 |
| Gauchito | 1,473 dwt | 100% owned | Spot |
| World Mitsubishi | 234,728 dwt | Chartered In | Time charter to 1974 — Consecutive voyages winter 1974-75 |
| Halcyon the Great | 226,692 dwt | Chartered In | Time charter expiring outward 1990 — inward 1990 |
| Humboldt | 219,087 dwt | Chartered In | Time charter 1974-80 — inward 1980 |
| Golar Robin | 215,923 dwt | Chartered In | Consecutive voyages to 1974 — Time charter 1974-79 — inward 1998 |
| Kollbryn | 99,347 dwt | Chartered In | Time charter expiring outward 1974 — inward 1974 |
| Sanko Bay | 59,200 dwt | Chartered In | Contract of Affreightment expiring outward 1976 — inward 1976 |
| J. T. Higgins | 212,010 dwt | Operated As Agent | Bareboat charter expiring 1995 |
| D. L. Bower | 212,010 dwt | Operated As Agent | Bareboat charter expiring 1995 |
| Texaco Darien | 78,170 dwt | Operated As Agent | Bareboat charter expiring 1987 |
| Chevron Frankfurt | 78,872 dwt | Operated As Agent | Bareboat charter expiring 1987 |

### REFRIGERATED SHIPS

| Ship | dwt | Ownership | Charter |
|---|---|---|---|
| Golar Frost | 7,400 dwt | 100% owned | Time charter expiring 1975 |
| Golar Borg | 7,400 dwt | 40% owned | Time charter expiring 1975 |
| Golar Freeze | 7,130 dwt | 100% owned | Time charter expiring 1975 |
| Golar Nel | 7,090 dwt | 15% owned | Time charter expiring 1975 |
| Golar Fruit | 6,090 dwt | 100% owned | Time charter expiring 1974 |
| Golar Tryg | 6,075 dwt | 15% owned | Time charter expiring 1974 |
| Golar Ragni | 9,072 dwt | Operated As Agent | Time charter expiring 1977 |
| Golar Girl | 9,072 dwt | Operated As Agent | Time charter expiring 1978 |

Column headers for chart: 1974 | 1975 | 1976 | 1977 | 1978 (each divided 1 2 3 4)

Timeline columns: 1974 | 1975 | 1976 | 1977 | 1978 (each divided into quarters 1 2 3 4)

## BULK CARRIERS

| Name | Size | Ownership | Note |
|---|---|---|---|
| Golar Sanko | 86,795 dwt | 100% owned | Bareboat expiring 1981 |
| Gaucho Laguna | 30,403 dwt | 100% owned | Contract of affreightment expiring 1976 |
| Gaucho Cruz | 30,403 dwt | 100% owned | Contract of affreightment expiring 1975 |
| Santos Vega | 27,021 dwt | 100% owned | Contract of affreightment expiring 1975 |
| Golar Arrow | 26,139 dwt | 51% owned | Time charter expiring 1987 |
| Golar Bow | 26,113 dwt | 51% owned | Time charter expiring 1988 |
| Martin Fierro | 15,780 dwt | 100% owned | Contract of affreightment expiring 1975 |
| Don Segundo Sombra | 15,230 dwt | 100% owned | Contract of affreightment expiring 1975 |
| Japan Oak | 53,640 dwt | Chartered In | Time charter expiring outward 1978 — inward 1978 |
| Japan Pine | 53,356 dwt | Chartered In | Time charter expiring outward 1977 — inward 1977 |
| Long Hope | 50,900 dwt | Chartered In | Time charter expiring outward 1978 — inward 1978 |
| Helvig | 36,000 dwt | Chartered In | Time charter expiring outward 1974 — inward 1974 |
| Agia Erini II | 31,904 dwt | Chartered In | Contract of affreightment expiring outward 1975 — inward 1979 |
| Gaucho Taura | 30,403 dwt | Chartered In | Contract of affreightment expiring outward 1975 — inward 1981 |
| Gaucho Pampa | 30,403 dwt | Chartered In | Contract of affreightment expiring outward 1975 — inward 1981 |

## PRODUCT CARRIERS

| Name | Size | Ownership | Note |
|---|---|---|---|
| Bruse Jarl | 32,000 dwt | 30% owned | Time charter expiring 1975 |

## DRILLING RIGS

|  |  |  |  |
|---|---|---|---|
| Norskald (Nor-101) | Semi-submersible | 39% owned | Drilling contract expiring 1976 |

## VESSELS ON ORDER

| Type | Size | Ownership | Note |
|---|---|---|---|
| LNG | 125,000 cu.m. | 95% owned | Delivery 1975 — Time charter expiring 1996 |
| LNG | 125,000 cu.m. | 95% owned | Delivery 1976 — Time charter expiring 1996 |
| LNG | 125,000 cu.m. | 95% owned | Delivery 1977 — Time charter expiring 1997 |
| LNG | 128,600 cu.m. | 100% owned | Delivery 1977 |
| LNG | 128,600 cu.m. | 100% owned | Delivery 1977 |
| Tanker | 410,000 dwt | 100% owned | Delivery 1977 |
| Tanker | 410,000 dwt | 100% owned | Delivery 1976 |
| Tanker | 410,000 dwt | 100% owned | Delivery 1978 |
| Product Carrier | 32,000 dwt | 100% owned | Delivery 1974 |
| Product Carrier | 32,000 dwt | 100% owned | Delivery 1975 |
| Product Carrier | 32,000 dwt | 100% owned | Delivery 1976 |
| Drilling Rig | Semi-submersible | 49% owned | Delivery 1974 — Drilling contract expiring 1976 |
| Drilling Rig | Semi-submersible | 65% owned | Delivery 1976 |
| Drilling Rig | Semi-submersible | 65% owned | Delivery 1976 |

FIGURE 15   Gotaas-Larsen Shipping Corporation Organization Chart

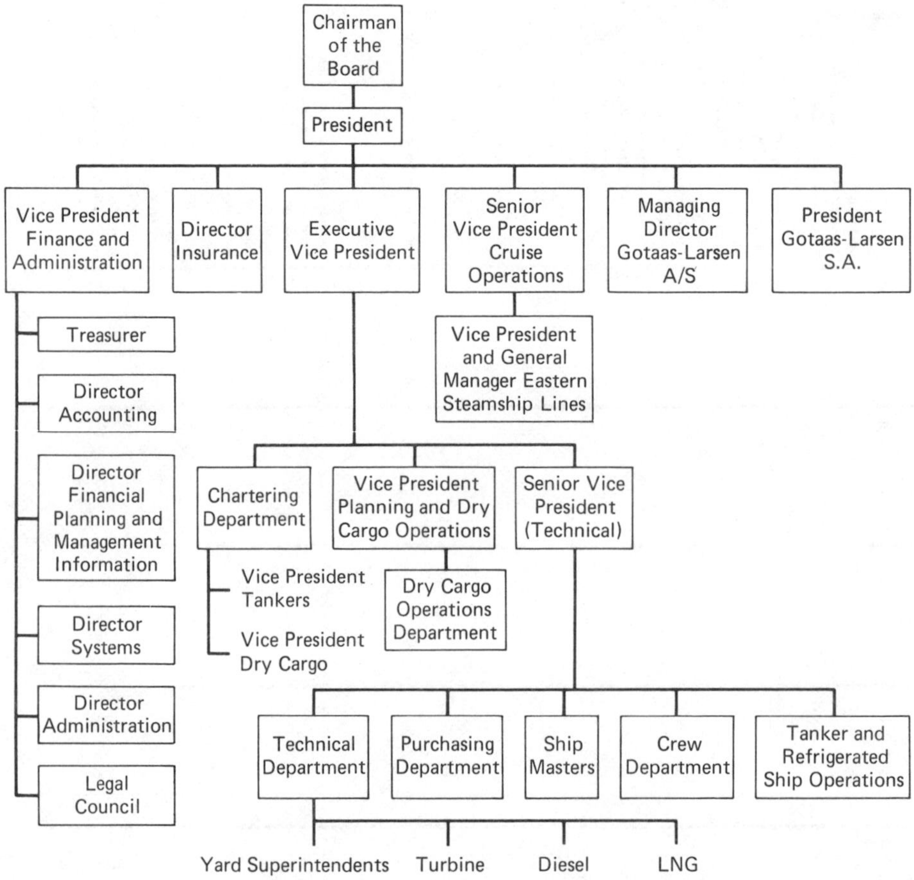

Mr. Krall (aged 54) graduated from New York University with a degree in business administration. He joined Gotaas-Larsen in 1948 and became its Treasurer in 1952. He became a vice president in 1965, Executive Vice President in 1970, and has been President since 1972. One of Mr. Krall's beliefs is that the way to run a company effectively is to limit the number of people managing it. He also believes that as the company grows, formal planning and control systems have to be instituted to help management make decisions, since the management has to become more impersonal. He believes that computers have created profound opportunities for the shipping industry. "They have made possible the building of very large ships, but they have also made possible the planning and control of the companies that own and manage these ships."

Mr. Grape (aged 41) joined Gotaas-Larsen as assistant to the President in 1970 after working as a tanker broker with Fearnley and Eger Chartering Co., Ltd., in Norway. In 1972 he became Executive Vice President and assistant to the Chairman.

Mr. Goldenberg (aged 42) is a graduate of the Harvard Business School. Before coming to Gotaas-Larsen, he worked in the planning group of IU International. During that time he was intimately involved with the IU planning system. He first came to Gotaas-Larsen as an internal consultant to help upgrade the planning system and make it compatible with that of IU. In 1972 he joined the Gotaas-Larsen management as Vice President for Finance and Administration.

### D.  Gotaas-Larsen's Strategic Posture and Philosophy

Gotaas-Larsen's current strategic philosophy is governed by what top management perceive as its strengths and weaknesses. Since Gotaas-Larsen is a publicly held company, it has audited financial statements. This circumstance is thought to give Gotaas-Larsen a slight advantage over privately held firms in getting funds from banks and other sources. Also, the fact that its management team has a very good operating record gives Gotaas-Larsen a competitive advantage in arranging new charters. Countering these strong points are several constraints under which the company operates. Gotaas-Larsen is a U.S.-based company. Compared with its foreign competitors, it is limited in its ability to siphon money through its series of foreign subsidiaries. One reason for this limitation is that U.S. taxes are paid when Gotaas-Larsen repatriates money from its foreign subsidiaries. Since Gotaas-Larsen has a relatively small management team, it is somewhat limited in its ability to go into businesses that require large numbers of workers.

Gotaas-Larsen's top management philosophy can be summarized as follows:

*Financial.*   It hopes to maintain a ratio of 60–70 percent debt to total capitalization. Under a constraint set by the parent company, it does not consider any new investments or business areas that will not yield at least a 15 percent DCF (discounted cash flow) return on equity before tax or a 20 percent average return on equity after taxes. It must also plan to satisfy IU International's needs for income and dividends.

*Trade.*   Gotaas-Larsen views shipping and other ocean activities and support services as its area of expertise and main line of business. However, because of its lean management organization, it will not enter trades such as containerized shipping or ocean liners, which require major, people-intensive management efforts. Consistent with this policy, Gotaas-Larsen has delegated away the management of its cruise business. Finally, because of risk considerations, Gotaas-Larsen shies away from any business or investment that is limited to one country.

*Chartering policies.*   IU wants to maintain a steady growth path for its reported earnings. Since Gotaas-Larsen contributes nearly 50 percent of IU's income, it is essential that Gotaas-Larsen also have a stable earnings pattern. To achieve this goal, the company follows a policy of sailing a large part of its fleet on medium- to long-term (2–10 years) charters (see Fig. 14). This policy avoids the high-risk, volatile spot market. In recent years, however, following a long-term chartering policy has also proved risky (in the absence of cost escalation clauses) because of the unexpectedly high rate of cost inflation in the industry.

*Investment.*  Gotaas-Larsen maintains a fleet of fairly new ships, and the company prides itself on being able to buy "new technology" ships early enough to make good returns. At the same time, however, every ship in the fleet is considered to be for sale at the right price. Of course, each investment must promise at least a 15 percent DCF return on equity before tax.

## II. PLANNING AND CONTROL AT GOTAAS-LARSEN

The Gotaas-Larsen planning system is centered on the company's basic operating entities, the individual ships (or projects). The sections that follow describe the planning and control system. The discussion is organized as follows:

Formal cycle of planning activities

Strategic search

Strategic planning

Computer usage in strategic planning

Capital expenditures

Operational planning and control

Insert 2 provides a brief overview of the levels of decisions that are made in shipping management.

### A.  Formal Cycle of Activities

To help structure and organize its planning and control activities, Gotaas-Larsen follows an annual formal planning cycle. The main outputs of the planning process are a 10-year strategic plan and a capital appropriation budget for the following year. Part of the strategic plan is further developed to form a one-year operating plan, which is used for control during the following year.

The formal cycle begins in March of each year with preliminary discussions (within Gotaas-Larsen's top management and with IU management) of broad long-range strategies for the company. This stage is followed by the preparation of preliminary plans by June. At the end of July, the preliminary plans are presented to the IU Board of Directors. At this presentation, major emphasis is placed on proposed changes from the previous year's long-range plan. After these preliminary discussions, a detailed strategic plan is prepared for presentation to the IU Board of Directors in September. Although the plan contains projections of activities for 10 years, only the first five years are presented to the IU. The first year of the plan is the current year, which is taken from the previous one-year operating plan.

The development of the one-year operating plan starts in August and is completed in October. The plan has details of monthly operating expenses and capital expenditures for the next 15 months (i.e., October of the current year through December of the following year). The capital-expenditure projections are sent to the IU Board for approval, and the rest of the plan is used for internal control. To keep the plan abreast of new developments, it is revised twice during the following year; the first revision is in April, when the remaining nine months are updated, and the

**Insert 2: Levels of Decisions in Shipping Management**

Shipping companies are characterized by a relatively centralized management structure. The management system of most shipping companies is called upon to make three types of decisions. The first type are those that chart the business directions of the company and may be termed "portfolio planning decisions." The second are the actual ship investment decisions, and the third are the ship operating decisions. Following are some key aspects of these three types of decisions.

*Portfolio Planning.* The portfolio planning problem has three main dimensions. The first is the choice of financial structure of the firm (i.e., the debt/equity ratio). The debt could be of different types, from mortgages on one vessel at one end of the spectrum through a corporate debt issue at the other end. The second important dimension is the allocation of capital to the different types of trades (e.g., tankers, bulk, cruise, etc.). Each trade has different characteristics and different returns to the capital invested. The third important variable is the chartering policy to be followed within each trade chosen (e.g., spot charter, short-term charters, long-term charters, etc.).

*Investment Decisions.* The investment decisions deal with the buying and selling of tonnage within the portfolio framework. Since the price of new tonnage is very sensitive to conditions in the industry, the timing of placing orders for new tonnage is a crucial determinant of the rate of return on each new ship bought. For new types of ships, ideas take a number of years in moving from the "drawing boards" to common usage. In buying ships involving new technology, timing is especially critical. Also there is a well-developed market for secondhand ships so that the average age of the company's fleet is a controllable variable.

*Operating Decisions.* These decisions are concerned with the day-to-day activities of running the fleet and are executed within the framework provided by the portfolio planning and the investment decisions. Operating decisions include things like scheduling ships, finding new charters, etc. Normally the ship's captain has control over voyage costs (e.g., the fuel consumed depends on the speed), and the chief engineer is responsible for the maintenance of the equipment. However, many of the operating decisions, such as setting up drydocking schedules, finding new cargos, and hiring crews, are made centrally.

Of course, these three levels of decision can be broken down much more finely. The planning and control process is designed to ensure that however they are broken down, they are made in a timely and appropriate fashion. The portfolio decisions limit that range within which the more specific goals and objectives of the company can lie. The investment decisions provide the assets that are required to achieve these goals and objectives. The operating decisions are the implementation phase of the strategy.

This overview is largely based on Lorange and Norman (1973).

second revision is in July, when the remaining six months are updated. Each operating plan has a three-month overlap with the previous one and a similar overlap with the next.

In addition to the one-year operating plan, a detailed plan of the expected operating expenses is produced each time a voyage is scheduled.

During the course of the year, the operations of the company are tracked by means of the accounting system. At the end of each month, the accounts are "closed," and income statements and balance sheets are prepared. Actual performance is compared with the expected performance expressed in either the operating plan or voyage plan, as is appropriate. On the basis of this comparison, deviations are diagnosed and corrective actions are taken if they are called for. Finally, funds-flow statements are prepared on a quarterly basis to help monitor the financial status of the company.

## B.  Strategic Search: A Key Component of Strategy Formulation

Although Gotaas-Larsen makes extensive use of its formal planning system, some key planning activities take place outside the formal system. One such activity is the ongoing search for new business opportunities. This process of environmental scanning is a chief responsibility of Messrs. Larsen, Krall, and Grape, all of whom maintain a wide range of contacts throughout the shipping world.

For example, Gotaas-Larsen's acquisition of liquefied natural gas (LNG) tankers and semi-submersible drilling rigs originated from the search activity of the top-level management of the company. Only after years of on-and-off analysis and consideration was the decision made to proceed with a more formal and thorough evaluation of the possible acquisition of these new types of ships. It was at that point that top management's ideas for developing these new lines of trade began to take operational form through the formal planning process. Thus many formal planning activities originated from ideas generated by top management through work outside the formal process.

For existing lines of trade, opportunities are often identified in the Operating, Technical, and Chartering Departments by line managers, who keep close tabs on conditions in the markets where Gotaas-Larsen is already operating. This environmental scanning is fairly easy because the shipping industry is very open, with much information available in shipping journals and through trade associations. The managers also maintain close contacts with ship brokers and shippers to keep track of demand for different kinds of ships. To monitor new technology or types of ships, the managers communicate with shipyards, which also contact Gotaas-Larsen occasionally to offer ships for which the orders have been canceled by another company.

## C.  Strategic Planning

Within the formal planning process, the first step in strategic planning each year is a discussion of the characteristics of Gotaas-Larsen's business in the next five to ten years and how it will differ from current business in terms of

Market characteristics

Market share

Technology and cost

Resources (organizational, financial)

Competitive, political environment

In thinking about broad strategies, top management is particularly attentive to the threats and risks that could affect the achievement of these strategies. Such threats and risks might include

Possible overcapacity in certain trades

Inflationary pressures on ship construction costs

New U.S. legislation

Political situations in potential market areas

Worldwide economic forecasts

These discussions form the basis for updating existing long-range plans and existing corporate goals and objectives. The plans and goals are reevaluated simultaneously because any gap between the two could be closed by changing either plans or objectives. In the goal-setting process for Gotaas-Larsen, the parent company plays an important role. This is necessary because if the intrinsic interests of Gotaas-Larsen were operating independently, it might change its current dividend policy. Negotiations concerning issues such as these are facilitated to a considerable degree by the fact that the Chairman of Gotaas-Larsen is a Vice Chairman of IU.

Once these broad strategic considerations have been agreed upon, a detailed long-range plan must be prepared. Mr. Goldenberg is responsible for the "production" of the plan. He carries out this responsibility in consultation with Messrs. Krall and Grape and with the assistance of a small planning staff.

At the detailed level, the long-range plan is thought of as consisting of "strategies," each of which is a ten-year operating plan for one vessel. These individual strategies are then aggregated into lines of trade, which are further aggregated to form the strategic plan for the company as a whole. Within this plan, financing arrangements are usually tied to individual projects. Exhibit 1 contains an annotated listing of the strategic planning information for a hypothetical ship.

As mentioned earlier, the search for new lines of trade and for new business within existing lines of trade is carried on outside the formal planning cycle. When the ideas begin to take definite shape, they are passed on to the professional staff working for Mr. Goldenberg. The ideas are translated into specific actions involving specific investments. Projections concerning the operating data for the ships are obtained from line managers in the other parts of the company. This data is converted to revenue and expense items and combined with the financing projections made by Mr. Goldenberg to produce income statements and funds-flow statements for further evaluation of the specific project. The projections for projects involving new lines of business are subject to special scrutiny as to reasonableness.

Along with updated plans for the existing fleet, these plans for new ships are keypunched by a clerk and fed into a computer system for strategic-plan consolidation. The output of this system is an aggregate strategic plan for the whole company. The system itself is based on the accounting relationships that define Gotaas-Larsen's

**Exhibit 1: Strategic Planning Forms**

The form included in this exhibit represents a subset of the detailed strategic planning information for a hypothetical ship. In the strategic planning cycle, plans of this sort are aggregated to produce a long-range projection of results, which is then used as the basis for modification of the long-range plan.

Revenues for this ship are set by contract until mid-1979. This arrangement can be seen from lines 2 and 6 of the form, which states that this ship is on voyage charter for six months and is then on time charter for the remaining months of the year. The time-charter rate during the chartered period is given in line 3. Revenues during this period can be calculated exactly by means of a formula involving the time-charter rate at which the ship is chartered and the size of the ship in deadweight tons. After mid-1979, revenues are not known with certainty since no charter exists. But line 4 gives an estimated voyage-charter rate (see line 6) based on the view of the future held by top management. For lack of exact information, the computer applies this estimated rate and the estimated voyage costs in line 6 to calculate revenue figures through the end of the 10-year planning horizon (line 7).

On the expense side, the uncertainties appear sooner. Running costs, the expected sum of lines 11 through 20 on the operational plan (see Exhibit 2), will be calculated by the computer for each year in the 10-year planning horizon on the basis of an estimate for the current year (line 11) and an estimated percentage escalation factor (line 10). Drydocking expenses (line 12) are estimated directly by the technical department on the basis of an assumed maintenance schedule corresponding to the ship's current condition, combined with an underlying notion of the cost escalation that will occur. Insurance expenses (line 14) will be calculated by the computer on the basis of the current year's estimated expenses and an escalation percentage (line 29).

If the data in lines 1-17 were complete, an estimated operating profit for each ship in each year could be computed. This calculation would be based on a combination of exactly determined figures and other estimates. Naturally, as the estimates extended further into the future, their accuracy would decrease. Nonetheless, such estimates are needed. Given the level of investment and the long lead times involved, the strategic-planning horizon in shipping is a long one and simply must involve estimates of unknown quantities.

The remainder of the detailed strategic planning information for a ship or project comprises more than 60 additional line items concerning not only additional details of revenues and expenses but also sources and uses of funds. (These items are not included in this exhibit since many of them cannot be understood without a detailed appreciation of accounting and finance in the shipping industry.) Since most ships are financed individually, it is possible to associate with each project its own financing arrangements. These arrangements constitute a commitment that is known with certainty many years into the future. For a given project there may be a number of financing choices with different kinds of effects on profitability, liquidity, debt/equity considerations, and so on. The proposed financing arrangement is entered as a series of numbers that is calculated outside the system. One of the purposes of companywide strategic planning considerations is to test the impact of choices among various possible financing arrangements.

| Item | Line | 1973 | 1974 | 1975 | 1976 | 1977 | 1978 | 1979 | 1980 | 1981 | 1982 | 1983 |
|---|---|---|---|---|---|---|---|---|---|---|---|---|
| Deadweight tons | 1 | 200,000 | 200,000 | 200,000 | 200,000 | 200,000 | 200,000 | 200,000 | 200,000 | 200,000 | 200,000 | 200,000 |
| REVENUES | | | | | | | | | | | | |
| Number of months chartered | 2 | | 6 | 12 | 12 | 12 | 12 | 6 | | | | |
| Time charter rate—chartered | 3 | | 3.00 | 3.00 | 3.00 | 3.00 | 3.00 | 3.00 | | | | |
| Time charter rate—unchartered | 4 | | 3.50 | | | | | 4.00 | 4.00 | 4.00 | 4.00 | 4.00 |
| Voyage costs—chartered | 5 | | | | | | | | | | | |
| Voyage costs—unchartered | 6 | | 677 | | | | | 750 | 1500 | 1500 | 1500 | 1500 |
| Total revenues | 7 | | * | * | * | * | * | * | * | * | * | * |
| EXPENSES | | | | | | | | | | | | |
| Brokerage commission—chartered | 8 | | .01 | .01 | .01 | .01 | .01 | .01 | | | | |
| Brokerage commission—unchartered | 9 | | | | | | | | | | | |
| Running cost escalation factor | 10 | | .08 | .08 | .08 | .08 | .08 | .08 | .08 | .08 | .08 | .08 |
| Running cost | 11 | 1441 | * | * | * | * | * | * | * | * | * | * |
| Drydocking | 12 | | 100 | 170 | 270 | 300 | 340 | 320 | 345 | 375 | 415 | 420 |
| Insurance escalation factor | 13 | | .04 | .04 | .04 | .04 | .04 | .04 | .04 | .04 | .04 | .04 |
| Insurance | 14 | 346 | * | * | * | * | * | * | * | * | * | * |
| Administration | 15 | | 20 | 22 | 24 | 26 | 28 | 30 | 32 | 34 | 36 | 38 |
| Depreciation | 16 | | 2000 | 2000 | 2000 | 2000 | 2000 | 2000 | 2000 | 2000 | 2000 | 2000 |
| Total expenses | 17 | | * | * | * | * | * | * | * | * | * | * |

*To be calculated by the computer

business. For each vessel or project, numerical extensions are performed and escalation factors are applied in producing dollar estimates across the 10-year horizon. Given these dollar figures, the accounting model underlying the system allows the production of pro-forma income and cash-flow statements for each ship, for each business segment, and for the company as a whole. At the corporate level, taxes can be estimated on the basis of predicted income and dividend policy. One of the special features of this system is that it allows alternative financing arrangements to be entered for any ship or project.

The final strategic plan is then presented to the IU Board. The plan presentation begins with a summary of the relevant financial, marketing, and operating factors. Threats and risks in the general operating environment are also discussed. After this general introduction, the strategic plan is presented, broken out by business line (crude carriers, product carriers, bulk cargo, liquefied natural gas tankers, oil drilling rigs, cruise, and miscellaneous). Within each business line the major capital appropriations are highlighted. This gives the Board early knowledge of the capital requests that are likely to come up for their approval. (Each appropriation in excess of $3 million must be approved by the Board.)

## D.  Computer Usage in Strategic Planning

Mr. Goldenberg believes that one of the key functions of the computer in strategic planning is to allow top management to compare the effects of different project combinations and financing arrangements. By performing the consolidations, the computer eliminates the large amount of clerical work that would otherwise be required to "fine tune" the plan.

During the first two years of the system's existence, Mr. Goldenberg sat at the terminal and ran the system himself. (A clerk had previously keypunched the details.) Recently the system has become stabilized, and other people have been given the responsibility to run it under his direction. This arrangement is preferable because it allows Mr. Goldenberg to obtain equally good results while putting his own time to better use.

The use of the system during the development of the 1974 version of the strategic plan was typical. First, the raw data for each individual project was put onto the system. For existing vessels, this was merely an update of the numbers already in the system. Next, the 10-year projections for each project were printed out. (Exhibit 1 shows a simplified format for these reports.) Mr. Goldenberg reviewed each of these reports to ensure that the estimates were reasonable. Special scrutiny was given to projects that were new or in an unfamiliar line of business. When all the individual projects had been reviewed, a first-cut estimate of corporate results was obtained by aggregation. That provided a preliminary estimate of corporate return on assets, debt/equity ratio, liquidity, smoothness of earnings growth, etc.

At this stage, Messrs. Krall, Grape, and Goldenberg studied the preliminary results and concluded that the plan was too ambitious in terms of new investments. After considering a number of alternative actions, they decided to sell one of the older vessels, eliminate the proposed purchase of two vessels, and delay the implementation of several other projects by a year. These modifications resulted in the accumulation of excess cash in several years of the plan. The next step was to use the excess cash to reduce previously planned loans for new construction. The result was a plan that management felt was satisfactory.

Since the plan has 10 years of projections, it is quite possible that new opportunities will result in the modification of projects in later years. However, the plan gives management a benchmark for evaluating these opportunities when they arise.

### E. Capital Expenditures

Most of Gotaas-Larsen's capital commitments are large and must be approved by the IU Board. A majority of these capital requests are not new to the Board because they have been part of previous strategic plans. However, because opportunities in all business areas are continuously monitored, particularly attractive projects (e.g. an attractive offer to purchase a ship) that were not in previous long-range plans do arise occasionally. If these projects are large, IU approval is still required.

Generally, most projects go through an initial screening process. The screening is done with the help of a commercially available time-sharing program for time-charter analysis. Estimates of investments and charter rates are input into the program, which then produces annual profit-and-loss (P&L) and cash-flow statements. By highlighting the charter rates required for the project to be successful, the program aids management in deciding which projects merit further consideration.

Once a project passes the initial screening, it is analyzed in greater depth. The analysis goes through the following steps.

*Economic analysis.* The economic analysis primarily consists of cash flow, discounted cash flow, and income calculations. This analysis emphasizes sensitivity of the cash flow to major assumptions about revenue and operating cost estimates. The major capital costs consist of the yard contract price, yard extras, superintendence and engineering, and interest on interim financing during construction. Initially this analysis is done on the basis of in-house estimates. However, as the project comes closer to fruition, the projected estimates are replaced by actual numbers.

*Negotiations with the yard.* The initial calculations are used to decide whether to talk to the yard owners at all. They also indicate the maximum price Gotaas-Larsen can afford to pay. The negotiations with the yard center on technical specifications, delivery dates, financing of the construction, and in some instances, permanent long-term financing for the ship after construction is completed.

*Capital appropriation request.* As negotiations with the yard are nearing completion, a capital appropriation request is made to the Board. Most new projects have already been discussed by the Board and have received their review before getting to the stage of a formal capital appropriation request. As a result, these requests are rarely rejected by the Board.

*Monitoring actual costs.* After the order has been placed, the actual costs must be monitored. A large part of the cost is fixed once the order is placed. However, some costs do change during construction (e.g., the amount of interest charged will depend on the construction period, the owner of the ship may change the specifications for equipment, there may be certain price escalation clauses, etc.). At Gotaas-Larsen, the technical staff execute the contract by approving plan changes and by having an inspector at the construction site.

*Financing.*   Once the construction nears completion, permanent financing must be arranged.

When a secondhand ship is to be purchased, the negotiations with the yard are replaced by negotiations with the seller, and there is no need to monitor actual costs.

## F.  Operational Planning and Control

Operational planning and control is carried out within the framework of the strategic plan. The 15-month operating plan is also used as a vehicle for setting detailed goals for the operating units. During the year, actual performance is continuously monitored and compared with the projections made in the operating plan. When performance deviates from predictions, problems are diagnosed, and appropriate corrective actions are taken.

### The Operating Plan

The strategic plan is nearing completion by the time operational planning starts in August. The strategic plan and performance in the recent past are used as a basis for operational planning. Unlike strategic planning, operational planning is highly decentralized. Each manager in the organization projects the performance of the operations under his control. These plans are reviewed by the Senior Vice President in each operating area (see organization chart, Fig. 15). They are then viewed as a commitment on the part of the manager, who is held accountable for the projected level of performance.

The plans are sent to Mr. Goldenberg's office. His staff check them for inconsistencies and other unusual features and then consolidate them. The clerical work of consolidation is done by an operational planning computer system. The input to the system consists of an operating plan for each ship (Exhibit 2 shows a sample plan). The system uses predefined accounting relationships to calculate revenues, expenses, profits, etc., and it produces an operating budget for each business segment and for the company as a whole. Decentralization of the preparation of the detailed plans makes it possible to utilize the expertise of managers in various parts of the organization. This decentralization is facilitated by means of a computer system that does the tedious work of consolidation.

Once the plans are consolidated, they are reviewed by top management. Changes may be negotiated with the line managers who prepared the plans. In general, there are few changes. A large number of the ships are on long-term charter, and the revenues cannot be altered. On the expense side, the major items are interest and depreciation, which are also fixed. The changes are usually in the expected revenues of ships whose charters expire in the next year, the marketing effort required in the cruise and cargo areas, and expected fuel and crew expenses. If income and cash flow are still not satisfactory, the management may decide to change the timing of the sale of a ship.

Mr. Goldenberg's staff are responsible for collecting the detailed plans. They feel that they get the cooperation of line managers, but that the line managers are sometimes not very enthusiastic about their role. Mr. Goldenberg's staff categorize the objections of the line managers into two general areas: (1) They do not like to be held accountable for uncertain results, and (2) they feel that the time committed to planning interferes with their regular work schedule. However, Mr. Goldenberg's staff believe that most of the line managers do realize the necessity of operational planning for the company, and that this is the basis of their cooperation.

*Performance Tracking*

To monitor the day-to-day operations of the company, a computerized general-ledger system is used. Although overheads are allocated to different operating units of the company for purposes of external reporting, a system approximating direct costing is used for management decision making.

To highlight any deviation of performance from plans, regular variance reports are produced. The general-ledger computer system produces a monthly operating report for each account for each operating entity. These operating reports are compared with the operating budget to generate variance reports. A detailed variance report pinpointing the costs for larger vessels is sent to Mr. Krall each month. In addition, quarterly summary reports are produced on each vessel showing yield, running expenses, operating profit, net profit, voyages completed, etc.

The general-ledger system also produces voyage reports that are used to monitor the profitability of individual voyages of ships on voyage charter. Before any ship is offered for a voyage charter, a time-shared voyage analysis program is used to evaluate potential charter arrangements. The input to this program includes ship characteristics, such as tonnage, speed, and fuel consumption, as well as voyage characteristics, such as distance, port changes, canal charges, and so on. The output of the program is an estimate of expected revenues, operating expenses, yield, and time-charter equivalent.[1] A voyage report from the general-ledger system provides a basis for comparison of actual versus estimated results. This report is particularly helpful to the Chartering Department in keeping up-to-date with shipping conditions in various ports. Variances from expectations in operating expenses often indicate that price schedules or other local conditions have changed, and that the new price levels should be included in future voyage planning calculations. A simplified voyage variance report is shown in Exhibit 3. These voyage reports are also used to produce detailed reports of the operating expenses of each ship on each voyage. These reports are sent to the Technical Department.

*Diagnosis and Corrective Actions*

The reports discussed in the last section are information sources for management action. Sometimes variances are simply accounting errors, but at other times they are symptoms of more serious problems. The most important use of the variance reports is as a feedback mechanism. They help in identifying emerging charter patterns and in updating cost data bases to be used in future planning. They sometimes lead to the establishment of task forces to study important problems. For example, one such group was set up to study the trade-off between ship speed and fuel costs when the price of fuel tripled in 1973.

---

[1]Time-charter equivalent is a standard measure for comparing the charter rates obtained by ships of different sizes.

## Exhibit 2: Operational Planning Forms

The form included in this exhibit contains a partial listing of a one-year operational plan for a hypothetical ship. This kind of plan is produced for budgeting and control purposes. Based on figures submitted by line managers, it is the standard against which actual operating performance will be compared. Many of the entries in the operational plan involve details that will not be mentioned here, although some points will be discussed. As lines 1 through 10 indicate, this ship will be on a voyage charter for the first six months of the year and on a time charter for the remaining six months. The difference in the detailed entries under each category reflects the difference in the contractual arrangements that apply. For instance, for the voyage charter, the revenue stream before commission is given by line 7 minus line 8. The time-charter equivalent on line 6 is present primarily to provide a standard of comparison for anyone reviewing the plan. During the time-chartered period, however, revenue is calculated by multiplying time-charter rate (line 3) by the size of the ship in deadweight tons (line 1) and by a conversion factor related to the length of time in the revenue period. The voyage costs on line 8 include fuel and port costs. These are listed only under

| Item | Line | Jan | Feb | Mar | Apr | |
|---|---|---|---|---|---|---|
| Deadweight tons | 1 | 200,000 | 200,000 | 200,000 | 200,000 | |
| TIME-CHARTERED PERIODS | | | | | | |
| Number of days chartered | 2 | | | | | |
| Time charter rate | 3 | | | | | |
| Brokerage commission | 4 | | | | | |
| VOYAGE-CHARTERED PERIODS | | | | | | |
| Number of days chartered | 5 | 31 | 28 | 31 | 30 | |
| Time charter equivalent—chartered period | 6 | 3.50 | 3.50 | 3.50 | 3.50 | |
| Monthly revenue collected | 7 | 0 | 1562 | 0 | 1633 | |
| Voyage costs—chartered period | 8 | 100 | 100 | 100 | 100 | |
| Brokerage commission | 9 | .02 | .02 | .02 | .02 | |
| Days off hire | 10 | | | | | |
| RUNNING EXPENSES | | | | | | |
| Wages | 11 | 55 | 55 | 55 | 55 | |
| Provisions | 12 | 10 | 12 | 10 | 10 | |
| Travel and subsistence | 13 | 4 | 4 | 4 | 4 | |
| Medical | 14 | 1 | 0 | 1 | 1 | |
| Other crew expense | 15 | 2 | 2 | 2 | 2 | |
| Stores | 16 | 10 | 10 | 10 | 7 | |
| Repairs and maintenance | 17 | 7 | 6 | 7 | 12 | |
| Drydocking | 18 | | | | | |
| Insurance | 19 | 30 | 30 | 30 | 30 | |
| Other running expense | 20 | 1 | 1 | 1 | 1 | |
| ADMINISTRATIVE EXPENSE | | | | | | |
| Research and engineering | 21 | 5 | 0 | 0 | 0 | |
| General administrative expense | 22 | 4 | 4 | 4 | 3 | |
| DEPRECIATION | | | | | | |
| Depreciation | 23 | 166 | 166 | 166 | 166 | |

voyage-chartered periods, because the shipowner absorbs these costs under voyage charters but not under the time charters. As one can see by comparing lines 4 and 9, the brokerage commission rate is higher for the short-term voyage charter than for the long-term charter. These rates are set on the basis of the amount of brokerage work required in consummating a charter and on the size of the contract. Since time charters involve much larger revenues, a smaller commission rate can be applied.

This information about revenue streams must be present as part of the operational plan. Once contractual arrangements have been settled, however, no action related to operational control can be taken on those items since income streams are fixed. To the contrary, the running expenses on lines 11 through 20 (except for insurance) are estimates that serve as goals for the operation of this ship. These figures are submitted by the technical department with the approval of whichever line managers are responsible for the particular operating activity.

The operating plan does not include financing arrangements for each ship, because they are not directly relevant to operational control. Financing is incorporated into reporting related to strategic planning, where such arrangements come into consideration.

| May | June | July | Aug | Sept | Oct | Nov | Dec |
|---|---|---|---|---|---|---|---|
| 200,000 | 200,000 | 200,000 | 200,000 | 200,000 | 200,000 | 200,000 | 200,000 |
|  |  | 31 | 31 | 30 | 31 | 30 | 31 |
|  |  | 3.00 | 3.00 | 3.00 | 3.00 | 3.00 | 3.00 |
|  |  | .01 | .01 | .01 | .01 | .01 | .01 |
| 31 | 15 |  |  |  |  |  |  |
| 3.50 | 3.50 |  |  |  |  |  |  |
| 0 | 1230 |  |  |  |  |  |  |
| 100 | 50 |  |  |  |  |  |  |
| .02 | .02 |  |  |  |  |  |  |
|  | 15 |  |  |  |  |  |  |
| 55 | 55 | 55 | 55 | 55 | 55 | 55 | 55 |
| 12 | 10 | 12 | 11 | 13 | 10 | 12 | 15 |
| 5 | 3 | 2 | 4 | 6 | 1 | 2 | 3 |
| 0 | 0 | 1 | 0 | 0 | 1 | 1 | 0 |
| 2 | 2 | 2 | 2 | 2 | 2 | 2 | 2 |
| 8 | 6 | 5 | 7 | 8 | 7 | 8 | 7 |
| 9 | 5 | 4 | 3 | 6 | 12 | 9 | 4 |
|  |  |  |  | 100 |  |  |  |
| 30 | 30 | 30 | 30 | 30 | 30 | 30 | 30 |
| 1 | 1 | 1 | 1 | 1 | 1 | 1 | 1 |
| 4 | 0 | 0 | 0 | 10 | 0 | 0 | 0 |
| 6 | 4 | 4 | 4 | 4 | 4 | 4 | 4 |
| 166 | 166 | 166 | 166 | 166 | 166 | 166 | 166 |

**Exhibit 3:    A Sample Voyage Variance Report**

Vessel:    PONTOBAYA
Voyage commencing:    04/07/74 at 1000
Sailed after completion:    06/12/74 at 1530

Days on hire:    Actual: 67.0
                 Estimated: 69.2

Cargo type:      Grain
   Tonnage:      25,492
   Rate per ton: 33.850

|                      | Actual     | Estimate   | Variance    |
|----------------------|-----------|-----------|-------------|
| FREIGHT REVENUE      | 862,908.44 | 862,908.00 | .44         |
| OPERATING EXPENSES   |            |            |             |
|   Commissions        | 56,516.34  | 56,089.00  | 427.34 −    |
|   Dispatch           | 19,386.81  | 19,076.00  | 310.81 −    |
|   Port charges       |            |            |             |
|     Loading          | 12,000.00  | 12,003.00  | 3.00        |
|     Discharge        | 9,000.00   | 8,594.00   | 406.00 −    |
|     Other            | 750.29     |            | 750.29 −    |
|   Bunker fuel        | 189,753.63 | 179,215.00 | 10,520.63 − |
|   Other              | 1,500.00   | 8,921.00   | 7,421.00    |
| TOTAL EXPENSES       | 288,889.07 | 283,898.00 | 4,991.07 −  |
| YIELD                | 574,019.37 | 579,010.00 | 4,990.63 −  |
| TIME-CHARTER         |            |            |             |
|   EQUIVALENT         | 9.12       | 8.91       |             |

## III. OVERVIEW: THE ROLE OF COMPUTER SYSTEMS IN PLANNING AND CONTROL AT GOTAAS-LARSEN

Planning and control at Gotaas-Larsen can be viewed as a series of activities that begins with defining the business mission and goals and ends with either choosing among strategic alternatives or taking corrective actions when performance deviates from operational plans. The purpose of separating general planning activities and the formal planning process from the specifics of the computer systems was to emphasize that computer systems are useful for only a subset of things that go on at Gotaas-Larsen (or anywhere else) under the rubric of planning and control. In the following review of the 10 general planning and control activities and the role computer systems play in each, this should become clearer.

1. *Defining Business Mission and Philosophy*

Computer systems play no role.

## 2. Setting Goals

Computer systems play no role.

## 3. Finding Business Opportunities

Computer systems play no role.

## 4. Evaluating Opportunities Individually

The time-shared programs for charter analysis are useful for some of the structured and quantitative aspects of this activity, such as calculating discounted cash flows, effective interest rates, and so on. Although these calculations are quite useful in the analysis, many noncomputerized considerations must be brought to bear, e.g., competition, political situations, market and economic trends, and relevant technological innovations. Furthermore, the same figures can be obtained manually with desk calculators. Thus the role of the computer in evaluating individual opportunities is primarily to make the quantitative part of the analysis easier.

## 5. Evaluating and Choosing among Opportunities
## in the Overall Context of Gotaas-Larsen's Resources

Here the strategic-plan consolidation system plays a central role. It is basically used as a feasibility tester and as a way of "fine tuning" the strategic plan. In the testing of feasibility, the main question being addressed is whether a series of individually profitable projects add up to a long-range plan that meets Gotaas-Larsen's requirements in all periods with respect to total return, cash flow, liquidity, risk exposure, debt/equity goals, taxes, and so on. This overall evaluation is very important, simply because it is quite possible for a series of individually profitable projects to add up to an overall corporate plan that is not feasible in one or more time periods from one or more of the viewpoints above. This feasibility-testing capability allows the VP of Finance to "fine tune" a strategic plan by testing the bottom-line effects of such modifications as the elimination of projects, changes in financing arrangements, changes in timing, and so on.

Although one might conceive of doing this kind of fine tuning manually, it would not be practical because of the amount of detail involved. This contention is supported by the difference between the previous planning calculations and the current calculations. Previously, the Chartering Department supplied estimated time-charter rates for categories of charters. Instead of planning vessel by vessel, the basic revenue break-out was no more detailed than

Voyage revenue

Time-charter revenue

Other revenue
_____
Total

Thus, by allowing the strategic plan to be stated at the level of individual ships or other projects, the computer system permits the "fine tuning" that was formerly impossible.

6. *Reporting and Justifying Strategic Plans to IU*

The strategic-plan consolidation system is useful in this area because its formats and terminology are consistent with those used by IU. For this reason, computer-generated reports can be submitted directly without much clerical transcription. Another useful by-product of the strategic-plan consolidation system is that its very existence lends greater credibility to the plan that is submitted. Thus the strategic-plan consolidation system serves a useful but relatively minor role in facilitating communication with people at IU.

7. *Setting Detailed Goals for Operational Units*

The operational-plan consolidation system serves the the same kind of role for short-range planning that the strategic-plan consolidation system serves for long-range planning. Specifically, it permits an operational planning and control process characterized by an extremely high level of detail, which extends down to specific monthly figures for every revenue and expense category for every account. Although such plans could surely be used for individual vessels and projects independent of computers, tight operational planning for the whole company based on this level of detail would not be feasible, particularly if such planning involved revisions and corrections at the lower levels of aggregation.

8. *Comparing Actual Performance to Goals*

The general-ledger system is used for generating monthly variance reports that could otherwise be generated by hand. Thus the role of the computer in this area is to by-pass a certain amount of clerical work in generating standard reports.

9. *Diagnosing Difficulties in Meeting Goals*

Computer systems play no role.

10. *Taking Appropriate Action*

Computer systems play no role.

★     ★     ★

At a more general level, the operational and strategic planning systems seem to have had impact in terms of both individual learning and operational capabilities. The more intangible impact of the strategic planning system in particular is that Gotaas-Larsen's top managers feel that it has helped them acquire a much stronger feeling for the business—its strengths, the constraints under which it operates, and the kinds of maneuvering room that are available. Thus they feel that the system has helped to clarify what their options are and how far they can go with them.

The more tangible impact of the operational and strategic planning systems has been in overcoming otherwise insurmountable clerical bottlenecks, which prevented the highly detailed type of corporate planning that is currently being done. The fact that this planning process is highly detail-oriented means that estimates at each level of aggregation are a direct summation of the opinions and experience of those who are immediately familiar with the items being estimated. This result is in contrast to the previous planning process, in which the Planning Department produced long-range plans based on trends in averages calculated for entire business segments. The person in charge of the mechanics of planning during recent years feels that his role has changed as a result of the system from one of producing plans to one of coordinating planning.

Another benefit of using a detailed planning process is that it is possible to "fine tune" a strategic plan. With a strategic plan based on less detailed data, the whole notion of fine tuning would be less meaningful and, in the extreme, would be reduced to a numerical exercise with little substance because of the inaccuracy inherent in the numbers being used.

To extend this point, consider the use of similar systems in other industries. For instance, one might ask whether it would be worthwhile to have such a planning system in a company that manufactured dresses and other fashion items. Although short-range planning and control might be susceptible to computer support, a detail-oriented long-range planning system would be of relatively little use in such a company, whether or not the system was computerized. The data needed for such a system simply would not be accurate enough to allow serious use of detailed long-range planning; i.e., long-range planning concerning general directions, marketing strategies, etc., could certainly take place, but not at a level involving estimated revenues from new product lines five years in the future.

In contrast, a detailed long-range planning system is feasible in shipping because many major cash flows are contractual in nature. For instance, since 94, 75, and 61 percent of Gotaas-Larsen's ships are currently chartered for 1974, 1975, and 1976, respectively, Gotaas-Larsen currently knows a substantial proportion of its revenues for those years. As for the ships not yet on charter for those years, they certainly will not go out of style. Although there can be major fluctuations in the short-term spot market, a long-term average cost curve does set a general lower bound on charter rates that will apply. On the expense side, the financing arrangements for each project are fixed by contracts. Although running expenses are variable, operating department estimates tempered by cost escalation factors provide a reasonable estimate of variable expenses. In total, this says that many of the numbers in a Gotaas-Larsen long-range plan are expected to be reasonably meaningful five or even ten years into the future. At a minimum, the fixed cash flows provide a framework within which the corporate risk inherent in the uncertainty in variable items can be analyzed. Given a top-level decision about the amount of risk that can be accepted, detailed strategic planning can proceed and can even include meaningful fine tuning. Thus the current strategic-planning process at Gotaas-Larsen was made practical by the effective use of computers, but only because the nature of the shipping industry determined that a reasonably large proportion of the information in the system is sufficiently accurate to allow meaningful estimates of future corporate outcomes.

### Questions for the Reader

1. Evaluate the strategic and operational planning systems at Gotaas-Larsen. Do these systems have a significant impact? For instance, could you counter a claim that the strategic planning system has little real impact on the business strategies that are actually followed?

2. Would it be possible to measure the impact of these systems on corporate profit? If so, what data would be needed, and how could the data be collected?

3. Is it possible that more could be done with computers to improve planning activities at Gotaas-Larsen? If so, describe some of the new systems or extensions to existing systems that might be built.

4. The implementation of the computer-based systems at Gotaas-Larsen did not encounter many of the difficulties discussed in the previous two cases. What are some of the possible reasons for the smoother implementations in this case?

5. Is Gotaas-Larsen unique in its requirements for planning and control systems? To what extent could Connoisseur Foods, the Great Eastern Bank, or IU International use similar systems? How might their planning and control systems be different?

# CHOICES FOR THE USER
# AND IMPLEMENTER

# PART TWO

All three case studies in Part One describe decision support systems. Each system is used to expedite or improve a decision making process; the emphasis of each is on flexibility and ad hoc utilization; each addresses issues of effectiveness rather than clerical efficiency. Despite these similarities, one of the messages that emerges from the case studies is that decision support systems can take on many different forms and can be used in many different ways. For example, just those three case studies include instances of the following.

Use by decision makers vs. use by intermediaries

On-line vs. off-line use

Systems based on data vs. systems based on models

Systems with one primary user vs. systems with many users

The chapters in Part Two expand on this theme of diversity by discussing the types of systems and usage patterns that were encountered in the author's exploratory survey involving 56 decision support systems. The thrust of these chapters is descriptive rather than normative. Chapter 2 uses a simple one-dimensional classification scheme to identify seven distinct types of DSS. Examples of each type are described briefly. Chapter 3 focuses on system content from another angle by asking the surprisingly elusive question "What do systems do that helps their users and supports decision making?" Chapter 4 discusses alternative patterns of system usage and reflects on the significance of on-line access to decision support systems. In effect, these chapters summarize what one finds when surveying current practice in the use of decision support systems.

CHAPTER **TWO**

Chapter 1 cited a series of common distinctions between decision support systems (DSS) and electronic data processing (EDP) systems. In effect, it said that computer-based systems can be categorized into two types (and that there is some overlap between the types). Early in the author's research it became clear that decision support systems are far from homogeneous. It seemed important to develop a classification scheme to help in understanding which issues were relevant to most DSSs and which were relevant mainly to particular types of DSS. This chapter introduces a taxonomy of DSS, briefly describes examples of each type of system, and discusses some of the key issues for systems of each type.

The taxonomy that eventually emerged is based on what can be called the "degree of action implication of system outputs," i.e., the degree to which the system's output can directly determine the decision. This is related to a spectrum of generic operations that can be performed by decision support systems. These generic operations extend along a single dimension, ranging from extremely data-oriented to extremely model-oriented:

Retrieving a single item of information

Providing a mechanism for ad hoc data analysis

Providing prespecified aggregations of data in the form of reports

Estimating the consequences of proposed decisions

Proposing decisions

Making decisions

The idea here is that a decision support system can be categorized in terms of the generic operations it performs, independent of type of problem, functional area, decision perspective, etc.[1]

From this viewpoint, the 56 systems in the sample fell into seven reasonably distinct types.

A.    *File drawer systems* allow immediate access to data items.

B.    *Data analysis systems* allow the manipulation of data by means of operators tailored to the task and setting or operators of a general nature.

C.    *Analysis information systems* provide access to a series of databases and small models.

D.    *Accounting models* calculate the consequences of planned actions on the basis of accounting definitions.

E.    *Representational models* estimate the consequences of actions on the basis of models that are partially nondefinitional.

F.    *Optimization models* provide guidelines for action by generating the optimal solution consistent with a series of constraints.

G.    *Suggestion models* perform mechanical work leading to a specific suggested decision for a fairly structured task.

Figure 16 demonstrates the rough parallel between the generic operations and the seven types of DSS. Figure 17 illustrates that the taxonomy can be collapsed into a simple dichotomy between data-oriented and model-oriented systems. Such a simplification loses a great deal of information, however, by grouping systems that differ in many significant ways.

---

[1]There are many ways to categorize computer-based systems. The most commonly used taxonomic schemes include the following.

Functional area: marketing, production, finance

Decision perspective: operational control, management control, strategic planning (see Anthony, 1965)

Problem type: structured vs. unstructured (see Simon, 1960, or Gorry and Scott Morton, 1971)

Computer technology: interactive vs. batch (see Keen, 1976)

For this sample of DSSs, none of these schemes seemed to be as useful as the one discussed in this chapter as a way of organizing the patterns that were observed. One of the difficulties with "functional area" was that many systems went across functions. "Decision perspective" had a similar problem, especially since systems used in short-run operational planning were often similar to longer-range planning systems in both mechanics and underlying concepts. "Problem type" was not useful because it was difficult to decide whether one business problem for which a computerized system could be used was more or less structured than another (especially since structure is in the eye of the beholder). Finally, the expected significance of the interactive vs. batch distinction was diminished greatly in the many cases in which decision makers were not the hands-on users.

FIGURE 16   *Parallels between Generic Operations and Types of DSS*

| Generic Operations | Types of DSS |
|---|---|
| Retrieving a single item of information | |
| Providing a mechanism for ad hoc data analysis | A.  File drawer systems allow immediate access to data items. |
| | B.  Data analysis systems allow the manipulation of data by means of operators tailored to the task and setting or operators of a general nature. |
| Providing prespecified aggregations of data in the form of reports | C.  Analysis information systems provide access to a series of databases and small models. |
| | D.  Accounting models calculate the consequences of planned actions on the basis of accounting definitions. |
| Estimating the consequences of proposed decisions | E.  Representational models estimate the consequences of actions on the basis of models that are partially nondefinitional. |
| | F.  Optimization models provide guidelines for action by generating the optimal solution consistent with a series of constraints. |
| Proposing decisions | G.  Suggestion models perform mechanical work leading to a specific suggested decision for a fairly structured task. |
| Making decisions | |

The remainder of this chapter describes these seven types of systems, provides examples of each, and concludes by comparing key issues across the various system types.

## I.  EXAMPLES OF EACH TYPE OF DECISION SUPPORT SYSTEM

### A.  File Drawer Systems

File drawer systems are basically mechanized versions of manual filing systems. The purpose of file drawer systems is to provide on-line access to particular data items, e.g., status information concerning entities ranging from overdue invoices and avail-

FIGURE 17    Data Orientation versus
Model Orientation of the System Types

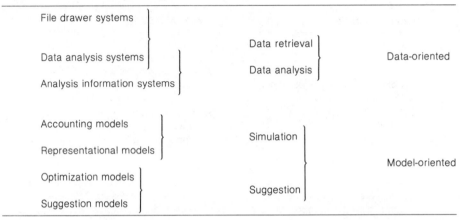

able seats on future airplane flights through inventory items, stock portfolios, lots flowing through a shop, etc.

1.  *Real-time Equipment Monitoring*

System A1 is used in the production of an inexpensive household fixture. At several stages in the production process, machine operators feed partially finished units into machinery that automatically completes the next step. The system was installed to help combat continual problems with material loss due to "creeping maladjustments" in machine settings. Every 15 minutes, messages concerning output and machine status are displayed automatically to the machine operators, who decide what action to take. Thus the system does the monitoring, and the operators take the corrective action.

2.  *Shop Floor Information*

System A2 is used in manufacturing complicated, high-technology hardware on a one-of-a-kind basis. The problem with this type of manufacturing process is that lack of a single part can bring the operation to a halt. Although it is often possible to "borrow" parts previously allocated to other assembly projects, doing so carries the risk of delaying completion of the project that "lends" the parts. An inventory system was developed to keep track of the location and current assignment of all parts on hand and all that have been ordered but have not yet arrived. The system provides access to this information via CRT screens. It is used daily by foremen in finding and reallocating parts. In addition, it is used by plant management in a weekly expediting meeting in which the current needs of various projects are examined and existing inventory is reallocated or transferred from project to project to maintain a smooth work flow.

*3. Shop Floor Information*

System A3 is used to facilitate the production of integrated circuits, the tiny silicon-based chips that perform the logical operations in modern computers, calculators, and switching systems. The system was developed to help improve the average yield rate of a newly designed manufacturing process that involves more than 50 steps. The input to the system consists of daily work reports submitted by each of more than 1000 machine operators. The system stores this information and maintains a history of each production lot by step. The history includes the yield at each step, the release date, the machine the work was done on, the worker, and so on. The system is used through CRT screens by section chiefs as an aid in monitoring work flow, detecting the source of yield problems, and avoiding production bottlenecks.

Typically, the hands-on users of file drawer systems are nonmanagerial personnel, ranging from clerks to foremen, who use the system to support their day-to-day operational tasks. The concept is very simple: People performing ongoing operational tasks should have immediate access to the most current version of the information they need. In the examples above, that information concerns internal operations. In other cases, it is proprietary commercial information to which access is sold, e.g., commodity and service trading systems which provide availability information concerning ships for charter throughout the world, lumber in stock in geographical regions, apartments for rent, etc.

---

**File Drawer Systems**

Type of operation: access to data items

Type of task: operational

User: nonmanagerial line personnel

Usage pattern: simple inquiries

Time frame: irregular use, but can be used daily

---

## B. Data Analysis Systems

Data analysis systems are typically used by nonmanagerial line or staff personnel in analyzing files of current or historical data. The portfolio management system in the Great Eastern Bank case is an excellent example of such a system.

*1. Budget Analysis*

System B1 is a budget analysis system used by division comptrollers in a bank as a way of expediting reviews of budgetary performance. In these reviews, comptrollers meet monthly with cost center managers to discuss the reasons for budget variances. Before the system was installed, each individual came to the meeting with a detailed standard printout comparing budgeted versus actual expenses in categories ranging from employee overtime to purchases of pencils. The system allows the comptrollers to browse through the data in these reports using a CRT screen and to check off and annotate the variances that are significant. The only variances included in the report sent to the cost center managers are the ones the comptroller is concerned with. When the meeting takes place, the cost center manager has had time to answer the comptroller's questions. As a result, the whole communication process is expedited, and less time is wasted.

### 2. Airline Data

System B2 is an on-line data retrieval and manipulation system used by staff personnel of an airline. The system's database consists of detailed quarterly operations data submitted by all airlines to the Civil Aeronautics Board. Although users can set up their own databases, much of the use made of the system consists of comparing the recent performance of various airlines to develop a better understanding of how each airline is progressing vis-à-vis its competitors. For instance, a trend of unusual productivity increases by one airline may constitute a warning of internal inefficiency for its competitors.

### 3. Generalized Financial Analysis

System B3 is a generalized financial analysis system used by financial analysts in an oil company. It serves as a tool that helps them analyze investment opportunities. In addition, it is used to consolidate divisional plans into a corporate plan. The original purpose of the system was to improve on a disorderly series of programs that did particular financial calculations for different organizational units. The lack of consistency in the definitions and assumptions used in these programs often led to confusion and disagreements. The new system is basically a language for financial analysis. By expressing an investment situation in terms of this language and supplying the appropriate data, analysts save time in performing their job and tend to produce reports that are reasonably consistent with other analysts' reports in format, style, and decision framework.

★     ★     ★

The data analysis systems in the sample fell into two categories: *tailored analysis systems* and *generalized analysis systems*. Tailored analysis systems are designed specifically to meet particular analysis requirements related to a definite job or task. The data in these systems is often historical, although current status information may be included. These systems allow analysts to manipulate the data and to produce analysis reports on an ad hoc basis. The portfolio management and media analysis systems described earlier in case studies are good examples of this type of system. Generalized analysis systems are specialized programming languages whose purpose is to allow users to perform fairly general kinds of analysis of databases and to program simple models. Such systems are viewed as off-the-shelf tools for use in many settings. Given a database in an appropriate format, some of these systems provide the user with the capability to analyze the data by means of such operations as data retrieval, pictorial representation, summarization of the data, and calculations. Others are oriented more toward facilitating the creation of simple models. Unlike tailored analysis systems, which address the special analysis needs of particular tasks, generalized analysis systems are designed to be readily transferable and relatively context-free. The border between file drawer systems and tailored analysis systems is fuzzy. Although there exist systems whose sole purpose is the retrieval of data items and other systems whose sole purpose is the analysis of files of information, systems also exist that attempt to serve both functions.

---

**Data Analysis Systems**

Type of operation: ad hoc analysis of files of data

Type of task: operational or analysis

User: staff analyst or nonmanagerial line personnel

Usage pattern: manipulation and display of data

Time frame: in some cases, irregular; in others, daily, monthly, quarterly, or yearly

---

## C. Analysis Information Systems

Throughout the first 20 years of computer-based "management information systems," one of the most common complaints was that these systems simply were not flexible enough to satisfy the changing information needs of managers. Typically, so-called management information systems were basically transaction-processing and record-keeping systems. Although these systems could be used conveniently to generate standard periodic reports, their requirements for consistency and efficiency precluded the generation of management information relevant to decisions or situations whose essential components varied over time. The purpose of analysis information systems is to provide management information through the use of a series of decision-oriented databases and small models.

### 1. Marketing Information

System C1 is a growing marketing information system in a consumer products company. Its databases include internal sales, advertising, promotion, and pricing data, plus a number of proprietary marketing databases purchased from marketing research firms. The system is used by staff personnel for many types of ad hoc reporting. In addition, it is used by a research group in developing methodologies for forecasting sales and analyzing the effectiveness of competitive actions. The data is accessed through a report generator and a statistical package. The marketing expert who initiated the effort was brought to the company with the general mandate to "support marketing." After four years of effort, he feels that the system is about two-thirds complete in terms of scope and content. Nonetheless, he plans to maintain a policy of adding other modules only when a definite need arises.

### 2. Sales Analysis

System C2 is a sales analysis system developed at a business equipment company. In addition to detailed sales data, it contains internally generated and purchased information about customers and potential customers, plus forecasts from industry sector economic models. It is used for product planning through the development of growth forecasts by industry sector, and of corresponding forecasts for product sales growth within industry sectors and geographical regions. Past success in providing management information has resulted in many requests for standard reporting applications. Since the system is viewed by its originator as a tool kit of data and small models for supporting ad hoc planning activities, he hopes to limit its use for standard day-to-day applications.

The basic idea underlying these analysis information systems is to recognize the incongruities between transaction processing systems and decision-oriented information systems, and to proceed accordingly. Analysis information systems are designed to extract relevant data from EDP systems and to augment that data with external data. By maintaining this type of analysis database, it is possible to access that data freely and without being constrained by the operational requirements of scheduling and running a large-scale corporate data center efficiently.

In some cases, such systems are basically vehicles by which a staff individual or group tries to have an impact on the ways in which decisions are made. The modus operandi is highly incremental: Start with an existing database and set of models. Identify a new business problem. Develop a solution that extends the system. Use the credit gained to expand the scope of future efforts.[2]

---

**Analysis Information Systems**

Type of operation: ad hoc analysis involving multiple databases and small models

Type of task: analysis, planning

User: staff analyst

Usage pattern: programming of special reports, development of small models

Time frame: irregular, on request

---

## D.  Accounting Models

Accounting models use definitional relationships and formulas to calculate the consequences of particular actions.

### 1.  Voyage Profitability Estimator

System D1 is a voyage profitability estimator used by a shipping company via time-sharing. This program performs a standard profit calculation, which is used to decide what charter rate should be charged for a particular ship on a particular voyage. The formula that is used involves ship and voyage characteristics, including tonnage, rate of fuel consumption, port costs, and so on. Because much of this data

---

[2]For a more elaborated discussion of this type of approach, see Montgomery and Urban (1970).

is stored in advance, what formerly required 15–20 minutes of calculation now requires 3–5 minutes of specification with the use of the terminal. In addition to merely saving time, this system makes it possible for charter clerks to explore trade-offs between speed and fuel consumption.

2. *Preliminary Budget Analysis*

System D2 performs preliminary calculations relevant to expense budgeting for production plants of a consumer products company. Starting with standard costs, the previous year's plant budget, and preassigned levels of production, it estimates budget variances that would apply if last year's budget was used for this year's production. The plant manager modifies the previous year's budget to take into account local conditions (e.g., requirements for exceptional maintenance) and assigned changes in production levels. He submits the new budget, which is consolidated with estimates and budgets from other areas, eventually producing a pro forma income statement for the company.

3. *Monthly Plan Calculations*

System D3 is a corporate budgeting aid used in a manufacturing company. The input consists of monthly production and shipment plans. Using simple formulas, the system determines levels of manpower that are needed and calculates costs of materials, inventory, and so on. The system is used to evaluate the adequacy of proposed operational plans, as reflected in the estimated bottom line. Typically, the system is used iteratively in an attempt to generate a plan that is sufficiently profitable and that meets the company's goal of maintaining reasonably level production in spite of the seasonal nature of its product.

4. *Source and Application of Funds*

System D4 is an on-line source and application of funds budget used for operational decision making and financial planning over a two-year horizon in an insurance company. The inputs are cash flow projections from various lines of insurance and investment areas. The output is an overall cash flow by month. The system output is used at weekly meetings of an investment committee to help in allocating funds across investment areas and to minimize the amount of cash that is left idle in banks.

Accounting models are typically used to facilitate planning by generating estimates of income statements, balance sheets, or other outcome measures. The inputs to these systems are estimates by business unit (product, department, etc.) of various elements of costs and/or revenues. Using accounting definitions and these estimates rather than actuals, such systems perform the kinds of extensions and additions that are performed by a clerk or a computer in producing a business statement. Such systems rarely contain mathematical descriptions of the mechanisms through which the firm's actions are related to outcomes in the market. For instance, it is typical to view sales as a fixed input rather than attempting to model it as a function of price or other competitive actions.

> **Accounting Models**
>
> Type of operation: standard calculations that estimate future results on the basis of accounting definitions
>
> Type of task: planning, budgeting
>
> User: staff analyst or manager
>
> Usage pattern: input estimates of activity; receive estimated monetary results as output
>
> Time frame: often periodic, e.g., weekly, monthly, yearly

### E.  Representational Models

Representational models include all simulation models that are not primarily accounting definitions, i.e., models that use at least partially nondefinitional relationships in estimating the consequences of various actions, environmental conditions, or relationships. Whereas an accounting model might start with product sales and prices that were determined external to the system, a representational model might start with only price and then calculate sales on the basis of a model representing the causal mechanisms by which price determines sales. Thus the market response model in the Connoisseur Foods case is a good example of a representational model. On the boundary between accounting definitions and representational models are systems such as E1, some of whose statements are definitions while others are cost accounting approximations to the relationships between variables.

### 1.  Top-down Budgeting Model

System E1 is used to support the yearly budgeting process in a large chemical company that has a hierarchy of mining sites, production facilities, inventory depots, and sales locations. One of the fundamental budgeting problems in a company of this sort is to develop plans and budgets that reflect the best interests of the company as a whole while also providing appropriate incentives to the people at each level. At the request of a new company president, the system was developed to help him and his budget committee evaluate yearly budgeting alternatives at a variety of planning levels. On the basis of individual models of each point in the flow pattern, the system calculates volumetric outputs and costs, which are then aggregated upward. These calculations help provide a rationale for the development of yearly budgets by allowing management to examine the profit impact of alternatives involving changes in volumes, prices, distribution patterns, production costs, transportation modes, inventory levels, raw materials sources, etc.

### 2.  Equipment Requirements Model

System E2 is used by an equipment manufacturer to help analyze individual customers' needs for the company's equipment. The development of the system began when it was perceived that similar variables determined the requirements of most customers. It was therefore possible to develop a general model of equipment usage that can be tailored to describe either the customer's current equipment configuration or alternative configurations. After the customer and salesman have agreed that a detailed equipment analysis is appropriate, a sales consultant collects equipment usage data over the course of several weeks. This data is used to parameterize the model, which can then be used to simulate the efficiency of different equipment alternatives, given the customer's workload. The comparison of alternatives is then presented to the customer for use in his decision.

3. *Risk Analysis Model*

System E3 is a commercial time-shared program for the analysis of potential investments or other situations involving uncertainty or risk. It is used by a diversified manufacturing company in analyzing acquisition and expansion decisions. The first step is to decide what factors will have a major impact on the project and then to state relationships expressing the impact of those factors on profit or other outcome measures. For instance, the main factors impacting a possible investment in a new factory include demand uncertainty plus possible changes in cost of labor, transportation, energy, and three raw materials. For each of these key factors, a range of uncertainty is given in the form of an estimated probability distribution. A simulation is then run several hundred times, with the values of key factors chosen at random from their probability distributions. The output consists of probability distributions for such performance measures as net present value, rate of return, etc. One of the main purposes of the exercise is to decide whether the potential investment has an unacceptably large downside risk.

★    ★    ★

It is possible to classify simulation models in terms of the uncertainty inherent in the relationships in the models themselves. Thus simulation models can be categorized along the following dimension.

Accounting definitions

Models in which the form of the relationship is accurate although parameter values may be inaccurate

Models in which the form of the relationship may not be a good representation of the underlying process

Clear-cut accounting models are at one end of the spectrum, and representational models are at the other end; many models fall between the two extremes.

The location of a model along the continuum above has many implications for its potential usefulness and acceptance. Accounting models are typically viewed as specialized adding machines that perform calculations a person would otherwise perform manually. Much of the effort in building such a model involves the clarification of accounting definitions and relationships that are internal to the company. On the other hand, representational models are frequently viewed as attempts to develop an understanding of the possible relationship between future actions and future outcomes. Much of the effort in building these models involves the creation of relationships that attempt to roughly describe the linkage between actions and outcomes. When one is using an accounting model, the accuracy of the model itself should not be an issue; rather, the main questions should concern the quality of the estimated values provided as inputs. When a representational model is being used, one of the main issues is whether or not the model is a reasonable representation of the situation being studied. At the same time, as in the Connoisseur Foods case, an important part of the benefits of such a model comes from the increased understanding that is gained by trying to develop explicit relationships describing how part of the business environment works. Related to accuracy, but only partially, is the credibility and acceptance of a model. In many cases, representational models tend to have credibility problems. Because they are approximations, it is often possible to question important relationships and to wonder whether these relationships produce misleading results.[3] At the same time, however, representational models that pass the test of credibility can be a very valuable source of understanding concerning the interaction between internal and external forces in the future.

---

**Representational Models**

> Type of operation: estimating consequences of particular actions
>
> Type of task: planning, budgeting
>
> User: staff analyst
>
> Usage pattern: input possible decisions; receive estimated monetary or other results as output
>
> Time frame: either periodic, as part of an ongoing process, or irregular, as a tool for ad hoc analysis

---

### F.  Optimization Models

Optimization models are used in studying situations that can be described mathematically as complicated puzzles whose goals involve combining the pieces to attain a specific objective, such as maximizing profit or minimizing cost.

#### 1.  Employee Training School Scheduling

System F1 aids in determining the start dates of three-week, 20-member training classes in a training school for service personnel who exhibit a high attrition rate. The person in charge of scheduling this school has a difficult problem. On the basis of current staffing and salary levels, estimated attrition rates, forecasted service demand (which is cyclical), costs of opening and running the school for each class, and some complex rules concerning consecutive start dates and school administration, the person in charge must generate a schedule of start dates. The schedule must satisfy most of the demand (except at the worst peaks) without being too expensive and without carrying too many extra employees during slack periods. A model was developed that helps the scheduler analyze this problem. Starting with the inputs listed above, the model uses a smoothing algorithm to generate a set of start dates with relatively (though not necessarily "optimally") low cost. The model

---

[3]The disputes concerning the World Dynamics model developed by Meadows et al (1972) and the Urban Dynamics model developed by Forrester (1969) are good examples of this issue.

is used iteratively in developing an understanding of the effect on the current year's plan of potential modifications in policy inputs, such as the maximum shortfall acceptable during peaks. The analysis continues until the scheduler adequately understands the ramifications of the various choices that can be made.

### 2. Long-range Plan Optimization

System F2 was used by a large oil company as an aid in integrating its production and marketing efforts. In an organization of that size, merely developing an adequate rationale for long-range planning and resource allocation was not a trivial task. A member of the operations research staff concluded that these questions could be viewed as a gigantic puzzle involving many potential sources of oil, many transportation routes, many alternative types of production, etc. By using a linear programming code to set levels of all major activities simultaneously and in a reasonably consistent manner, it seemed that the goal of integrating production and marketing might be attained. The system itself was developed over the course of several years and required a major rethinking of the way planning was done.[4]

### 3. Material Usage Optimization

System F3 was used by a consumer products company faced with short-run supply problems. For many of the raw materials the company used, both availability and price had suddenly begun to fluctuate. One way of making the best of a bad situation was to respond to the fluctuations by adjusting product recipes to meet production requirements at minimum cost. A staff analyst visualized this problem as a puzzle involving a large number of fixed inputs that could be used in many different combinations (product recipes) in producing certain fixed outputs. It took him only two weeks to set up a simple linear programming model that produced an optimal set of product recipes on the basis of the somewhat simplified assumptions built into the model (e.g., differences in setup flexibility in different plants were not considered). The system was used sporadically over the course of a year as a way of providing guidelines for production adjustments. When the supply situations stabilized, the system was no longer needed.

★　　★　　★

In each of these examples, an optimization model was used as an analysis tool rather than as a way of generating a definitive answer that could be acted on directly. In other words, each situation had enough structure to permit the development of an optimizing model that could be used as part of the analysis. Many applications of optimization techniques, such as linear programming, are of this type. There are other types of applications, however, in which there is enough structure to make it possible for a model to produce a direct suggestion of action. These models will be described in the next section.

---

[4]This system is described in detail by Rosemary Stewart (1971). For a technical overview of a planning optimization model, see Hamilton and Moses (1974).

---

**Optimization Models**

Type of operation: calculating an optimal solution to a combinatoric problem

Type of task: planning, resource allocation

User: staff analyst

Usage pattern: input constraints and objectives; receive an answer that maximizes the objective consistent with the constraints

Time frame: either periodic, as part of an ongoing planning process, or irregular, as a tool for ad hoc analysis

---

## G. Suggestion Models

Suggestion models generate suggested actions on the basis of formulas or mathematical procedures, which can range from decision rules to optimization methods. The purpose of such systems is to expedite or bypass other procedures for generating the suggestion. In a sense, suggestion systems are even more structured than optimization systems, since their output is pretty much "the answer," rather than a way of viewing trade-offs, the importance of constraints, and so on.

### 1. Calculating Level of Contract Activity

System G1 is a curve-spreading module of a budget consolidation system used by a company that works under long-term research and development contracts. In the development of monthly and yearly financial budgets for the company and each of its divisions, departments, and cost centers, it is important to spread the total contract dollars over the course of the contract in such a way that there is a smooth flow of activity within years and from year to year, consistent with the life cycle of the contract. Lacking formal procedures for doing so, sales planners who analyze these contracts formerly contended with an excessive amount of ad hoc calculation and recalculation. The burden of the calculations detracted from their ability to do their basic job, i.e., analyzing the contracts. With the curve-spreading module, the sales planner concentrates on analyzing the contract in order to generate several key assumptions concerning the project life cycle, and to choose one among the ten calculation procedures that are appropriate for various contracts. The curve-spreading module performs the horizontal spread over time, after which other modules perform vertical consolidations across departments and divisions.

### 2. Insurance Renewal Rate Calculation

System G2 performs some complicated calculations needed in adjusting the rates on particular group insurance policies. It performs them on the basis of the historical relationship between premiums and claims for those policies. The system was developed to eliminate part of the clerical burden associated with renewal underwriting and to help ensure that rate calculations are consistent and accurate. Using the system has become part of the job of a large number of underwriters in an insurance company. Instead of calculating renewal rates by hand and in a relatively undisciplined manner, the underwriters fill out coded input sheets for the system, which calculates a renewal rate under a series of standard statistical and actuarial assumptions that may or may not apply to the policy. Upon receiving the output, the underwriter reviews the accompanying documentation and decides whether these calculations correctly represent the situation. If not, the coding sheet is modified in an appropriate manner and resubmitted.

### 3.  Optimal Inventory Allocation

System G3 was used to expedite the assembly of a standard piece of electronic equipment over the course of a one-year production contract. Each unit of equipment contained 10 diodes, each of which had a particular resonant frequency. Because of problems in producing the diodes, this measurable frequency varied from one diode to the next. Because of peculiarities of the electronics, 200 among the millions of different combinations of diodes of particular frequencies could be used in any unit of the equipment. The weekly input to the system was the inventory on hand of each type of diode. Using linear programming, the system maximized the number of units produced with this inventory. The output of the optimization fed a program module that generated a separate circuit diagram for each unit to be assembled. In this way, a complicated manual matching problem (analogous to Little League scheduling) was automated.

### 4.  Pricing Cardboard Boxes

System G4 automates the pricing of cardboard boxes on the basis of such standard factors as dimensions, type of joints, coatings, printing, reinforcements, and so on. Traditionally, prices for boxes had been taken from a standard industry price book, which dates from the 1930s. The system incorporates these rules, thereby automating the procedure for generating base prices. In addition to performing day-to-day calculations, the system is being used by the company's president to explore the relationship between the cost structure implied by the outdated price book and the actual cost structure in his plant.

★    ★    ★

The suggestion models in the sample were a potpourri of applications with a single common theme, i.e., performing a calculation whose output was a specific recommendation for action. These applications differed greatly in impact and significance. The user of an optimal bond-bidding model stated that it had increased the profits of his bank because neither he nor any other person could possibly match the model's performance in generating solutions to an intrinsically combinatoric problem of choosing bond coupon rates that satisfy a series of complicated constraints at minimal cost to the bond underwriter. The developer of a system that calculates rates for group insurance policies felt that this system had probably saved money by preventing rate errors that had occasionally gone unnoticed. The implementer of a system that forecasts production requirements by product line and type felt that this system had had an important impact on production planning since only very aggregate forecasts had been available previously. On the other hand, most of the remaining suggestion systems in the sample had their primary impact through saving time and/or annoyance by allowing someone to avoid spending several hours each week doing a task manually (and perhaps less than optimally). For most decision support systems, it is extremely difficult to estimate benefits convincingly. For instance, it is difficult to estimate the dollar benefit of "a more thorough analysis." As indicated above, however, this problem is much less a factor for suggestion models since the outcomes can be evaluated more directly.

---

**Suggestion Models**

Type of operation: performing calculations that generate a suggested decision

Type of task: operational

User: nonmanagerial line personnel

Usage pattern: input a structured description of the current instance of a repetitive decision situation; receive a suggested decision as output

Time frame: daily use in some cases; periodic use in others

---

## II. COMPARISON OF THE TYPES OF DSS

By merely asking what type of operation a decision support system performs, it was possible to classify each of 56 DSSs into one of seven categories. The categories range from type A, systems whose basic purpose was to retrieve simple aggregations of raw data, through type G, systems whose basic purpose was to suggest actions based on formulas or mathematical procedures. Aside from performing different types of operations, do the various types of DSS actually differ in significant ways?

Figure 18 summarizes some of the important characteristics of the systems of each type encountered in the sample. Each entry in Fig. 18 is an attempt to describe in a single qualitative phrase the commonalities or predominant values of each characteristic within the systems of each type. (The sample contained 7, 8, 3, 11, 12, 6, and 9 minicases of systems in categories A through G.) Without getting into an elaborate methodological discussion, there is clearly some question of whether or not these minicases constitute a sufficient basis for generalizations by type. On the other hand, many of the commonalities by system type in the data were relatively striking. In many instances, for example, most or all of the occurrences of a particular problem were within one type of system or two types with a similar characteristic.

To the extent to which its summary characterizations are accurate, Fig. 18 indicates that systems of various types do differ in many significant ways. Consider, for instance, the notion of the "key role" in successful system usage. Since the planning and analysis systems (C through F) were often used through intermediaries who structured and performed much of the analysis, the success of these systems was especially dependent on the ability of the intermediary to maintain effective communication with decision makers. In the systems for operational tasks (especially A and G), intermediaries were not a main issue because the hands-on user was the decision maker.

The key usage problem varied greatly across the sample. In the systems for operational tasks (A and G), user motivation and training were major issues, especially since the system development efforts were often initiated by the users' superiors. In the data analysis systems (B), a recurrent problem was that system implementers and proponents incorrectly assumed that potential users would figure out how to apply the systems; in the more successful cases, either users were trained to use the system in a relatively repetitive manner, or the implementers themselves were the users. For the representational and optimization models (E and F), the key impediment to successful usage was a lack of understanding of how the model worked and what it really represented. This was a direct consequence of the fact that the users of these models were typically intermediaries rather than decision makers.

Although the implementation patterns of the systems varied greatly, it was interesting that most of the data analysis systems, analysis information systems, and representational models (B, C, and E) were initiated by internal or external entrepreneurs. These individuals often found themselves in a position of attempting to sell their innovative ideas to managers and potential users. On the other hand, the need for most of the file drawer systems and accounting models (A and D) was identified by users or their superiors. One possible inference is that the latter types of DSS are more easily visualized and appreciated by nontechnical personnel.

Key design and implementation problems varied by system type. Since the file drawer systems (A) were all used by a large number of people and often involved procedural changes in the way data was collected and reported on a day-to-day basis, the process of defining the data and handling the procedural changes was especially important. The data analysis systems (B) were typically viewed as a way of making it convenient to analyze specialized databases. In addition to the previously mentioned problem of deciding how to use these systems in changing situations, it was often difficult to assess the degree to which the analysis had a significant impact on decisions. The analysis information systems (C) in the sample were entrepreneurial efforts that grew incrementally. A key issue noted by the developer in each case was that of focusing usage appropriately and controlling the mix of projects that were undertaken. The purpose of most of the accounting models (D) in the sample was to compute the combined result of planning inputs submitted by people in different parts of the company. A significant problem for these systems was to get people to participate seriously in the planning process by submitting numbers that were well thought out. The trade-off between richness and understandability was a key issue for both representational models and optimization models (E and F). As these models became richer and more detailed, they also became more difficult to explain. For suggestion models (G), the key design issue was whether or not it was actually possible to develop a standard method or set of rules for computing a suggested decision. In half these cases in the sample, the specification of the method was considered a major breakthrough.

Systems of different types brought different kinds of change. File drawer systems, accounting models, and suggestion models (A, D, and G), brought changes in organizational procedures and information handling methods. The successful use of data analysis systems (C) by line rather than staff personnel seemed to require major changes in the user's job image. The success of advanced models (primarily E and F) often required changes in the way people thought about situations and solved problems.

Finally, the main technical challenges varied in a manner quite consistent with the generic operation performed by the system. In the data-oriented systems, the main technical challenge involved attainment of an appropriate balance between

FIGURE 18    Characteristics of Particular System Types

| Type | Type of Task | Hands-on User | Decision Maker | Key Role | Key Usage Problem |
|---|---|---|---|---|---|
| File drawer system | Operational | Nonmanagerial line personnel | Nonmanagerial line personnel | Hands-on user | User motivation and training |
| Data analysis system | Operational or analysis | Nonmanagerial line personnel or staff analyst | Nonmanagerial line personnel, manager, or planner | Hands-on user | Can people figure out what to do with the system? |
| Analysis information system | Analysis | Staff analyst | Manager or planner | Intermediary | How effective is the intermediary? |
| Accounting model | Planning | Staff analyst or manager | Manager or planner or line personnel | Intermediary, feeder | Integration into planning process |
| Representational model | Planning | Staff analyst | Manager | Intermediary | Understanding |
| Optimization model | Planning | Staff or nonmanagerial line personnel | Manager or nonmanagerial line personnel | Intermediary | Understanding |
| Suggestion model | Operational | Nonmanagerial line personnel | Nonmanagerial line personnel | Hands-on user | User motivation and understanding |

FIGURE 18 (continued)   Characteristics of Particular System Types

| Type | System Initiator | Key Design and Implementation Problem | Key Change Issue | Key Technical Problem |
|---|---|---|---|---|
| File drawer system | Managerial | Defining the data; handling procedural changes | Changing information sources and procedures | System crashes; retrieval from large database |
| Data analysis system | Entrepreneurial | Deciding how to use system, especially if off-the-shelf; assessing impact on decisions | Unfreezing job image and way of approaching problems | Flexible retrieval from broad database; generality vs. power |
| Analysis information system | Entrepreneurial | Focusing usage and development; controlling mix of projects | Using the system as a vehicle for change | Flexible retrieval from broad databases |
| Accounting model | User or managerial | Getting people to participate seriously in the planning process | Unfreezing procedures people are familiar with | Checking consistency of intention, meaning of numbers |
| Representational model | Entrepreneurial | Richness vs. understandability | Unfreezing ways of approaching problems | Modeling technology |
| Optimization model | Mixed | Richness vs. linearity and understanding | Unfreezing ways of approaching problems | Modeling and solution technology |
| Suggestion model | Mixed | Designing rules sensibly | Unfreezing standard procedures; avoiding a fear reaction | Task modeling |

flexibility and efficiency in retrieval from a database. In model-oriented systems, developing the model itself was the main technical challenge since current modeling methods are insufficient for many types of analysis of the future.

## III. CONCLUSIONS

In light of the continual state of confusion that has surrounded such terms as management information system (which usually isn't used by management), interactive system (which rarely interacts with decision makers), distributed processing (which has many meanings currently), the need for understandable taxonomies in the computer applications field should be eminently clear. The findings described here—both the taxonomy itself and the fact that DSSs of various types differ in many important ways—illustrate that the term "decision support system" can have vastly different connotations for different people. Consider, for instance, the respective viewpoints of a user of a file drawer system and of a user of a very large optimization model. Whereas the file drawer user might conclude that the essence of decision support lies in on-line access to data, the optimization user might feel that on-line access is completely beside the point since each run of his DSS might require two hours of preparation and setup. Rather, he would probably identify accurate and complete modeling as the key issue in producing a useful DSS. Although the opinions of both users might be appropriate with regard to their own systems, neither conclusion would be appropriate for all, or even most DSSs. Thus, whether it is this particular taxonomy or another, a classification scheme for DSSs is needed merely to help users and implementers communicate their experience in this emerging area.

The comparative findings in the previous section indicate that key implementation issues vary across the different types of DSS. These findings complement the growing body of knowledge concerning the general topic of implementation.[5] This knowledge is useful because it provides guidelines for implementers and alerts them to early warning signals that may be symptomatic of incipient implementation difficulties. The comparative findings provide an additional framework for anticipating and avoiding potential problems. For instance, while implementing a data analysis system, a designer should be especially concerned about the user's willingness and/or ability to figure out how to apply the system in novel situations. In developing an accounting model, the implementer should put special effort into assuring that the input estimates are well thought out. In developing a representational model or optimization model, the implementer should be concerned about possible misunderstandings of what the model means and how it can or cannot be used.

Finally, one of the main implications of the taxonomy itself is that there are many different ways to use computers in supporting decision making. In designing a DSS, one of the first steps is to choose the type of system that will be developed. A potential use of the taxonomy is as a guideline in this process. In other words, a system designer might attempt to sketch out a system of each type as a potential "solution" to the "system design problem" and would then combine the most useful features of each solution into the final design. Thus the taxonomy would provide a

---

[5]For instance, see Schultz and Slevin (1975) or the *Management Science Special Issue on Implementation*, currently in press.

substantive framework that would help in generating quite different approaches for supporting a particular decision. Whether this would actually be a fruitful exercise is a question that has not yet been explored. Nonetheless, the sample did contain indirect supporting evidence in the form of several cases at least suggesting that the exercise of generating alternative designs might be useful. In the Connoisseur Foods case, a consultant felt very strongly that a representational model was needed for advertising decisions, whereas several users were more worried about the unavailability of data. After a period of trial and error, an effective procedure was developed in which a staff specialist provided briefings based in part on his use of a representational model (E) and in part on his use of a data analysis system (B). In the Great Eastern Bank case, a portfolio analysis system was installed to help portfolio managers think about portfolios from many different viewpoints (e.g., risk profiles, industry breakdowns, detailed sorted listings, etc.). After initial experience with this data analysis approach (B), it became clear that many portfolio managers wanted displays of what a portfolio would look like if particular decisions were made. To handle these "what if" inquiries, an accounting model (D) was added to the system. As a result, system usage increased. In these and other cases, the consideration of different types of systems led to a better overall solution. The reader is encouraged to return to the case studies and the examples in this chapter, and to try to identify alternative approaches that might have been used in each instance. Wherever alternative approaches seem practical, compare them. Which would be easier to design and use? Which would do a better job in supporting decisions?

# USING DECISION SUPPORT
# SYSTEMS TO INCREASE THE
# EFFECTIVENESS OF INDIVIDUALS

CHAPTER **THREE**

It was stated at the outset that DSSs focus on improving individual effectiveness rather than on increasing the efficiency of data storage and retrieval. How do they do this? In what ways do DSSs increase effectiveness? The sample provided numerous examples of each of five different routes for accomplishing this goal.

*Improving Personal Efficiency*

"Doing these monthly scheduling calculations used to take two days of my time, . . . and when I made a mistake and didn't catch it right away, I'd just boil from the aggravation of doing the same things over again. With the new system, most of the calculations are done automatically, and I can spend my time getting people to agree about what the plan really tries to accomplish."

*Expediting Problem Solving*

"One problem we had was that the data was all over the place. When you're running a regulatory agency and you produce decisions that are out of line with previous rulings, you're in trouble and deserve to be in trouble. With this new system, a detailed and carefully indexed summary of all of our past rulings is immediately available. Instead of looking through reams of reports, our lawyers and economists can use the computer to get a much better view of what has happened in related industry groups and geographical areas."

*Facilitating Interpersonal Communication*

"Before we set up this corporate planning model, the company used to plan based on three sets of forecasts—those of the marketing VP, the production VP, and finance VP. Unfortunately, there was hardly any relationship between these forecasts, and the whole exercise was frustrating. Now we can put the forecasts into the model and immediately see how or if the whole thing fits together. As a result, the VPs find it much easier to get together with each other to figure out what we should really do as a company."

### Promoting Learning or Training

"The idea of present value and discounted cash flow has been around for ages. Not in this company. Would you believe that until three years ago, a dollar next year was considered just about as good as a dollar now in our planning decisions? One of the results of bringing in that cash flow model has been a major improvement in our appreciation of how money works."

### Increasing Organizational Control

"One of the results of bringing up our distributed inventory control system is that literally hundreds of usable spare parts have come out of the woodwork in many sites. We had a significant saving by just shifting spare parts instead of buying new ones."

Each of the five routes for improving effectiveness will be discussed in turn. Of these, the last three are especially noteworthy because their significance in many settings had not really been anticipated by system designers themselves. Instead, what often happened was that the users discovered one or more of the latter three types of use for a system that the designers had developed with the purpose of improving personal efficiency or expediting problem solving. In these cases, the system designers had had an overly limited view of the potential avenues of applicability for their systems. Although the cause is open to speculation, a reasonable guess in some instances is that the designers were overconcerned with and enamored of the technical details of their systems and did not appreciate the true nature of the user's environment. In other instances, serendipity is an equally plausible explanation, with the users simply being innovative in applying a tool creatively.

## I. IMPROVING PERSONAL EFFICIENCY

One of the ways to help people become more effective is to help them become more efficient. At minimum, this should allow a person either to perform the same task in less time or to perform the same task more thoroughly in the same length of time. More optimistically, increased efficiency may mean that the person is performing a more appropriate task in a different way and using less time and effort. The main point is that there is no inconsistency in saying that a DSS increases effectiveness by improving efficiency. Remember that we are not talking about the efficiency of a cog in a rigid, unbending system for processing large masses of transactions and/or data. Rather, we are talking about the efficiency of people whose basic job is to exercise discretion, judgment, and creativity. Although it may be more difficult to measure relative efficiency in such jobs, it should be clear that relative inefficiency can only dilute the possibilities for exercising discretion, judgment, and creativity.

Without belaboring the point, we can say that the principal impact of some decision support systems (especially accounting models and some suggestion models) is to automate intrinsically clerical tasks that are performed by people who are not clerks.

"Although my job description says I'm a financial analyst, in the past I have really worked as a high-powered clerk about 70 percent of the time. If I was paid for every time I've done a multiplication on my pocket calculator, I'd be rich. . . . But things are improving. Our new planning system has actually taken over a fair percentage of the hackwork I used to do whenever the division's plan changed. With the new system, I only enter the changes instead of entering the changes and then adding up all the numbers."

The result of automating the clerical component of decision-related tasks is often to improve consistency and accuracy, and to allow people to spend more of their time on the substantive rather than clerical aspects of their jobs.

"With this system, I come to work each day feeling much more like a financial analyst. A much larger part of my time is now devoted to thinking about what the numbers mean rather than just generating the numbers."

Among the best examples of DSSs that increase efficiency are accounting models that consolidate plans submitted by people in various parts of a company.

"About a month before the final corporate plan is due, each division submits its approved plan. Since these plans have all been developed on the system, we can generate a total corporate plan immediately. The last month in the cycle is spent in finding soft spots in the total plan and fine tuning. Before the system was put on the computer, it took a week to add up the numbers and retype the results after each round of changes. Since we can now do that almost immediately, we can do many more iterations and can produce a more coherent and better integrated plan for the corporation."

---

**For the Reader**

Consider the three case studies in Part One and the systems described in Chapter 2. Which of these systems have their primary impact through increasing personal efficiency? Which are unrelated to efficiency?

---

## II. EXPEDITING PROBLEM SOLVING

Almost all decision support systems are viewed as expediting some part of a problem-solving process. In explaining how a DSS contributes to problem solving, people who were interviewed usually started by describing the information that was provided or the calculations that were performed. For most systems, the actual impacts on problem solving were noted under three headings:

Permitting fast turnaround

Improving consistency and accuracy

Providing better ways of viewing or solving problems

### A. Fast Turnaround

"Permitting fast turnaround" was cited frequently as a major contribution of decision support systems. Among systems for operational tasks, (e.g., shop floor information systems) this meant that the required data item(s) could be obtained quickly, often within seconds or minutes.

"One of the simplest and most successful DSSs in the bank is an on-line system that lists the current plan for sources and uses of funds by month over the next two years. It was especially valuable during a recent period of tight money markets. When the bank learned of opportunities to make investments on extremely short notice, the system could be used to evaluate the expected benefits of these investments. Had the system not been available, the bank might not have responded in time in several lucrative situations."

This kind of immediate turnaround was also seen as especially valuable in production expediting meetings and group planning sessions when particular information was needed on the spur of the moment.

"We went to the boss with a proposal based on an $8\frac{1}{2}$ percent interest rate. He said we had done a good job and asked whether we had done the analysis for $8\frac{3}{4}$ percent and 9 percent. We had, of course, but then he asked the clincher: 'What is the highest interest rate at which this venture will still yield a profit?' He was amazed that I could get the answer for him before the meeting was over. When Joe rushed in with the answer 15 minutes later, you could see that he was ready to give us the go-ahead."

Finally, as mentioned above, for planning systems whose purpose was to consolidate plans submitted by people in various parts of the company, a typical perception was that the system reduced a two-week clerical and typing job to a simple computer run, thereby allowing more time for planning iterations among the people involved in the process. The ability to "test more alternatives" was cited frequently as a key impact of model-oriented planning systems.

Another aspect of fast turnaround that was considered important was that it was very helpful in debugging retrieval requests and programs (especially in data analysis systems and analysis information systems). Instead of forcing the user to wait until the next day to discover an incorrect specification or a grammatical error, on-line or otherwise rapid turnaround facilitated the rapid discovery and correction of such errors.

Although the fast turnaround afforded by on-line systems was seen as advantageous in these ways, I was surprised that very few situations were encountered that could be described as "interactive problem solving," i.e., a search process involving a single person (especially a decision maker) sitting at a terminal for a prolonged period, adaptively exploring a problem space in an attempt to find the best possible action. More typical user behavior involved performing a preconceived series of runs that tested the effect of various values of particular variables, such as interest rates, go vs. no-go decisions, alternative investment timings, etc. In those relatively rare instances where interactive problem solving occurred to the greatest extent, the purpose was typically one of developing a report that would look good to someone else rather than of trying to find an answer on which the user would act. The issue of interaction between people and machines will be discussed further in Chapter 4.

## B.  Consistency and Accuracy

Another of the cited contributions to problem solving was "improving consistency and accuracy." Typical examples are a plan analysis system and an underwriting renewal system. One of the main impacts of the former is that people throughout the company have common, explicit definitions of most of the accounting and planning terms that are encountered. In addition, plans developed by means of the system tend to reflect a particular style and discipline, as a result of which it is much easier to compare alternatives and to consolidate divisional plans. Where an underwriting renewal system was instituted, improved accuracy was a very important issue since clerical underwriting mistakes in the customer's favor sometimes went unnoticed at significant cost to the company. In addition, since almost all underwriting decisions are generated through one system, the supporting documentation is consistent. This has helped the sales force make much more effective use of the documentation they received.

### C. Better Ways of Viewing Problems

The last contribution to overall problem solving, "providing better ways of viewing or solving problems," was also cited in a range of situations. One of the purposes of the portfolio management system in the Great Eastern Bank case was to help portfolio managers move away from a security-oriented decision process and toward a portfolio-oriented process (see p. 27). One of the main impacts of system F3 (Chapter 2) was that it changed management's view of raw material utilization. Whereas formerly the allocation of raw materials to finished products had been based on product priority schemes, the rationale changed to an overall optimization of production mix subject to raw material constraints. In general for data-oriented systems, "providing better ways of viewing or solving problems" typically meant that there now existed access to information that had been previously either unavailable or available but in unusable form. For simulation, optimization, and suggestion systems, "providing better ways of viewing or solving problems" implied new methodologies and sometimes a substantial amount of change.

## III. FACILITATING INTERPERSONAL COMMUNICATION

One of the most unexpected mechanisms by which the DSSs in the sample increased individual effectiveness was the facilitation of interpersonal communication. This occurred in at least two ways: (1) The DSS provided individuals with tools of persuasion. (2) The DSS provided the organization with a vocabulary and a discipline that facilitated negotiations across subunit boundaries.

### A. Tools of Persuasion

The personal use of decision support systems as persuasion tools was rather interesting. In a rough sense, this type of use could be broken out further into two categories: proactive, or "offensive," use in persuading someone else to do something; and reactive, or "defensive," use in persuading someone that the user had done a good job earlier.

*Examples of Offensive Use*

1. A data retrieval and manipulation system first received wide exposure when it was used by a number of the company's top executives in

exploring and manipulating a large database of public industry information in an attempt to develop a good quantitative rationale for a proposed merger. In this case, the desired "decision" was clear. The decision support system helped the users by facilitating the creation of arguments that would be used in convincing a government regulatory agency that the merger should be approved.

2.    A commercial media selection system was used offensively by the sales staff of magazines that wanted to sell their advertising pages to potential advertisers. After they had developed a rationale, their sales pitch was that a computer-based analysis indicated that their advertising pages would be a good, cost-effective buy for the client's advertising dollars.

3.    A system used in consolidating and fine-tuning strategic investment plans in a shipping company also served a beneficial function in negotiations with banks. The user of the system said that banks and other sources of financing seemed to be uniformly impressed by the careful computer-based analysis on which the financing requests were based. The resulting edge in credibility was small but, in his opinion, noticeable.

4.    A model for calculating optimal production recipes in a chemical plant was used to demonstrate that the plant was operating under inherently inefficient production goals. These goals were being set by a marketing group without much consideration of the raw material shortages under which the plant was operating. At one point, it occurred to the plant manager that he could use this system to investigate whether the marketing group was setting goals that resulted in grossly suboptimal plant utilization, thereby making him appear inefficient as a plant manager. When he ran the model under a series of different production mix goals, it became clear that this was so. The plant manager used these results to persuade marketing to change his plant's production mix.

*Examples of Defensive Use*

1.    When asked whether he ever made direct use of a case-tracking system, the head of an adjudication group in a government regulatory agency said he remembered only one instance. He had spent a lunch hour trying to generate a report that made his group's recent performance appear as favorable as possible in spite of some unfortunate delays and problems that made the standard progress report look rather bad.

2.    A one-year budgeting model was used by the new president of a large company to help him understand the budgeting alternatives that existed, but also to help him discount what people in various areas claimed concerning their own budgetary needs.

3.    A model for generating optimal training schedules was used to develop class schedules for a training school for a company's service personnel. This had been an extremely frustrating job because it was always difficult to justify the budget on explicit grounds. With the model, the

scheduler could protect himself very easily by saying, "Using these assumptions concerning attrition, acceptable peak time shortfalls, etc., this is the best budget. If you [the budget cutter] would like me to change these assumptions, I would be glad to generate a new budget. What level of shortfall do you suggest?" Thus the system not only helped the scheduler make the decision but also helped him defend it.

4.    A risk analysis model was applied to a particular proposed venture. Many people suspected that the venture might not be worthwhile, but no one knew exactly why. When a risk analysis was performed, the reason became clear: The venture had a very substantial downside risk. In addition to sealing the decision, the system provided a rationale that allowed the decision makers to defend their decision with an understandable explanation for the people who had proposed the venture.

A cynic might contend that the people in these situations were somehow taking advantage of or abusing systems designed for quite different purposes. A more practical conclusion would be that these systems simply served to improve the users' effectiveness in their organizations by helping them communicate with other people. It is likely that at least as much of the benefit from using many decision support systems comes from this sort of thing as from any direct impact on the way individuals solve problems.

## B.  Tools for Facilitating Communication across Organizational Units

In addition to serving as tools for individual persuasion, DSSs were also useful in facilitating communication across organizational boundaries. This seemed to occur in one of two ways: (1) through standardizing the mechanics of negotiation processes and (2) through providing a common conceptual basis for decision making.

### 1.  Standardizing Mechanics and Vocabulary

Even before EDP systems became pervasive, business organizations growing in scope and complexity came to recognize the need to develop systems for planning and coordinating the overall business effort. Inconsistencies across organizational boundaries in definitions and procedures have been a continuing stumbling block in these efforts. Even after the blossoming of EDP systems for standardizing transaction processing, many of these inconsistencies remained.

"One of the problems we had in producing a corporate plan was that the meaning of terms such as 'contract initiation date' differed across divisions. In one division this was when the contract was signed; in another it was when the work began."

Since planning and control processes involve negotiation, the lack of consistent definitions and even of something as seemingly unimportant as consistent document formats reduces the effectiveness of these negotiation processes in large organizations. One of the main benefits from certain decision support systems for planning accrues from the fact that the system defines a discipline and format that are common across organizational boundaries.

"One of the problems we always had with corporate planning was that we couldn't talk to each other. We'd come in with our divisional plans and go round and round trying to allocate resources fairly, . . . and when we finished we'd discover that our definition of product cost included overhead items that another division didn't include. When we went to the computerized planning system, we had to all agree to the meaning and format of everything in the system. It took us three years of corporate plans to get the system straightened out. The real value of the system came from that effort. Now we can talk to each other."

2. *Providing a Common Conceptual Basis for Decision Making*

One of the purposes of some of the model-oriented systems in the sample was to provide a common conceptual basis for decision making, i.e., to combine separate potential decisions of various people by filtering these decisions through a single model that would estimate the total result. In these cases, the system became an implicit arbiter between differing goals of various departments. Instead of arguing from their own divergent viewpoints, the marketing, production, and financial people could use the model to demonstrate "objective" effects of one group's proposals on other groups' actions and on the total outcome. As a result, the issues were clarified, and the negotiation process was expedited. The same kind of facilitation was noted by users of the previously mentioned shop floor information system, which helped in work-scheduling discussions and problem investigations by providing immediate access to "objective" information about "who did what, when, and how well, on any production lots in the shop."

## IV. IMPACT ON LEARNING OR TRAINING

Although they are comparatively rare, some DSSs are designed with the specific goal of fostering organizational or personal learning. An example is the market response model described in the Connoisseur Foods case. Much of the anticipated and actual value of that model came in the form of an improved understanding of the market environment in which the key brands of Connoisseur Foods operated. By developing the models in a group setting and then tracking their accuracy over time, Connoisseur Foods personnel attained a much more thorough understanding of the potential effects of competitive actions.

Quite frequently learning occurs as a by-product of initial and ongoing use. Learning as a by-product seems to occur in two forms: the learning of new concepts and the gradual development of a better understanding of the business environment (i.e., new facts rather than concepts). Among other systems, two of the analysis information systems were perceived as sources of new concepts. These concepts emerged when standard types of analysis were developed for such repetitive problems as forecasting and the analysis of past promotions and advertising efforts.

"One problem we had was that everyone seemed to be pulling product forecasts out of the air. The division vice president asked us to try to develop consistent and understandable methods for producing these forecasts. After a period of trial and error, in which we learned more about how the forecasts were being made, we worked with the marketing people to develop a forecasting concept based on combining what we call the 'objective' and the 'subjective' components. It was fascinating to watch them come to understand what they had actually been doing."

On the other hand, the use of a number of planning models aimed primarily at evaluating alternatives resulted in a better understanding of the business environment, either through a better understanding of specific relationships or through a better feeling for such specific policy issues as the amount of leverage that was available under certain circumstances.

> "An almost intangible benefit we feel we have derived from our strategic planning system is a stronger feeling for the business in terms of its strengths, the constraints under which it operates, and the kinds of maneuvering room that are available. By generating and discussing projected financial statements under a series of investment alternatives and economic conditions, we feel that the system has helped clarify our options and how far we can go with them"

A somewhat unexpected type of DSS impact was found in the explicit use of a number of systems as training tools. An example is the insurance renewal rate system. Using this system, a class of underwriter trainees were able to work out more than 100 settlements of real cases. As a result, these new underwriters were able to do competent work much sooner than previous classes of trainees had been. For the on-line shop floor information system, it was observed that new foremen were very enthusiastic about system usage, but "old-timers" resisted the system. One explanation for the enthusiasm was that the system was a de facto training tool for the newcomers. It helped them figure out how things happened in the shop and allowed them to do reasonably good expediting, even before they felt confident in their knowledge of exact work locations and personal identities. On the basis of this sample of two, it is interesting to speculate about the use of training as a general leverage point in promoting the acceptance of certain decision support systems by defining part of newcomers' jobs in terms of the system and its overall methodology and viewpoint. A key problem would be finding an appropriate strategy for coping with any kind of "future shock" syndrome that might emerge among the old-timers.

## V.  IMPACT IN OVERALL CONTROL

In addition to helping individuals perform their own jobs, a number of DSSs were extended to provide data for purposes of overall organizational control. Once again, an example is the insurance renewal rate system, which was extended to include management reports comparing final decisions incorporating underwriter judgment with initial renewal calculations based totally on standard formulas. The purpose of the review was to ensure that underwriters were "giving away" neither too much nor too little. A similar type of management review took place for a credit-scoring system used in a bank with branches throughout a metropolitan area. With this system, credit-scoring calculations for all loan requests were retained and analyzed. One purpose was to ensure that loan officers were neither accepting too many risky loans nor rejecting too many marginal but reasonably secure loans, particularly in the poorer areas of the city, where most of the clientele were scored as marginal risks. Finally, it is interesting to note that this type of review was considered but judged impractical for the portfolio analysis system in the Great Eastern Bank case. The difficulty was that no one had a normative model of the portfolio decision process that was comprehensive enough to be useful in reviewing and criticizing a portfolio manager's performance over a wide range of portfolios with vastly different requirements.

## VI. UNDERLYING AGENDAS IN DSS USE

In a very rough sense, two levels of system purpose can be discussed: the "manifest" and the "underlying." The manifest purpose or impact of a system involves what might be called "objective" business tasks of the organization. As above, examples of these include the following.

Data manipulation

Problem solving

Interpersonal communication

Learning or training

Overall control

All the decision support systems encountered were designed to have an impact on at least one of these objective business tasks. Many had impact on several, some on most of these tasks. In addition to these "objective" or "manifest" purposes and results, interviewees' personal versions of the history of some systems also revealed interesting underlying agendas, usually of a personal nature. Some examples follow.

### Individual Power Struggles Through System Development

"One divisional vice president just wouldn't give us access to his sales history. This left a glaring gap in our [analysis information] system until the president of the company wanted a particular report. Suddenly we had the divisional data, but not without a fair amount of private kicking and screaming."

### Attempts to Become Visible in the Organization or to Build Empires

"The guy who built the planning system was a real opportunist and was proud of it. The first time the system worked well, he was sure that everyone knew about it."

### Attempts to Impress People with the Appearance of Being Modern

"I'll have to admit that we were taking advantage. Every time he objected, we'd pull out another printout he didn't understand and we'd insist that these new methods led to only one conclusion. If he wanted to do business the way his grandfather did, OK, but we had the word, or so we claimed."

### Attempts to Experiment with New Technology

"I think their main reason for using that type of CRT screen was to see what they could do with it. Around here, people aren't penalized for trying new things as long as they stay within budgets and do good work."

Isolating and clarifying underlying agendas is extremely difficult. Consider, for instance, the distinction between a person who is demonstrating general ambition by trying to do a good job and another who is motivated by some kind of planned Machiavellian scenario. Observing this kind of thing is especially complicated because different individuals sometimes have different opinions about what is happening. For very good reasons they may be quite cautious about the manner in which they verbalize their perceptions.

Two books that shed significant light on some of the basic issues in this area are *Parkinson's Law* by C. Northcote Parkinson and *Computers and Bureaucratic Reform* by Kenneth Laudon. Parkinson uses a humorous and flippant style to describe some very serious phenomena. He begins by stating that work expands to fill the time available for completion. Adding this to the fact that organizational rank is often determined in part by the number of subordinates one has, Parkinson concludes that bureaucracies tend to expand, regardless of whether the real workload is increasing.

The significant issue in the DSS area is that the development and use of DSSs does require people. This issue came to the fore at one stage in the development of a rapidly growing analysis information system in a rapidly growing company. After the team working on the system had grown to twelve members, the developer of the system was described by an executive vice president as being "just about the most expensive guy in this division." Eventually, this system was dismantled in favor of a more decentralized approach, in which one or two programmer-analysts were assigned to each of five organizational subunits.

Although Laudon's book is primarily concerned with government bureaucracies, much of what he observes is quite relevant to business organizations. In describing critical functions that information fulfills for government agencies, he includes the following.

Maintaining the agency's reputation with clients, the public, and its own employees

Preserving autonomy by controlling the release of information to political executives and legislatures

Preserving public ignorance concerning the informal accommodations that may be needed for an agency to survive and function effectively

As in government agencies, control over information of this sort is a significant base of power in business organizations. Laudon cites an article by Anthony Downs (1967) that discusses the strongly divergent interests related to information in city politics. It is in the interest of operating departments to prevent outsiders from having detailed knowledge of how things are done in the departments. Possession of such information by outsiders would surely pose a threat to a department's control over its own behavior and its traditional sphere of influence. On the other hand, it is in the interest of city planners and budgetary officials to promote the development of centralized data systems in order to gain control over information channels within operating departments.

The basic point is that underlying agendas of this sort do exist and can be taken into consideration in analyzing how decision support systems are used.[1] Of the

---

[1]Keen and Gerson (1977) argue that these issues should be aired explicitly.

many ways to enhance effectiveness, increasing an individual's power, image, or visibility may be every bit as legitimate as increasing that individual's ability to manipulate and use data in "objective" business tasks. At the same time, of course, understanding these motives and deciding whether they really are desirable is extremely difficult. Increasing the power and visibility of one individual or group will often have negative effects on others. Furthermore, as Graham Allison (1971) demonstrates in his analysis of the Cuban missile crisis, one reality may actually consist of many different realities for different observers. The reader is encouraged to think about the possible existence of underlying agendas in the three case studies of Part One and in those presented later in the text.

## VII. EVALUATING THE IMPACT OF DECISION SUPPORT SYSTEMS

The purpose of this chapter has been to discuss some of the ways in which DSSs increase the effectiveness of individuals. How can one assign a monetary value to effectiveness-oriented benefits of the type described? What is the dollar value of facilitating interpersonal communication or expediting and improving problem-solving activities?

Typically, users and/or implementers have had little to say concerning the monetary impact of DSSs. In general, these systems were designed to help people do a better job in relatively unstructured decision making. In most cases, there was no convincing way to "prove" that money had been saved or earned.

"How could I possibly assign a dollar value to the use of this system? All I know is that when we go to the Executive Committee with an investment plan whose details have been filtered through this system, they have much less trouble wading through the numbers, and they seem to get to the crucial issues more quickly. We find it invaluable in doing our investment analysis, and they find the consistent definitions and formats useful in facilitating their deliberations. Everyone is happy. . . . Although they can be real penny pinchers on some issues, they've never even asked what the system costs because it really does the job."

"When the guys with the green eyeshades came around asking for a cost-benefit justification for the system, we tried to resist at first, but then we caught on. We played their game. They wanted a cost-benefit justification, and we gave it to them. The system would save 27.5 minutes of staff-analyst time a day; it would result in plans that were 0.1 percent more profitable, and so on. We didn't believe any of that, and I don't think they did, either. But since some high-powered people wanted that system, they stopped giving us a hard time. . . . At this point, we've put three man-years into the effort. I think we make some of our decisions on a more rational basis now but don't really know what that's worth. I certainly don't know whether the decisions we made recently are different from what they would have been without the system."

As exemplified above, most respondents in the research interviews found it very difficult to deal with the evaluation of decision support systems. Whenever this point was pressed, respondents usually stated that they simply did not know of any reasonable way to show that a decision had turned out to be "*x* dollars" better than it would have been without the system. With two types of exceptions, if a DSS flourished, it was because people found it useful in doing their jobs, not because they could prove that it saved money.

The two types of exceptions included a number of systems that led to clerical savings of a rather standard variety and a few systems that led to demonstrable improvements in decisions, as evidenced by lower inventories, less material loss, more accurate pricing, better bidding decisions, etc.

> "Each of these price quotations used to take 15–20 minutes. Now it takes five minutes."

> "The foreman had the same annoying puzzle everyday. He would receive a bunch of orders for rolls of paper of different lengths and different widths and would have to do a mental juggling act to decide how to cut up his existing stock of large rolls in a way that filled the orders without producing excessive scrap loss. Since I wanted a clear-cut demonstration that the new system saved money, I kept a record of his decisions and then ran the same situations through the system. The foreman didn't mind, because the whole point of the system was to help him be a foreman rather than a mental juggler."

> "By installing our distributed inventory system, our total parts inventory shrank from $20 million to $18 million in the first year, and service levels improved. Do you know the cost of carrying $2 million of extra inventory?"

Excluding exceptions such as these, the general feeling among respondents in the interviews was that searching for demonstrable monetary savings would simply be missing the point in the area of decision support systems.

Unfortunately, there is another side to this issue. If it is difficult to assign a monetary value to the impact of an existing DSS, imagine how difficult it is to estimate the potential benefits of new systems. Decision support systems are investments of time, money, and energy. Most companies do not invest time, money, and energy unless an adequate payoff seems likely.

> "We wanted to go to an on-line inventory system, but the project approval committee basically just laughed us out. Money has been tight, and they have had to be tough on approvals. When we came in with a proposal listing a clear-cut bunch of costs but mainly intangible benefits, they just weren't impressed."

> "In this company, you spend two hours justifying what you do for every hour you actually do anything. We don't have many decision-oriented systems, because we could never get them through our justification procedures."

> "Since any project costing over $10,000 goes through a budget committee, we try to break up much of our innovative decision support work into small pieces and then do it out of discretionary funds or "borrow" the time from other projects. We go to the budget committee only when we have something we know will sell. This isn't a very good way to do things, because many of the big wins in this area seem to occur when people risk some time and effort in figuring out how a system can be used."

Thus the fact that the monetary value of many DSSs is difficult to estimate or evaluate does not imply that this is a nonissue. Although small DSS efforts are often funded through discretionary budgets of staff groups, large DSSs sometimes go through standard project selection procedures, in which estimated costs and benefits are a primary consideration. It is quite possible that many potential DSS efforts have failed to get off the ground because their sponsors could not present a convincing defense of the potential monetary benefits of the system.

The reader is encouraged to try to develop a method for estimating the costs and benefits of a DSS and then to think about how this method might have been applied to the DSSs in the case studies or in the examples in Chapter 2. This method would be likely to consider the full range of effectiveness-oriented benefits covered in this chapter. Special attention might be given to two questions: How can one estimate the dollar impact of the system on the final decision? How can one estimate the value of improving the process whereby decisions are reached? Prior to attempting to develop such a method, it might be interesting to read discussions of the evaluation of information systems (e.g., Carlson, 1974; Keen, 1975b) or overviews of cost-benefit analysis for information systems (e.g., King and Schrems, 1978).

CHAPTER **Four**

Much of the initial promise of computer-aided decision making was based on the belief that top managers would begin to make many of their key decisions while working over computer terminals. In part, this viewpoint was an outgrowth of the dreams and expectations of computer scientists in the late 1950s and early 1960s. For instance, Licklider (1960) spoke of the expected development of "man-computer symbiosis," a cooperative interaction between people and computers resulting in a partnership that would "think as no human brain has ever thought and process data in a way not approached by the information-handling machines" known at that time. In this partnership, the people would set goals, formulate hypotheses, and determine criteria, and the computers would do the routine work necessary to facilitate these decisions.

Throughout the 1960s, for every proponent of this view, there was either a system failure or a skeptic to challenge the feasibility and/or the significance of direct managerial use of computers. For instance, Dearden (1966) stated that "the latest vogue in computer information systems is the so-called real-time information system." He concluded with the personal opinion that "of all the ridiculous things that have been foisted on the long-suffering executive in the name of science and progress, the real-time information system is the silliest."

Initial attempts to provide top management with direct access to computers met with little success. A typical scenario for the time was given by Chambers (1970). Shiny new terminals were rolled into executives' offices and were demonstrated. Soon they weren't being used. The terminals were then rolled into the secretaries' offices, where they stayed shiny and new—and unused.

Despite the initial lack of general success in this area, some researchers began to demonstrate that possibilities did exist. One of the first to demonstrate the feasibility of management decision making aided by an interactive computer system was Scott Morton (1967, 1971). As also described in Keen and Scott Morton (1978), an interactive system developed as a research tool became an integral part of a monthly decision process aimed at coordinating production and marketing plans for a line of laundry appliances. On the basis of experience with this system, Scott Morton (1967) concluded that in order to help in "management problem solving, a computer system must be a flexible interactive system that is easily used by a manager ignorant of computers." With his work and that of Gerrity (1970) and several others, the dream had been translated into the glimmerings of a reality.

Current practice finds itself in an intermediate position regarding the examples cited above. Although the technology has advanced to the point where on-line managerial decision-making applications are feasible in some situations, direct on-line use of computers by managers is still the exception. In the survey of current practice, four distinct usage patterns appeared repeatedly. This chapter will discuss some of the advantages and disadvantages of each of the patterns. It will also discuss the significance of interactive use in existing systems.

## I. ROLES IN SYSTEM USAGE

A good way to begin a discussion of usage patterns is by pointing out that the use of DSSs can involve a number of different roles:

A *user* is a person who communicates directly with the system in either on-line mode or off-line mode and receives and decodes its outputs.

A *decision maker* is a person who makes business decisions on the basis of the outputs of the system.

An *intermediary* is a user who filters and interprets system outputs before the decision maker receives them and who explains the meaning of the results to the decision maker.

A *maintainer* is a person who ensures that the system is kept up-to-date and who supervises its mechanical aspects, e.g., the coding and keypunching of data.

A *feeder* is a person who provides data for a system, but who may not use it directly for decisions or may not derive benefit from it for other reasons. This role is common in budgeting and planning systems, in which people at various organizational levels are required to provide information that is later digested and consolidated by the system.

In some cases, one person either occupies or manages all five roles simultaneously. An example might be a sales information system that was conceived, implemented, and maintained by a marketing VP. At the other extreme, the five roles may be occupied by totally different individuals or groups. Corporate planning systems sometimes have this type of role structure. Not surprisingly, the systems that seem simplest to implement and use are those with the smallest number of people in the various roles. For instance, if one person is the decision maker, user, and maintainer, the amount of time and effort required for communication and coordination related to the system will surely be less than it might be otherwise.

## II. FOUR USAGE PATTERNS

The first three of the cited roles are useful in understanding the advantages and disadvantages of the four common patterns of DSS usage. Figure 19 illustrates the differences in these patterns in terms of the way the decision maker communicates with the system.

### 1. Subscription Mode

The decision maker receives reports that are generated automatically (and in a standard, repetitive manner) by consolidating existing information or information sub-

FIGURE 19    Patterns of System Usage from the Decision Maker's Viewpoint

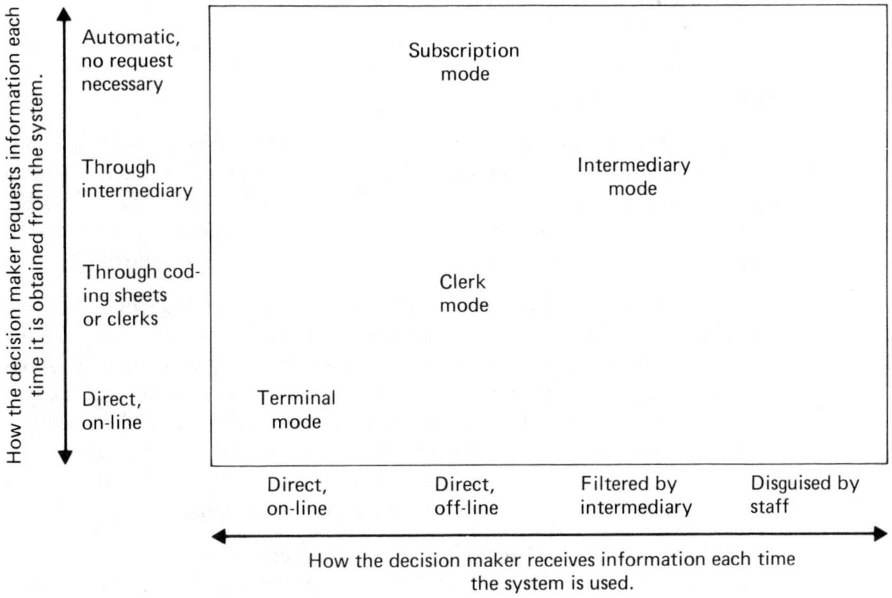

mitted by people other than the decision maker. Example: the source and application of funds budget (System D4 in Chapter 2).

2.  *Terminal Mode*

The decision maker employs direct, on-line access to the system. Functioning as the direct user, he or she frames the questions, interprets the responses, and uses the answers in making decisions or directing the search for further information. Examples: the shop floor information systems (A2 and A3, Chapter 2) and the portfolio analysis system (Case 2).

3.  *Clerk Mode*

The decision maker uses the system directly but in off-line mode rather than on-line. He or she frames the questions and submits them to the system by filling out a coding form or telling someone else exactly what is to be done. The decision maker proceeds with other work until the answer is returned. Example: the insurance rate renewal system (G2, Chapter 2).

4.  *Intermediary Mode*

The decision maker uses the system through substantive intermediaries, who conceptualize and perform the analysis and report their findings. In the extreme case, the DSS is basically the tool of the intermediary rather than of the decision maker, and it may not even be mentioned in the final report (thereby avoiding issues such as the "mystique of the computer"). Examples: the sales analysis system (C2, Chapter 2), the market information system (C1, Chapter 2), and the raw material usage optimization system (F3, Chapter 2).

## A. Comparison of Usage Patterns

Subscription mode is the standard pattern of usage for EDP systems. The basic idea is to define the information that is needed on a repetitive or exception basis, settle on standard report formats, and develop systems for consolidating and delivering the information. Although this approach has proved effective for many purposes, it does have shortcomings. Probably the most important of these is inflexibility.

> "We have 300 products that are sold by each of 400 sales branches. We have what is supposedly a top-notch transaction system that records every sale we make and then produces a 300-page report every month describing in great detail what happened. Unfortunately, that report is virtually useless for analyzing what is really going on—questions such as which sales divisions are improving vis-a-vis others or which advertising campaigns are giving us the biggest bang for the buck. To find out anything important, I have to get a clerk to spend a day or two retabulating a computer output! It's ridiculous."

An important part of the problem with subscription mode systems is that the information and report formats that are useful today may not be adequate for decision needs two months hence.

> "The thing the computer guys don't want to understand is that I'm worried about different problems each month. They want me to tell them today exactly what standard reports I'll need next year to solve next year's problems. Who knows what we'll be worried about next year? The brands that we're trying to get on course right now may not even be around next year. If they had their way, they would program up a special report and send it to me monthly forever, even if it was full of zeros because the brand was discontinued."

Thus, unless a subscription system can be modified on short notice, it will probably be unable to service decision-making needs in a timely and cost-effective manner. (This was precisely the motivation of all analysis information systems in the sample.) An additional problem is unnecessary paper. One of the most common complaints about many standard reporting systems is that most of the reports are never used. In fact, some companies have taken the position that paper reports should be generated and distributed only when requested specifically.

The second and third usage patterns, terminal mode and clerk mode, build on the notion of direct user requests for information or computation. The difference between these two patterns is only in the technology used. The advantage of direct, on-line access to the DSS is that the user gets immediate feedback instead of having to wait hours or days until the answer returns. Thus the user, whose concentration will not be broken by delays, can pursue a line of thought to a logical conclusion (either in the form of a decision or a set of questions that must be answered through other means).

> "For our foremen, everything takes five minutes—five minutes checking with the downstream foreman, five minutes readjusting a machine, five minutes

---

**Modes of Information System Usage: An Example from Everyday Life**

Most people who have bank accounts have used the bank's information system in at least several of the four modes.

*Subscription Mode*

Each person with an account receives a computer-generated statement through the mail without requesting it each time.

*Terminal Mode*

If the bank has an automatic-teller terminal, one can usually learn one's latest recorded account balance without asking a clerk. It is necessary only to insert a bank identification card and then press a button indicating the question being asked.

*Clerk Mode*

If the bank does not have an automatic-teller terminal, one can obtain one's latest recorded account balance by requesting the information from a bank clerk. The clerk obtains the information either from a card file or through a terminal and then tells the person what the balance is.

*Intermediary Mode*

In deciding what type of car loan to apply for, a potential applicant usually speaks to a loan officer, who describes the alternatives and helps the borrower decide how to proceed.

*Question:* In the bank setting, what are the advantages and disadvantages of each of these modes? Would it be possible to transact all personal banking in any one of these modes?

---

telling Charlie not to be late again. The on-line in-process inventory system fits in with the job. The big weekly computer printout is completely out of date in a day or two, and if they had to phone up some clerk to get information, they would probably just do without it."

On the other hand, there are many situations in which on-line access is not especially important. For example, in the insurance rate renewal system, underwriters fill out coding forms describing the policies, and they obtain results only after these forms have been checked, keypunched, and submitted. Operating in off-line clerk mode allows underwriters to do underwriting and keypunchers to take care of clerical details.

"We thought about training our underwriters to use computer terminals and frankly just didn't see much advantage. Why bother them with the computer when a clerk can be trained to do the data input more cheaply and efficiently?"

The fourth pattern of DSS usage is intermediary mode. Unlike the first three usage patterns, in which the decision maker was viewed as the direct user of the system, intermediary mode positions the DSS as the tool of a staff person or intermediary. The advantage of this arrangement is that the decision maker can relegate the analysis to someone else, thereby saving time that can be devoted to other chores. Furthermore, the intermediary or staff person often brings specialized experience or training and as a result is particularly knowledgeable or adept at doing the type of analysis involved. The obvious disadvantage is that as decision makers become further removed from the analysis process, they also become less aware of how the details fit together, where the methodology has shortcomings, which data, assumptions, or relationships are most tenuous, and so on. The result is often that decision makers do not have an adequate basis for evaluating the analysis on its own merits. Instead, they must rely on their confidence in the staff person and the agreement between the results and their own intuition. It is noteworthy that many on-line DSSs are used in this pattern. The fact that the system is on-line does not have a major effect on the way the decision maker explores the problem, but it can have quite beneficial effects by allowing the staff person to perform the intermediary role more quickly, thoroughly, and efficiently.

Figure 20 summarizes the most obvious advantages and disadvantages of each of the usage patterns. It should be clear at this point that no one of these usage patterns is best in all situations. One generalization that seemed to apply across the sample was that the likelihood of direct DSS usage by a decision maker was inversely proportional to the amount of staff help that was available. It remains a matter of conjecture whether this situation will change when technology improves to the point where people can develop systems more easily and can communicate with computers more directly.

### B. Changes in Usage Patterns

One of the interesting aspects of usage patterns for a number of systems was that the patterns changed over time. As people gained experience with the systems, they came to realize the disadvantages of current patterns and the possible benefits of others. Several examples follow.

*Terminal Mode to Intermediary Mode*

"We put the terminals in top executives' offices but soon found that the terminals weren't being used. Since they really wanted their information predigested and summarized, our only choice was to go back to staff briefings."

*Intermediary Mode to Terminal Mode*

"We set up the system at the request of the new division president and assumed that we would use it to provide him with information for fine-tuning the budget. Pretty soon he caught on to the mechanics of using the system and even had a terminal put in his office. He really uses it, too, maybe because he doesn't want us to know everything he's thinking about."

*Terminal Mode to Clerk Mode*

I had had experience with computerized planning systems and was brought in to develop such a system here. After several years, the use of the system set-

FIGURE 20   Advantages and Disadvantages
of Four System Usage Patterns

| Pattern | Advantages | Disadvantages |
|---------|-----------|---------------|
| Subscription mode | Convenient, simple, and automatic | Inflexible |
| | Requires no user interaction with computers | Inadequate when requirements change continually |
| Terminal mode | Convenient and simple for highly structured, repetitive tasks | Requires the user to be trained concerning the detailed contents and use of the system |
| | Provides immediate response to simple queries | Often infeasible with unsophisticated users in nonroutine tasks |
| Clerk mode | Does *not* require user training concerning the detailed contents and use of the system | Slower than terminal mode because it requires the extra step of requesting that someone else obtain the information |
| | Reasonably convenient if the "computer clerk" is readily available | The hands-on user (the "computer clerk") may have other responsibilities that reduce availability |
| Intermediary mode | Decision makers not burdened with details of system Decision makers can use their time more appropriately | Decision makers are distant from the details of the analysis and may not appreciate its strengths and weaknesses |
| | Benefit to decision makers from a system consisting of the intermediary and the computer Good for defining and studying previously unstructured problems | Special knowledge and intuition of the decision maker may not enter the computer-based analysis |

tled down a lot, and I saw no reason why I had to push the buttons, especially since I had been given additional responsibilities. I've trained my assistant to take care of the computer details, and now I just tell him what alternatives I want him to get the numbers on."

*Clerk Mode to Terminal Mode*

> "In this regulatory agency we have a lot of young hotshot lawyers and econo-
> mists. We didn't really expect them to condescend to go near a computer ter-
> minal and assigned two computer types to do their database inquiries. The
> system is really easy to use, and we found that a majority of them didn't want
> to bother tracking down the help. They just used the terminal themselves. But
> a minority of them wouldn't go close to a terminal."

★      ★      ★

Finally, the interactive market system to be described in Case 5 involves a
commercial media analysis system used in the following three modes.

*Clerk Mode*

About 50 percent of the hands-on users of the system are secretaries or very junior
analysts, who simply type specifications for previously requested reports and return
the output to their superiors.

*Intermediary Mode*

About 35 percent of the hands-on users are empowered to make a limited range of
substantive analysis decisions, and they can request additional reports to pursue
interesting situations revealed by initial reports.

*Terminal Mode*

Up to 15 percent of the users are full project directors, who have total freedom in using the system.

The main thrust of these examples is that system usage pattern is a choice. It is
often a choice that can be modified as users and implementers gain experience with a
system and develop a feeling for its true potential in the setting. One of the strong
messages from the interviews was that a flexible attitude and tailoring to individual
tastes was much more successful than dogmatic insistence on a particular usage pattern.

## III.  MORE ON THE SIGNIFICANCE OF INTERACTIVE
## USE OF DECISION SUPPORT SYSTEMS

We noted at the beginning of the chapter that much of the initial promise of computer-aided decision making was based on the belief that top managers would begin
to make many of their key decisions while working over computer terminals. To
date this has not happened. Although interactive computation is available, top managers rarely use computers directly. In the remainder of this chapter we will discuss
some of the reasons why interactive usage by top managers has not (yet) become a
dominant pattern.

Let us first consider some of the well-known advantages of on-line access to
computers:

1.    Rapid turnaround allows computer users to obtain answers to isolated
      questions more or less immediately, rather than tomorrow or next

month. This means that reservation clerks can obtain up-to-the-minute information on openings. It also means that staff analysts can respond quickly to the new policy proposed in the executive committee. For example, they may even be able to generate pro forma statements before a meeting ends.

2.  Rapid turnaround helps the computer user avoid the annoyance of interrupted concentration while waiting for output. This is especially important in expediting the analysis of a database and in testing complicated models.

3.  Rapid turnaround allows people to consider more alternatives. On-line access to models makes it feasible to play with them and to do a certain amount of fine-tuning of plans. When asked whether this capability led to significant improvements or insights, almost all the respondents said that they could not quantify the improvement but felt that it was not negligible.

4.  Rapid turnaround alleviates annoyances related to debugging. Everyone who has used a batch system appreciates the pain of returning the next day only to discover no results at all because the question was not asked correctly or a comma was misplaced.

5.  On-line computation is essential for applications that involve monitoring and controlling production processes in real time.

Although these advantages of on-line computation are very real, they are related primarily to convenience and efficiency rather than to the substance of decision making per se. In the research study, the most clear-cut substantive impact of interactive computation occurred in a number of cases in which an on-line decision support system was seen as an impartial resource that could be used to focus and clarify a negotiation process. One of the earliest examples of this sort of usage is described by Scott Morton (1967, 1971). He built a CRT-based information system that was used in monthly planning meetings in evaluating the impact of alternative schedules on both marketing and production performance for a large household appliance. Before the system was installed, the production and marketing managers had had a difficult time reconciling their mutually contradictory goals. The ongoing use of the model helped them appreciate their mutual dependency and greatly facilitated the development of plans that were satisfactory to both parties.

A more recent example, which has been used in several public sector settings, is the GADS system developed by IBM Research, San Jose (see Carlson et al., 1974). In one application, several teams of police personnel developed and evaluated alternative combinations of police "beats," with the ultimate goal of aggregating 248 city zones to 40 beats that were both balanced and equitable. The system provided instantaneous evaluations in terms of call-for-police-service statistics, and the user teams brought to bear their personal knowledge of the geography and character of each neighborhood. The result was a group problem-solving climate in which computerized facts and personal knowledge and judgment could be brought to bear freely and productively.

A final example is a shop floor information system (A3, Chapter 2) that contained detailed historical information by lot and production step. This information could be displayed through standard retrieval commands concerning productivity by combinations of operator, machine, lot, production step, and so on. Aside from its use by production foremen in monitoring work flow and pinpointing yield problems, it became an implicit arbiter of day-to-day disputes concerning who had worked on what lot and when, and why a lot was late or below standards.

In all three of the cases cited above, the fact that the system was on-line affected the substance of a group-negotiation or problem-solving process. Of particular significance was the fact that the system facilitated communication by clarifying where things stood, separating questions of judgment from questions of fact, and helping people focus on the same things at the same time.

Instances such as these demonstrate that on-line computation can have an impact on decision making. Nonetheless, most of the people interviewed in the research study concurred with the common belief that top-level decision makers are very hesitant to use computers interactively. There has been much conjecture on this topic. A remarkably diverse collection of reasons for the hesitancy have been cited (both in the literature and in the interviews for this research). Some are briefly noted in the following paragraphs.

### Lack of a Natural Language Interface

Computer scientists and artificial intelligence aficionados have been especially vocal proponents of the view that managers won't be able to use computers effectively until they can communicate with them in English.

### The Managerial Environment

Carter (1975) and many others have noted that most executive decision making requires neither large amounts of detail nor immediate response. In his famous article on "Management Misinformation Systems," Ackoff (1967) states that too much rather than too little information is usually the problem.

### Managers' Work Habits

Mintzberg (1971, 1973) studied managers at work and concluded that their work is characterized by "variety, fragmentation, and brevity." These characteristics of managerial work, plus Mintzberg's observation that managers exhibit a strong preference for verbal media, do not bode well for the widespread acceptance and use of terminals by managers.

### Managers' Cognitive Style

McKenney and Keen (1974)[1] have studied individual differences in the ways people receive and process information. For instance, they compare "systematic thinkers" with "intuitive thinkers." By their definition, systematic thinkers tend to approach a problem by structuring it in terms of a method likely to produce a solution, whereas intuitive thinkers avoid committing themselves in this way and tend to use trial-and-

---

[1]And others, for example, Bariff and Lusk (1977), Carlisle (1974), Doktor and Hamilton (1973), Driver and Mock (1975), Larreche (1974), and Stabell (1974).

error strategies in problem solving. To the degree to which computer systems tend to force unnaturally systematic approaches on managers, and to the degree to which managers tend to be intuitive thinkers, one would anticipate problems in having managers use computers.[2]

### Managerial Status

Many observers have surmised that managers will avoid using any device that resembles a typewriter since typing is viewed as a secretary's (low-status) job.

Although there is at least some truth in each of these rationales for managerial hesitancy to use computers interactively, an alternative conclusion is also plausible: Most existing decision support systems simply don't do anything that should entice an executive to use them interactively.

For business problems with enough structure to allow the evaluation of alternatives by means of models, it seems that it should be possible to list feasible values of parameters, list the dimensions of the objective function, and then simply perform a series of runs using these values. For repetitive business situations, in which problems can be identified through prespecified exception reports, interaction would not be needed. Although interaction would be useful in exploring novel problems and/or unfamiliar situations (given that the appropriate data and models had somehow found their way into the system previously), it is reasonable to wonder whether the identity of the person hunched over the computer terminal should really matter very much on the average (adequate competence and knowledge assumed).

There is also an important normative question here: Why should decision makers use computers interactively? Despite what seems to be a common belief that the direct use of DSSs by decision makers should be encouraged, Chapter 5 will cite a number of anecdotes about the misuse of systems by people who were sold on a system's capabilities without really understanding either the capabilities or the associated limitations of the system. The common theme running through these examples is that there is a great danger of misuse of a system when it is not under the control of someone who understands the details. Given that it is difficult to build models that are genuinely robust, and given that masses of historical data are difficult to interpret or even interrogate without models of some sort, a possible conclusion is that the direct use of decision support systems by nonexperts should be discouraged rather than encouraged. A more sanguine view is that nonexperts should use interactive systems only when the task is very simple or when a knowledgeable intermediary is present.

The belief that interactive use might be important for managerial decision making is based in part on the idea that there are many "unstructured" or "semistructured" problems that can be handled most effectively through the process of "interactive problem solving," i.e., a search process involving one or more persons (preferably decision makers) sitting at a computer terminal adaptively exploring a problem space in an attempt to find the best possible conceptualization of the problem and the best possible course of action.

---

[2]See p. 19 in the Connoisseur Foods case.

Reports of such behavior were extremely rare in the research study. In the most common usage pattern for on-line systems, most of the thinking occurred off-line. Typically, the on-line system users came to the terminal with a prior idea of which reports they would request or how they would test the effects of a range of values of particular variables. In most of the instances where interactive problem solving was mentioned, the purpose was to develop a report that would look good to someone else rather than to try to find an answer the user would act on. A prime example: When asked whether he had ever made direct use of a case tracking system, the head of an adjudication group in a government regulatory agency said he remembered only one instance. He had spent a lunch hour trying to generate a report that made his group's recent performance appear as favorable as possible in spite of some unfortunate delays and problems that made the standard progress report look rather bad. This sort of usage seemed especially remarkable because it far outweighed the types of interactive problem solving I had expected to find.

## IV. CONCLUSIONS

The preceding can be summarized as follows:

1.    Current decision support systems are used in any of four patterns.

2.    On-line systems have clearly brought their users significant benefits of efficiency and convenience.

3.    Interactive computing sometimes has a major substantive impact in group planning processes.

4.    There is some question whether current DSSs can do anything that should entice individual executives to use them directly.

5.    It is conceivable that nonexperts should be discouraged from rather than encouraged to use on-line systems without the help of expert intermediaries.

Where does this leave us on the impact of "interactive use" on the decision support systems used today? The first and most obvious point is that, regardless of the identity or role of the hands-on user, responsive and well-engineered tools or systems are preferred to cumbersome, unresponsive, unmanageable tools or systems. In terms of the benefits listed above, on-line computational tools are often more responsive, more manageable, and more useable than off-line tools, especially in nonrepetitive situations.

The second point is that interaction for its own sake is not the main issue. Nominally interactive decision support systems encountered in the sample exhibited a wide range of successful usage patterns. Several were used directly by managers. Many were used by staff analysts in response to or in anticipation of requests by managers. In four or five instances, respondents stated explicitly that the manager was never shown a computer output and was hardly aware that a computer had been used in developing what appeared to be a normal staff analysis. Across this range of usage patterns, the key issue was not whether the user or manager could talk to a computer to get the required answers, but rather whether a combination of people, data, models, and technical tools could provide these answers in a convenient, timely, and cost-effective manner.

What is important in decision support systems is primarily "responsiveness" rather than "interactiveness," where responsiveness is a combination of the following.

1. Power—the degree to which the system (including its human elements) can answer the most important questions.

2. Accessibility—the degree to which the system can provide these answers in a timely and consistent manner.

3. Flexibility—the degree to which the system can adapt to changing needs and situations.

From this perspective, the type of interface, the scope and type of model, the identity of the user, and many other issues are in some sense a series of design decisions whose overall objective is to attain a cost-effective degree of responsiveness. For many decision situations, the best responsiveness for the price is attained by hiring staff people to do analyses more or less outside the company's computer systems. For many other situations, strong reliance on computer technology is simply a better choice. For a third group, there are no truly satisfactory choices because the most important questions (e.g.: What will really happen next year?) seem to defy any formal or systematic combination of human intelligence and computer technology.

Ever since the notion of "interactive" computing was conceived in the 1950s, there has been a great sense of anticipation in the jargon surrounding this field. In reality, interactive computing has been a great boon in terms of the convenience and efficiency of computer users. Occasionally it has had a direct impact on the quality of decision making processes. In some cases, it may have created an environment in which some sort of person-computer synergy could occur. But it hasn't been a panacea—*yet*.[3]

---

[3]See Keen (1976) for a discussion of similar issues with a somewhat different thrust.

# TOWARD SUCCESSFUL
# IMPLEMENTATION

# PART THREE

Implementation—more accurately, the lack thereof—has been a significant problem throughout the history of computer-based systems. One of the chief aims of the research study was to attain a better understanding of the key issues related to the successful implementation of decision support systems. Chapters 5, 6, and 7 present data and conclusions in this area. Chapter 5 demonstrates that an implementation problem exists by documenting some of the difficulties encountered in the use of the systems in the sample. These difficulties are representative of what can happen when system implementation is undertaken with insufficient planning, background experience, and of course, luck. Chapter 6 begins the discussion of the implementation process per se by describing four different implementation patterns that were used in developing the systems in the sample. An interesting quandary is defined by the fact that the pattern with the lowest average success rate was also the pattern by which a preponderance of the genuinely innovative systems in the sample were developed. In Chapter 7, the idea of implementation risk factors is used as a way of describing the kinds of things that inhibited successful implementation. Since the basic purpose of implementation analysis is not only to identify incipient problems but also to do something about them, a series of implementation strategies are also discussed. The main idea on which Part Three is based is that the likelihood of successful implementation can be enhanced by an appreciation of both the problems that sometimes occur in the development and use of DSSs and the approaches that practitioners have taken in addressing these problems. For the interested reader, references to other literature on implementation is also provided.

Chapter 8 concludes Part Three with a brief look at the trends that are likely to affect implementation success in the next decade. Although the issues raised in Chapters 5, 6, and 7 will not go away in the 1980s, most of the trends that are cited will almost certainly have a positive impact on the implementation of decision support systems in the near future.

CHAPTER **FIVE**

The previous three chapters have been concerned with types of decision support systems and ways in which these systems are used successfully. Unfortunately, DSS usage is not always a sure path to Elysium. Difficulties are sometimes encountered. The purpose of this chapter is to describe some of the problems that reduced the effectiveness of the systems in the sample. An appreciation of the kinds of things that can go wrong should help future implementers anticipate and avoid similar pitfalls. The five categories of problems that will be discussed are technical problems, data problems, conceptual design problems, "people" problems, and "fundamental limitations." Although they are often interrelated, the only way to handle them cogently is to discuss them separately.

## I. TECHNICAL PROBLEMS

In order to understand the technical problems that were encountered, it is important to start with the distinction between technical *constraints* and technical *problems.* The nature and scope of all decision support systems are constrained by the available technology. When applied to the development of small accounting models and other relatively small systems, the technology is not a binding constraint since existing technology is certainly powerful enough to drive such systems effectively (disregarding, for the moment, problems with telephone lines and annoyance due to slow response). On the other hand, when applied to very complex models and broad databases, the existing technology tends to become a binding constraint, which prevents the development of many systems that are otherwise conceptually attractive.

> *Example:* Most large corporations collect a great deal of data about their business environment. This includes many types of information about competitors, products, customers, government regulation, and potential future developments in these areas and many others. It is conceivable that much of this information could be stored, processed, and accessed by means of computers. This type of computerized database for environmental scanning might be a very valuable tool for tactical and strategic planning if it were possible for managers or staff people to browse through the database in the same way they might browse in a library. Unfortunately, database technology has not yet reached the stage where this is feasible.

The following discussion of technical problems encountered by the systems in the sample will not include speculation as to the manner in which existing technology became a problem by preventing the development of systems of grander scope or nature. Rather, the problems will be those that occurred in attempting to utilize current technology in applications that can be handled by current technology.

In addition to differentiating between technical constraints and technical problems, one should also differentiate between *transient* and *persistent* problems. The former are situations in which a recently developed or recently modified system has not yet been debugged completely. The latter are situations in which the system requires a major overhaul or redesign effort in order to perform its function adequately. In the research study it became clear that noncomputer personnel tended not to differentiate between transient and persistent problems, and they were quick to conclude that a system that was still in a shakedown phase simply didn't work. (This problem occurred in the Great Eastern Bank case.)

If for the present we exclude fundamental limitations (we will take them up later in the discussion), it often seems that out-of-pocket cost is the real basis of what are usually called the "technical" problems in systems that are currently feasible. If system builders could spend more for larger computers, redundant terminals, better software, more and better programmers, and so on, many of the so-called technical problems encountered with DSSs (but not necessarily whole computer installations) could be swept under the rug. Typical examples include:

Insufficient response time (up to 15 minutes) in a shop floor system. (A system revision was needed, but no one was available to make it.)

Insufficient response time (15 seconds) in another shop floor system. (A totally dedicated computer would have improved response.)

Formation of queues around on-line terminals. (More terminals could have been used.)

Inability to run adequately large models due to limited core memory. (Programmers were required to use a small in-house computer.)

One should not infer, however, that all systems in the sample experienced only mundane technical problems such as the above. Some of the problems of several systems resulted from their stretching the state of the art. The portfolio management system in the Great Eastern Bank case accessed a very large database of portfolio information. It required an advanced technical design, which interposed a minicomputer between the user terminals and a large IBM 370. Debugging that complicated arrangement was quite difficult and resulted in delays. In an effort to get back on schedule, a temporarily unreliable version of the system was made available to users, who experienced frustration because of its erratic performance during the period of debugging that remained. The commercial media selection system in the Interactive Market Systems (Case 5) also employed a very advanced technical design in order to permit the extraction of any logically conceivable cross-tabulation that could be produced from a large proprietary marketing database. To attain the required efficiency, consultants wrote extremely complicated code, some of which was in assembly language. Although the system worked, almost two years passed before it was clearly documented and adequately understood by the regular systems staff.

Note that the discussion above of technical problems didn't start by differentiating between hardware and software problems. Other than problems with telephone lines, many technical problems seemed to result from an interaction of the power of the software and that of the hardware. For instance, slow response could be ameliorated by better-tailored software or by faster computers. Once again, for systems well within the constraints of existing technology, the real basis of technical problems seemed to be cost-effectiveness rather than technical trouble with hardware or software per se.

The basic issue here is the allocation of finite resources. In most cases where the state of the art is not being stretched, seemingly persistent technical problems are actually transient problems that have not been fixed because of resource-allocation decisions that may (or may not) be quite reasonable. Given a choice of improving an existing system or developing a new system to meet a more pressing need, it may well be entirely rational to develop the new system. Given a choice of hiring an additional programmer to improve a DSS or hiring an additional staff analyst to make better use of existing systems and to perform other tasks, it may well make sense to hire the analyst. Given a choice of tolerating some disuse of a multi-user system or of destroying goodwill by forcing everyone to use the system in a consistent manner, it may well be appropriate to tolerate the disuse. Thus the fact that a DSS is running in an imperfect manner does not necessarily mean that it must be changed. Instead, the changes should (and usually do) happen only when they have sufficient priority to warrant whatever efforts are required.

## II. DATA PROBLEMS

Although various systems in the sample experienced a range of data problems, most of them seemed to be of two types: problems due to the nature of the data per se and problems associated with the feeder role.

### A. Problems Due to the Nature of the Data

The problems with data per se were the standard ones: It wasn't correct, it wasn't timely, it wasn't measured or indexed properly, too much of it was needed, or it didn't really exist.

Stewart's (1971) description of data inaccuracy problems in a long-range planning system is typical for model-based applications. The reasons for the problems included the speed of transition from a research model to an operational model, the difficulties of collecting accurate data about new processes, and a lack of technical expertise in finding errors early. A considerable amount of extra work resulted.

Among the data-oriented applications in the sample, incorrect data entered systems for a variety of reasons, ranging from inappropriate formatting to keypunch errors. The most interesting cases in which this was a problem were those where the problem persisted because people were not motivated to clean up the data files. An example is a shop floor information system whose database was a historical file of daily work reports by each production worker. Ideally, one of the first jobs each morning for each section chief should have been to check the computer printout of the previous day's work forms in order to monitor throughput and to correct such errors as transpositions in lot numbers. Since the section chiefs didn't really need the system in monitoring their sections' throughput, they tended to slough off checking the computer printouts. In some cases they did the checking weekly rather than daily. As a result, a significant fraction of the recent data on the system was inaccurate. The level of inaccuracy was not such that the system could not be used, but it was serious enough to give people who were unenthusiastic about the system something to complain about. Apparently plant management did not feel that the problem had high enough priority to warrant a serious crackdown. Similar problems occurred for a regulatory agency's case tracking system and for a planning system (G1, Chapter 2) that performed complicated calculations in spreading contract dollars across years by month. In the case tracking system, the source of the difficulty was that the logic of the initial system was so complicated (e.g., 65 separate processing statuses, a number of which were on the same desk) that it was a hindrance rather than an aid to people in performing their jobs. As a result, case-processing personnel submitted data to the system but didn't check it and didn't really care whether it was right. The problem was solved by means of a total system revision that simplified the logic, tightened controls, and led to procedures that actually helped people with their work. For the planning system, the problem was that people just didn't check the system's answers carefully. In addition to the fact that errors sometimes crept through, the potential benefits of the feedback aspects of system usage were lost.

Several of the data-oriented systems encountered difficulties related to untimely data. The database of the portfolio management system in the Great Eastern Bank case contained only the actual contents of portfolios. Since five days elapsed between buy or sell decisions and the completion of those transactions, the database was perpetually five days out of date. Since action on the majority of the portfolios was relatively infrequent, this was often not a major concern. However, for certain accounts involving frequent trades, portfolio managers found it necessary to maintain separate manual records in order to keep current. The source of the data in a shop floor information system was daily work reports submitted by production workers and nominally checked by section chiefs through a computer printout the next morning. As a result, the accurate data in this system was typically two or more days old. Though acceptable for some expediting and problem finding, this was inadequate for the analysis of very recent production.

Inappropriate measurement or indexing of data results in the standard "apples and oranges" problem—the nemesis of an experienced practitioner in large-scale LP systems.

> "For some reason, the data from transaction-oriented EDP systems is *never* in the right units for use in optimization efforts. For instance, it is invariably true that when you want coefficients in dollars per ton, the EDP system always provides data in dollars per hour. If you need shipments by geographical area, EDP systems always give it to you by product type only."

In the sample, this issue was mentioned in connection with some data analysis systems and analysis information systems. For a commercial media selection system, it arose with regard to the applicability of certain proprietary databases to particular marketing analysis situations. Industry market data is generated on the basis of a wide range of measurement assumptions and with various periodicities, such as bimonthly, quarterly, 13 periods per year, and so on. When the measurement assumptions and periodicity of this data conflicts with that of such external sources as these proprietary databases, people in industry find it difficult to assimilate all the data into a unified, coherent viewpoint. As a result, they tend to disregard data not consistent with industry standards. The same problem applied to a data-retrieval and manipulation system that included a standard industry-wide database of quarterly operating information that was submitted to a regulatory agency and later made public. In attempting to use this database to compare the major companies in the industry as a sort of problem-finding exercise, it was extremely difficult to decide whether many of the differences were due to real differences in performance or merely different measurement assumptions. A final example is an analysis information system that went through a period of serious strain following a sales branch reorganization. The result of the organizational change was that the indexing of historical information was no longer consistent with that of current and future information. The major effort required to recast the past to make it consistent with the future cut into the time available for production runs for the users, who had come to rely on this system as a primary source of sales analysis. The minor uproar that ensued eventually led to the resignation of the main intermediary and system developer, a person who was difficult to replace.

A commonly heard complaint is that many management science models require too much data.

> "One of the problems with our corporate model was that it would never hold still. Each year the company would do something a bit differently, and we would have to send our troops out to get the data that was needed for the new coefficients."

This complaint was emphasized in comments concerning two long-range capacity-planning models for electric utilities. These models contain very detailed representations of generating capacity, and they go so far as to simulate on-line decisions made by computers in balancing the load across the regional power grid. Even with the help of outside consultants, almost a year elapses in developing the supply, demand, cost, and technological projections that are required as inputs. Typically, three days of analysis are required after the model runs, just to be sure that the outputs make sense. In spite of this complexity, the model is used because it remains the company's best tool for doing long-range capacity-planning analysis.

Finally, there is the ultimate data problem—not that it isn't quite correct, timely, or consistent but, rather, that it simply doesn't exist. This was mentioned as a major problem by the proponents of a generalized planning analysis system. They felt that this was one of their most serious frustrations in trying to develop acquisition and divestiture analyses for ventures involving the subsidiaries of a company attempting to diversify its interests. A fine anecdote concerning this problem is provided by Montgomery (1973): In a pharmaceutical company, management wanted to study the effectiveness of past advertising and other marketing expenditures. Monthly data on sales calls to doctors for virtually all competitors had been collected for many years. Unfortunately, this information had not been viewed as a resource with long-term value, and it had always been discarded after two years. In contrast, at another drug company, much of that data had been stored by a staff man, who simply squirreled it away in a drawer. This data allowed the company to go much further in studying marketing effectiveness.

A summary of the foregoing data problems is given in Fig. 21.

FIGURE 21    Summary of Data Problems

| Problem | Typical Cause | Possible Solutions (in some cases) |
|---|---|---|
| Data is not correct. | Raw data was entered inaccurately. | Develop a systematic way to ensure the accuracy of raw data. |
| | Data derived by a person was generated carelessly. | Whenever derived data is submitted, carefully monitor both the data values and manner in which the data was generated. |
| Data is not timely. | The method for generating the data is not rapid enough to meet the need for the data. | Modify the system for generating the data. |
| Data is not measured or indexed properly. | Raw data is gathered according to a logic or periodicity that is not consistent with the purposes of the analysis. | Develop a system for rescaling or recombining the improperly indexed data. |
| Too much data is needed. | A great deal of raw data is needed to calculate the coefficients in a detailed model. | Develop efficient ways of extracting and combining data from large-scale data processing systems. |
| | A detailed model contains so many coefficients that it is difficult to develop and maintain. | Develop simpler or more highly aggregated models. |
| Needed data simply doesn't exist. | No one ever stored data needed now. | Whether or not it is useful now, store data for future use. (This may be impractical in some cases because of the cost of storing and maintaining data. Furthermore, the data may not be found when it is needed.) |
| | Required data never existed. | Make an effort to generate the data or estimate it if it concerns the future. |

## B.  Data Problems Associated with the Feeder Role

Although data is always produced and submitted by people, the problems directly associated with the feeder role can be thought of as somewhat separate from most of the problems above relating to the intrinsic nature of data. A favorite anecdote of a well-known practitioner illustrates the basic data-from-people problem.

"Once I got into a conversation with this guy who was very proud of his company's large-scale linear programming model. Well, the matrix was 1000 by

3000, and I started asking where they got all those numbers from. Naturally, the matrix was less than one percent dense, but that still left at least 10,000 numbers that were needed. Getting more specific, I asked how they obtained a particular number, such as the number of pounds of X that were produced in a particular plant per ton of input Y. It seemed as though the scenario went like this: The assistant LP guy in New York sent a memo to the plant manager in Kansas City. He sent it to the head of manufacturing, whose secretary gave it to the deputy director of engineering, whose overworked staff assistant had no one else to give it to and therefore made up a way of calculating the number without spending too much time, although for appearances he did wait two weeks before sending it back . . . How much money would you bet on that number?"

Of the systems in the sample, the one most susceptible to similar scenarios was probably a linear programming model for long-range planning (F2, Chapter 2). Virtually all the complex model-based systems in the sample encountered the same basic problem to some degree.

Thus a question for people in feeder roles was simply: "Why bother?" For a system that maintained the location and status of a large inventory of interchangeable and reusable equipment spread across a large number of sites, local inventory managers had little motivation to report changing the status of a piece of equipment from "spare" to "in use" or vice versa. A case tracking system in a regulatory agency shared the same motivational problem until procedures were revised to ensure that the system was useful to the feeders. In the first stages of a bank's credit scoring system, the experienced loan officers resisted filling out the forms because they felt (perhaps with reason) that the system wouldn't be of direct use to them (as opposed to the inexperienced loan officers, whom it would definitely help).

Five planning systems posed a more direct threat to people in a feeder role. In each of these cases, not only was there a question whether personal benefit would be derived, but there were also some underlying issues concerning loss of autonomy and revelation of ignorance.

> "Frankly, we developed the sales forecasting model because the division vice president wanted it, and not because the marketing people wanted it. They were scared of the whole effort because they didn't want to publicize the 'quality' of the forecasts they pulled out of their back pockets."

> "They didn't want us to help them improve their estimating procedure. They felt that it was a matter of art, not science, and they wanted to leave it that way."

In three of these cases, these apprehensions were partially addressed by stretching parts of the system to provide benefits for the production and marketing people in the feeding role.

> "We were changing our basic budgeting process. Instead of merely estimating budget cost items, plant managers would have to submit fixed costs (independent of level of production) plus variable costs (dependent on level of production) in many categories. They tended to resist this because they hadn't really known what those costs were in most categories. To sell the system to them, we put in special modules that calculated previously unavailable budgetary performance results. We related these results to their new budget

inputs. Soon they saw that *they* were also getting much better outputs as a result of providing the new inputs.

Intermediate between the "why bother?" and "perceived threat" sentiments are the feelings of people who must submit their own plans to a bottom-up budgeting system. On a conceptual level, the basic motivational problem for such systems is to get people to submit realistic estimates of what can be done with a reasonably ambitious but probably attainable level of effort. On a mechanical level, the problem is somehow to motivate people to put aside their minute-to-minute work and to think seriously about their future plans. In one company, the problem was summed up very concisely by a skeptic.

> "Expense budgeting here is very simple. Everyone goes off and meditates and comes back needing a 10 percent across-the-board increase for his area. When that is trimmed to 7 percent, everyone moans but usually somehow seems to make ends meet."

A last example of the foibles of the feeder role is provided by a risk analysis system used in evaluating new ventures. In analyzing a proposed acquisition, the director of management science obtained estimates of a number of key parameters, such as overall demand, price and cost levels, etc., from each member of a planning committee. When the director of corporate planning discovered that his estimates were vastly different from those of the company president, he was horrified and asked the director of management science whether he should scale up his estimates in order to be in line with the boss. Although it was pointed out that one of the main purposes of the exercises was to expose the differences in people's intuitions and opinions, the corporate planning director went to the next meeting with great trepidation. (A more far-reaching example of exactly the same phenomenon was the process whereby field reports on the Vietnam war reportedly went through a series of rose-colored filters on their way through the information channels to Washington.)

## III. CONCEPTUAL DESIGN PROBLEMS

This section concerns nontechnical problems related to the design of the systems in the sample. Two types of conceptual design problems were encountered: problems related to assumptions concerning people and those related to software and modeling.

### A. Assumptions about People

It appears that the designers of a number of systems were overoptimistic with regard to users' willingness and/or ability to figure out how to use systems. In one way or another, the assumption that users could figure out what to do led to rather similar disappointments for a number of systems.

> *A shop floor information system.*   It was assumed that section chiefs could figure out how to use 13 CRT reports to help them control and expedite the production process. The manual demonstrated how to obtain the reports but not how to use them. Little formal training was provided. Many section chiefs did not learn to use the system effectively.

*On-line budget analysis system.*    One part of this system was a free-form analysis capability that allowed users to retrieve and manipulate budget data on an ad hoc basis. Although the standard and repetitive parts of the system were used on a monthly basis, these routines for ad hoc analysis were almost never used.

*On-line retrieval system for executives.*    This system was produced to allow a top executive to scan through the corporate database. No use was ever found for the system.

*On-line retrieval and manipulation language.*    This is an "Englishlike" command-driven APL-based language, which was designed to allow nonprogrammers to analyze data in a large database. Although there was some more or less experimental use by nonprogrammers, when things settled down, almost all use was by programmers, many of whom used the language mainly for its automatic report-generating features.

*Generalized planning and modeling system.*    In spite of efforts to encourage use by line managers and others throughout the organization, the only users are members of the department that developed the system. Typically, people are "happy to have this department's analysts develop model-based analyses for them, provided that they don't have to do much work themselves."

*Corporate policy model.*    Operating at an aggregate level, this system models the impact of various corporate policy parameters on corporate outcomes. It was developed at the suggestion of an external consultant with the intention that it should be available for policy analysis. It has been used only once, and that analysis had no impact.

*Curve-spreading system for estimating contract income streams.*    According to the implementer, this system was developed with a large number of "bells and whistles" to encourage deeper analysis when nonstandard situations arose. The "bells and whistles" are almost never used.

The recurring pattern here is simply overoptimism on the part of system designers and advocates, who assume that noncomputer personnel will figure out how to use computerized systems to solve their business problems. One possible inference from this series of disappointments is that in order to attain system usage by noncomputer personnel, it is often necessary to tell them *exactly* how they should use the system for particular business problems they encounter. If this is true, the prescriptive implication is that training programs should be geared toward system use on real business problems rather than toward the explanation of the system's capabilities. Furthermore, if the implementer cannot produce this kind of training program, he should not be surprised if a low level of usage occurs. Disregarding the question of whether it is even possible to specify in advance the exact usage patterns for complicated or genuinely innovative systems, it appears that the likelihood of successful implementation is reduced wherever usage patterns cannot be predicted accurately.

### B. Conceptual Design Problems Related to Software and Modeling

Several repetitive patterns emerged in this area: designing inflexible systems, attacking the wrong problem, and attacking the easy problem. These will be discussed briefly.

In two instances in the sample, systems were strained badly or died as the result of corporate reorganizations. As mentioned earlier in the section on data problems, one of the analysis information systems encountered severe difficulties when historical data became inconsistent with future data because of a sales branch reorganization. Likewise, an old version of a planning model was abandoned as the result of a reorganization, only to have its basic logic resurrected several years later in the form of the current version. The conceptual design problem here is building systems that are truly flexible, i.e., designing data structures and forms of modeling logic that will allow graceful upgrading through organizational changes. Neither of these is handled well by formal mechanisms of current technology.

Several systems seemed to attack either the wrong problem or a problem that wasn't the main one. An advertising model was designed to aid in analyzing marketing actions related to particular brands. Unfortunately, marketing budgets in this company were also allocated across many other brands for which models did not exist. Furthermore, there was a situation of mutual cannibalism among brands in the sense that increases in one brand's sales were often at the expense of other brands sold by the same company. In this situation, brand models were being phased out in favor of an overall budget allocation model. Another example is a bank's regional growth potential model, developed as an input to branch location decisions. In fact, because of a corporate policy of high growth, these decisions were being made in a very simple ad hoc manner. Whenever it was possible to build or acquire a branch at reasonable cost, this was done. Later antitrust actions ended geographic growth altogether. As another example, Stabell (1974) reports on a portfolio management system that was similar to the one in the Great Eastern Bank case but was designed to support a somewhat different decision process from the one in effect in that bank. The system was designed to support a portfolio-oriented process that determined purchases and sales starting with the needs of particular portfolios. In fact, the real process started with attractive purchases or sales of securities and then searched for a match with portfolios. One of the reasons this system was underutilized was that it was not oriented toward the decision process that actually existed. All three of these cases shared the conceptual design problems of attacking the wrong problem or a problem that wasn't the main one.

Stewart (1971) describes a long-range planning model based on linear programming. She reports that one observer felt that the basic approach in linear programming—"pressing ahead and making all decisions on a marginal basis"—makes sense as a way of optimizing an existing situation, but it doesn't help people think through more fundamental problems. In each of these four cases, the implementer entered the situation with the prior intention of implementing a rather specific system with a definite orientation, thereby exemplifying the much discussed "Have technique will travel" syndrome.[1]

---

[1]"Have technique will travel" was coined by Heany (1965). Also see Churchman and Schainblatt (1965), Grayson (1973), Hammond (1974b), and McKenney and Keen (1974) for discussions of related issues.

A last and somewhat more obscure (some might say nonexistent) conceptual design problem involves "attacking the easy problem" rather than tackling the more important questions head on. This is exemplified by many computerized budgeting and/or planning systems that contain no formal mechanism for modeling the world outside the firm. For instance, one would normally think that price, quality, advertising, and so on would be controllable variables, which are partial determinants of sales through some difficult-to-model mechanism external to the firm. To the contrary, the accounting models in most current budgeting and planning systems assume that price, advertising, and sales are all fixed quantities determined outside the model itself. The model then cranks out what the bottom line will be if these assumptions are correct. Although this is very useful in performing the relevant calculations rapidly and effectively, it seems that the key issues for decision making are skipped altogether, i.e., finding the combination of controllable variables, such as price, quality, advertising, etc., that is most appropriate in terms of the market mechanisms external to the firm. The reason these mechanisms are rarely modeled in decision support systems is obvious: Current modeling technology is not very good for this kind of problem.

> "You don't install the company's first telephone today and invite the chairman of the board to make a long-distance call tomorrow. We're not very high on our learning curve in using computers for planning. So what if the computer only adds up the numbers. It sure speeds things up, and that's important. Maybe we'll try to put in a fancier model next year—when I'm in some other job. The problem we've had up to now is that we just can't model the market accurately."

Nonetheless, this kind of fundamental limitation constrains the scope and usefulness of most decision support systems.

## IV. "PEOPLE PROBLEMS"

The whole area of "people problems" related to decision support systems is extremely unwieldy because of the difficulty of uncovering and separating cause and effect. It is often difficult to decide whether a particular behavior or opinion is a "people problem" or a rational response to shortcomings of the system or other circumstances. A commonly encountered example is the situation in which a system does go down, but fairly infrequently. Invariably, some people will be pleased that the system is up most of the time, and others will be outraged that the system is down part of the time. Is the expectation of perfection a people problem, or is the lack of perfection a technical problem?

Given the rather general types of data that were obtained concerning the sample, it is not possible to delve deeply into the people problems that were encountered. However, we will take a rough and often figurative cut at them by discussing *syndromes* on the one hand and *manifestations* on the other. Syndromes are the things people complain about and the emotions they feel, whereas manifestations are the resulting disuse and misuse of systems.

### A. Syndromes

In a discussion of syndromes, a simple analogy is helpful for putting things into proper perspective. Instead of thinking about the use of computers, consider the complaints and negative emotions that arise in connection with the use of an automobile. In an admittedly impressionistic form of argument, a series of these complaints and annoyances are listed below, along with paraphrases of corresponding concerns that were voiced with regard to specific decision support systems in the sample. Although some of the complaints are related to technical issues, the irritations and frustrations that are generated are often perceived by implementers, enthusiastic users, and other proponents as people problems related to a general unwillingness or inability to use computers.

## 1.  *Operating Performance*

THE CAR WON'T START

"When I had to do the demo for the executive VP, I was praying that the computer would be up."

"When we tried to give the demo for the new users, the system went down. Some of them never forgot that."

I CAN'T GET THE CAR INTO GEAR

"The system is awkward to use. It is hard to remember what comes when."

"The system got more and more complex as we added special-purpose bells and whistles. At one point, you had to put in 50 numbers to get one lousy report."

I HAD A FLAT TIRE

"Sometimes the computer goes down in the middle of a lengthy report specification, resulting in an hour of retyping."

"With improper recovery procedures, full four-hour reruns were needed even when the computer went down near the end of a run of the old version."

I'M CAUGHT IN A TRAFFIC JAM

"At 11:00 A.M. response time is five minutes!"

"Sometimes there are queues of unit men in front of the CRTs!"

I'M DELAYED BY A SPEED LIMIT

"It takes weeks to gather and input the data for this model. Why can't we try something quicker?"

I'M GETTING 5.8 MILES PER GALLON

"This fancy retrieval language may save a little time, but it's rather expensive for anything other than trivial reports; that's why I don't use it."

*2. Maintenance*

INSURANCE

"Documentation is a pain. EDP people spend so much time documenting that they never get anything done."

"If one of these programmers leaves, we'll be in trouble because this system has no documentation."

REPAIRS

"Why is it that systems are never quite right?"

"When the company reorganized, the planning model died."

"When the company reorganized, the past data in the system was no longer consistent with future data."

RUST AND CORROSION

"When responsibilities changed, the new guy in charge of that area wasn't interested in the system. As a result, the data got worse and worse."

THE TRUSTED MECHANIC

"Turnover has killed off more models around here than anything else."

"We experienced a turnover of the bright young guys assigned to the task of building the model. Two of them left the company, two were moved to other and better jobs, one is still with us. Naturally, they didn't bother to document their work properly."

*3. Other Drivers*

THEY DON'T KNOW HOW TO DRIVE AT ALL

"It took months of checking the computer's addition before those people believed the computer could add accurately."

"They kept manual records in their desks and never used the computer."

THEY DRIVE YOU OFF THE ROAD

"The comptroller didn't like our planning system and told me to get my terminal out of his vacant room and never to bother his people again."

"We have the system but don't have any money to run it during this budget year."

THEY PROBABLY WANT TO DRIVE YOU OFF THE ROAD

"Some of the cost accountants were scared to death that the computer would replace them."

"When it was demonstrated that the optimization model produced paper-cutting solutions with less trim loss than those formerly produced by the guy who used the system, his boss (who was not very bright) actually tried to lower his salary since a computer could now do his job."

THE DRIVERS IN THIS TOWN ARE CRAZY

"Financial people are some of the most unimaginative people around."

"These guys are good engineers, and it's amazing that they can't visualize what a financial simulation is."

"The managers of this company came up through sales. They really know how to sell peanut butter but haven't got a clue when it comes to analyzing the dependence of market forecasts and production levels."

"Marketing guys are always overoptimistic in their aggregate forecasts and are never willing to be pinned down to product line forecasts."

"The guy's a computer nut. If he had to add up five numbers, he'd run off and write a program."

This extended analogy between cars and computers illustrates the following points: (1) When someone says "I don't like using this decision support system because . . . ," it is quite difficult for an observer to distinguish between the personal and technical aspects of the real reason for the statement. Furthermore, the perceptions of the observer (whether a member of the organization or an outsider) are *always* biased by his own viewpoints and knowledge concerning both people and technology. In other words, although it is possible to observe and report difficulties in the form of such manifestations as misuse and disuse, the syndromes are quite elusive. (2) The analogy itself is useful in emphasizing that many of the mysteries that arise in relation to the use of decision support systems are essentially identical to some of the mysteries encountered in mundane day-to-day living. Why does one person react to a car's failure to start by tinkering with its carburetor and another person merely become infuriated, venting his rage by cursing mechanics, who he knows must all be thieves? Thus the challenge of "explaining" people's attitudes toward and use of decision support systems is very similar to the challenge of explaining their attitudes toward and use of automobiles. Although certain patterns can be inferred from evidence related to overt behaviors, it is much more difficult to substantiate any claims concerning patterns in underlying motives. On the basis of the general type of data that were gathered, no such claims can or will be offered.

## B. Manifestations

On the other hand, the data do reveal several patterns concerning the manifestations of people problems in the form of disuse and misuse of systems. In the section on conceptual design problems, we discussed the clearest pattern of disuse that occurred, namely, that noncomputer people were often either unable or unwilling to discover how to apply existing decision support technology to their problem-solving tasks. Another pattern of disuse suspected with regard to some planning systems was that these systems really didn't have much impact on decisions. The vague feeling was that the systems produced a lot of numbers that decision makers looked at but didn't really incorporate into decisions.

As for misuse rather than disuse, a number of comparable examples were cited.

> *Corporate investment plan consolidation.*   When the system came up, people tried to use it in inappropriate ways. For instance, a very rough tax projection calculation was used by the tax department as the basis of estimates in areas that required more careful analysis. The implementer had to ask them to back off from this type of use.

> *Long-range planning optimization.*   In some cases, "what if" questions were incorrectly framed, or the results were incorrectly interpreted.

> *Annual corporate budget consolidation.*   People tended to waste money by doing an excessive number of runs. "Corporate plan iterations came out faster than anyone could read the results." When the implementer tried to control system usage by citing the time-sharing budget, the budget was merely increased.

> *Competitive bidding model.*   "When the model was 95 percent debugged, an interesting bond-bidding situation arose on short notice. As a test of the model, we tried to use it to find an optimal solution. Well, the bond market guy just about ripped the page off the printer and ran out and made that bid. I almost had a heart attack when I found out. A mistake could have killed the whole effort. We were lucky."

Like any other organizational activity, developing and using DSSs involves a learning curve for both implementers and users. The common thread through these and other examples encountered is that there is a substantial danger of misuse of model-based systems when they are not under the direct control of someone who genuinely understands how the model should be used and the degree to which it is or is not valid under various conditions or assumptions.

## V. FUNDAMENTAL LIMITATIONS

Until now in this chapter, we have been concerned with difficulties that arise in the kinds of systems that are being built and used today. In order to complete the picture, it is important to say something about the fundamental limitations that constrain the types of systems that can be built.

### A.  A Four-Question Genie

To think about these fundamental limitations, imagine that decision support systems are free. What should one want from a DSS that was free and could do virtually anything? One would probably want a magic genie that could answer the following four questions at any level of depth.

1. *What really did happen in the past?*

   *Examples:*    What was the process by which the Cuban missile crisis occurred and by which it was resolved? Why did company X double its sales last year?

2. *What is happening right now?*

   *Examples:*    To what extent does the health of the U.S. economy depend on military expenditures? How are the promotion policies of Company X affecting employee morale?

3. *What will happen in the future?*

   *Examples:*    Will a Democrat or a Republican be elected next time? What will the price of gold be four years from now?

4. *What can I do to shape the future to my desires?*

   *Examples:*    What can the United States do to improve the human rights situation in the world? What action can we take to increase our market share without reducing our profits?

   Unfortunately (or perhaps fortunately), no one knows how to build a computer system that can answer questions such as these. What happens in current DSSs is that the system contributes in one way or another to users' attempts to do whatever they can to answer one or two of these questions themselves. In summary, the fundamental limitation of existing DSSs is that no one knows how to build the kinds of models that would be needed in order for the magic genie to answer *any* of these four types of questions definitively.

### B. Types of Variables

To explore the problem of limitations further, let us consider the kinds of variables that can be handled and the kinds of questions that can be answered by existing DSSs.

Variables can be classified along a dimension ranging from highly tangible to highly intangible. Tangible variables are easily perceived and measured. Example include time, physical entities (e.g., car, person, loaf of bread, dollar), transactions (e.g., sale of an item, hotel reservation), and locations (e.g., marketing department, Chicago).

Most of the entities in existing DSSs represent instances or aggregations of tangible variables. Most of the models in existing systems express relationships involving tangible variables. Some of the relationships are accounting definitions, and others are approximations stated in terms of parameters (e.g., levels, rates, time lags) that must be derived or estimated. In merely dealing with tangible variables, one encounters a number of key issues that are often difficult to resolve.

1. *In any situation, which are the independent and dependent variables?*

*Example:* Do expectations about the proper role of women determine the characteristics of most women, or alternatively, do the characteristics of most women determine expectations about the proper role of women?

*2. What is the relationship between independent and dependent variables?*

*Example:* If advertising is set at $1,000,000 next year, what will our net sales be?

*3. To what extent is it possible to manipulate dependent variables by setting values of controllable independent variables?*

*Example:* How much is it possible to increase our sales by increasing our advertising effort?

Any attempt to develop the four-question genie would surely require infallible methods for resolving these types of issues. Such methods do not exist currently. Worse yet, the world in which decision makers operate consists of much more than just tangible variables. First, there are intangible variables, such as politics, status, ethics, and satisfaction. In addition, there are composite variables, such as scenarios (i.e., chains of events), strategies or plans (i.e., connected series of anticipated actions leading to the accomplishment of goals), situations (i.e., dynamic entities, the sum of whose parts does not suffice in describing the whole). Given the difficulty of merely representing or measuring such variables, it is not surprising that they are excluded from most DSSs.

These distinctions between types of variable serve mainly to indicate that existing DSSs are significantly limited in scope. Current decision support systems are most useful for manipulating tangible variables both in analyzing past events and in evaluating alternatives for action in the future. Some systems make no pretense of establishing the relationships among tangible variables. Rather, they facilitate the manipulation of these variables by users who have complete responsibility to draw causal inferences and policy conclusions. Model-based systems, on the other hand, do include explicit relationships between variables. Although these relationships are relatively easy to describe in some cases (e.g., the flow of in-process goods through a production operation), in others the representation and calibration of relationships, even among tangible variables, remains a challenging enterprise (e.g., estimating the effect of advertising on sales). Capabilities with regard to intangible and composite variables are far less powerful because of problems of conceptualization, representation, and measurement. It is reasonable to hypothesize that the current lack of capabilities in these areas is one of the main reasons why current decision support systems are not more helpful in management decision making.

## C. Types of Questions

Another way of viewing the fundamental modeling limitations under which existing systems operate is to catalogue the types of questions they can and cannot answer. Consider four common types of questions that arise repeatedly in day-to-day business activities.

*1. Factual, noninferential (i.e., questions involving direct retrieval and aggregation of data from a database)*

*Example:*   How much of brand X did we sell in sales branch 24?

2. *Factual, inferential (i.e., questions of fact requiring interpretation and inference on the part of the answerer)*

*Example:*   How much of brand X did we sell in the sales branches that aren't doing well?

3. *Causal, inferential (i.e., questions concerning causality rather than fact)*

*Example:*   Why are we doing badly in sales branch 35?

4. *Predictive (i.e., questions involving the future rather than the past)*

*Example:*   If we adopt this new advertising campaign, how much will we sell next year?

Current decision support systems in business organizations can answer factual, noninferential questions and a rather constrained set of predictive questions stated in the form "Under these assumptions, which are generated subjectively, what will be the outcome?" Although these systems can help their users answer inferential questions, the systems themselves almost never contain models that allow factual or causal inferences to be drawn automatically. In part, this limitation is due to the common lack of an explicit model or structure for drawing inferences. It is also due in part to the current inability to ensure that computer programs will apply some semblance of common sense in drawing inferences correctly. The result is that significant parts of the processing must still be done in the head of the user.

> "Our computers can retrieve information and can do huge numbers of calculations, but they can't tell us what the outputs mean. Our managers and staff don't have to do as much pencil pushing anymore, and they use better quantitative approaches, but things haven't changed that much—we still pay *people* for their ability to think, plan, and evaluate."

There is no necessary contradiction in saying that DSSs are quite limited in scope and that many different types have been used successfully. The basic point is that one should not overestimate what can be done with a computer. We have not yet taught computers to think. Although DSSs have been very useful in many settings, there are still many decision situations in which DSSs cannot be developed to genuinely address the main issues. Frequently these are situations in which the main issues involve intangible or composite variables or in which no model exists for describing and performing the required inferences and predictions.

## VI. SUMMARY

Although decision support systems can be very useful, they are not guaranteed to succeed completely in solving all problems under all circumstances. Five types of difficulties in DSS usage have been described. All have occurred in the past and will occur in the future. Once the potential problems in each category are understood, however, they can be anticipated and avoided through appropriate action on the part of implementers, potential users, and managers.

CHAPTER **SIX**

It has long been recognized that the process of introducing change is a key determinant of the ultimate success or acceptance of that change.[1] Since the implementation of a decision support system always constitutes some kind of change in a work environment, it is clearly worthwhile to study the implementation of these systems. This chapter begins by presenting a normative description of the process by which systems projects should take place. This normative description is useful in appreciating the impact on project success of two key variables: the degree to which the user initiated the project and the degree to which the user participated in the development effort. Combinations of high or low values on these two variables are conceptualized as implementation patterns. Data and examples are provided to demonstrate the significance of these patterns, which are also reinterpreted in terms of six common implementation situations. The chapter ends with a quandary: Many of the most innovative systems in the sample were developed through the implementation pattern with the highest probability of difficulties. Chapter 7 will extend the discussion of implementation from this point by describing an approach for identifying implementation risk factors and developing implementation strategies.

## I. A NORMATIVE VIEW OF THE
## CHANGE PROCESS IN SYSTEMS PROJECTS

There are many ways to view the process whereby systems are implemented. One approach is to assume the existence of a fairly distinct problem area and then to describe the mental or physical steps the system designer (or implementation team) does or should go through in specifying and implementing the exact algorithm or program that is utilized. Many versions of this systems analysis paradigm can be found in the literature. For instance, Scott Morton (1973) argues that the systems analysis sequence illustrated in Fig. 22 is especially relevant to decision support sys-

---

[1]An extensive literature on social change is devoted to describing the characteristics of different types of change processes and the general determinants of successful change across a wide range of situations. An important subset of the change literature concerns the implementation of computer-based systems and/or management science techniques, e.g., Rubenstein et al. (1967), Radnor et al. (1968, 1970), Kolb and Frohman (1970), Powers and Dickson (1973), Hammond (1974a, 1974b), Zand and Sorenson (1975), Ginzberg (1975, 1976).

FIGURE 22   *Decision-Oriented Systems Analysis and Design (as described by Scott Morton, 1973)*

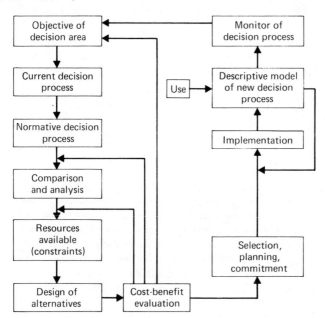

tems.[2] Figure 22 basically says that the design of a decision support system should start with a comparison of the current decision process with the desired process. A cost-benefit analysis of alternative system designs should then take place. After one of the alternatives is chosen and the system is implemented, the new decision process should be monitored, leading to possible changes in the new system.

An alternative approach that provides a great insight into the success or failure of many projects is to focus on the process by which change takes place. The Lewin-Schein theory of change is a concise and elegant description of this process. The theory states that change consists of three steps:

Unfreezing: creating an awareness of the need for change and a climate of receptivity to change.

Moving: changing the magnitude or direction of the forces that define the initial situation; developing new methods and/or learning new attitudes and behaviors.

Refreezing: reinforcing the changes that have occurred, thereby maintaining and stabilizing a new equilibrium situation.

---

[2]Many textbooks (probably starting with Gregory and Van Horn, 1963) have cited a paradigm of this sort, although the details vary. Gerrity (1971) notes that this particular "decision-centered" approach differs from other approaches, such as machine-centered design, data-centered design, process-centered design, and information-system design. Kling (1977) differentiates user-centered vs. machine-centered software designs.

Zand and Sorensen (1975) applied this change theory directly and demonstrated that success in handling the issues at each step was strongly associated with overall success in a large sample of projects involving the implementation of management science methods. Figure 23 lists some of the key issues at each step that are cited by Zand and Sorensen.

FIGURE 23    Favorable and Unfavorable Forces
at the Three Stages of Change

|  | *Favorable* | *Unfavorable* |
|---|---|---|
| **Unfreezing** | 1. Top and unit managers felt the problem was important to company.<br>2. Top managers became involved.<br>3. Unit managers recognized a need for change.<br>4. Top managers initiated the study.<br>5. Top and unit managers were open, candid.<br>6. Unit managers revised some of their assumptions. | 1. Unit managers could not state their problems clearly.<br>2. Top managers felt the problem was too big.<br>3. Unit managers did not recognize need for change.<br>4. Unit managers felt threatened by the project.<br>5. Unit managers resented the study.<br>6. Unit managers lacked confidence in the management scientists.<br>7. Unit managers felt they could do the study alone. |
| **Moving** | 1. Unit managers and management scientists gathered data jointly.<br>2. Relevant data were accessible, available.<br>3. New alternatives were devised.<br>4. Unit managers reviewed and evaluated alternatives.<br>5. Top managers were advised of options.<br>6. Top managers helped develop a solution.<br>7. Proposals were improved sequentially. | 1. Management scientists could not educate the unit managers.<br>2. Needed data were not made available.<br>3. Unit managers did not help develop a solution.<br>4. Unit managers did not understand the solution of the management scientists.<br>5. Management scientists felt the study was concluded too quickly. |
| **Refreezing** | 1. Unit managers tried the solution.<br>2. Utilization showed the superiority of the new solution.<br>3. Management scientists initiated positive feedback after early use.<br>4. Solution was widely accepted after initial success.<br>5. Unit managers were satisfied. | 1. Management scientists did not try to support new managerial behavior after the solution was used.<br>2. Management scientists did not try to reestablish stability after the solution was used.<br>3. Results were difficult to measure. |

---

*FIGURE 23    (continued)*

---

6. Solution was used in other areas.
7. The change improved the performance of the unit.

4. Standards for evaluating results were lacking.
5. Top managers ignored the solution recommended by the management scientists.
6. Solution was incompatible with the needs and resources of the unit.
7. Top managers did not encourage other units to use the solution.

---

Reprinted from "Theory of Change and the Effective Use of Management Science" by Dale E. Zand and Richard E. Sorensen, published in *Administrative Science Quarterly*, vol. 20, no. 4 (December 1975), by permission of *The Administrative Science Quarterly*. © Cornell University.

Figure 24 presents a more elaborate version of change theory as applied specifically to the relationship between the user and the designer of a system.[3] The Kolb-Frohman model in Fig. 24 is strongly normative. It suggests a pattern of interactions between designer and user that should increase the probability of successful implementation. Ginzberg (1975, 1976) performed an empirical study in which he hypothesized that success in implementation efforts is positively correlated to the quality of the implementation process. Measuring the quality of the process as the degree to which key issues were resolved at each of the seven stages, he concluded that projects that conformed closely to the normative process in Fig. 24 actually did succeed more often than those that deviated significantly.

## II. IMPLEMENTATION PATTERNS IN THE SAMPLE

Although the case study data from the sample of 56 decision support systems did not contain detailed information about each of the seven stages, information collected about the history of the systems was quite consistent with change theory and the conclusions cited above. This can be demonstrated by categorizing each of the system implementations in terms of two factors: (1) the degree to which the user initiated the system development effort; and (2) the degree to which the user participated in the system development effort. Both the Lewin-Schein and Kolb-Frohman models imply that these variables should be associated with successful implementation. For instance, one would imagine that the unfreezing and moving stages of the Lewin-Schein model should be facilitated by a high degree of user initiation and user participation. Likewise, a high degree of initiation and participation should increase the chances of success in the first five stages of the Kolb-Frohman model.

The data from the sample support these hypotheses. Both the theoretical justifications above and the common wisdom imply that the needs of users must be con-

---

[3]The individual steps in Fig. 24 come from the model of the consulting process developed by Kolb and Frohman (1970). The application of the model to system development is based on Ginzberg (1976).

FIGURE 24   A Normative Model of the Consulting Process in System Development
Activities

1.  Scouting: User and designer assess each other's needs and abilities to see if there
    is a match; an appropriate organizational starting point for the project is selected.

2.  Entry: User and designer develop an initial statement of project goals and objec-
    tives; commitment to the project is developed; user and designer develop a trust-
    ing relationship and a "contract" for conducting the project.

3.  Diagnosis: User and designer gather data to refine and sharpen the definition of
    the problem and goals for the solution; user and designer assess available re-
    sources (including commitment) to determine whether continued effort is feasible.

4.  Planning: User and designer define specific operational objectives and examine
    alternative ways to meet these objectives; impacts of proposed solutions on all
    parts of the organization are examined; user and designer develop an action plan
    that takes account of solution impacts on the organization.

5.  Action: User and designer put the "best" alternative into practice; training neces-
    sary for effective use of the system is undertaken in all affected parts of the orga-
    nization.

6.  Evaluation: User and designer assess how well the goals and objectives (speci-
    fied during the Diagnosis and Planning stages) were met; user and designer de-
    cide whether to work further on the system (evolve) or to cease active work (ter-
    minate).

7.  Termination: User and designer ensure that "ownership" of and effective control
    over the new system rest in the hands of those who must use and maintain it; user
    and designer ensure that necessary new patterns of behavior have become a
    stable part of the user's routine.

sidered in developing systems and that users should participate actively in implementing them. Nonetheless, the users did not initiate 31 of the 56 systems in the sample and did not participate actively in the development of 38 of the 56. The results,
illustrated in Figure 25, are not surprising. Intended users neither initiated nor played
an active role in implementing 11 of the 25 systems that suffered significant implementation problems. Conversely, there were relatively few such problems in 27 of
the 31 systems in which the users played a more active role in initiating or implementing.

FIGURE 25   Systems Resisted by Users

|  | Few or none of the intended users were involved in implementing system | All or most of the intended users helped implement system |
|---|---|---|
| Intended users did not initiate | 11 of 25 systems | 0 of 6 systems |
| Intended users helped initiate | 2 of 13 systems | 2 of 12 systems |

Although the data in Fig. 25 are consistent with both common sense and the theoretical models cited above, they should be a bit mystifying: If high initiation and participation are so significant, why were both present in only 12 out of 56 implementations in the sample? Furthermore, if there are good reasons why systems are not always developed under ideal circumstances, what are some of the key warning signals of incipient implementation difficulties? The remainder of this chapter discusses various aspects of the implementation patterns that produced the results cited in Fig. 25.

Figure 26 indicates part of the rationale behind each of the four implementation patterns.

*FIGURE 26   Four Implementation Patterns*

| | | |
|---|---|---|
| *Initial stimulus*<br><br>Managerial<br><br>Entrepreneurial | Nonuser initiation<br>Low participation | Nonuser initiation<br>High participation |
| User | User initiation<br>Low participation | User initiation<br>High participation |

Degree to which the system is imposed on the user

Turnkey system — Provides data and checks — Implementation team — User develops system

Degree of user participation
in system definition and development

## System Initiation

The initial push to develop a decision support system seemed to be of three types: user stimulus, managerial stimulus, and entrepreneurial stimulus. Systems initiated through user stimulus were those in which the user perceived the need and pushed for the initial implementation efforts.

> "We just couldn't do all we wanted to in our capacity as staff analysts. We decided to look into the possibility of using computerized tools to do some of our repetitive calculations. When our in-house EDP staff couldn't—or wouldn't—help, we went outside."

Systems initiated through managerial stimulus were those in which the user's organizational superiors perceived a need for a decision support system for the user.

> "I was never satisfied with the way brand managers made their budget committee presentations. There was never an adequate rationale for justifying an individual budget request or for comparing requests. I decided that the brand managers needed a rational method for developing their budgets and asked our internal consultants to work with them in developing such a method."

Initiation through entrepreneurial stimulus implies that a person inside or outside the organization made a concerted effort to sell people in the organization on an idea for a system which he or she would like to implement. The entrepreneur could have been a staff person, an MIS or management science person, an outside consultant or other commercial interest, or an experimenter who wished to use the organization as a test bed for a technique.

> "Our company markets a pretty good database system. My job is to make our potential customers aware of the possible benefits of the system by demonstrating that it will reduce their programming requirements while greatly reducing turnaround time for certain types of applications."

> "Our budgeting system certainly didn't spring forth full-grown. It started as a special project for one large division that really had a bad budgetary control problem. When the system produced good results, we decided to try to expand it to encompass every division in the company. We got the Executive Committee to agree and then tried to sell it to users in the other divisions."

Managerial and entrepreneurial stimulus were often intertwined since there were many cases in which an entrepreneur made a significant effort to sell the concept to a manager (who might then "convince" a subordinate as to its merits). This is why managerial and entrepreneurial stimulus are lumped into one category (low initiation) in Figs. 24 and 25.

### User Participation

The degree to which the user participated in definition and development varied widely. Some systems were presented to the user on a turnkey basis.

> "They sold us a standard program for doing risk analysis. They had developed it and marketed it over several years. The result is that we don't have to deal with a million details they have resolved. From day one, we had a program that we could use by simply providing the input data."

Other systems were developed with little user participation in conceptualization but some participation in data gathering and checking.

> "Basically, I was transferred here to develop a way to keep track of the current status of all of our construction projects. Since I had had some experience with our procedures for handling construction projects, the approach was relatively obvious. I wrote the program and gave some demos. A couple of the report formats changed a bit, but the basic idea of the system never changed."

In contrast to these examples of low-participation implementations, there were many implementations that had a very high level of user participation. One common approach for maintaining a high level of participation is the implementation team.

> "It was a new kind of system for us, and we didn't want to produce something that would turn out to be useless. We used a team approach, in which the man in charge was the technical liaison in the marketing department. His responsibility was to be sure that the system met the needs of the marketing group. The other members of the team were a lead programmer, a junior programmer, a marketing manager, and a marketing analyst. After agreeing on a system definition, we met once a month to monitor the project's progress."

The extreme case of user participation is the implementation in which the implementer is the user.

> "This (sales information) system is my group's vehicle for having an impact on this business. Whenever we do an analysis for someone, we ask ourselves whether that kind of analysis will come up again. If so, we try to avoid losing the work we put in. We do this by adding a new module to our system of analysis procedures and data."

Both common sense and behavioral theory imply that a high degree of user initiation and participation should increase the chances of success. Nonetheless, both factors were favorable in only 12 of 56 systems in the sample. The examples above indicate that this seeming inconsistency is (usually) not due to some sort of suicidal tendency on the part of system implementers; rather, it is a result of the realities of system development activities in most environments. In a sense, the heart of the issue is not really high or low values of initiation and participation but, rather, the characteristics of fundamentally different situations.

### Six Implementation Situations

In order to focus this point more clearly, Fig. 27 "names" and locates six generic implementation situations in terms of a slightly modified version of the framework used in Fig. 26. The particular situation names that are used are meant metaphorically rather than pejoratively. Each situation will be discussed briefly.

1. "Join hands and circle round" defines the spirit of the normative implementation literature[4] and is consistent with most empirical findings that are reported. Other things being equal, the accepted wisdom is that high levels of user initiation and participation are associated with higher probabilities of success. The basic assumptions here are that no solution is obvious in advance and that the client/user is buying a cooperative problem definition and problem-solving effort in addition to a product, such as a system or recommendation.

   > "I joined this insurance company with the charter of developing some kind of computerized assistance for investment planning. Since they didn't know exactly what they wanted, and I wasn't sure what I could deliver, we spent a lot of time groping around trying different things. Some kinds of financial analysis worked fine, and there were duds. . . . At this point, we have systems that are used throughout the company but certainly have a way to go, and I'm not at all worried about working myself out of a job."

2. "Service with a smile" is a situation in which the client/user is actually buying a product rather than a service.[5] The form and content of the

---

[4]The normative implementation literature (as distinguished from the empirical or theoretical literature) is primarily concerned with providing advice for systems implementers and users, e.g., Ackoff (1967), Wagner (1971), Hammond (1974a,b).

[5]This distinction is made by Keen (1975a).

FIGURE 27    *Six Generic Implementation Situations*

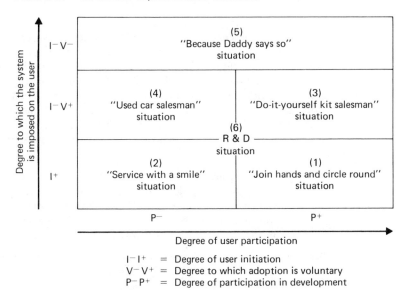

$I^- I^+$ = Degree of user initiation
$V^- V^+$ = Degree to which adoption is voluntary
$P^- P^+$ = Degree of participation in development

product are relatively clear-cut, and the main issue is that of completing the project to specifications within time and budget constraints. The literature on systems analysis, project management, and large-scale software development is especially relevant here.

> "The project itself was no great mystery. The input was fixed. We could not change the piecework tickets that the workers turned in. The outputs were a series of on-line displays that were pretty well understood. Our problem was to develop computer software that would store and maintain the inputs and produce the displays cheaply and reliably. . . . But the technical design wasn't as simple as we originally thought. The first version of the system answered some on-line queries in two seconds and others in five minutes. Back to the drawing board!"

3. The "do-it-yourself kit" salesman situation is basically an effort to convert a low-initiation, low-participation implementation situation into a more favorable one. The basic strategy here is to use guile and sleight of hand to convince the client/user that the product is needed and then to obtain his involvement in its development, regardless of who initiated it.

> "When people come to our corporate staff group with analysis requests that can be addressed using our financial analysis system, we tell them we'll work on their problem, but suggest that they come to our next two-day system demonstration. In those sessions, they must bring an analysis problem of their own. By solving the problem themselves in the course of the demo, they learn

that the system really is useful and often use it themselves thereafter."

4.   The "used car salesman" situation is that in which an entrepreneur is attempting to sell a particular idea, model, or capability. Although "have technique, will travel" is the prevailing strawman of the normative implementation literature, the selling of existing products usually isn't viewed with as much horror. The "used car salesman" situation has a comparatively high risk of implementation difficulties. Nonetheless, it is also a route through which significant innovations are sometimes introduced since new ideas often originate outside of the settings in which they are applied.

> "Decision-tree analysis is now a very common way to provide structure for complex decision situations. It wasn't always that way. Someone came up with the inspiration that a decision tree is a powerful tool. The rest of it was perspiration—going around convincing other people that it was a really useful approach."

5.   "Because Daddy says so" is a very common situation, in which a subordinate is obligated to comply with the decisions, whims, or desires of a superior. Many repetitive circumstances fall under this heading.

> Ensuring that systems provided to subordinate groups will be used in the desired manner:
>
> "We monitor the credit decisions of our loan officers. We want to know that they are usually within our guidelines for granting and refusing loan applications."
>
> Imposing a system on a "user" and forcing compliance to certain usage patterns:
>
> "Admittedly, the cost budgeting system was designed mainly to service the needs of large divisions of the bank. The really small divisions find it a nuisance more than anything else because cost budgeting isn't a major problem for them. The bank simply decided that the overall benefits of being able to do fast bankwide budget consolidations outweighed the minor inconvenience of data entry by small divisions."

This implementation situation applies not only in business organizations but also in a wide range of governmental settings, e.g., the implementation of legislative enactments.[6]

6.   The R & D situation starts with a preimplementation attempt to develop new concepts or products. The placement of this situation squarely in the middle of Fig. 27 is motivated by the fact that the results of R & D efforts can enter the regular implementation stream through any of the

---

[6]"Because Daddy says so" is studiously avoided in the management science implementation literature although it is addressed in the planned change and political science literature. For instance, see Bennis, Benne, and Chin (1969), Derthick (1972), Pressman and Wildavsky (1973), Bardach (1977).

other five situations. On the one extreme, there were cases in the sample in which management scientists stated that they tried to anticipate user needs. Further, the results of well-hidden R & D efforts to develop new concepts tended to emerge magically six months later in situation (1) type discussions of these same needs. On the other extreme, results of R & D efforts also surfaced in a number of implementations of types (4) and (5), in which the installation and use of a system was mandated by management decree. Several instances of this situation were minor disasters in which the "users" went through the motions of using the system but never allowed it to affect the substance of their work. Consider, for instance, the reaction of the brand manager who was forced to use the model in the Connoisseur Foods case. On the other hand, there were also major successes in which the uniform use of a system was enforced as a vehicle for more adequate organizational planning or control. (Examples are discussed in Chapter 3 in the section concerning impact on control.)

## III. CONCLUSION

One easy way to summarize the basic differences between the various implementation situations is to highlight the perspective of each concerning the user and implementer. In (1) and (2) the system is being *built for* the user; in (3) and (4) it is being *sold to* the user; in (5) it is being *forced upon* the user. In (1) and (2) the user and implementer have the common goal of creating the system or product that best suits the user's needs and desires. In (3) and (4) the commonality is diffused somewhat by the implementer's intention to sell a particular product whether or not it is what the user really wants. In (5) the goal is that of manipulating the user in order to achieve whatever compliance is required.

In talking about the implementation of decision support systems and management science methods, people usually think about a slightly schizophrenic combination of "built for" and "sold to" situations, and they almost always take the viewpoint of the implementer. The substance of the discussion, whether empirical or normative, is usually that on the average, situation (1) leads to better results than (2) or (3), both of which dominate (4) and (5) in turn. From this it follows that implementers should consider doing what they can to move implementation environments in the direction of situation (1). Without disputing this conclusion, we note that one of the basic points illustrated by the examples above is that, although "sold to" and "forced upon" sound menacing compared with "built for," it is clear that many implementations are and *should be* instances of each of these three types of thrust. Furthermore, it is clear that many, if not most, implementations involve at least some component of each member of the "built for," "sold to," and "forced upon" trinity. For instance, most systems *built for* one client must also be *sold to* some of his superiors and peers and will likely involve extra work forced upon subordinates and/or peers. The obvious conclusion is that it may not always be possible to apply the standard prescription that one should attempt to move in the direction of situation (1).

This chapter has discussed four implementation patterns (high or low initiation and participation) and then reinterpreted these patterns in terms of six implementation situations. Both theoretical and empirical arguments have suggested that the likelihood of successful implementation increases to the extent to which the user has initiated the system and participated in its development. However, whereas the taxonomy in Chapter 2 and the usage patterns in Chapter 3 were viewed as positive choices for the implementer, implementation patterns pose more of a quandary.

For instance, consider the possible conclusion that the low-initiation, low-participation pattern should be avoided totally. The problem is that many of the genuinely innovative and ultimately successful systems in the sample were developed through this pattern. As innovations, they embodied significant change and therefore involved a greater inherent risk of implementation difficulties. On the other hand, many of the systems resulting from user initiation seemed to do little more than to mechanize existing practices. Although such mechanization can be very beneficial, and although one certainly cannot suggest that major innovations must come from outside sources, it is conceivable that a general insistence on user initiative in system development would lead to more systems that merely mechanized existing practice and fewer systems that engendered any kind of significant change in approach. Some of the most successful systems in the sample were the result of lengthy R & D efforts that preceded any attempt either to unveil the concept or to implement the system. This adds further weight to the notion that the key issue is not only to identify high-risk projects but also to decide what to do to increase the likelihood of successful implementation, regardless of a priori risks. Chapter 7 will present an approach for analyzing these risks and developing appropriate implementation strategies.

# IMPLEMENTATION
## RISK FACTORS AND
## IMPLEMENTATION STRATEGIES

CHAPTER **SEVEN**

In the research study, a substantial part of each interview concerned questions under the general heading of "factors either in favor of or opposed to successful implementation." After some initial interviews, it became clear that the question as posed was incomplete. In addition to identifying factors that were especially relevant to their situations, implementers and users seemed quite interested in discussing what they did in response to these conditions. The properly posed question should have contained three parts:

1.  What situational factors favored or opposed successful implementation?

2.  What actions were taken in response to these factors?

3.  What determined whether these actions were successful?

The previous chapter introduced the notion that many systems must be implemented under circumstances that are at least partially unfavorable. This chapter presents data from the sample concerning both key early warning signals and strategies that were devised to keep implementation efforts on course. (It should be noted at the start that these warning signals and implementation strategies were relevant across all of the implementation situations described previously.)

The basic normative conclusion of the chapter is that practitioners should perform what may be called an "implementation risk analysis" in addition to (or despite the lack of) a cost/benefit study in the initial stages of a project. Such an analysis begins with the identification of an "ideal implementation situation." Deviations between the existing circumstances and the ideal are identified as risk factors, i.e., conditions that decrease the likelihood of successful implementation. For each risk factor that is relevant, a corresponding implementation strategy should be devised. If adequate implementation strategies cannot be devised, the project should be abandoned or deferred if at all possible.

This chapter is divided into three major sections. The first section provides a conceptual introduction to the idea of risk factors and implementation risk analysis. The second section presents empirical data about the types of situations in which each of eight risk factors had a significant impact. The third section discusses situations involving the use of each of 16 implementation strategies that were observed in the sample. The basic purpose of the chapter is to use implementation risk analysis as a way to organize and present a great deal of information about implementation situations.

## I. IMPLEMENTATION RISK ANALYSIS

As part of its work in reducing the incidence of heart attacks, the American Heart Association maintains an active advertising campaign that stresses a series of "risk factors" that tend to increase the likelihood of heart attacks. The basic contention is that the risk of suffering a heart attack increases in correspondence to the deviation of a person's life style from an ideal life style never stated explicitly in the advertising because it is best described as follows: The person

weighs 120–123 pounds;

neither smokes nor drinks;

eats mostly grains, vegetables, and fish and never eats chocolate eclairs;

gets 10 hours of sleep each night;

runs six miles per day, supplementing the exercise of a full-time occupation as a shepherd; and

lives in a pristine, unpolluted mountain valley just southeast of Shangri-La.

Not a very interesting person, perhaps, but one whose likelihood of having a heart attack is relatively low.

It is possible to use the same type of metaphor in thinking about implementation. Let us start by defining implementation as a process or sequence of events whose purpose is to accomplish a goal. For this particular sample, implementation can be defined more specifically as a process of converting an initial conception of a system into a tool that is used effectively. Two possible summary measures of the quality of an implementation process are (1) the degree to which effective usage is achieved; and (2) the degree of difficulty encountered in attempting to accomplish effective usage. In this study, the latter was the more practical measure of the implementation process. First, it was much easier for respondents to describe what happened during an implementation than to recall exactly what the initial goals were (especially since the initial goals were often vague). In addition, the systems in the sample were in different phases of their life cycles. Some had been used for years, whereas others were still in a technical and organizational shakedown phase. As a result, focusing on difficulties encountered provided a better basis of comparison.

Using the second criterion, one could rank an implementation effort on the following dimension.

(Successful)      Smooth implementation: No problems are encountered.
.
.
.          Difficult implementation: Much trial and tribulation precedes effective use.
.
.
(Unsuccessful)    Terminated implementation: Effective use is never achieved.

Note that this one-dimensional view is really a combination of two dimensions: degree of goal achievement and quality of process.

|  | *Goal achieved* | *Goal not achieved* |
|---|---|---|
| *Process easy:* | 1. Smooth implementation | 2. Smooth rejection |
| *Process difficult:* | 3. Difficulties surmounted | 4. Difficulties not surmounted |

Since data were collected on systems that were being used, whether effectively or not, category 2 was automatically neglected in the sample. Note also that, although not a major issue in the sample, smooth implementation may actually be counterproductive if the purpose of a system is to force change on people in an organization.

Based on the second success criterion, and given that instances of "smooth rejection" were excluded, a simple principle seemed to apply across the sample:

> The likelihood of a successful implementation process is positively related to the certainty with which that process can be planned.

In a restatement of this principle in terms of decision support systems, it is possible to propose an ideal implementation situation *for such systems* by imagining a case in which the implementation process could be planned and controlled with maximum certainty:

> The system is to be produced by a single implementer for a single user who anticipates using the system for a very definite purpose that can be specified in advance with great precision. Including the person who will maintain it, all parties affected by the system understand and accept in advance its impact on them. All parties have prior experience with this type of system, the system receives adequate support, and its technical design is feasible and cost-effective.

Across the entire sample, the more closely the implementation situation conformed to this ideal, the more likely it was that the implementation would go smoothly. Conversely, system development efforts that began under quite different circumstances seemed to encounter many implementation difficulties. Whether or not success was achieved ultimately, the histories of the latter systems were cluttered with high levels of discouragement and exasperation.

Consider the ways in which any actual implementation situation can differ from this ideal situation. At least eight types of deviations can occur that reduce the certainty of the implementation process.

Nonexistent or unwilling users

Multiple users or implementers

Disappearing users, implementers, or maintainers

Inability to specify purpose or usage pattern in advance

Inability to predict and cushion impact on all parties

Lack or loss of support

Lack of prior experience with similar systems

Technical problems and cost-effectiveness issues[1]

These deviations can be conceptualized as "implementation risk factors," i.e., factors that increase the likelihood of implementation difficulties. Note that these risk factors are a series of deviations from an ideal situation, *which rarely occurs.* Just as a large percentage of cardiac problems would disappear if people really could live like the ideal person, a large percentage of implementation problems wouldn't exist if implementation situations were of the ideal type. In both cases, however, the comparisons with an ideal are useful because they highlight areas where action to reduce the risks inherent in the situation may be in order.

Using risk factors, one can perform an implementation risk analysis prior to the development of a system by proceeding as follows:

> List every way in which the implementation situation for the proposed system currently deviates or soon may deviate from the ideal; i.e., list every risk factor that seems to be applicable. For each characteristic in which it deviates, design a course of corrective action that will either reduce the deviation itself or control its consequences. If there is no feasible way to reduce either the deviations or their consequences to tolerable levels, explain to interested parties the specific problems that are blocking effective implementation, and move on to the next system unless forced to do otherwise.

This kind of analysis can be employed as a discipline for anticipating trouble, or it can be formalized as part of the organization's procedures for selecting and authorizing projects. It can be used even if a formal cost/benefit study is thought inappropriate (as in many decision-oriented projects that are deemed potentially beneficial despite the impossibility of quantifying their potential benefits convincingly).

It should be stressed that identifying sources of risk is only the first stage of the analysis. The second stage is to develop general approaches and specific strategies for avoiding these potential stumbling blocks. Although the term "implementation strategy" has been used in a fairly general sense by many others,[2] in an attempt to develop this concept further, we will define "implementation strategy" here as a conscious course of action undertaken to minimize the effects of risk factors inherent in implementation situations. Contrary to the assumptions implicit in much of the normative implementation literature, the view taken here is that particular implementation strategies should be viewed as neither desirable nor harmful, a priori. Independent of context, there should be no reason to assume that any particular implementation strategy is relevant or irrelevant, effective or ineffective, good or

---

[1]Each of these risk factors could be interpreted as a cluster of related factors (e.g., nonexistent user and unwilling user) whose dynamics and impact were relatively similar in the sample.

[2]For instance, Chin and Benne (1969) identify power-coercive, political-economic, and rational-empirical approaches to planned change, Radnor et al. (1970) mention "bargaining" and analytic implementation strategies, and Bean et al. (1975) mention "mixed strategies" with respect to project portfolios of operations research and management science groups. In general terms, Reisman and de Kluyver (1975), Roberts (1977), and Hammond (1974b) discuss strategies for implementing system studies and corporate models.

bad. In fact, if we take this view to the extreme, any strategy that "always works" should be viewed skeptically since it is likely to be either trivial or underspecified.

Data from the sample concerning implementation risk factors and implementation strategies will be presented in turn and explained in more detail.

## II. IMPLEMENTATION RISK FACTORS

Although the implementation risk factors cited above are probably reasonably general, note that the situations and corresponding risk factors cited here are not meant to be absolute or universal in any sense. Rather, these risk factors are especially relevant to the systems in one particular sample. Since organizations differ in size, purpose, dynamics, etc., it is likely that an organization applying implementation risk analysis would start with factors such as those described below but would also include risk factors that were especially relevant within its own context. Such risk factors could be identified by comparing recent project successes with recent disappointments.

Figure 28 summarizes the ways each of the risk factors "operated" in the systems in the sample. The basic idea underlying Fig. 28 is that in facilitating an anticipatory analysis of a proposed implementation, research results should provide information and guidance beyond the mere identification of risk factors that may be relevant. For instance, in the majority of the cases in which risk factor 2 (multiple users or implementers) was present, the main problem it produced was inadequate communication and an inability to incorporate varied interests of different individuals. In turn, since most of these situations involved voluntary rather than mandatory use of the system, the result was uneven usage and, in several cases, considerable dispute as to the value of the system. Turnover of personnel is a fact of life; risk factor 3 became most significant in situations in which the system was a vehicle of a person who left or in which the system initiator left before the system was installed. The result in the cases in the sample was severely reduced usage. Although it is often difficult to predict exactly how a system will be used, in the sample this became a major problem when system designers and advocates were unduly overoptimistic in assuming that noncomputer personnel would figure out how to use the new system. The result was disuse. Finally, what were posed as technical problems and cost-effectiveness issues in various systems were often very similar in nature. Typically, it could not be proved either that an existing system had been beneficial or that the expenditure of time and talent necessary to correct technical shortcomings of a system was really worthwhile. In both instances, the result was a general weakening of the system due to inadequate support.

Instances of each of the risk factors will now be discussed in turn.

### 1. Nonexistent or Unwilling Users

The risk of having nonexistent or unwilling users is especially high for systems that are not initiated by their potential users and that are developed with little active participation by the users. In the sample, this happened under a number of circumstances:

    a)    An internal or external entrepreneur (typically a consultant or staff analyst) develops a new procedure or methodology and then attempts to sell it to its potential users.

FIGURE 28 *Summary of Data Concerning Risk Factors*

| Risk Factor | Problem | Typical Situation | Result |
|---|---|---|---|
| 1. Nonexistent or unwilling users | Lack of commitment to use the system | System not initiated by potential users and developed without their participation | Disuse; uneven use; lack of impact |
| 2. Multiple users or implementers | Communication problems; inability to incorporate interests of many people | System involving voluntary use by many individuals or coordination among many people | Uneven use |
| 3. Disappearing users, implementers, or maintainers | No one available to use or modify the system | Worst case: system is the vehicle of a person who leaves, or system initiator leaves before system is installed | Reduced use or disappearance of the system |
| 4. Inability to specify purpose or usage pattern | Overoptimism on part of system designer and advocates | Assumption that noncomputer personnel will figure out how to use the system | Disuse |
| 5. Inability to predict and cushion impact | Lack of motivation to work or change work pattern without receiving benefits | No benefits from the system to people in the "feeder role"; forced changes in organizational procedures | "Why bother" syndrome; fear and/or annoyance |
| 6. Loss or lack of support | Requirements for funding; obstruction by uncooperative people | Lack of budget to run system; lack of management action to use system effectively | System death or disuse |
| 7. Lack of experience with similar systems | Unfamiliarity leading to mistakes | Developing an innovative system aimed at substantive change rather than automation per se | Technical problems; bad fit of solution and problem; misuse or disuse of system |
| 8. Technical problems and cost-effectiveness | Cost of maintaining or improving system | Advocacy situation: no adequate way to estimate value of system either before or after potential improvements | Failure of system to meet needs; either limps on or is discarded |

*Example:*   The director of management science in a bank developed a cost-budgeting system for one division of the bank. Having produced a working system, he attempted to sell the same approach to the other divisions. Some were enthusiastic; others thought the system would not help them. Eventually the system was imposed on all divisions by top management. Some of the "users" were very half-hearted in using the system.

b)   Management hears about the latest technique or system and assigns someone to implement such a system without a clear idea of how it will be used and who will use it.

*Example:*   An external consultant told the president of an insurance company that the company had no adequate way of making tactical decisions, such as the number and deployment of field agents. He suggested that a corporate model be developed to study this and similar issues. The model was developed but remained in limbo because no one could identify a pressing problem that it could help solve.

c)   An implementation team designs a system for use by a large number of people, some of whom have no desire to change their current practices.

*Example:*   A shop floor information system (A3 in Chapter 2) was developed at the request of the management of a factory that was obtaining low yield rates in manufacturing integrated circuits. The system was to provide information for shop foremen, some of whom found the system quite useful while others neglected it. In general, the system was least accepted by old-timers with 10 or more years of experience and best accepted by newer foremen.

Chapter 6 demonstrated that lower user initiation and participation tends to increase the likelihood of implementation difficulties. In the sample of 56 decision support systems, 44 percent of the 25 that were developed with low user initiation and participation encountered unwillingness or inability to use the system on the part of potential users. Of the 31 remaining systems only 17 percent experienced such difficulties.

The details of the unwillingness problem differ widely among the systems studied. In four of them (see the example given under b above), the problem meant that the system had little or no impact because it received little use. In the Connoisseur Foods case, it meant that the experience with one particular approach led to a better appreciation of what was feasible in the situation, and that result led to efforts to develop a more appropriate decision support system. For nine systems (e.g., the Great Eastern Bank case and the example given under c above), it meant that acceptance by individuals varied widely, with significant use by some and little or no use by other potential users. In most of these cases, there existed some combination of bad communication and false expectations, which led people to believe that greater or more uniform levels of usage would occur.

## 2.  *Multiple Users or Implementers*

All of the systems that had more than five users experienced different levels of use by different people. The degree of usage by individuals varied from heavy to none for a number of the systems that were used independently and individualistically for operational tasks. This range of usage tended to alarm implementers and maintainers of a number of systems. It was their feeling that since the system existed and worked, people should use it.

One explanation of the problem is that with a large number of potential users, it is quite difficult to obtain the high levels of user initiation and participation that tend to lead to high commitment and usage. An example here is the portfolio management system in the Great Eastern Bank case. This system had 50 potential users. The 10 potential users who were members of the implementation team became the most active users of the system, whereas many of the others who did not participate used the system only when required to do so. On a more general level, the issue with multiple users and implementers is simply that the larger the number of people involved in anything, the harder it is to maintain communication and to incorporate individual interests. In the political science literature, Derthick (1972), Pressman and Wildavsky (1973), and Bardach (1977) provide fine examples of this phenomenon in analyses of federal programs that failed.

3.  *Disappearing Users, Implementers, or Maintainers*

Turnover among users and/or implementers of systems was cited frequently as a serious problem in the development and use of decision support systems. Typical comments concerning these problems include the following.

> The original guy who thought of this system and his replacement have both moved into line positions in different areas of the company. It is not clear who is going to push this system to keep it going.
>
> Observation concerning a budget analysis system

> When I moved from the other consulting company to this one, this account came with me quite gladly because I was the one who really knew what was going on in this system.
>
> Implementer of a costing and pricing system

> Turnover of client personnel isn't that much of a problem for us. As a matter of fact, it's sometimes an advantage in the sense that they know we're experts in maintaining these systems and that we'll be available for years to come and can help keep the ball rolling even if their own guys come and go.
>
> Principal of a technical consulting company

> One of the reasons why managers don't get involved with decision support systems is that they realize that it will take them a year to really learn how to use the system. They also realize that they will probably be in a different job by that time.
>
> Implementer of a commercial marketing system

> Turnover has killed off more models around here than anything else.
>
> Implementer of a planning model

> Because of frequent turnover among sales planners, we have had to train some users of the system from scratch every year.
>
> Implementer of a financial planning system

If one of these programmers leaves, we'll be in trouble because this system has no documentation.

Implementer of a complex simulation model

We experienced a turnover of the bright young guys assigned to the task of building the model. Two of them left the company, two were moved to other and better jobs, one is still with us. Naturally, they didn't bother to document their work properly.

User of a corporate model

Apparently turnover was a problem for a whole gamut of roles. The disappearances of initiators, implementers, users, and maintainers were all cited as serious problems. The themes that pervade these examples can be summarized as follows: The degree to which turnover affects any particular system seems to depend on such contingencies as the stage in its development, the type of system, and the degree to which the system is basically a vehicle of or for the individual who is leaving. If the initiator leaves at an early stage in system development, the system's chances of successful implementation may decrease drastically unless that person's replacement thinks it is important to carry on in the same direction. If a system is developed for one user (e.g., some of the model-based systems) then that user's departure may well signal the demise of the system. If a system is primarily a vehicle of one staff person, then its usefulness may not recover from that person's departure. On the other hand, turnover may not have a serious impact on system survival if the system has been widely accepted, if there are many users, if it is well documented, if a number of knowledgeable people do the maintenance work, and so on. In the planning preliminary to implementation of new systems, it might be possible to take some of these factors into account in assessing the system's degree of exposure related to potential turnover problems.

### 4. Inability to Specify Purpose or Usage Pattern in Advance

A number of systems in the sample were developed without a clear notion of exactly how they would be used. As illustrated by the examples given in Chapter 5, Section III (conceptual design problems), the result was often a disappointingly low level of system usage. The implications of this pattern of overoptimism on the part of system designers and advocates were also discussed in the same section.

### 5. Inability to Predict and Cushion Impact on All Parties

The systems in the sample encountered a number of problems involving people other than users, implementers, and maintainers. Many of these problems involved individuals occupying what might be called feeder roles, in which they provided data for a system, but either didn't use it directly or didn't derive benefit from it for other reasons. Such situations are common in budgeting and planning systems, in which people at various organizational levels are required to provide information that is later digested and consolidated by the system. As discussed in Chapter 5, Section II (data problems), questions for people in feeder roles range from "why bother" to how to avoid loss of autonomy and/or revelation of ignorance. In addition, other situations occurred in the sample in which new systems in one area had such effects as modified reporting formats that rippled into other organizational units, thereby causing a certain level of annoyance. Conceptually, the entire problem was simple: The development and maintenance of a computerized system sometimes had implications, either through changing formats or causing more work, for people who received little benefit from the system. Not surprisingly, the reaction was often annoyance and sometimes belligerency. Although the basic issue is simple to describe, totally satisfactory accommodations were not always achieved.

### 6.  Lack or Loss of Support

Business organizations operate through people and budgets. Correspondingly, the general notion of support subsumes both management action and funding. Situations in which the issue was funding were often relatively mundane: People wanted to develop systems and required authorization. Where the issue was management action, the situation sometimes involved forcing people to use systems or to comply with unfamiliar formats or requirements. Specific situations here ranged from a budgeting system in which management enforced standard definitions to a marketing model in which management required direct participation by an uninterested brand manager. In these cases and many others, a lower level of support would have minimized the effectiveness of the system or would have killed it altogether.

Other than in a number of instances where there was controversy about the cost-effectiveness of systems, lack of support was not an overriding concern for most of the systems in the sample. In a Darwinian sense, one would expect this: Without a reasonable level of support, a system would not have survived and would not have found its way into the sample. For two file drawer systems in manufacturing environments and for a data analysis system and a representational model in corporate planning environments, partial lack of support led to a limbolike existence. Although enough resources had been provided to keep the applications alive, little definitive action had been taken to establish the systems firmly since the overall management attitude in each case ranged from indifference to tolerance. The long-term survival of these systems was by no means obvious.

### 7.  Lack of Experience with Similar Systems

Obviously, gross incompetence by implementers or users of systems will tend to lead to bad results. A less trivial notion of competence is worth mentioning, however. This is the idea of competence vis-à-vis a particular system effort. As an analogy from the field of medicine, a highly competent general practitioner might not perform particularly well if called on to do brain surgery. In the sample, there were a number of instances where unfamiliarity led to problems. In terms of the implementer's performance, unfamiliarity led to technical and conceptual design problems (see Chapter 5), which included designing systems with poor response, designing systems using inappropriate computer languages, and designing systems that were technically infeasible. In terms of the user's performance, unfamiliarity led to the disuse and misuse problems also discussed in Chapter 5. Like any other organizational activity, developing and using decision support systems involves a learning curve for both implementers and users. Whenever a new type of system is attempted, the result is as much a research effort as it is a development effort. As a result, the risk of encountering stumbling blocks is greater.

### 8.  Technical Problems and Cost-effectiveness Issues

As discussed in Chapter 5, many of the technical problems that were encountered in the sample could also be viewed as cost-effectiveness issues. In many cases, higher levels of redundancy, more programming work, better software, larger computers, etc., could have solved what were called technical problems. On the opposite side, many systems were the object of considerable skepticism concerning their cost-effectiveness. Typically, skepticism took the form of complaints on the part of people who were not enthusiastic about the system in the first place. For precisely this reason, it was difficult, if not impossible, to decide whether much of the cost-effectiveness discussion was really concerned with that issue or with other unspoken agendas. As discussed in the section on system evaluation at the end of Chapter 3, cost-effectiveness was a somewhat irksome issue with regard to decision support systems since it was extremely difficult to quantify the dollar impact of a system in terms of better decisions. As a result, whether or not cost/benefit studies were produced, people actually seemed to make decisions on the basis of what they admitted were gut feelings about whether systems were worthwhile. Although the point was never pressed in the interviews since it appeared to be rather sensitive, cost-effectiveness rationales often seemed to be somewhat strained for those systems that had exceeded their budgets or that were not being used as effectively as was originally hoped.

## III.  IMPLEMENTATION STRATEGIES

As described above, the first stage of implementation risk analysis is the identification of the risk factors that may apply in the implementation situation. However, merely identifying risk factors is not enough. The next stage of the analysis should be the formulation of possible strategies for dealing with either the risk factors themselves or their consequences. As in any decision, the choice of strategies will be based on a series of considerations, such as resource requirements, likelihood of success, and situational limitations of each of the strategies.

Once again, the analogy with heart attack risk factors is useful. Assume that a cardiac risk factor analysis has determined that a person is 15 pounds overweight. The possible strategies include reducing food input, going on a special diet, getting more exercise, and doing nothing. Each of these strategies has certain advantages and certain disadvantages. Although it might not show dramatic effects quickly, reducing food consumption would probably work if the person had the willpower to persevere (and that might be doubtful). Going on a special diet might yield major results quickly but might not have lasting effects. Furthermore, each diet strategy might bring side effects, such as irascibility or lack of stamina. Getting more exercise might not work without a simultaneous change in eating habits, and sudden imposition of a strenuous exercise program might precipitate trouble. Doing nothing would avoid the disadvantages and possible side effects of the other strategies but would also reap none of their benefits. Depending on the person's values and situation in life, doing nothing and merely accepting the risks in their current form might be the preferred alternative.

The second stage of implementation risk analysis is deciding what to do about each risk factor that is in effect. In the sample, a total of 16 discernible implementation strategies were observed. They can be classified into four categories:

1.    Divide the project into manageable pieces

2.    Keep the solution simple

3.    Develop a satisfactory support base

4.    Meet user needs and institutionalize the system

In general terms, each of these categories may seem obvious. Given a choice, who would want to provide a system that does not meet user needs or that does not have a satisfactory support base? However, a number of distinct strategies exist under each heading. And as outlined in Fig. 29, every one of these strategies has certain advantages and certain pitfalls, just as did the strategies for losing weight. In the following discussion, instances of effective and ineffective application of strategies under each heading will be included. Just as in any management situation, past results with particular approaches can help people find the leverage points they need and can help them anticipate and avoid potential difficulties similar to those encountered by others. However, there is no magic formula.

### A.  Divide the Project into Manageable Pieces

Three different strategies fell under this general heading: Use prototypes, use an evolutionary or modular approach, and develop a series of tools in the form of databases and small models. Although each of these strategies had the same general objective, they were used under different circumstances. Each was used quite successfully in some cases and less successfully in others.

### 1.  Use Prototypes

Development through a series of prototypes is a strategy sometimes used in implementing systems that are sufficiently innovative in their organizational settings to verge on being research efforts. The idea is to produce and test a relatively inexpensive running version of the system before committing the firm to the expense of a full-fledged version. The purpose of the strategy is to minimize the risk of spending a large sum of money on a system that cannot be used effectively or that turns out to be infeasible technically.

The prototype strategy is especially useful when the success of the effort hinges on one or several relatively untested concepts. It seeks to test the key issue as a discrete first step in system development, and it is particularly appropriate for large, expensive systems. In the sample, this strategy was used in seven systems to test one of two types of feasibility: technical feasibility and the usefulness of the underlying concept. Technical feasibility was a serious issue in systems for portfolio management, media analysis, and renewal underwriting. For instance, the commercial viability of the media analysis system was based on an assumed capability to extract information from a large survey database of characteristics and media habits for 1500 people. It was necessary to be able to generate any logically conceivable cross-tabulation of consumer characteristics against their media habits.

After the prototype demonstrated the efficiency (economic viability) of the technical approach that was chosen, further development continued. For all seven systems, there was a question concerning the feasibility of the underlying concept. For instance, since the validity of using linear programming for long-range planning

FIGURE 29  Summary of Data
Concerning Implementation Strategies

| Implementation Strategy | Typical Situation or Purpose | Pitfalls Encountered |
|---|---|---|
| 1. Divide project into manageable pieces. | To minimize the risk of producing a massive system that doesn't work. | |
| Use prototypes. | Success of the effort hinges on relatively untested concepts. Test these concepts before committing to a full-fledged version. | Reactions to the prototype system (in an experimental setting) may differ from reactions to a final system in day-to-day use. |
| Use an evolutionary approach. | Implementer attempts to shorten feedback loops between self and clients and between intentions and products. | Requires users to live with continuing change, which some people find annoying. |
| Develop a series of tools. | To meet ad hoc analysis needs by providing databases and small models that can be created, modified, and discarded. | Limited applicability. Expense of maintaining infrequently used data. |
| 2. Keep the solution simple. | To encourage use and to avoid scaring away users. | Although generally beneficial, can lead to misrepresentation, misunderstanding, misuse. |
| Be simple. | Not an issue for inherently simple systems. For other systems or situations, it may be possible to choose between simple and complicated approaches. | Some business problems are not inherently simple. Insisting on simple solutions may result in skirting the real issue. |
| Hide complexity. | The system is presented as a "black box" that answers questions using procedures not presented to the user. | Use of "black boxes" by nonexperts can lead to misuse of the results because of misunderstanding of the underlying models and assumptions. |
| Avoid change. | Given a choice of automating existing practice or developing new methods, choose the former. | New system may have little real impact. Not applicable to efforts purporting to foster change. |

*FIGURE 29 (continued)*

| Implementation Strategy | Typical Situation or Purpose | Pitfalls Encountered |
|---|---|---|
| 3. Develop a satisfactory support base. | One or more components of a user-management support base is missing. | Danger that one support-gaining strategy will be applied without adequate attention to others. |
| Obtain user participation. | The system effort was not initiated by users. The usage pattern is not obvious in advance. | With multiple users, difficulty of getting everyone involved and incorporating everyone's interests. With sophisticated models, reduced feasibility of user participation in model formulation and interpretation. |
| Obtain user commitment. | The system has been developed without user involvement. The system is to be imposed on users by management. | It is difficult to obtain commitment without some kind of quid pro quo or demonstration that the system will help the user. |
| Obtain management support. | To obtain funding for continuation of the project. To obtain management action in forcing people to comply with the system or use it. | Management enthusiasm may not be shared by users, resulting in perfunctory use or disuse. |
| Sell the system. | Some potential users were not involved in system development and do not use it. System is not used to full potential by the organization. | Often unsuccessful unless real advantages can be demonstrated convincingly. |
| 4. Meet user needs and institutionalize system. | A system is to have many individual users in an ongoing application. | Since strategies under this heading are somewhat incompatible, emphasis on one may exclude another. |
| Provide training. | The system is not designed in close cooperation with *all* potential users. | Frequent difficulty in estimating the type and intensity of training that is needed. Initial training programs often require substantial reformulation and elaboration. |
| Provide ongoing assistance. | The system is used by an intermediary rather than a decision maker. The system is used with the help of an intermediary who handles mechanical details. | If the system is used by an intermediary, the decision maker may not understand the analysis in sufficient detail. |

FIGURE 29 (continued)

| Implementation Strategy | Typical Situation or Purpose | Pitfalls Encountered |
|---|---|---|
| Insist on mandatory use. | The system is a medium for integration and coordination in planning. The system purports to facilitate work of individuals. | Difference between genuine use and half-hearted submission of numbers for a plan. Difficulty in forcing people to think in a particular mold. |
| Permit voluntary use. | Avoid building resistance to a hard sell by allowing voluntary use. | Generally ineffective unless the system meets a genuine felt need or appeals to an individual intellectually or otherwise. |
| Rely on diffusion and exposure. | It is hoped that enthusiasts will demonstrate the benefits of a system to their colleagues. | Ineffective; perhaps as much an excuse for lack of positive action as it is a real strategy. |
| Tailor systems to people's capabilities. | People differ in their ability and/or propensity to use analytic techniques. | Not clear how to do so. In practice, systems seem to be built to people's requirements, not their capabilities. |

was far from obvious in one large company, a small version of such a system was implemented in a subsidiary in order to test the idea. Companywide implementation was attempted only when the experience in the subsidiary indicated that the concept was sound.

Another example was a system requested by a recently appointed company president to help him get a good fix on the overall budgeting process in the company. Given a relatively vague mandate to try to design something that would help, the developers produced a prototype that demonstrated to the president's satisfaction how a much larger system would work. As described by Stabell (1974), a less successful outcome of the prototype approach was experienced by a system that began as an experimental prototype built to investigate the possibility of on-line support of portfolio managers. It turned out that the use of the prototype in analyzing portfolios was much more active and varied than the use of the final operational system. Apparently the difference stemmed from the fact that the portfolio managers were unfamiliar with the portfolios presented during the experiment and therefore found it important to display them in many different ways in order to learn about them. In contrast, their use of the system in examining their own portfolios in day-to-day work was much less active because of familiarity. An alternative explanation is that the high level of initial usage was primarily a result of the expectations raised in the experimental situation.

## 2.  Use an Evolutionary Approach

To some extent, most systems are developed through an evolutionary or modular approach. Although these terms may seem to connote the trivial idea that most systems are developed gradually and piece by piece, they can be used in a nontrivial sense to describe conscious design strategies by which implementers attempt to shorten the feedback loops between themselves and their clients and between their intentions and their products.[3] When a consciously evolutionary approach is used, an initial system is put up quickly and then modified incrementally to suit the user's needs. As a result, user feedback tends to be reasonably accurate because it concerns a system in use rather than one that is only imagined. The modular approach is an attempt to build systems in very small, discrete pieces, which can be tested and, under some circumstances, used separately. The purpose of both approaches is to minimize the risk of producing a massive system that doesn't do the job and/or can't be changed easily.

The prototype strategy and the evolutionary strategy address the same problem but in somewhat different types of situations. Whereas the prototype approach is especially appropriate for large, expensive projects based on an untested concept, the evolutionary approach applies to smaller systems serving a number of different functions, typically with a life cycle of ongoing periods of use and modification. Modular organization and programming tend to be effective for both approaches.

The problem with an evolutionary approach is that it requires flexibility from the user and willingness to live with continuing change. One user of a corporate model found this expectation quite annoying: "Why is it that the model is never quite right? If our company produced things that aren't quite right, we would go out of business!" Several on-line systems for operational decision making experienced serious user attitude problems when brought up in usable but incomplete versions in an attempt to get back on schedule after development delays. In each case, many users formed a poor impression of the system, which was difficult to overcome. In the words of one implementer, "We found ourselves fighting our way out of a hole. We learned that we should never bring up a system for use unless it is at least 95 percent reliable."

## 3. Develop a Series of Tools

The strategy of developing a series of tools in the form of databases and small models was mentioned explicitly by developers of five systems for analyzing sales or planning data.[4] The feeling was that standard EDP systems could not serve the needs of sales and planning analysis. Since analysis needs change, and since many useful types of analysis are of an ad hoc nature, systems were developed that consisted of one or more databases and a series of small models that could be created, modified, and discarded easily.

For systems developed under this strategy, out-of-pocket charges for storing and accessing large amounts of data were noted as a serious problem. In two instances, managers in a budget pinch were tempted to wonder whether such systems were really needed. Another pitfall of this approach is its sheer reliance on databases. For example, serious difficulties arose in the use of one system as a result

---

[3]For an elaboration of this approach in the analysis of consumer products, see Urban and Karash (1971). In a similar vein, Drake (1973) states that success of the projects in his sample seemed to be enhanced by developing a preliminary model and then embellishing it on the basis of experience.

[4]This approach is suggested by Montgomery and Urban (1970).

of a company reorganization that caused the system's historical data to be inconsistent with current and future data. A major effort was required to recast past data to make it comparable with current and future data.

## B.  Keep the Solution Simple

Next to "obtain user participation and management support," "be simple" is one of the most commonly offered bits of implementation advice.[5] From most viewpoints, the appeal of simplicity is quite direct: Simple solutions are easier to understand, easier to implement, and usually easier to control and modify than complicated solutions. The rub, of course, is that many business problems are not really amenable to simple solution. For instance, developing a genuinely simple model that gets to the heart of a complex business planning question is no mean feat. In an attempt to abide by the rule of simplicity when no simple solution is readily available, the choice is either to solve only the parts of the problem for which simple solutions are available or to disguise complex solutions to make them appear simple. In practice, the desire for simplicity leads to at least three distinct strategies: Use simple solutions, hide complexity, and avoid change. The third strategy is grouped with the other two because some of the problems associated with change are quite similar to those associated with complexity.

### 1.  Be Simple

If it was mentioned at all, the strategy of "being simple" was typically broached with regret. For inherently simple systems, it wasn't an issue. Although "being simple" was rarely mentioned as a conscious strategy in other cases, an inability to be simple was sometimes seen as a serious problem. This was especially true for data analysis systems and models that are difficult to validate (e.g., a model for predicting the level of sales on the basis of the level of advertising). Two data analysis systems encountered difficulties because they became too complicated mechanically. The first, which was developed for commercial use, went through a stage in its development when it was necessary to "put in too many numbers to get a few numbers out" when requesting simple reports. In order to make system usage more convenient, parts of the user interface were revamped. The second, a generalized planning system, "had so many options that you had to be very knowledgeable to use it." The unresolved conflict here was between providing powerful tools for people who wanted them and providing simple tools in order to get people to use them. Two other analysis systems attempted to position themselves in the latter camp but with relatively little success: A data retrieval system for executives was so simple that it didn't have enough power to be useful, and a system purporting to make data manipulation tools palatable for nonprogrammers never really caught on except as a simplified report generator for use by programmers.

Lack of conceptual (rather than mechanical) simplicity was a serious problem with a number of model-oriented systems. These models tended to be understood only by the technical people who ran them. When used effectively, these models were thought of as tools for helping staff people do an analysis that could be reported to management like any other type of staff analysis. For two planning models for

---

[5]For instance, see Hammond (1974b).

which some level of direct management involvement with the formal analysis tools was considered important, lack of simplicity was all the more serious. After all, how could management make correct decisions on the basis of an analysis done with tools they did not understand completely?

### 2.  Hide Complexity

One response to the perceived need for simplicity is to design systems in such a way as to hide their complexity. Although not mentioned often in the interviews as a conscious strategy, it is a strategy suggested implicitly by some of the MS/MIS literature.[6] In the sample, hiding complexity was not a significant issue for data-oriented systems since most of the complexity in these systems resided in the mechanisms for extracting data from computer files and then consolidating it into useful reports. Typically, users didn't seem to care how this was done, as long as the results were accurate and cost-effective.

For some model-oriented systems in the sample, much of the complexity resided in the model itself. For these systems, hiding complexity was a dangerous strategy. If nonexperts were allowed or encouraged to use model-oriented systems directly, the result of the strategy was sometimes misuse of the system (see examples in Chapter 5, Section IV B). However, most of the systems in the sample avoided this issue, either by keeping nondefinitional models in the private domain of staff experts who understood very well what the models could and could not do, or by using the models to produce numbers whose validity could be verified easily (e.g., the prices and circuit diagrams generated by systems G1, G3, and G4 in Chapter 2). On the other hand, there were several interesting examples in which nonexperts were directly involved in the use of nondefinitional models. In systems containing marketing mix and LP planning models, respectively, staff intermediaries were always present to ensure that the models were being used correctly and, in some instances, to carry the ball. Another system, which calculated suggested insurance renewal rates, also provided extremely complete documentation as backup for all rate suggestions.

### 3.  Avoid Change

A parallel strategy that can be used to minimize the difficulties in implementing systems is to avoid change. For example, in the development of an on-line inventory control system, a decision was made to retain the same data items and report formats that appeared in the old batch system, but to gain benefits by providing immediate access to current data. Likewise, one of the key factors leading to the success of a commercial media selection system was that it started with an established body of marketing analysis concepts, which were well understood throughout the advertising industry. As a result, the related selling task was reduced to selling a mechanical tool rather than selling both a concept and a tool.

Unfortunately, the strategy of avoiding change is not available for systems whose purpose is to foster change. In a system that changed the way one-year budgets were reported, people with budget responsibility for production locations had a

---

[6]This view is exemplified by Scott Morton's (1967) initial conclusion that a computer system used for management problem solving should be a "flexible interactive system that is easily used by a manager ignorant of computers."

generally difficult time with the change from submitting only monthly budgets in terms of line items to submitting an additional yearly budget in terms of fixed and variable costs. In the Connoisseur Foods case, changes in thinking implied by a model-based method for analyzing marketing mix were quite difficult for some of the users to absorb. The problem of imposing a formal model on a person not trained in formal techniques was illustrated vividly, if jokingly, through a paraphrase of a typical comment by a brand manager being forced to work with the model.

> "I just don't understand this kind of stuff. It simply is not my bag. I'm an idea man. I'm intuitive. I just don't understand equations and that kind of stuff. I just use them when I have to put them on reports. I look at ads and see if they turn me on. I look at promotions and see if they turn me on. I try to get a feel for the market. It's an intuitive thing. . . . In summary, I'm an intuitive animal, so don't bother me with the facts."

In fact, a retreating position was taken with regard to this modeling effort, with more attention being paid to the needs and capabilities of the managers and more data-oriented analysis being provided.

### C.  Develop a Satisfactory Support Base

Four distinct strategies were employed that belong under this general heading: Obtain user participation, obtain personal commitment, obtain management support, and sell the system. One of the interesting aspects of these strategies is that applying one without adequate attention to the others leads to ineffective implementation. This will be illustrated by a discussion of each strategy in turn.

### 1.  Obtain User Participation

The term "user participation" can imply anything from help in providing data to very active participation in the design of the system. The objective need for "user participation" in the design of most systems whose specifications aren't perfectly obvious in advance is reasonably clear: User participation reduces the probability that the final system will be based on misunderstandings. A more psychological need for user participation stems from the fact that it helps in fostering commitment to the use of the final system.

The strategy of obtaining user participation, which is a relatively simple affair for small, easily defined systems, becomes much more difficult in proportion to the size of the system and the degree to which it is basically a research project. For at least five systems of this type, a task force approach was used. A development team was formed to decide on specifications and to monitor the progress of the implementation. (Case 4, the computer-assisted underwriting case, describes such an implementation effort.) This approach, though reasonably successful in most instances, did have a serious flaw, in that it was sometimes impossible to get enough users directly involved in the process. A result in the Great Eastern Bank case was that, of the 50 potential users, only 10 were enthusiastic initially, and all 10 were members of the development team.

Another basic problem suggested by the experience in the sample is that substantive participation in model formulation and interpretation seems to be rather unlikely when the system involves a high level of mathematical sophistication. That is, in the development of such systems, it was almost always necessary that an expert choose the modeling technology, define the model, and clarify its meaning, while user participation was limited to providing data and/or parameter values. This approach was satisfactory for an optimization-based planning system, but it encountered difficulties in two simulation-oriented systems, in which some of the users were basically dragged through an experience they found taxing and unpleasant.

One interesting and very direct way of using the participation strategy was employed in conjunction with a system for analyzing sales and marketing data. Here each new module or application that is developed goes through a three-stage development process. The first stage is general uncommitted discussions of any current problem areas with which user groups are concerned. Following research by the management science staff, the second stage is a brief formal problem statement written in conjunction with the user group. In addition to a description of the problem, it contains a statement of the methodology that will be applied and the level of resources that will be required. The third stage is the formal request for authorization of out-of-pocket expenses. In effect, that request formalizes the user participation strategy, even for relatively small projects, and has been used quite effectively.

## 2. Obtain User Commitment

The strategy of attempting to obtain personal user commitment was utilized for some of the systems that were not initiated by the users and other people involved. Manifestations of a lack of personal commitment existed in many forms but often derived from a variation on one of three repetitive scenarios.

a)   Management hears about the latest technique or model. Management assigns someone to implement such a system without any clear idea of what the benefits will be or who will use it.

Under these circumstances, no one is really committed to the project's successful end use. Once the technical tools are developed, the project goes into limbo because no one is really eager to use it. This scenario occurred in a data retrieval system for use by executives, a five-year corporate policy model in a financial organization, a customer population growth model, and an account profitability analysis system in another financial organization.

b)   Management is persuaded to decree mandatory use for a tool or technique for which users feel no particular enthusiasm or commitment.

This kind of problem occurs frequently in budgeting and planning systems. When participation is mandated, unenthusiastic participants respond with half-hearted involvement. They submit the numbers—in effect, feeding the system but not using it in any meaningful way. This issue arose to some extent in almost every planning/budgeting system encountered.

c)   In order to expand a system in partial or ongoing use, it is necessary to obtain cooperation and participation from people in other areas of the company.

This kind of problem is typical in planning systems in which numbers submitted by one group have a direct impact on numbers generated by another group, e.g., the effect of marketing forecasts on production forecasts.

In a number of systems, the danger of these scenarios of noncommitment was anticipated, and explicit attempts were made to obtain personal commitment from users. An example is a real-time production monitoring system that was installed in a production plant on a turnkey basis to reduce material loss. In order to obtain commitment from users, posted notices invited plant personnel to receive on-the-job training concerning the workings of the system. Full responsibility for running the system was then given to the people who did well in the training course. In the designing of an on-line inventory control system that serviced a number of users in the receiving, stores, and production areas, a very definite attempt was made to provide one or more retrieval reports that would be especially useful to the people in each area. A similar strategy was employed by the designers of a yearly budgeting system motivated by the needs of top management and received rather unenthusiastically by marketing and production people, who thought it wouldn't really help them. At every stage, the designers made a point of providing them with a quid pro quo in the form of sales and material usage reports that made the system useful to them. Finally, a similar strategy was used at a stage in the development of the insurance renewal pricing system when there were some transient problems stemming from lack of system understanding by underwriter supervisors. In addition to the provision of training aimed specifically at the supervisor's needs, a team of supervisors was formed to define a weekly supervisor's report to be generated by the system. In this way, they were encouraged to "buy a piece of the action."

### 3. *Obtain Management Support*

In the sample, the strategy of "obtaining management support"[7] was applied for two basic reasons: to obtain funding and to obtain management action that would force people to comply with a system or use it. Appealing for management support was not uniformly successful. For seven systems, the basic concept was sold to management first rather than to the users. It turned out that management enthusiasm was not shared by the middle- and lower-level people who were actually to use the systems. As each situation developed, serious questions arose as to whether the application would ultimately become effective. In four cases, the situations had not been resolved. Although enough resources had been provided to keep the applications alive, little definitive action had been taken to institutionalize the systems since the overall management attitude in each case ranged from indifference to tolerance. In the other three cases, more effective management action was taken as a result of the strategy of obtaining management support. When the portfolio management system was not being used as actively as was desired in the Great Eastern Bank case, management instituted mandatory account review procedures involving reports generated on the system. The purpose was to augment training programs by getting the more reluctant portfolio managers involved with the system. The belief was that they would gradually come to use it effectively if they had more exposure to it. In a budgeting system that could be used in a limited way on a solely divisional basis, a management decree was obtained that required all divisions to use the system, thus permitting companywide consolidations and the performing of other budget analysis

---

[7]Management support has been cited often as a key requirement for successful utilization of corporate computing facilities. This notion was first popularized by Garrity (1963).

via the system. In implementing an insurance renewal pricing system, the implementation team had been very sensitive about not forcing people to use the system. When it became apparent that one whole underwriting department was not using the system because department managers were unconvinced of its merit, management produced a decree. Subsequently everyone used the system, which turned out to be a great success.

### 4. Sell the System

The strategy of attempting to "sell the system" was used mainly when potential users had not been involved in the implementation. This strategy was mentioned explicitly by people involved in a number of systems. Typical comments: (1) "After the initial system was set up, we made a presentation in an attempt to sell it to management." (2) "This system really needs a strong marketing effort by the management science guys." Among the most interesting selling efforts encountered were the following three.

A real-time system for monitoring the largely automatic production of an inexpensive consumer item was installed in order to minimize material loss due to creeping maladjustments in machine settings. During the initial installation, the implementation team's effort to monitor the system led to the discovery of expected but previously unsubstantiated cheating by piecework employees. Somehow, more pieces were leaving many machines than were entering them. In scrupulous avoidance of embarrassing anyone publicly, the reply to this type of activity was a private comment that the monitoring machine had to be checked because it was registering an impossible result. Soon the employees were "sold" on the new system: They knew very well that it worked.

A somewhat more direct selling procedure was used to convince people of the merits of a sales forecasting system. The pitch was very simple: Compare manual monthly forecasts for the year with the system's forecasts. At the end of the year, both sets of forecasts were rather far off in many months, but the system's forecasts were closer to actual in ten months and had 33 percent less total error than the manual forecasts.

A similar strategy was used during the initial installation of a system that minimized scrap loss in the manufacturing of cardboard boxes. As part of the input routine for specifying the orders to be cut, the implementer insisted that the person in charge also submit his manual solution to the cutting problem. Since the system outperformed the person consistently, the system was sold quite easily. (Incidentally, the person in charge was quite happy to tend to other chores while the computer dealt with the mathematical puzzle.)

### D. Meet User Needs and Institutionalize the System

A number of strategies address issues related to meeting user needs and/or institutionalizing the system. They include providing training programs, providing ongoing assistance in using the system, insisting on mandatory use, allowing voluntary use, relying on exposure and diffusion, and building systems to suit the particular capabilities of users.

There is a certain amount of overlap between some of these strategies and contradictions between others. Unlike strategies for developing a support base, where difficulties tend to arise from focusing on one strategy and ignoring others, the issue here is more one of direct choice among strategies that go in opposite directions.

### 1. *Provide Training Programs*

Training programs of one sort or another are usually provided for systems other than those designed in very close cooperation with all potential users. Many of the training programs encountered in the sample were not totally successful. Implementers of systems tended to have trouble estimating the type and intensity of training that were needed for many systems. For instance, implementers of five systems mentioned that their initial training programs proved insufficient and required substantial reformulation.

> "The first training program just bombed out. We gave them our dog and pony show, and they walked out frowning. They just didn't see what we were getting at . . . I'll have to admit that we weren't very well prepared. For the time being, we're going after them individually and solving problems for them."

Many different problems were encountered in attempting to apply the training strategy. For three systems, the problem was at a very basic level: Management would not commit human resources to provide a formal training program.

> "One reason why the foremen haven't utilized the system fully is that they have had about the most half-hearted training program imaginable. Joe and I programmed the system and are now assigned to other projects. When we get a chance, we go down to the shop floor to try to catch a foreman's attention and show him how the system can help him. But that's awfully haphazard, and I know we miss a lot of opportunities to have some real impact."

For the system above and three others, it was assumed that providing a familiarity with the system's concepts would be sufficient to obtain proper use. This expectation proved overoptimistic. The potential users of an automated inventory of programs and data for use by application programming groups simply balked, saying there was no reason to change their existing procedures in order to be able to use the system. The new training strategy in this effort was to sit down with each application group, go through an improved sales pitch, and demonstrate that the system would help in their new, rather than existing, applications. The general finding in two systems for analysis related to operational decision making was that the majority of potential users either could not or would not figure out how to use the system to help with their work. In each case, the revised training approach was oriented toward user problems rather than toward system functions.

The contrast between the training strategies employed for two general planning and analysis systems is instructive. In the first case, the system never seemed to catch on, despite training demonstrations provided for divisional staff and other potential users. These individuals seemed enthusiastic about the possibility of using the system, but they never really used it unless corporate planning people basically did all the work for them. In contrast, the training program for the other system fostered immediate and active involvement. In order to attend the training workshops, people were required to bring their own financial analysis problems. They learned to use the system by working on those problems. When the workshops ended, many users were enthusiastic. Not only did they know how to use the system, but they had also proved to themselves that it could help them.

The normative conclusion here is that well-thought-out training programs seem to be required for systems whose hands-on users are personally uninvolved in implementation. Furthermore, for systems that people use voluntarily or on an individual basis, the training should be directed not toward explaining system capabilities but, rather, toward demonstrating how the system can be used to solve problems encountered in the users' jobs. If the implementers believe the system is relevant to user problems but think that users are the ones best qualified to figure out how it should be used, they are likely to be headed for a disappointment. (The exceptions are statistical packages and other tools intended for use by sophisticated analysts.)

### 2. *Provide Ongoing Assistance*

As mentioned earlier, many systems in the sample were used through staff intermediaries who were responsible for maintaining the system. The strategy of providing ongoing assistance in such systems needs no further discussion. It is more interesting as applied to those systems in which the people responsible for maintaining the system are not the people who run the system. Two examples of the effective use of ongoing assistance involved systems for contract-oriented budget consolidations (G1 in Chapter 2) and group insurance rate calculations (G2). The former contained complicated curve-spreading methods that calculated smoothly varying monthly values of activity for each contract over its life cycle. Since this system was used only once a year, the sales planners who performed the contract analysis would not have much practice with the mechanical aspects of the system. In recognition of that fact and to expedite the process, a system maintenance person ensured that forms were filled out correctly, that card decks were submitted properly, and that sales planners' questions were answered.

The rate calculation system was used quite similarly. The underwriter analyzed the claim experience for each policy and filled out a coding sheet. The system maintenance person checked the coding sheet for completeness before it was submitted. Computer outputs were checked for gross errors (e.g., those resulting when a number is punched in the wrong place) before being returned to underwriters for review. In this way, the underwriters had to contend only with underwriting, and the maintenance person ensured that system details were taken care of.

### 3. *Insist on Mandatory Use*

The strategy of insisting on mandatory use is employed in two types of situations: those in which people use systems to help in their individual functions and those in which people use systems as a medium of integration and coordination in organizationwide tasks, such as budgeting and planning. For the latter, some level of mandatory involvement is often required in order that the total plan can be consolidated. For a number of planning systems, there certainly was a difference between genuine use and half-hearted submission of numbers for the plan. At least five systems were encountered in which a "why bother?" attitude on the part of people in system feeder roles expanded into a perception of direct threat through loss of autonomy and revelation of ignorance.[8]

Mandatory use of systems that people use as individuals seemed to be even more tenuous unless the task was relatively programmed, e.g., a program that calculated time-charter rates for ships. The problem is illustrated by the market model in the Connoisseur Foods case. Among other considerations, insisting that a brand manager use this particular model in his thinking simply didn't work very well, because the brand manager was uncomfortable with the whole idea of using models.

An interesting issue related to mandatory use arose in two shop floor information systems and a portfolio management system in the Great Eastern Bank case. In each of these systems, usage was very uneven. Some foremen or portfolio managers used them extensively, while others used them rarely, if at all. If an attempt had been made to require mandatory use of the systems in day-to-day work (excluding mandatory portfolio review procedures), it surely would have failed, because the foremen and portfolio managers had other sources of similar information. In order to force people to use these systems, it might have been necessary to eliminate the batch reports they received or to insist on some outward demonstration of system usage through system logs or through the generation of paperwork. In each case, it was thought that forcing the situation would gain little and might cause some very serious problems whenever the system went down.

### 4.  Permit Voluntary Use

Permitting voluntary use is a strategy applicable to systems that people use as individuals. The idea is to avoid building resistance to a hard sell but to encourage use of the system only when it appears really likely to help. As a strategy for encouraging use, this proved rather ineffective, since it was attempted with only partial success in six systems. The problem was that without a strong push, people tended not to be especially eager to change the way they did their jobs.

> "On numerous occasions we have gone to potential users in our various divisions and subsidiaries and have demonstrated our planning analysis system. Typically, they are very impressed and go away saying that the system certainly seems to be useful. But they never come back to use the system. Instead, they always come back to us in our corporate staff function and ask us to use the system to perform an analysis for them."

People seemed to respond favorably to the voluntary approach under two circumstances: The system met a genuine felt need (e.g., did clerical work for them), and/or the system appealed intellectually or otherwise (e.g., contributed to their image of being "with it"). The felt-need enticement seemed by far the more powerful.

These two circumstances coincided in an on-line shop floor information system that tracked the flow of production lots of integrated circuits through a 50-stage process. The system was used by two types of foremen: the "old-line" foremen, typically high school graduates who had worked in the plant more than five years, and the "new-line" foremen, typically college graduates who were being rotated through the shop on their way to other positions. In addition to lacking the inclination to use the system, the old-line foremen claimed not to need to use it since

---

[8]Many related issues are discussed in Argyris (1970, 1971).

their experience helped them track down problems and their causes. The new-line foreman found the system interesting, labor-saving, and quite valuable in tracking down problems.[9] Several said that it was basically the way they learned about the flow of material through the shop and that they would have trouble operating effectively without it. An old-line foreman (aged 28) whose area was at the end of the process said that he rarely used the system because he was at the end of the line. The new-line foreman immediately preceding him said that it was a shame he didn't use the system since, as the person who generated the promise dates for the delivery of production lots, he was the person who needed the information most. In summary, there was both felt need and curiosity on the part of the system's voluntary users and neither on the part of its nonusers, most of whom seemed to be doing a reasonable job nonetheless. Since overall percentage yields were at a rather low level, management was starting to think about the new ways of using the system but wasn't sure that changes would be effective.

### 5.  Rely on Diffusion and Exposure

The strategy of relying on diffusion and exposure is rather similar to the voluntary usage strategy, except that less effort is devoted to training. The idea is that the people who are enthusiastic initially will demonstrate the benefits of a system to their colleagues, who will then make an effort to learn how to use it for the advantages they perceive in it. In the sample, this strategy was cited explicitly in situations under which two conditions applied: The system wasn't being used fully, and direct training or mandated use was impractical because of some combination of lack of management commitment and lack of an effective training method. As a strategy for implementing systems, relying on diffusion and exposure seemed to be rather ineffective. In some cases, it may have been as much an excuse for inaction as it was a real strategy.

### 6.  Tailor Systems to People's Capabilities

An issue that comes up repeatedly in general discussions of computer applications is that there are great differences among people with regard to their ability and/or propensity to use analytic techniques. Issues related to this topic are explained insightfully by McKenney and Keen (1974), who stress that people with different cognitive styles tend to be especially adept at different kinds of tasks. Although many systems in the sample were designed or modified to suit the requirements of individuals, building systems to suit the particular capabilities of individuals was never mentioned as a conscious strategy. The closest anyone came in this direction was a corporate management science director who said that his general rule of thumb was to attempt to build systems only for those people who seemed likely to be able to use them effectively, and to avoid computerized approaches altogether for others. The policy of many companies is to proceed from the opposite direction by hiring people with analytical skills, rotating them through training programs or management science groups, and then spreading them throughout the organization in line or staff positions. One goal of this policy is to foster greater acceptance of analytic approaches through the placement of people who can and will adopt these methods.

---

[9]The same types of reactions have been cited by many others, e.g., Dickson and Simmons (1970).

## IV. CONCLUSIONS

The standard wisdom in designing and installing computer projects includes the suggestion that a cost/benefit study should be performed at the outset to ensure that the proposed project is a worthwhile application of the organization's time and resources. Typically, the cost/benefit study proceeds from the premise that implementation will be accomplished smoothly and that the system will operate as initially planned. However, since smooth implementation is probably as much the exception as it is the rule, and since projects often evolve into systems quite different from those initially envisaged, these studies sometimes degenerate into futile exercises with little real impact.

This chapter has introduced the notion of implementation risk analysis and suggested that such an analysis should be performed in addition to (or despite the lack of) a cost/benefit analysis. Just as it is possible to employ the formal procedure of estimating the costs and benefits resulting from proposed projects, it is also possible to develop a formal procedure for anticipating and avoiding some of the problems that may arise in implementation. This is viewed as a two-stage process. The first stage is the identification of those implementation risk factors that tend to increase the likelihood of implementation difficulties in the situation at hand. Such risk factors are found by comparing the existing situation with what would be the ideal implementation situation. The second stage in the process is the identification of and choice among potential strategies, either for reducing risk factors themselves or for minimizing their manifestations. If the second stage yields no really good strategies for overcoming key risk factors, then postponement or cancellation of the project should be considered. Although there is certainly much generality in the risk factors and strategies cited earlier, it is quite likely that other observers studying other systems would find some risk factors and strategies that were omitted here or would choose different conceptualizations for those that were found. This is all well and good since the main point is only that implementation risk analysis may constitute a feasible and worthwhile procedure, which can be used in avoiding implementation difficulties. The particular risk factors and strategies mentioned here should be viewed only as a starting point, which can be expanded or modified on the basis of the implementation experience and special circumstances of any company in which this sort of analysis would be used.

In an application of implementation risk analysis, the underlying notion of an "ideal implementation situation" will lead directly to an intriguing dilemma for management. Many of the truly innovative systems in the sample were precisely those that would have been judged quite risky by a risk analysis prior to implementation. And they were risky, as evidenced by a higher rate of implementation difficulties and a lower rate of success than for the systems adhering more closely to the ideal situation. The quandary here is analogous to the risk vs. return decision with regard to stock portfolios. It is possible to weed out those systems with high risk, but the result will be that most of the systems actually authorized will be those that start close to the ideal situation, i.e., small, user-initiated, efficiency-oriented projects that automate an existing, well-understood function and involve little or no research and little or no change in the way things are accomplished. The projects avoided will be those that are initiated by management or internal entrepreneurs in an attempt to produce fundamental improvements in decision making, organizational control, planning methods, etc. Just as the ideal life style for minimizing cardiac risk is a virtually unattainable abstraction, the ideal implementation situation is only a model that is useful in anticipating implementation difficulties and in trying to develop strategies that increase the likelihood of success. In fact, this model may well lead to a sort of conscious mixed strategy whereby development groups are expected to maintain a portfolio of projects, some of which are routine and low in risk while others are more innovative and higher in risk. Thus the fact that an ideal implementation situation can be characterized does not necessarily mean that all system development efforts undertaken must fit that characterization exactly.

Implementation risk analysis obviously cannot guarantee implementation success. In many cases, most of the ideas it highlights might have been considered anyway. Its primary value is that it serves as an organized, disciplined approach for anticipating stumbling blocks that may arise. Although there is no way to prove that the more tortuous implementations in the sample would have been facilitated by this type of analysis, it is likely that implementers using this kind of analysis would have been far more attentive to risk factors that came back to haunt them.

## CHAPTER **EIGHT**

This book has attempted to capture the state of current practice in decision support systems. It has attempted to maintain balance by citing both the positive and the negative. It has described things that work well—various types of systems, system usage patterns, and system benefits. It has also described some of the implementation and usage problems that are frequently encountered in current practice. The book has focused on the present. To a large extent, it has underplayed the technical aspects of systems themselves while stressing the behavioral aspects of their implementation and usage.

The purpose of this final chapter is quite different from that of the rest of the book. In describing trends for the future, it introduces a time dimension and set of concerns that are lacking in the other chapters. Its main message is that future possibilities will be defined by two sets of developments:

Gradual advances in the expectation levels, technical awareness, and quantitative skills of decision makers in organizations

Dramatic improvements in the basic technology of decision support systems

The discussion of future trends begins with a brief overview of where things stand currently in terms of the way DSSs are used. An analogy between building a DSS and building a home points to the identification of three areas in which current trends are leading to further DSS usage. Next, a brief historical note on the past evolution of DSS technology provides perspective concerning the technical aspects of the trends that are now in motion. Although frontiers of the possible are being pushed back rapidly, the chapter ends by citing the diffusion of existing knowledge as perhaps the key issue for decision support systems in the next decade.

### I. DSS: WHERE WE ARE

Figure 30 presents Keen's (1976) sketch of how many decision support systems work. This picture is useful in highlighting a number of key aspects of current DSSs.

1.  The manager/decision maker usually communicates with a person (the intermediary) rather than with a computer or computer terminal.

2.  The intermediary's job is to help translate the manager's concerns into a set of specific questions posed in a framework that makes these questions amenable to quantitative analysis.

3.    The intermediary may or may not communicate directly with a computer and often works with a computer specialist—whether a staff assistant or a programmer—who actually deals with the computer.

4.    The computer specialist may face a variety of situations. If a DSS that is complete and in place can be used to perform the analysis, the job is usually done with dispatch. However, to the degree to which new data must be gathered and new programs or models developed, the computer specialist may not be able to service the intermediary's request in time to help the decision maker. Conversely, to the degree to which the components—data, prewritten program modules, etc.—are readily available and useable, the chances of a timely and cost-effective response will improve.

FIGURE 30    *Operational Scheme of Many Decision Support Systems*

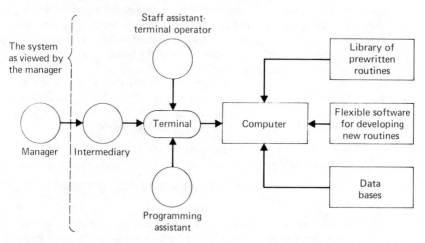

Source:    Peter G. W. Keen, " 'Interactive' Computer Systems for Managers: A Modest Proposal." *Sloan Management Review*, Fall 1976, p. 9. Figure reprinted by permission.

It does not take a communication expert to recognize the difficulties inherent in the way most current DSSs are built and used. The steps above are not unlike the situation of a pair of lifelong apartment dwellers who decide to have a house built for them:

They talk to an architect.

The architect tries to figure out what they really want.

The architect expresses to a builder his or her idea of what should be built.

The builder tries to meet the architect's specifications, finding it easiest and cheapest to do so wherever standard, prefabricated modules can be used.

By the time the house is ready, it may be no longer be the house the apartment dwellers want because they have seen many other houses in the interim. In fact, it may not even be what they initially wanted, because they simply didn't have the vocabulary and trained perspective necessary to describe exactly what they wanted (even under the unlikely circumstance that they really knew what it was).

Although the analogy between the creation and use of a DSS and the construction of a home is by no means perfect, it does highlight several key generalizations that apply across a wide range of situations.

1.   The similarity between the end product and what the user or initiator really wanted or needed is proportional to the user's knowledge and expertise concerning the desired product. (An architect or builder will have better luck than a baker or candlestick maker in visualizing and describing a house that is to be built.)

2.   The similarity between the end product and the user's initial intention is inversely proportional to the number of translation/communication steps in the flow of information from the user to the person who actually puts the pieces together. (If the baker or candlestick maker is also a practicing architect and builder on the side and actually builds the house, the final product will probably be closer to the initial intentions.)

3.   The amount of time and effort that is required to produce the end product is proportional to the fraction of the product that must be created from scratch for this particular project; conversely, the project is expedited to the degree to which it can be put together using standardized, prefabricated parts. (It is easier to buy an existing home than to build a new one.)

Where are we with regard to decision support systems, and where are things moving? Stated simply, favorable trends are in motion under each of these three headings. In combination, these trends produce movement toward increased DSS usage that is fueled by the synergy between increased understanding on the part of users and improved tools and techniques for system builders. In many ways, the technical advances have been the driving force that has made possible the increased demand for systematic support of decision making. Nonetheless, as is obvious from earlier discussions of implementation issues, technical advances alone do not automatically create systems that help people solve important problems in organizations. Since this book has stressed the human side of this relationship, the next section will provide a brief picture of where the technical side has been and where it is going. The subsequent section will then bring these threads together.

## II. TECHNICAL ADVANCES

The first commercial use of digital computers occurred in the 1950s. Today computers play such an essential role in the day-to-day operations of business and government that many large organizations would simply creak to a halt if their computers went on strike. A tool that was barely at the periphery a quarter of a century ago is now at the core of large-scale business activities. How can one account for the vast inroads that computers have made in this short length of time?

## A. Advances in Hardware

The basic driving force in the growth of computer applications has been a literally astounding series of technical advances. The insert contains quotations that illustrate the magnitude of the advances that have taken place in computer hardware. The cost-effectiveness improvements that have occurred and are continuing are unprecedented in the history of technological change.[1]

Regardless of the specifics cited, the basic thrust of most discussions of technological improvements in computing is that the computing engines themselves are both more powerful and cheaper. However, as anyone who has ever sat 20 minutes in a traffic jam knows, having a more powerful engine doesn't ensure that more can be accomplished. Even the most powerful computer imaginable is useless if not programmed effectively.

## B. Advances in Programming

Fortunately, advances in hardware have been accompanied by advances in programming technology. The first computer programmers wrote programs in internal machine languages that correspond to the set of elementary instructions deep within the bowels of the computer. Those languages forced programmers to decompose every thought into a series of minute arithmetic and logical operations. Resorting again to the analogy to building a house, the programmer was in a position similar to that of an architect. In addition to deciding exactly what was to be accomplished, the programmer was forced to go through a substantial translation process in order to express the desired processing in a form the computer could deal with. This translation process required the programmer to make many computer-related choices (e.g., data format, program structure, naming conventions, etc.) that were basically irrelevant to the business problem at hand. As a result, anyone who later attempted to change a program needed to understand not only what the program was supposed to accomplish but also the design choices that were made in writing it. And design choices often came back to haunt future programmers in the same way that design choices come back to haunt people fixing the plumbing or making modifications to a building. Just as the short-sighted choice of running pipes through a concrete foundation rather than through accessible spaces can lead to untold hardships when changes are needed, an unfortunate choice of program structure or data format can turn a minor embellishment into a major rewrite of a program or system.

A great deal of progress has been made in expediting this translation process. The advent of general-purpose compilers, such as Fortran and Cobol, allowed programmers to express themselves much more directly and succinctly. In effect, compilers performed part of the translation from the mental image to the machine code for what had to be accomplished. The result was that programmers spent a smaller proportion of their time dealing with program design choices and a greater proportion describing the substantive processing that was required.

---

[1]Since most data processing texts provide a summary description of the various "generations" of computers that have been used, this will not be done here. The electronic technology that is now in use is discussed in the special issue of *Scientific American* (Sept. 1977) devoted to microelectronics. Predictions of future hardware capabilities are contained in Turn (1974), Withington (1976).

---

**Insert: Advances in Hardware**

Perhaps the key element in the growth of data processing by computer is the fact that with the advent of microelectronics the cost of computer hardware has steadily decreased as capacity and performance have steadily increased. Since 1960 the cost of a computer divided by its operating power (measured in millions of operations per second) has dropped by more than 100. In the same period the cycle time (the time it takes to do an operation) of the largest machines has decreased by a factor of 10.

L. Terman

In past 20 years the speed at which calculations can be performed has increased by six orders of magnitude, or roughly a million times. What is more, the cost of computation has fallen dramatically. Minicomputers available today for about $1000 can nearly equal the capabilities of very large machines that cost as much as $20 million 15 years ago. By 1985 a medium-scale minicomputer may cost less than $100.

W. Holton

The technology of digital storage is perhaps the most rapidly changing sector in microelectronics. Over the past decade operating speed and reliability have increased by at least an order of magnitude as physical size, power consumption and cost per bit of storage have been reduced by factors ranging from 100 to 1000.

D. Hodges

Progress since then [1960] has been astonishing, even to those of us who have been intimately engaged in the evolving technology. An individual integrated circuit on a chip perhaps a quarter of an inch square can now embrace more electronic elements than the most complex piece of electronic equipment that could be built in 1950. Today's microcomputer, at a cost of perhaps $300, has more computing capacity than the first large electronic computer, ENIAC. It is 20 times faster, has a larger memory, consumes the power of a light bulb rather than that of a locomotive, occupies 1/30,000 the volume and costs 1/10,000 as much. It is available by mail order or at your local hobby shop.

R. Noyce

The statements on technological progress quoted above are from *Scientific American*, September 1977, special issue on microelectronics. The articles are as follows: Lewis M. Terman, "The Role of Microelectronics in Data," p. 163; William C. Holton, "The Large-Scale Integration of Microelectronic Circuits," p. 82; David A. Hodges, "Microelectronic Memories," p. 130; Robert N. Noyce, "Microelectronics," p. 65.

---

Many significant developments have followed and continue in this same basic spirit. Database systems have provided an increasingly attractive methodology for storing and retrieving data. The basic concept underlying these systems is to store not only the data itself but also a standard definition of the data in terms of its format, location, linkage to other data, access restrictions, and so on. By automatically applying this definition of the data whenever a program or inquiry uses the data, a programmer or system user can express what must be accomplished without expending a substantial amount of time and effort providing information that is already available. Although few of the systems in the sample used commercial database systems, a repetition of the same survey two years later would have uncovered many more instances of the effective use of such systems.[2]

Specialized languages and standard programs for solving repetitive problems have also provided major improvements in this direction. Specialized problem-oriented programs, such as linear programming codes, statistical packages, etc., were used in the optimization and data analysis systems in the sample. Where applicable, these programs had a major impact because they made it unnecessary to re-invent the wheel each time a standard technique was applied. The language APL was used with great success in setting up new decision support systems quickly. The special advantage of APL is that expert APL programmers can express complicated ideas quite tersely. By greatly reducing the amount of code that must be written and debugged, APL reduces the time lag between the conception of a system and completion of coding.[3] This type of impact was considered a key issue for most of the seven systems in the sample that were written in APL. Conversely, the fact that most of the others were in Fortran or Cobol resulted in longer delays in coding and program modification.

## C. Hardware vs. Software Trade-offs and Future Directions

Although programming developments such as these have been extremely important in expediting the system building process, these advances have not kept pace with the rapid decrease in the cost of hardware, as indicated in Fig. 31. While computer costs per unit of work have plummeted, personnel costs per hour have increased. Thus, although improved programming techniques have allowed overall productivity to increase, the standard forecast is that human costs will continue to exceed computer costs in data processing in the foreseeable future.

Where are we and where are we going? In terms of decision support systems of the types described in this book (and other business data processing systems), the key stumbling block to greater use and acceptance is that it simply takes too long (varying from weeks to months to years) and requires too much effort (whether in weeks or years) to bring the concept of a system to the point where it can be tried out

---

[2]See Carlson (1977) for the proceedings of a conference on decision support systems, in which several interesting database applications are described. For more general information about the database approach and the details of its computer implementation see *Computing Surveys*, special issue on database systems, March 1976, or virtually any of the database texts that have been published recently. These include: Date (1976), Haseman and Whinston (1977), Kroenke (1977), Martin (1976), Sprowls (1976), Tsichritzis and Lochovsky (1977), Wiederhold (1977).

[3]APL was first described by Iverson (1962). A number of APL texts have been written, e.g., Gilman and Rose (1970). The significance and special characteristics of APL are also described by Canning (1976) and Keen (1976).

FIGURE 31    Hardware/Software Cost Trends

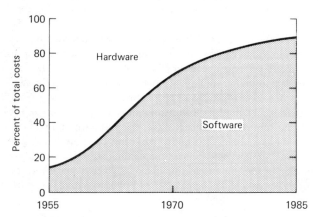

Source:   Barry Boehm, "Software and Its Impact: A Quantitative Assessment." *Datamation*, May 1973, pp. 48–59.
Reprinted with permission of *Datamation* magazine, © copy-
right by Technical Publishing Company, a division of Dun-
Donnelley Publishing Corporation, a Dun & Bradstreet company, 1978. All rights reserved.

realistically.[4] If it were possible to create and modify decision support systems in the
time span of hours or days, the use of these systems would expand greatly. Much of
the success of database systems and languages such as APL stems from the fact that
they begin to address this issue for a limited set of situations in which the data are
readily available and neither the data nor the models are too complex.

ɪr this is indeed the main issue, then the direction for future developments is
clear. These future developments will facilitate programming, debugging, and program modification in the following ways.

1. Increasing the degree to which the user and/or programmer can specify
   the required processing in the terms in which they think about the problem.

2. Decreasing the degree to which the user and/or programmer must make
   choices about computer-related details in which they are not especially
   interested.

3. Increasing the degree to which the program is self-explanatory in
   expressing the processing that is desired.

---

[4]The costs of the systems in the sample ranged from several thousand dollars to more
than a million, and from several weeks of working time to many years. Since programmer productivity was considered peripheral to the main thrust of research, detailed data
in this area were not gathered. For more extensive information concerning the time and
cost involved in writing programs, see Boehm (1973), Wolverton (1974), and Brooks
(1974, 1975).

These three types of facilitation are all directed toward telling the computer what should be done rather than exactly how it should go about performing the required processing.

Past improvements along these lines have been accomplished by developing large, complicated programs capable of creating machine code corresponding to inputs (whether higher-level language programs or retrieval requests) that are convenient for people to deal with. Future improvements will continue in the same mode. With programming viewed as a process of translating from the idea of what is to be done into instructions for a computer, future advances will place more of the burden of this process on the computer.[5] At each stage, this has been and will be possible mainly because of the economics of rapidly declining computer costs per unit of work versus increasing human costs. The ultimate implication of these advances will be a major facilitation of the communication chain between manager, intermediary, and computer specialist, as well as increased possibilities of collapsing parts of that chain completely.

### D.  Other Advances

Until the late 1960s, the trend in computer hardware was toward larger, more powerful computers that operated at lower cost per unit of work. The prevailing model, proposed by Herb Grosch and accordingly called Grosch's Law, stated that the power of a computer was proportional to the square of its cost.[6] The obvious economic implication was to build even larger computers. In the 1960s, the first computers were built that had enough processing power to permit them to be shared simultaneously through terminals by independent users. Under this time-sharing arrangement, each user operated under the illusion of having exclusive use of the machine (unless too many others were also using the machine, and then each user felt like the driver of a car in a traffic jam).

The development of time-sharing was quite important for decision support systems because it permitted the delivery of a substantial amount of computing power to many remote users, none or few of whom could afford to dedicate an expensive computer to occasional decision support activities. An additional development of great significance was the technical feasibility of using CRT displays in decision support systems. In 1965–1967, Michael Scott Morton expended monumental effort in providing the technical basis for one of the first successful experiments with CRT-based decision support in a corporate environment.[7] Today, however, the use of CRT displays has become almost second nature because of advances since then. The result is that information can be delivered to decision makers (and/or their staff intermediaries) in a more timely manner and a more usable format. It is virtually certain that the development of improved query languages (which are logical extensions of the trends in programming cited earlier) will further shorten the chain of time and people between a decision maker's information request and the response.

Two technological trends that were barely in evidence in the systems in the sample are likely to have major impacts on the DSSs of the future. One is the rapid

---

[5]See Cardenas (1977) for a recent discussion of automatic program generation.

[6]See, for instance, Solomon (1966), Knight (1966, 1968).

[7]See Scott Morton (1967, 1971), or Keen and Scott Morton (1978).

advance of communication and computer network technology. The other is the rapid advance of microelectronics, which will soon turn the hand-held calculator boom of the 1970s into a "personal computer" boom in the 1980s. By themselves, the new developments in communication and networking will greatly expedite corporate data processing by allowing that processing to be distributed across the corporation in a more logical way. For instance, it will become much more feasible to have local control of data and data entry while having at the same time centralized control of data standards and centralized access to almost any data in computer-readable form. Extending the minicomputer revolution that began to reverse Grosch's Law in some computing environments in the early 1970s, the trend toward personal computers will allow people to employ the computing power of what are currently large computers without suffering the annoyance of traffic jams and interference from other users.

Although it is not yet clear what impact the confluence of these two sets of developments will have for future decision support systems, it is likely that many dramatic changes will occur. It is quite possible that the "information utility" concept[8] that was conceived in the 1960s will start to become a reality in the 1980s. Builders of DSSs will be able to purchase or lease standard modules that can be transferred immediately over phone lines into the memories of their personal computers. Both internal corporate data and proprietary commercial data will be available in the same manner. Some of the standard off-the-shelf modules will be report generators; others will be easily tailored query languages, statistical packages, graphical display packages, etc. As noted earlier, the key stumbling block to greater use and acceptance of DSSs is that it simply takes too long and requires too much effort to bring the concept of a system or type of analysis to the point where it can be tried out realistically. The combined power of network technology plus personal computers may have a profound impact in alleviating much of this problem in situations where the data exist and the models are reasonably well understood and not too complex. The degree to which it will help when the data are not readily available or the models are not well understood is much more questionable.

## III.  THE HUMAN COMPONENT

Although technology provides tools that are essential for building DSSs, no amount of technology automatically creates these systems. People identify the need for them, people build them, and people use them. As the tools continue to improve, the limiting factor in the development of decision support systems will be the skills and abilities of system designers and users.

Two major trends on the human side of the ledger bode well for future systems. The first is simply that with each year computers are less the untamed beasts they used to be. The basic fact from which future developments will spring is simply that the ground has been broken. Learning to deal with computers has been an arduous process in many companies. Many initial attempts to develop and use computer systems were less than successful because no one really understood the nature of the beast. A significant part of the problem resulted from the inherent complexity and uncertainty of dealing with an entity whose technical components few people had

---

[8]See Sprague (1969).

mastered and whose human components few people could manage effectively.[9] In many ways, the beast has been tamed. Little more than a quarter of a century after the first commercial applications, computerized data processing has become an essential part of the business practices of medium and large organizations and many small ones as well. Although problems still arise in both the components and their interfaces, it is increasingly likely that the problems will be perceived quickly and remedied in an appropriate manner.

The second major trend is education. Most business and engineering students receive an exposure to computers and quantitative techniques. Many become quite skilled in these areas. As these people enter and rise through the ranks of business organizations, they are generally more receptive to the use of computers and analytic methods than most current managers, who often come from very different educational backgrounds. Perhaps more important, members of this new generation bring to their jobs not only a greater familiarity with the ideas but also an expectation that the use of the tools is part of their jobs.

The second trend was quite apparent throughout the interviews in the research on which this book is based. Many of the system designers and intermediaries are of that new generation. Although they had varying degrees of tolerance for the slow pace of change and the reluctance of some of their superiors to adopt systematic approaches to decision making, they were strikingly similar in their acceptance of and enthusiasm for the tools and concepts at their disposal.

## IV. CONCLUSION

What are reasonable expectations concerning decision support systems in the relatively near future? The trends cited above lead in the same direction: People who build the systems will be able to deliver them more quickly and more cheaply. People in positions to use decision support systems will be increasingly knowledgeable about what can be done and increasingly likely to use the systems effectively. In combination, these trends should lead to much wider application of computers in decision-supporting roles.

Admittedly, this forecast is safe and unstartling, especially if the reader expected claims that DSSs would do $X$ by 1980 and $Y$ by 1990 and $Z$ by 2001. Regardless of whether one research group or another is developing astounding new applications, and independent of technical advances that are on the drawing board now, the basic fact is that little of what is currently possible has yet been attempted in most organizations. For instance, despite extensive experience with EDP systems, many organizations have used no more than one or two of the seven types of DSS discussed in Chapter Two.

Rather than technical innovation, the key issue for decision support systems in the next decade may simply be the diffusion of the idea that computers can be used to support (rather than replace) decision makers. In many ways, this diffusion process may be nontrivial. One reason is that the cost justification of DSSs can be difficult. Quantifying the impact of replacing ten clerks with one computer is one thing, but quantifying the impact of improved individual effectiveness of line personnel is quite another. A second reason is that the implementation of DSSs requires a com-

---

[9]For an interesting view of the process by which companies learned to deal with computer systems, see Nolan (1973) or Gibson and Nolan (1974).

bination of technical and interpersonal skills; Chapters 5 through 7 illustrated some of the problems that can arise and the kinds of responses that are available.

In spite of these effects, it is clear from the many examples that have been cited that decision support systems have caught on to a certain degree. People in organizations have begun to accept the legitimacy of using computers to facilitate decision making and communication processes. After some false starts, they have also attained much more realistic expectations about what can and cannot be done, both technically and organizationally. Although the continued improvement of technology cannot ensure the instantaneous success of the diffusion process, it will surely provide some of the impetus and alleviate some of the resistance.

The main purpose of this book has been to contribute to this diffusion process by providing both overviews and detailed case studies of the kinds of things that have been done in the area. "Formulas for success" have been avoided throughout because the data on which this book is based contained one or more counterexamples to every surefire path to DSS Nirvana I know of. Approaches that are fine in one setting simply don't work in others. In light of this fact, the book has emphasized choices. There are many types of systems, various ways to develop and use systems, and many possible strategies for attaining successful implementation. The opportunities in the area are many; the same can be said for the challenges. I hope that this book will help in identifying the former and surmounting the latter.

# ADDITIONAL
# CASE STUDIES

# PART FOUR

Part Four contains five additional case studies, whose purpose is to extend and solidify the reader's understanding of decision support systems. In approaching each case, the reader should remember to ask the seven general questions proposed in the introduction to Part One as a way of outlining one's understanding of a decision support system. One measure of the success of this book is simply whether the reader now has a better understanding of what those questions mean.

The first case, Case 4, concerns a computer-assisted underwriting system that had a major impact on day-to-day work in an insurance company. Case 5 describes the development and use of an advertising analysis system sold commercially through time-sharing. The facilitation of budgeting and planning activities of a bank is described in Case 6. Case 7 describes the evolution of a decision support system used by a temporary regulatory agency in Washington, D.C. Finally, Case 8 describes a data retrieval and analysis system used by an airline. At the end of each case is a series of questions about key issues that are raised or illustrated strongly in that case.

# EQUITABLE LIFE:
# A COMPUTER-ASSISTED
# UNDERWRITING SYSTEM

## CASE FOUR

## I. INTRODUCTION

CAUSE, Computer-Assisted Underwriting System at Equitable, was developed to help insurance underwriters calculate renewal rates on group insurance policies. Simply stated, the problem faced by the underwriter is as follows: A group insurance policy (health, life, weekly indemnity or a combination of these) has been in force for a period of time. During that time, premiums have been paid by the policyholder at a specified premium rate, and claims have been received and paid by the insurance company. Approximately nine months into a policy year, the underwriter must perform a complicated but structured analysis to determine the premium rate that should be offered for the policy renewal for the ensuing year. Although a rather comprehensive theory underlies this determination, a number of special circumstances may call for adjustments in the renewal rate. Furthermore, even in regular cases, the rate determination often involves anywhere from 500 to 1000 calculations. CAUSE was developed to eliminate part of the clerical burden associated with renewal underwriting and to help ensure that rate decisions would be based on consistent and accurate calculations.

This case begins with a brief overview of group insurance underwriting and the general problems attacked by CAUSE. The initial conception of computer assistance for underwriters is discussed. Next is a description of its use and impact. The final two sections on the implementation of CAUSE cover technical and human issues.

---

This case is based on the following four sources of information.

1. A paper by Mr. James Johnson, system architect and project leader, entitled "The Implementation of Computer Assisted Underwriting." Subsequent to the writing of the case, this paper appeared in *Interfaces*, Vol. 6, No. 2, Feb. 1976, pp. 2–13.
2. Interviews with project team members and underwriters involved in implementation and use of the system.
3. System documentation.
4. A task force report, which recommended development of the system.

I would like to thank the Equitable Life Assurance Society for permission to publish this paper, and Mr. Johnson for his interest and support.

## II. THE PROBLEM ADDRESSED BY CAUSE

### A. Group Insurance from an Underwriting Perspective

Although it is impossible in a few pages to provide an adequate explanation of how group insurance really works, a bit of general background concerning underwriting is helpful.

### 1. *Obtaining New Business*

Figure 32 represents the underwriting view of the process of obtaining new group insurance business. The first step is the initial contact and negotiation between a field representative and a potential policyholder. Policyholders are usually corporations or municipal organizations that wish to provide coverage for their employees in one or more of the following types of insurance: life, health, weekly indemnity, accidental death and dismemberment. In some instances, new business prospects are considering leaving their current insurance carrier in favor of another carrier. In others, the prospects are considering modifications in coverages with their current insurance carrier.

FIGURE 32   *New Business in Group Insurance*

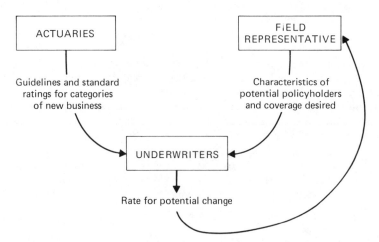

Upon being notified of the characteristics of the potential customer and of the types of coverage desired, an underwriter has the responsibility of setting a premium rate (monthly rate per employee). This rate is usually obtained directly from a rate manual developed on the basis of guidelines and standard ratings that have been generated by actuaries for various categories of new business. In determining these guidelines and standard rates, actuaries apply an extensive body of actuarial theory, which combines discounted cash flow analysis with the statistical analysis of the incidence of illness or death based on demographic characteristics (particularly the population's age distribution).

Within this framework of actuarial theory, the standard rates are set at a level that is likely to yield the following results.

It will cover the expected level of claims.

It will provide a reserve that will cover future claims incurred in the current year and other liabilities. The desired reserve is usually calculated as a function of earned premiums and at a rate dependent on the mix of coverages in the insurance plan in order to dampen the effect of random fluctuations in claims.

It will provide a desired year-end dividend for the policyholder.

It will meet administrative costs and commissions.

It will provide a small contribution to the insurance company's surplus.

An additional consideration not covered by actuarial theory is that the rate must be competitive. Since there is a very high level of competition among insurance companies, rates based on the five considerations above are occasionally adjusted (subject to state regulations) in order to entice new business or maintain existing business.

2. *Renewal of Existing Business*

Figure 33 represents the underwriting view of the renewal of existing coverages. Although rates for new business are usually established in accordance with a manual of premium rates, the rates for annual policy renewals are adjustments of the previous rate based on claim experience from the particular policyholder. The analysis produces a rate basis change factor, $F$, which is the ratio of the required premium to the current premium.[1] This rate basis change factor is applied to the case as a whole to determine the total premium needed. The adjustment must then be allocated to major lines (life, weekly indemnity, and health) and then to individual coverages. Although there exists a definite theory and structure for these calculations, the process tends to become rather complicated for a number of reasons, as suggested in the following paragraphs.

*Number of calculations involved.*    Typically, renewal underwriting for a single policyholder involves 500 to 1000 calculations.

*Multiple categories and procedures.*    Case characteristics, which determine the set of formulas relevant for any particular case, can be classified in 20

---

[1] A simplified formula for this factor is

$$F = SLR/ (1 - m - r),$$

where SLR is the significant loss ratio, $m$ is the required margin as a fraction of the required premium, and $r$ is the estimated retention.

The significant loss ratio is the ratio of incurred claims to the premium at the current rate basis. For small cases, where experience is less significant in a statistical sense, the experience for a policyholder is fully or partially pooled with that of similar policyholders.

In dollars, margin equals premiums minus benefits and minus retention for services, administrative expenses, and profits. If the actual margin is positive, a dividend is paid.

FIGURE 33   *Renewal of Existing Coverage*

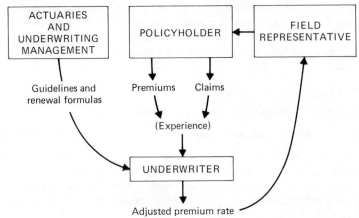

major categories, each of which can lead to 2 to 13 alternative calculation procedures. In addition to many that are not listed, these categories of characteristics include:

The way coverages are combined for dividend purposes

Financial arrangements for underwriting (including retrospective, prospective, premium stabilization reserve, pooled, and many other arrangements)

Financial arrangements for premium payment

Renewal tables applicable (depending on the size of the policy)

Type of reserve arrangements

Factors governing life rerating

Method of determining what experience is relevant

The complete classification of a case and the selection of the appropriate calculation procedure cannot be given by the underwriter (or determined by the computer) at the start of the renewal calculation. Many of the important logical choices can be made only after considerable preliminary calculation and summarization. Experienced underwriters weave their way through a web of calculations, logical decisions, more calculations, and so on. They can often tell at a glance that a number of decisions do not have to be made and can therefore bypass many intermediate steps. Inexperienced underwriters often have difficulty in deciding which decisions and calculations are actually required.

*Allocation.*   With a rate basis change factor obtained for the case as a whole, the allocation of the adjustment to the major lines and to individual coverages would ideally leave each coverage with the same margin. This solution is impractical, however. The fact that the data for some coverages may not be statistically significant would lead to wide rate fluctuations from year to year that would be difficult to justify to policyholders. There are no firm guidelines for allocation, although two practical alternative procedures are in common use.

*Incomplete information.*    In order to allow the policyholder time to decide whether to renew the policy, the rate basis change factor must be determined on the basis of approximately nine months of experience. Where seasonal or other factors apply, direct extrapolation may be insufficient.

*Special situations.*    There are many circumstances under which the policy experience is not truly representative of the case or under which the standard guidelines are not entirely applicable. An example of the former is the occurrence of one or more unusually large claims; of the latter, a change in the way the policy is being administered by the policyholder's insurance department or the existence of unusual inflationary trends peculiar to a locality or industry segment.

*Competitive considerations.*    Field representatives sometimes request modifications in rates in order to meet competitive pressure. The underwriter must then respond by striking a balance between prudence and lost business.

## B.  More Detail Concerning Underwriters and Their Jobs

The group insurance area employs approximately 120 underwriters whose experience and skill vary widely. Typically, the most experienced underwriters handle from one to five very large cases, which are monitored on a monthly basis, whereas less experienced underwriters each handle a larger number, often from 15 to 45, of the 4000 group cases in force. The disproportionate significance of major policies is indicated by the fact that in a recent year, nearly 80 percent of dividend-generating coverages had annual premiums of less than $25,000 and in aggregate produced less than 10 percent of all group premiums. Since 30 to 40 percent of all policies have year-end anniversary dates, the underwriting workload is particularly high in the fall. Prior to the development of CAUSE, many underwriters worked several evenings a week during that period.

Underwriting functions are spread among several divisions, each of which has a manager and several assistant managers and supervisors. (Figure 34 illustrates the location of these divisions within the group insurance area.) The primary role of the managers is to ensure that the underwriting function is carried on effectively and accurately. This role can be broken into two major components. One is the maintenance of an environment of ongoing training for the less experienced underwriters. The other is quality control over the output of underwriters by means of spot checks and other forms of follow-up. Quality control is important because gross errors simply do not disappear. Since field representatives must explain premium rates to customers, they sometimes provide prompt feedback about incorrectly determined rates, particularly if the rates are too high. Other errors become obvious at the time of the next rate renewal, when incurred claims do not correspond to the expectations expressed in the premium rate.

FIGURE 34    *The Organization of the Group Insurance Area*

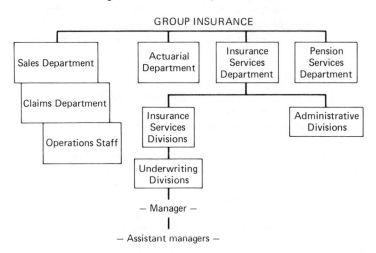

The underwriters themselves are salaried employees. They are evaluated primarily on their ability to do their job accurately and within time deadlines. Although it is impractical to monitor the accuracy of each renewal determination, a combination of spot checking and the level of complaints received from the field gives a supervisor a general impression of the quality of an underwriter's work.

Becoming an underwriter involves what is basically an apprenticeship. As indicated earlier, the job involves a detailed familiarity with a large number of benefit structures and with complicated and sometimes confusing analysis techniques. A former manager of one of the underwriting divisions stated that it probably takes five years to produce a trained underwriter. In the process of developing the operating logic of CAUSE, the implementation team came to understand one of the key reasons for the length of the period required to build expertise. Traditionally, underwriters had been trained to rely heavily on their experience and to think in terms of specific situations with which they were familiar. This was fine for experienced underwriters but very difficult for inexperienced underwriters, particularly since, as was eventually shown, more than 100 billion different situations could conceivably arise. Allowing this narrative to get a bit ahead of itself, we note that one of the key issues in developing CAUSE was the need to organize and codify this multitude of possibilites into an explicit and inclusive framework.

For inexperienced underwriters, the imposing conceptual task of mastering the necessary knowledge was compounded by the logistics of the job.

For any given case, information could be required from up to 18 sources.

It was often necessary to work on several cases simultaneously over long periods of time.

It was necessary to interface with a number of other departments in order to develop and implement a decision.

Largely because of the combination of these conceptual and logistical problems, turnover among first-year underwriters was high. One unfortunate result of the high turnover rate was that a relatively small percentage of the people in the divisions (often the experienced underwriters) seemed to end up doing a very large part of the useful work that was done. This fact plus time pressures and other work conditions, such as insufficient clerical support, late receipt of cases, incomplete reporting from field offices, etc., led to a morale problem among some underwriters.

To help assess the potential impact of computer-assisted underwriting, the feasibility study that ultimately led to the development of CAUSE focused on the work process of underwriters in determining renewal rates. The steps in the process were mapped out as indicated in Fig. 35.

FIGURE 35:   Steps in the Renewal Underwriting Process

1. Descriptive information is assembled from various source documents to provide a complete picture of the benefit structure.

2. Current and historical premium and claim statistics and population and exposure data are gathered, enabling the underwriter to project current year financial results and anticipate future claim expenses.

3. On the basis of the plan design, claim history, and current exposure, the underwriter performs the calculation required for trend analysis and projection of claim expenses.

4. Upon completion of this analysis, experience-adjusted premium rates are established in accordance with underwriting rules, which are designed to provide sound underwriting margins.

5. Depending on case complexity, review of the underwriting action may be required at supervisory, managerial, or executive levels.

6. Administrative action is initiated by issuance of a rate memorandum.

7. The underwriting action and supporting detail, together with appropriate advice for the policyholder, are communicated to the field representative.

8. Inquiries and appeals presented by the field representative and/or client are reviewed.

A time use study based on the breakdown of activities given in Fig. 35 concluded that the time an average underwriter spends in processing renewals can be broken down as follows:

|  | Time, % |  |
|---|---|---|
| Clerical |  |  |
|   Gathering descriptive information | 11 |  |
|   Numerical extraction | 14 |  |
|   Calculating significant loss ratio | 5 |  |
|   Other computations | 14 |  |
|   Issuing a rate memo | 6 | 50 |
| Analysis and decision-making activities |  | 18 |
| Other |  | 32 |
|  |  | 100 |

It is important to note that this breakdown relates to less than 50 percent of an average underwriter's total time, since underwriters have responsibilities other than determining renewal rates.

## III. THE INITIAL CONCEPTION OF COMPUTER ASSISTANCE FOR UNDERWRITERS

### A. Organizational Background

The origins of CAUSE date to around 1970. At that time, there was growing concern about the existing administrative EDP systems in the group insurance area. Though relatively sophisticated when developed around 1962, those systems were approaching the end of their useful life. As a result of this problem and the usual difficulty in maintaining effective communication between user groups and the systems department, development projects were not progressing at an adequate rate. This, of course, was not a unique situation. What was uncommon was that the problem was identified and addressed at an early stage.

After significant study, the action taken was the adoption of a task force approach for identifying key issues to be addressed in planning new systems. These task forces consisted of highly qualified people from both technical and user areas. After a number of initial successes for this approach, the Group Insurance EDP Task Force was formed in December 1970 to study the whole framework of EDP support for administrative operations.

### B. Opportunities and Problems

The initial goal of the Group Insurance EDP Task Force was to evaluate a proposed overhaul of computer systems related to all aspects of group insurance. An interim report discussed a number of general problems that stemmed from the fact that the existing systems were eight years old. Those systems had served their purposes well, but they were starting to become outdated from two viewpoints: technical efficiency and effective use. Stated simply, the technical component was that the computer equipment available in the 1970s would be much more powerful and efficient than the early 1960s equipment for which the systems were designed. In terms of effective end use, it was clear that many procedural and managerial aspects of the business had changed, and consequently, problems had begun to arise that existing systems were not designed to address. In addition, during the 1960s users and management had learned a great deal about the possibilities for effective computer use and had begun to see many opportunities for improvement. In comparison with what people increasingly understood that computer systems ideally might do, the accomplishments of existing systems were incomplete for some purposes and untimely for others. Management reports were also found to be lacking. Finally, a number of complex and sometimes redundant manual processes that were performed apart from the existing EDP systems might be expedited by revised systems.

The interim report concluded that an earlier proposal for system modifications was aimed primarily at technical-efficiency shortcomings of the existing systems and tended to neglect some of the effective end-use problems and opportunities cited above. After further study, the Task Force suggested a more general overhaul of administrative systems. Part of the overhaul would lead toward computer-assisted underwriting. The following opportunities and problems were identified.

1.  As the time study had indicated, less than 20 percent of underwriters' time spent on renewals was devoted to analysis and decision-making activity, whereas 50 percent of that time was devoted to clerical and arithmetic work.

2.  Virtually all calculations performed by underwriters were viewed as repetitive and probably susceptible to mechanization. The complex nature of group underwriting requires the employment of individuals with high technical competence. Current practice required that those highly trained individuals perform the calculations manually.

3.  Accounts generating minimal premium income might be renewed more or less automatically, subject to underwriter review. As mentioned earlier, nearly 80 percent of dividend-generating coverages had annual premiums of less than $25,000 and in aggregate produced less than 10 percent of all group premiums. Consequently, a disproportionate amount of underwriting effort went into the part of the business portfolio that produced relatively little income. The Task Force suggested that mechanizing the renewal of a large number of small cases would substantially reduce the renewal workload in the underwriting divisions.

4.  Established underwriting procedures were not interpreted and followed consistently. There were a number of reasons, such as the large number of inexperienced personnel, the volume of work that had to be handled, and the time pressure for renewals, particularly during peak periods.

5.  Input data for the underwriting process were derived from multiple manual and EDP sources. As many as 18 distinct source documents in varying formats had to be consulted for large cases, and up to 13 source documents were needed for small cases.

6.  Most of the needed information had been recorded in one or another EDP system at some point, but it was not available in the form most usable by underwriters. For example, because the level of aggregation was either too high or too low, underwriters had to perform a considerable amount of manual compilation and transcription from EDP reports and worksheets onto other worksheets.

## C. Proposal for a New Underwriting System

After citing the opportunities and problems above, the Task Force report proposed that computer-assisted renewal underwriting offered an opportunity to eliminate routine clerical work and reestablish the underwriter as an analyst and decision maker. Together with a new underwriting experience ledger and a text-editing facility for descriptive information, a computer-assisted renewal underwriting system could save about 50 percent of almost 100 production underwriters' time.

As pictured in Fig. 36, the proposed system encompassed the following.

1.    Collection of necessary premium, claim, and rate data.

2.    Calculation of experience-adjusted premium rates based on established projection formulas.

3.    Presentation of experience-adjusted premium rates and supporting data in a form convenient for review by the underwriter, explanation to the client, and administrative application of the adjusted rates in premium billing and collecting systems. In addition, there would be a convenient mechanism for overriding computer rate results wherever underwriters' judgment determined that these results were inappropriate.

FIGURE 36    The Underwriting System as Initially Conceived

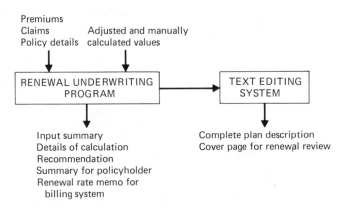

The proposed benefits of this system included the following.

1.    Significant production cost savings.

2.    Elimination of routine clerical work.

3.    Increased accuracy.

4.    Reduction in verification procedures.

5.    Prompt notification of rate action to the field representative, to the agent or broker, and to the customer.

6.    Complete statistical data supporting the underwriter's action.

7.    Production of experience-adjusted premium rates at intervals dictated by underwriting requirements, rather than by rigid, predetermined schedules.

The proposal also predicted that upon full implementation of the system, reductions in the activities of underwriters, expressed in percentages of time, would be as follows:

|  | *Renewals* | *Applications* | *Other* |
|---|---|---|---|
| Gathering descriptive information | 90 | 90 | 50 |
| Numerical extraction | 90 | 90 | 50 |
| Calculating significant loss ratio | 90 | 90 | 90 |
| Other computations | 90 | 90 | 50 |
| Review time | 0 | 0 | 0 |
| Rate memo preparation | 90 | 90 | 90 |
| Other | 0 | 0 | 0 |

## IV.  THE SYSTEM THAT WAS DEVELOPED

Instead of proceeding in chronological order through the design and implementation of CAUSE, this section discusses the system as it is currently used. Given the context of how CAUSE is used, the last two sections of the case will backtrack to discuss a variety of implementation issues.

### A.  The Philosophy of CAUSE

The CAUSE program is basically a simulation of much of the logical thought process that might be followed by a moderately experienced underwriter. On the basis of a painstaking enumeration of the logical and numerical steps in the process, CAUSE was designed to produce a pricing decision "according to the book." An underwriter analyzing the case manually would decide from the feel of the numbers whether the data and guidelines were representative and appropriate. Adjustments from the "book" solution would then be made only on discovery of significant departures from the assumptions underlying the calculations. The philosophy of CAUSE is to perform the standard calculations that lead to a standard pricing decision, but then to leave the underwriter responsible for discovering the departures and compensating for them on the basis of both judgment and experience. Thus CAUSE attempts to assist underwriters in standard aspects of their jobs, not to replace them.

### B.  The Technical Scope of CAUSE

CAUSE consists of 23 production programs composed of more than 200 FORTRAN subroutines, two assembly-language subroutines, and 24 COBOL modules. The main underwriting program consists of 154 subprograms and runs in 512K of core. The production system consists of 63 jobs. The system resides on a commercial time-sharing computer rather than on the in-house 370/168. Although some editing of previously entered data is performed on-line, most of the runs are done on an overnight basis.

## C. The Process of Using CAUSE

Figure 37 outlines the steps in reviewing a case via CAUSE. The first step, preparing input, is more time-consuming than the Task Force envisaged, because the general overhaul of administrative systems has not been completed. As a result, underwriters must still obtain the required information (coverages, claims incurred, premium rates, etc.) manually from a number of different source documents. Since filling out extensive input forms is described as a bit of a "hassle," some of the input is prepared by part-time clerical help, and the underwriter completes the more complicated input forms.

Before the input forms are keyed to tape, they are reviewed for omissions and other obvious errors by the CAUSE production team. This two-person team is responsible for maintaining a smooth interface between the underwriter and the computer. In addition to checking the initial input forms for errors, their activities include arranging for key-taping of data provided by underwriters, arranging for transfer of rate data from a computer file, activating all production runs, performing on-line editing to correct input data and to enter overrides, reviewing the computer output, and maintaining all underwriter guidelines tables and other parameters used by the system.

After the input is checked by the production team, it is keyed to tape and later transmitted to a commercial time-sharing system, where most of the computer runs take place overnight. Because of the time required for input checking, keying, transmission, and output checking, turnaround time is two days. With direct on-line data entry, turnaround time could be reduced. However, it was decided that the benefits of improved turnaround did not exceed the increased costs of on-line data entry.

As stated earlier, CAUSE underwrites a case by the book, following the same procedures that a careful and conservative underwriter would follow. CAUSE output includes a pricing recommendation and supporting material that substantiates the recommendation, both to the underwriter and to the policyholder and field representative. The underwriter reviews the output and considers questions such as those in Fig. 38.

The judgment aspect of underwriting consists primarily of evaluating these issues to determine whether or not the "book" solution is applicable. CAUSE does not perform this evaluation and was not intended to do so.

Strictly speaking, experienced underwriters do not go through each question in Fig. 38 explicitly. On the basis of experience, they have developed intuition that helps them identify exceptional circumstances without going through lists of questions. However, in order to design CAUSE in such a way that it would be able to handle these circumstances through overrides submitted by underwriters, it was necessary to list the questions very explicitly, along with all possible corrective actions that might apply.

Thus, as indicated in Fig. 37, CAUSE contains a set of overriding techniques enabling the underwriter to modify the system's underwriting action if any combination of exceptional circumstances arises. The overrides are noted in red on the original input forms. The production team enters the overrides using an on-line data entry terminal, and the calculations are rerun overnight. It was decided that a relatively small volume of on-line data entry for overrides was economically justifiable, in spite of the fact that on-line entry of the mass of the data would be too expensive.

FIGURE 37   Steps in Renewal Underwriting Using CAUSE

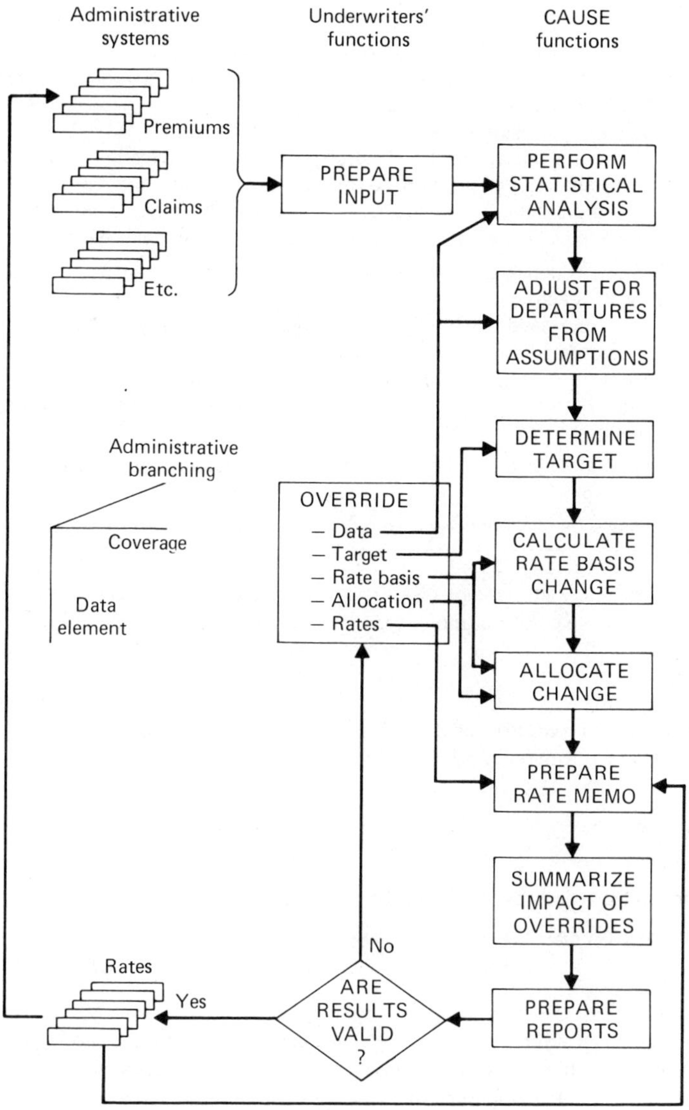

Administrative systems | Underwriters' functions | CAUSE functions

Premiums

Claims

Etc.

PREPARE INPUT

PERFORM STATISTICAL ANALYSIS

ADJUST FOR DEPARTURES FROM ASSUMPTIONS

Administrative branching

Coverage

Data element

DETERMINE TARGET

OVERRIDE
— Data
— Target
— Rate basis
— Allocation
— Rates

CALCULATE RATE BASIS CHANGE

ALLOCATE CHANGE

PREPARE RATE MEMO

SUMMARIZE IMPACT OF OVERRIDES

Rates

Yes

No

ARE RESULTS VALID ?

PREPARE REPORTS

FIGURE 38:    Issues Resolved by Underwriting Judgment in
Determining Whether to Modify the "Book" Solution Generated
by CAUSE

---

1. Is there any evidence to indicate that the premium, claim, and other data entered into CAUSE are not representative?
   a. Is there a gross error in the data supplied to CAUSE?
   b. Is there a change in the trend of premiums or claims sufficiently large to invalidate the procedure used to forecast loss ratios and margins?
   c. Has there been an unusual occurrence of claims, that is, claim activity unlikely to be repeated in the near future on that particular case?
2. Is there any evidence to indicate that the standard renewal guides are not appropriate for the case?
   a. Does the case exhibit significantly higher inflationary tendencies than are incorporated in the renewal guides?
   b. Does the case exhibit unusual variability (or lack of variability) in claim activity from year to year, such that the standard margin for statistical variability is inappropriate?
3. Are there competitive or other business reasons that warrant the use of modified renewal margins?
4. Is the allocation of the increase among coverages and branches satisfactory?

---

Approximately 40 percent of all cases require no reruns. The reruns that are required are due to a combination of reasons, which break down roughly as follows:

|  | *Percentage* |
|---|---|
| Erroneous preparation of input forms (including copying errors and misunderstanding of the source data or the input forms) | 45 |
| Updating experience to monitor cases from month to month | 18 |
| Keying errors | 2 |
| Personal preferences in interpreting guidelines | 30 |
| Competitive reasons or case-specific knowledge | 5 |
|  | 100 |

Figure 39 is a summary report for a test case to illustrate the scope of the program. Package I exhibits the raw premium and paid claims data as of the time the renewal action is calculated (usually two or three months before the next policy anniversary).

Package II estimates the incurred experience through the end of the current policy year. It is primarily for information purposes, although in certain types of cases the renewal action may be affected by these figures.

Package III, the significant package, is designed specifically for input to the underwriting calculation. The package is a statistical fiction designed in concert with the required margin tables and renewal guidelines. The premiums are those expected the following year if the underwriter does *not* take any renewal action at the next anniversary, excluding growth in the number of lives covered. The incurred claims

FIGURE 39

DATE MAR 25 74     CAUSE UNLIMITED

PACKAGE SUMMARY

| POLICY NUMBER | DIVIDEND NUMBER | ANNIVERSARY DATE | EFFECTIVE DATE | TYPE OF ACCOUNT | P K | FIELD OFFICE | DIV. | ANALYST | CLAIM PAYMENT |
|---|---|---|---|---|---|---|---|---|---|
| XX-XX | | JUNE 1 1974 | JUNE 1 1974 | SA | 0 | 14 | 3 | TEST | 3 |

| | PACKAGE I CURRENT 9 MONTHS | | | PACKAGE II ESTIMATED CURRENT YEAR | | | PACKAGE III RENEWAL ANALYSIS | | | PACKAGE IV EST. NEXT YEAR END | | |
|---|---|---|---|---|---|---|---|---|---|---|---|---|
| | PREMIUM | PAID CLAIMS | RATIO | PREMIUM | INCURRED CLAIMS | RATIO | PREMIUM | SIGNIFICANT CLAIMS | RATIO | PREMIUM | PROJECTED CLAIMS | RATIO |
| EMPLOYEE LIFE | 36197 | 22500 | 62.2 | 48263 | 38830 | 80.5 | 53663 | 42202 | 78.6 | 53663 | 43378 | 80.8 |
| DEPENDENT LIFE | 2147 | 0 | 0.0 | 2863 | 182 | 6.3 | 2863 | 494 | 17.3 | 2863 | 491 | 17.2 |
| TOTAL LIFE | 38344 | 22500 | 58.7 | 51125 | 39012 | 76.3 | 56526 | 42696 | 75.5 | 56526 | 43869 | 77.6 |
| A D & D | 1502 | 0 | 0.0 | 2003 | 452 | 22.6 | 2003 | 1705 | 85.1 | 2003 | 1699 | 84.8 |
| WEEKLY INDEMNITY | 13253 | 6550 | 49.4 | 17671 | 8692 | 49.2 | 17671 | 9018 | 51.0 | 17671 | 8916 | 50.5 |
| NEW YORK DISABILITY | 1300 | 660 | 50.8 | 1733 | 1021 | 58.9 | 1733 | 1027 | 59.2 | 1733 | 1017 | 58.7 |
| WEEKLY INDEMNITY TOTAL | 14553 | 7210 | 49.5 | 19404 | 9713 | 50.1 | 19404 | 10044 | 51.8 | 19404 | 9933 | 51.2 |
| EMPLOYEE HEALTH | | | | | | | | | | | | |
| BASE PLAN - TOTAL | 18108 | 30116 | 166.3 | 24144 | 40823 | 169.1 | 24144 | 44978 | 186.3 | 31241 | 50133 | 160.5 |
| MAJOR MEDICAL | 3260 | 2604 | 79.9 | 4347 | 3274 | 75.3 | 4347 | 3758 | 86.5 | 4347 | 4141 | 95.3 |
| MEDICARE | 0 | 2347 | 0.0 | 0 | 3148 | 0.0 | 0 | 0 | 0.0 | 0 | 0 | 0.0 |
| TOTAL EMPLOYEE HEALTH | 21368 | 35067 | 164.1 | 28491 | 47245 | 165.8 | 28491 | 48736 | 171.1 | 35588 | 54274 | 152.5 |
| DEPENDENT HEALTH | | | | | | | | | | | | |
| BASE PLAN TOTAL | 44002 | 44849 | 101.9 | 58669 | 64024 | 109.1 | 58669 | 67148 | 114.5 | 75915 | 76380 | 100.6 |
| MAJOR MEDICAL | 4569 | 998 | 21.8 | 6092 | 981 | 16.1 | 6092 | 1373 | 22.5 | 6092 | 1447 | 23.7 |
| MEDICARE | 0 | 3172 | 0.0 | 0 | 4187 | 0.0 | 0 | 0 | 0.0 | 0 | 0 | 0.0 |
| COB | 0 | -2143 | 0.0 | 0 | -2587 | 0.0 | 0 | 0 | 0.0 | 0 | 0 | 0.0 |
| TOTAL DEPENDENT HEALTH | 48571 | 46826 | 96.4 | 64761 | 66606 | 102.9 | 64761 | 68521 | 105.8 | 82007 | 77827 | 94.9 |
| COVERAGE TOTAL | | | | | | | | | | | | |
| BASE PLAN | 62110 | 74965 | 120.7 | 82813 | 104847 | 126.6 | 82813 | 112126 | 135.4 | 107156 | 126513 | 118.1 |
| MAJOR MEDICAL | 7829 | 3602 | 46.0 | 10439 | 4256 | 40.8 | 10439 | 5131 | 49.2 | 10439 | 5588 | 53.5 |
| MEDICARE | 0 | 5469 | 0.0 | 0 | 7334 | 0.0 | 0 | 0 | 0.0 | 0 | 0 | 0.0 |
| COB | 0 | -2143 | 0.0 | 0 | -2587 | 0.0 | 0 | 0 | 0.0 | 0 | 0 | 0.0 |
| TOTAL HEALTH | 69939 | 81893 | 117.1 | 93252 | 113851 | 122.1 | 93252 | 117258 | 125.7 | 117595 | 132101 | 112.3 |
| TOTAL PACKAGE | 124338 | 111603 | 89.8 | 165784 | 163028 | 98.3 | 171184 | 171702 | 100.3 | 195527 | 187602 | 95.9 |

ESTIMATES INCLUDE AN ESTIMATED ANNUAL POOLING CHARGE OF 1232. DOLLARS AND REINSURANCE OF 67. DOLLARS

do *not* represent what is expected the following year. Roughly speaking, the Package III incurred claims are those expected if no inflation in claim costs takes place. The allowance for inflation is built into the required margin tables.

Package IV is an estimate of the next year's experience, based on an assumption that the recommended premium rates are charged and that claims follow the anticipated inflationary trend. It provides a rough check on the renewal action.

Figure 40 illustrates the analysis of Package III and the renewal recommendation. The underwriting factors presented in the figure have been modified to preserve their confidential nature.

## D.  Management Control Information

Management and supervisory personnel receive a weekly production report, which provides a one-line summary of the action taken for each case. The summary compares the "book" rate action with the results of any override. This report is an important management control tool because it allows managers to keep aware, in a rough sense, of the kinds of decisions the underwriters are making. Even at the vice-presidential level, it has become possible to show an interest in what is going on and to obtain a sense of the kinds of decisions that are being made without becoming bogged down in the details of case-specific calculations. It is interesting that whereas the majority of overrides were originally in the direction of reduced premium rates as compared with book decisions, more recently the overrides have appeared to fluctuate evenly about the book decisions. To some degree, this demonstrates the fact that the system tracks decisions by management, such as changing margin requirements because of inflation.

Another management control report prepared by the production team is a backlog report that lists for the current month and two succeeding months the number of cases that have anniversaries, the number that have received initial action, and the number that have received final action. This report gives managers a good early warning of whether work backlogs are mounting, and it encourages corrective action before the underwriters become swamped.

## E.  The Impact of CAUSE

As of this writing, CAUSE has been completely operational for more than a year. Renewal rates for all small cases and many large cases are now calculated via CAUSE. A number of types of impact have been observed, in terms of both the underwriting process and the quality of underwriting output.

> *Process: calculating vs. reviewing.*   Prior to the installation of CAUSE, a large component of renewal underwriting was performing numerical calculations. By doing a case manually on a yellow pad, an underwriter could get a feel for the validity of the premium and claim data. This helped to evaluate whether or not the "book" solution required an override. With CAUSE, the underwriting process is more involved with reviewing supporting material to make this evaluation. Many underwriters were initially uncomfortable unless they went through the calculations by hand, both to be sure that the computer had used the correct procedures and to get a better feel for the numbers. With additional experience, most underwriters gained confidence in CAUSE and

FIGURE 40

```
DATE   MAR 25   74                    CAUSE UNLIMITED

                      ANALYSIS OF PACKAGE III

POLICY   DIVIDEND  ANNIVERSARY   EFFECTIVE   TYPE OF   P   FIELD   DIV.   ANALYST  CLAIM
NUMBER   NUMBER    DATE          DATE        ACCOUNT   K   OFFICE                  PAYMENT

XX-XX             JUNE  1 1974  JUNE  1 1974  SA       O   14      3      TEST     3
```

| | PACKAGE AMOUNT | PCT OF PREMIUM | LIFE AMOUNT | PCT OF PREMIUM | ADDD AMOUNT | PCT OF PREMIUM | W.I. AMOUNT | PCT OF PREMIUM | HEALTH AMOUNT | PCT OF PREMIUM |
|---|---|---|---|---|---|---|---|---|---|---|
| PREMIUM AT CURR RATE | 165,784 | | 51,125 | | 2,003 | | 19,404 | | 93,252 | |
| PACKAGE III PREMIUM | 171,184 | | 56,526 | | 2,003 | | 19,404 | | 93,252 | |
| POOLED PREMIUM | 1,299 | .8 | 1,232 | 2.2 | 67 | 3.3 | | | | |
| PREMIUM LESS POOLING | 169,885 | | 55,294 | | 1,936 | | 19,404 | | 93,252 | |
| | | | | | | | | | | |
| PAID CLAIMS | 163,490 | 96.2 | 42,696 | 77.2 | 1,705 | 88.1 | 9,613 | 49.5 | 109,476 | 117.4 |
| CHANGE IN M+Q RESERVES | 2,945 | 1.7 | | | | | | | 2,945 | 3.2 |
| CHANGE IN I+U RESERVES | 408 | .2 | | | | | 325 | 1.7 | 83 | .1 |
| RES STRENGTHENING ADJ | 4,054 | 2.4 | | | | | | | 4,054 | 4.3 |
| LAG | 699 | .4 | | | | | | | 699 | .7 |
| STATE PLAN ASSESSMENT | 106 | .1 | | | | | 106 | .5 | | |
| INCURRED CLAIMS | 171,702 | 101.1 | 42,696 | 77.2 | 1,705 | 88.1 | 10,044 | 51.8 | 117,258 | 125.7 |
| INC CLAIMS LESS POOLING | 170,404 | 100.3 | 41,464 | 75.0 | 1,638 | 84.6 | 10,044 | 51.8 | 117,258 | 125.7 |
| EST NORMAL RETENTION * | 17,602 | 10.4 | | | | | | | | |
| INC CLAIMS + EST RET | 188,006 | 110.7 | | | | | | | | |

RECOMMENDATION BASED ON PACKAGE III

| | PACKAGE AMOUNT | PCT | LIFE AMOUNT | PCT | ADDD AMOUNT | W.I. AMOUNT | HEALTH AMOUNT | |
|---|---|---|---|---|---|---|---|---|
| NORMALIZED UNPOOLED | 194,240 | | 63,220 | | 2,214 | 22,186 | 106,620 | |
| ADJ FOR 72 WAGE PRICE | 198,329 | | 63,220 | | 2,214 | 23,086 | 109,808 | |
| INC CLAIMS + EST RET | 188,006 | 94.8 | | | | | | |
| | | | | | | | | |
| PROSPECTIVE RENEWAL | | | | | | | | |
| ESTIMATED MARGIN | 10,323 | 5.2 | | | | | | |
| REQ PROSPECTIVE MARGIN | 29,238 | 14.7 | | | | | | |
| ADDL PROSP MARGIN NEEDED | 18,916 | 9.5 | | | | | | |
| ADDL PREMIUM NEEDED | 25,192 | 12.7 | | | | | | |
| WAGE-PRICE LTD EXP ADJ | -1,486 | -.7 | | | | | | |
| ADDN TO NORMAL PREM | 23,706 | 12.0 | | | | | | |
| TOTAL PROSPECTIVE PREM | 219,244 | | | | | | | |
| | | | | | | | | |
| PSR/RETRO RENEWAL | | | | | | | | |
| MARGIN IN NORM PREM | 6,234 | 3.1 | | | | | | |
| MARGIN FROM PSR ACCT | 0 | | | | | | | |
| NET EST MARGIN WITH PSR | 6,234 | 3.1 | | | | | | |
| REQUIRED MARGIN | 3,885 | 2.0 | | | | | | |
| ADDITIONAL RETENTION | 2,338 | 1.2 | | | | | | |
| ADDL RET + MARGIN REQ | -12 | - | | | | | | |
| ADDN TO NORM PREMIUM | -12 | - | | | | | | |
| | | | | | | | | |
| ADDL PREM DUE TO RECALC | 5,400 | | 5,400 | | | | | |
| ADDN TO PACK III BILLED | 24,343 | | | | | | 24,343 | |
| TOTAL ADDITIONAL PREMIUM | 29,743 | | 5,400 | | | | 24,343 | |
| TOTAL BILLED PREMIUM | 195,527 | | 56,526 | 10.6 | 2,003 | 19,404 | 117,595 | |
| PCT CHANGE IN RATE | | 17.9 | | | | | | 26.1 |
| PCT CHANGE IN RATE BASIS | | 14.2 | | | | | | 26.1 |
| | | | | | | | | |
| NORMALIZING FACTOR | 1.12211 | | | | | | | |
| YEAR END ADJUSTMENT | 12.1 | | | | | | | |
| OBJECTIVE LOSS RATIO | 87.7 | | | | | | | |

* PREVIOUS YEAR'S NORMAL RETENTION WEIGHTED BY MAJOR COVERAGE PREMIUM

began to appreciate the extent to which it reduced tedious paperwork. On the other hand, at least until other administrative systems are changed, the tedium of the yellow pad has been partially replaced by the tedium of the input form.

*Accuracy.* CAUSE has greatly reduced the risk of gross errors in arithmetic calculations. Formerly, a combination of time pressure, the complexity of the calculations, and the inexperience of some underwriters had resulted in a very serious accuracy problem, primarily in the 90 percent of cases that were classified as small. According to one assistant manager, periodic quality control reviews had revealed arithmetic and logical errors that were close to appalling in some instances. With CAUSE, a solution within guidelines is guaranteed, even if sophisticated adjustments may be overlooked. Previously, erroneous high rates had generated complaints from field representatives, whereas erroneous low rates had often slipped through. Since most of the undetected errors were almost certainly on the low side, it is likely that premium income increased with the implementation of CAUSE.

*Uniformity.*   Previous to the use of CAUSE, there had been considerable variability in the detailed application of guidelines and formulas. Often these variations would not result in major errors in the final premium rates, but they would result in confusion whenever a second underwriter got involved in a case, either in supervising or in taking over a case previously handled by someone else. In other words, there was a good chance that the other person's calculations would be difficult to follow and interpret. Even when only one underwriter is involved, the second year's considerations are simplified because the prior year's results are in a consistent standard form.

*Communication.*   Consistency in reports and procedures has facilitated communication with other underwriters, with supervisors, and even with field representatives, who now receive rate memos and supporting documentation that are consistent across all cases.

*Turnover.*   Because of the large amount of knowledge that must be mastered by trainees, underwriter turnover is a serious problem. CAUSE has reduced the severity of the turnover problem in two ways. First, it has facilitated training. A recent training class completed the underwriting on more than 200 cases in the time that previous classes were able to gain experience with only a negligible number of live cases. Second, CAUSE serves as a way of leveling out the experience of underwriters by helping new underwriters attain general competence much more quickly.

*Overtime.*   Before CAUSE existed, high case loads during the autumn forced salaried underwriters to work up to three nights a week to keep from becoming totally swamped. Much of the overtime during peak periods has now been eliminated. Work backlogs during these periods have dropped correspondingly.

*Rule changes.*   At one point during the period of price and wage controls (1971–1973), a directive from the Price Commission dictated a change in several important underwriting guidelines. As a result, it was necessary to recalculate renewal rates in hundreds of cases. Without CAUSE, the recalculation effort would have created serious work backlogs, not to speak of annoyance at having to repeat the renewal calculations. With CAUSE, the recalculation was done automatically, using the existing data files after a special subroutine was programmed. The complexity of underwriting has increased in recent years and continues to increase. Thus it is important to be able to update underwriting procedures through both retraining and reprogramming rather than through the single mechanism of continuous retraining.

*Management control.*   For the first time, management has good tools for reviewing and monitoring renewal actions. Previously there was a quality control spot check at the supervisory level, but there was little in the way of control reports for higher managers.

Although there is general agreement that CAUSE has been a success and a worthwhile investment, it is difficult to place a definite monetary value on its impact either on the mechanics of the underwriting process or on the improved consistency and accuracy of underwriting decisions. On the process side, monetary savings were initially anticipated because of the drastic reduction in the clerical component of underwriting. To date, such savings have not been realized, largely because most of the input to CAUSE is still manual rather than automatic. On the output side, Mr. Johnson estimates that premium income may have increased five to eight million dollars per year as a result of closer adherence to guidelines and the elimination of arithmetic miscalculations made under heavy time pressure. Balanced against the range of tangible to relatively intangible benefits listed above are the development costs, which were approximately half a million dollars, and the ongoing operational costs, which amount to approximately $25 per case.

An important impact of CAUSE, one that is virtually impossible to evaluate monetarily, is that it has facilitated two major organizational changes toward a more effective decentralized management approach. (Since the details and purposes of these changes are peripheral to the purposes of this case, they will not be discussed.) In part, these changes became feasible because of two outgrowths of the implementation of CAUSE. The first was a general reduction in requirements for underwriter specialization, a force that had previously restricted the possibilities for reorganization. The second was the new capability to audit output quality, which permitted decentralization while maintaining uniform standards of guideline application. The opinion among management is that these organizational changes would not have been practical without CAUSE.

★   ★   ★

The two final sections of this case flesh out the development of CAUSE by discussing key technical and human aspects of the implementation effort. Of special interest in the technical approach was the use of a series of prototypes to demonstrate the system's feasibility to different audiences. Of special interest on the human side of the implementation is the careful handling of those issues by the implementation team.

## V.  TECHNICAL ASPECTS OF THE DESIGN AND IMPLEMENTATION OF CAUSE

### A.  Implementation Goals

From the first day of the project, the primary concern was implementation. This concern was reflected in plans, research, system architecture, program design, and phasing. There were four implementation goals.

---

Section V is based on an early version of the paper by James Johnson that was cited earlier.

1.    To demonstrate technical and economic feasibility at an early stage.

2.    To minimize the future shock resulting from the interaction between the underwriter and the computer, as well as from changes in underwriting procedures.

3.    To modify underwriting procedures where appropriate and develop management monitoring mechanisms.

4.    To minimize input prepared manually and minimize computer running costs.

The first goal addressed the need for interest, support, and confidence in the project team by management. The second goal addressed the underwriting audience. The third addressed the effectiveness of the process, and the fourth, its efficiency. The strategy was to develop four successive versions of the system, using a prototype concept, with each version dedicated to one of the goals above. This approach contrasts with a massive one-pass approach that would attempt to balance all goals simultaneously.

## B.  Phases of Development

Figure 41 illustrates the development cycles of CAUSE through the first three prototypes. In a sense, a complete system development cycle from conceptual design through program test was repeated for each version of the system. These versions will be described in sequence.

*FIGURE 41   Development Cycles*

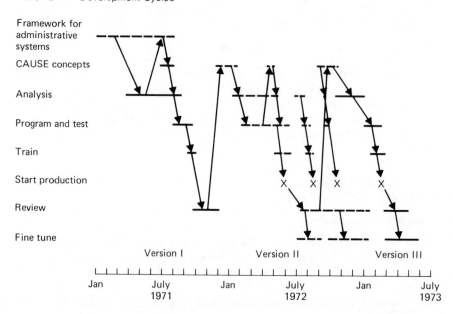

## 1.  Version I

Version I of CAUSE was capable of performing all the underwriting functions for a limited range of case characteristics. Development was based on a detailed analysis of all underwriting functions. A number of renewal cases were studied quite carefully to help generate a model of the process and of the sequence and rationale for choices that were made. Version I was coded and tested in six weeks. The program consisted of 26 subroutines. Twenty-two cases were then underwritten by CAUSE in parallel with their manual renewal, and the processing time and accuracy of the results were analyzed. Version I successfully demonstrated the concept of computer-assisted underwriting to those who participated in the test. A research program was undertaken to resolve more than 70 procedural questions brought to light in this first experiment. The experiment itself also yielded considerable additional insight into the underwriting process. For an investment of one-twentieth of the total cost of the project and one-tenth of its elapsed time, feasibility was demonstrated to management.

## 2.  Version II

Version II handled common types of cases in a manner generally familiar to underwriters. In developing this version, the project team strongly resisted pressures to change practices to conform more closely with theory. In some gray areas of "judgment and experience," algorithms and tables were devised on the basis of expert opinion. A steering committee of project team members, underwriters, and actuaries reviewed all concepts and calculation procedures. During this phase of the project, the main CAUSE program grew to 87 routines. Analysis occupied four months; coding and testing took three months. An additional three months were spent bedding down the system and production procedures, extending the range of cases handled to accommodate common situations originally thought to be rare, modifying report formats, and adding new reports. The wage-price rules were encoded. A training program was undertaken to introduce the standardized underwriting practices, as well as procedures for using the system.

## 3.  Version III

The initial thrust was toward developing management information. A statistical summary file containing the key results from each renewal was created. The weekly production report from each renewal was created. The weekly production report from this system provides a one-line summary for each case, which compares the "book" rate action with the results of any override. In addition to functioning as a management tool, the report was helpful in pointing out common overrides that might well be programmed. A number of less common situations, such as exclusions from retrospective agreements, were analyzed and incorporated into the program so that cases with high dollar volume could be processed. Although the project team had initially anticipated being able to identify considerable improvements in the underwriting guidelines and calculation procedures, they found that underwriting concepts generally withstood detailed analysis.

CAUSE was extended in a number of ways. Report formats were modified in response to suggestions from underwriters. A supervisor's summary was developed. Additional flexibility was implemented in input methods, processing procedures, and override options. A new round of training was undertaken. Considerable attention was directed to developing tools to assist the production team. A number of on-line editing procedures were standardized in the form of production jobs. The turnaround time was reduced by a day. The main CAUSE program grew to 154 routines over a period of ten months, although most of the programming effort was concentrated in a six-week period.

### 4. Version IV

Version IV, still underway, is concerned with the interfaces with the administrative EDP systems and with data processing efficiency. The first step in this direction was the development of an automatic interface feeding rate skeletons from the administrative EDP systems to CAUSE, reducing manual input by roughly 50 percent. In addition, three key routines out of more than 200 were rewritten to reduce run time by 20 percent. Current research addresses the goal of providing data at the appropriate level of detail when working directly from the administrative database.

### C. Program Design Concepts

The program design concepts essential to the rapid development of CAUSE were the following.

Off-the-shelf architecture

Off-the-shelf report generators and edit routines

Table driven/parameterized design

Suitable language (FORTRAN)

Structured programming

Standardized record formats

Use of time-sharing

The CAUSE architectural concepts are to a large degree independent of the underwriting application. The concepts and many of the coding techniques were developed in financial planning and production control applications for other companies. The basic framework is to all intents a package program. Input and output processing utilize generalized subroutines. The internal layout of data is standardized. This approach made it possible to get Version I up and running in six weeks, provided flexibility, and enabled the project team to concentrate on synthesis of the underwriting logic.

Report preparation is accomplished with generalized report subroutines. The sequence, editing, and content of report lines are specified in dictionaries maintained on disk storage. In many instances, additional report lines can be added, existing report lines can be deleted, or the editing can be changed without changing the program. Calculations are broken down into simple steps so that intermediate results can be presented in backup reports.

Underwriting guidelines and reserve factors are contained in 32 tables maintained on disk storage. Two versions of each underwriting table are maintained, with the effective table keyed to the anniversary date of the policy. Table changes are made by the production team and are usually implemented within half a day of approval.

The database design is much less sophisticated than the program design. Each day's input is maintained in a separate sequential disk file. If a case must be updated or rerun, it is located by reference to a manually prepared index card. Older cases are periodically purged to tape. This approach places heavy responsibility for file control on the production team, but it greatly simplifies the database design.

## VI. HUMAN ASPECTS OF THE IMPLEMENTATION OF CAUSE

### A. Awareness of the Issues

Although the technical aspects of the implementation of CAUSE were carefully planned, the Task Force was always cognizant of the fact that successful technical implementation would not ensure successful use and institutionalization. For this reason, many of the human aspects of implementation were also carefully planned and monitored. Given the scope of the project and the past history of communication problems between user groups and systems people, it was considered quite important that effective lines of communication be established and maintained.

The first step in accomplishing this goal was the formation of a steering committee that kept close tabs on both the technical development and the way system use developed. Upon reflection, it was clear to the project team and steering committee that the project would have to address four "credibility audiences": themselves, user management, system development management, and the underwriters. Version I of CAUSE addressed the first three audiences, convincing the project team, steering committee, and finally user and systems management that the project was feasible technically and that it was very likely to yield beneficial results. Given the enthusiasm and commitment of these three audiences, the project proceeded into Version II, which addressed the underwriters' concerns. During this and succeeding phases, it was important to monitor the acceptance and use of CAUSE by the 120 underwriters and the supervisory personnel. At each stage, underwriters were encouraged to express any reservations they might have, particularly since their comments would provide advance warning of major design problems.

The prototype approach to implementation played an important role in facilitating communication, in that it helped everyone maintain a realistic view of the progress that had been made and of the problems that were being encountered. One result was that approvals could be obtained quickly from the viewpoint of the technical people and could be considered and granted confidently from the viewpoint of the steering committee. Note also that the implementation was carried out by a small, highly skilled project team (averaging four people), who worked together quite effectively. The technical members developed a deep interest in improving the environment for underwriters. The group members responded by spending a great deal of time in helping the systems staff obtain an in-depth knowledge of underwriting.

## B. System Introduction

When the CAUSE project was initiated, underwriters expressed some reservations about the feasibility of mechanizing the complex sequence of logical choices and calculations required in determining renewal rates. They argued that a great deal of judgment and experience were required at each stage, and that judgment and experience simply could not be computerized. The countering argument was that a large part of the standard wisdom of experienced underwriters could probably be expressed in formulas, decision trees, and tables. The end product seems to represent a conclusion intermediate between these views. It was possible to program rules and decision trees that would produce a "book" solution, but experience and judgment still had to be exercised in finding errors and in adjusting the calculations to compensate for special situations.

In May 1972, Version II of CAUSE became operational for solving a simple set of cases. By May 1973, Version III was in full operation. That first year of operation was a busy period, involving a range of tasks related to system introduction and modification:

Adding new features

Correcting errors

Changing report formats

Training underwriters

Training the production staff

Solving workflow problems

Revising the overall administrative process

Training new project team members

Largely because feedback was actively sought from the underwriters who were learning to use the system, the introduction period went as well as could be expected. People realized that this was a complicated system, and they understood that it would evolve from the intermediate version that was first used into a final version that would incorporate their insights and concerns. Given that the project team maintained its credibility by correcting bugs and resolving procedural questions as they arose, the underwriters were generally cooperative in providing feedback and in accommodating to procedural changes.

## C. Resolving Residual Implementation Problems

Most of the work on the technical aspects of system development and improvement was completed by the beginning of 1973. In reviewing the project's progress through early 1973, the team concluded that the technical implementation had proceeded quite well and, in particular, that it had been under control at all times. Nonetheless, there remained some "loose ends," which were basically residual problems related to system acceptance and effective use. The team therefore concluded that it should "switch gears" and begin to spend most of its time training people to use the system effectively and modifying certain details of the system and its documentation to reinforce the training. Management concurred with this analysis, which also concluded that it would be desirable to avoid exerting too much direct pressure to use the system. The idea was that future efforts should be directed at convincing underwriters that CAUSE was not merely an imposed procedural change in the way they did their jobs. Rather, it was a change that addressed their problems and would help them do a better job under better conditions.

Thus, although implementation concerns had been addressed throughout system development, it was felt that additional effort from the project team would be helpful in establishing CAUSE as a standard component of renewal underwriting. This effort would have two types of motivation: to take full advantage of the opportunities afforded by CAUSE and to resolve a number of residual implementation issues that had not been totally resolved during the primarily technical part of system development. Notes exist from an April 1973 meeting of the CAUSE project team, at which many of the residual issues were discussed. Those notes are the basis of the following discussion of the issues and the actions that were taken in resolving them.

*Input problems.* Many of the forms that were being turned in by underwriters were incomplete and/or inaccurate.

This problem was due in part to the exacting and somewhat boring nature of input preparation. Many underwriters were occasionally using the first computer run to debug the data, just as a computer programmer sometimes uses a compiler to help find errors in the code instead of doing a lot of tedious prior checking at a desk. In using the first run this way, underwriters submitted possibly incomplete or unrepresentative raw data and then examined the CAUSE calculation documentation generated in the production of the "book" renewal rate.

In some instances, however, incomplete or inaccurate input was indicative of difficulties ranging from misunderstanding to occasional carelessness. To catch and correct these problems, the production team assumed the responsibility of checking the input forms. When the time seemed appropriate, the production team consciously changed its feedback style from being very forgiving and supportive to being direct and critical whenever badly prepared forms were submitted. This approach, supplementing the learning curve that was in effect, reduced the error rate to an acceptable level.

As a stopgap in relieving part of the chore of input preparation, part-time clerical help was recruited to prepare some of the simpler input forms, leaving the more complicated ones for the underwriters. Eventually, when the administrative EDP system is complete, the whole question of manual input should become minimal.

*Calculations done by hand.* It was observed that a number of cases were being put into CAUSE after being done manually. This fact was obvious because of the high incidence of overrides on the first input forms. The extent of this double work could not be stated with certainty, although it was thought to be as high as 20 percent in the division handling most of the small cases.

Part of the problem was that some underwriters wanted to check the logic employed by CAUSE until they became convinced that the program really worked. Many of them had heard of disasters with other computer systems, and they were reluctant to delegate their responsibility without being absolutely sure of the system. Certainly the underwriters could not be faulted for this kind of concern.

To help them gain confidence in CAUSE, the underwriters were encouraged to request full backup reports for a number of cases so that they could check CAUSE's handling of a case to their satisfaction. Full backup is now rarely requested, and the general confidence problem has faded away.

*Disuse by supervisors.*   Some supervisors had not learned to use the system. Some assistant managers in the division handling most of the small cases had never completed a case from input preparation through output analysis. Having been too busy to spend enough time to do a sufficient number of cases using CAUSE, they had not become comfortable with the CAUSE decision process.

This problem was confronted directly by an accelerated training effort. Time was spent in developing separate training sessions aimed at the respective needs of supervisors, experienced underwriters, and new trainees. A working group of supervisors was formed to design a supervisor's summary, which was then implemented. Supervisors were thus encouraged to buy a "piece of the action."

*Disuse of manuals.*   Some underwriters had not read the CAUSE manual and a large number of subsequent releases that updated the manual as new features were added. As a result, some errors occurred and some questions seemed to be asked repeatedly. One of the problems here was that the original manual was incomplete and that the numerous updating releases were in a form such that it was not always possible to find the information needed for a specific problem.

The training manual has now been completely rewritten and has been entered into a text-editing system so that it can be updated and reissued easily.

*Limited understanding.*   CAUSE seemed to require a broader knowledge of both underwriting concepts and system details than the inexperienced underwriters possessed.

To some degree, this problem resulted from the fact that CAUSE did calculations and presented results that were not normally relevant in the types of cases assigned to inexperienced people. As in the problem of disuse by supervisors, the solution was an improved training program. Exposure to these additional calculation procedures accelerated the professional development of the inexperienced underwriters, but the transition was a bit of a jolt. The training program for new underwriters was completely redesigned as well.

*Order of training.*   There were 120 underwriters, who were to be trained in groups of eight or fewer. For a while, some underwriters wondered why others were being chosen for CAUSE training before they received their own training. That is, was there some special significance to the choice? The rationale that someone had to go first was not accepted by everyone, but the issue disappeared as training progressed.

*Resistance from a manager.* The manager of one of the divisions handling large cases was indifferent to CAUSE. His attitude was reflected by the division's assistant managers. One of the weekly CAUSE management control reports going to top management registered no renewals through CAUSE in that division. In that exceptional situation, a decision had to be made about whether people should be forced to use the system at that time. Until then, the project team had urged management not to issue edicts concerning system use, especially until everyone was comfortable with the system's ability to handle new situations. Since CAUSE was being used effectively in the other divisions, management decided to tell that manager that they really did expect cases to be done through CAUSE insofar as possible. That manager never became enthusiastic about CAUSE but conformed with the directive from top management.

One of the important points here is that the system provided the information to pinpoint the few areas where direct action was required. It was therefore possible to avoid blanket statements that would offend the majority, who had cooperated to the extent to which their business caution allowed.

*Input and procedural changes.* There had been many changes in input forms, output reports, and calculating procedures. Although most underwriters appreciated the reasons for the changes, many were finding the changes annoying.[2]

Given the complexity of the calculations in CAUSE, an evolutionary approach was essential. If the system was to be built and debugged, people would simply have to live with the fact that there would be many changes until all the procedures were correct and the new features were added.

*"Long" turnaround.* The normal processing cycle for CAUSE made it impossible to do a case at the last minute. Although it is possible to do a case on a same-day basis using CAUSE, doing so is costly and therefore impractical, except on rare occasions. With CAUSE, the minimum elapsed time per case increased from half a day to three or four days. Even with a subsequent one-day reduction in turnaround, the longer time requirement involved changes in work-distribution planning, work habits, and so on. To facilitate these changes, a number of control procedures were instituted to prevent cases from being left to the last minute.

*Program errors.* At the time the analysis was made, there were still some errors in certain calculating routines, but they have been corrected, and the system now works quite smoothly. In the period from May 1973 to May 1974, only one program error was uncovered. At the point in the program where the error occurred, someone had inserted the remark, "This situation should never happen at this point." This renewed certain people's faith in the First Rule of Underwriting: "Never say never."

---

[2]Some underwriters also blamed the project team for such procedural changes as wage-price calculation procedures, which would have been necessary with or without CAUSE.

## D. Growth of Acceptance

All in all, Mr. Johnson estimates that at least 25 percent of the development cost of CAUSE was directly related to addressing the human aspects of implementation. This is not at all surprising when one considers the number of people involved in the use of the system. In retrospect, Mr. Johnson feels it was important that the decision was made to allow the project team to continue working on the acceptance of the system after its technical installation. This continuing effort has helped in bringing about the kinds of impacts discussed earlier by encouraging the acceptance of the system. Around May 1973, it was estimated that 20 percent of the underwriters used CAUSE effectively and liked it, 20 percent were strongly opposed, and 60 percent were indifferent. As indicated above, the system had undergone considerable change and growth during the year prior to May 1973. Compounding natural tendencies to be skeptical about new ways of doing things, these continual changes had produced some of the indifference and resistance reflected in the percentages. During the year, as the system settled down considerably, attitudes became much more positive. By October 1974, the general feeling was that they were running around 80 percent strongly favorable and 20 percent indifferent. Probably the strongest measure of the success of CAUSE is the fact that it has been institutionalized. It has become part of the definition of renewal underwriting and has had a major impact on both the process of underwriting and the quality of the decisions produced.

### Questions for the Reader

1. Compare the process of renewal underwriting before and after CAUSE.

2. Compare CAUSE's approach for supporting decisions with that of the systems in the other case studies you have read. Would it be possible to develop a system similar to CAUSE to support the decision makers in those other settings?

3. Do you think that CAUSE has affected the evaluation of individual underwriters? For instance, do you think it has increased or decreased an individual's ability to demonstrate his or her talent, skill, and ambition?

4. If you were a member of an underwriter's union (if such a union existed), would you have favored or opposed the initial effort to develop the system? Would you have favored or opposed the system that was actually developed?

5. Simon (1960) predicted that a substantial part of management decision making would be automated within a decade. To what extent does the success of CAUSE imply that this prediction could come true in the next decade or two?

6. Did the prototype-development methodology have a major impact on the success of CAUSE? Would this approach have been helpful in the implementations described in the other case studies?

7. Discuss possible changes or embellishments in CAUSE. For instance, might it be advantageous to have the underwriters bypass the production team by interacting directly with the system through CRT terminals (as was done in the Great Eastern Bank case)? Alternatively, might it be possible to further automate the underwriting process, thereby reducing the need for underwriters?

# INTERACTIVE MARKET SYSTEMS:
# A MEDIA DECISION
# SUPPORT SYSTEM

## CASE FIVE

### I. INTRODUCTION

The problem of allocating advertising dollars to media is important to three distinct groups of people.

> Advertisers, who have money for advertising and want to reach potential consumers of their product.

> Media representatives, who have advertising space they want to sell to advertisers.

> Agencies, who are principally involved in trying to get advertisers and media people together in an efficient and effective way.

This case describes the development (from 1969 to 1974) and use (in 1974) of a series of advertising analysis programs that are among the principal products of Interactive Market Systems, Inc. (IMS). Additional IMS services not mentioned in this case include a range of support services for media decisions and general marketing decisions. What will be called "the system" in this case is a combination of a database of market research information and a series of programs that apply specialized types of analysis to that database. The case stresses that there may be a range of alternative approaches for supporting a particular type of decision. Additional emphasis is placed on usage patterns in general, as well as on differences among different types of users.

### A. Statement of the Problem

In any mass market, the advertising media serve an information dissemination function that helps potential consumers of a product and the producers of a product to get together in the marketplace. Since the producers are relatively few and the consumers relatively many in such a market, it is the problem of producers to reach the

---

This case is based in part on a technically oriented case study written by David Ness and Christopher Sprague (1972), implementers of the early versions of the system described here. The cooperation and support of Leon Liebman, President of Interactive Market Systems, are appreciated.

consumers to inform them of the characteristics of the product. In order to accomplish this objective, advertising media exist as an effective channel of communication. Before placing an ad, however, the advertiser should ask a number of questions.

Who are the potential consumers for the product?

What are their media habits (for example, what magazines do they read, and what television shows do they watch)?

How can we effectively use the media to reach the consumers?

What tactics should be used (for example, what content should be put in the ad, what characteristics of the product should be emphasized, and what should the frequency of advertisements be)?

For the most part, the system described here addresses only the first three questions above. The thrust of the system is to aid in identifying potential consumers and analyzing their media habits in order to determine the overall strategy of an advertising campaign. Tactical questions are left for resolution by the advertisers and their agencies.

## B.  How Can the Problem Be Addressed?

Since the three questions of concern are significant to virtually everyone who advertises, a great deal of thought and effort has gone into the development of appropriate methods for studying the problem. For example, a number of syndicated databases are collected periodically and are made available for advertisers, media, and agencies to purchase. One such database is the well-known "Simmons Sample," collected annually by W. R. Simmons and Associates Research, Inc. Throughout this case, the Simmons database will be used as a surrogate for a list of databases, which would include ORC, TGI Storch, Canadian Print Measurement Bureau, and other syndicated and proprietary media studies to which a client might subscribe.

The Simmons database consists of responses collected in an annual survey of more than 15,000 representative consumers. In addition to completing a leave-behind questionnaire, each consumer provides responses to two questionnaires administered by an interviewer. The purpose of this effort is to elicit a profile of the consumer on four separate kinds of dimensions:

Demographic characteristics (income level, number of people in family, location of residence, etc.).

Consumption habits (information about consumption of widely used products by brand, with a number of detailed questions about heavily advertised products in particular).

A description of media habits, consisting of a two-week television diary and two separate measurements of magazine readership.

Psychographic information about the consumer's self image and ideal image.

In disaggregated form, the data represent some 10 to 15 thousand bits of information from each consumer.[1]

From these data, Simmons and other similar companies prepare a large number of cross-tabulated summary reports, which might consist of information, for example, about magazine readership of nonsmokers, smokers of filtered cigarettes, smokers of menthol cigarettes, and smokers of unfiltered cigarettes. Figure 42 provides a sample cross-tabulation of the magazine preferences of beer drinkers.

These pretabulated reports often prove useful to advertisers, agencies, and the media. However, since the reports necessarily represent only a small fraction of the information available in the total sample, it has been customary for users of the information to request that specially prepared reports be generated to their specifications. Providing such reports normally involves processing requests through a batch-oriented computer system and necessarily entails delays in obtaining responses to the requests. The delays range from eight to 72 hours, depending on the nature of the problems involved in producing the batch run. It was to help cut down on the delays that the principals of IMS became interested in attempting to develop a time-shared facility for accessing this large database. Their general hypothesis was that if they could cut down on the delays involved in the process, potential users of the information might be likely to use it more extensively and effectively.

## II. THE SYSTEM

As mentioned earlier, for the purposes of this case, the "system" consists of a series of advertising analysis programs. This section will describe four types of analysis that are among the products of Interactive Market Systems. To eliminate the delays mentioned above, these products are delivered to the user through a commercial time-sharing system. We will begin with a description of the user language, i.e., the manner in which the user of the system specifies the reports desired, and then describe four types of advertising analysis reports that can be generated by means of the system.

### A.  The User Language

A substantial amount of time in the early development of the system was invested in creating a simple and straightforward user-oriented language. This language would allow the user to specify reports in a clear and concise way and would provide for relatively simple and direct interaction with the system. The development of the user language was important for two reasons. First, users of the preexisting batch-processing system had not formulated the requests for their reports themselves. Instead, their requests were typically telephoned to a company representative, who then reformulated the requests in the language of the computer system that would generate the tabulated reports. Thus the representative functioned as a technical intermediary between the users of the data and the computer system. If an on-line strategy was to

---

[1]The data for each consumer in the sample are coded in terms of a "0" or a "1" for each possible response. For instance, age is broken down into three categories: 18 to 34, 35 to 49, and 50 and over. Thus age information for a 45-year-old consumer would be coded as 0,1,0 in the three categories.

FIGURE 42    Cross-Tabulation of Beer Consumption versus Magazine Readership, in Percentages. *

| | Saturday Review | Newsweek | Time | Esquire | Sports Illustrated | Playboy | Field and Stream |
|---|---|---|---|---|---|---|---|
| Number of glasses consumed† | | | | | | | |
| Heavy | 7.2 | 6.4 | 9.1 | 9.2 | 9.9 | 9.3 | 10.5 |
| Medium | 16.1 | 18.8 | 18.4 | 20.1 | 19.4 | 23.4 | 24.2 |
| Light | 12.8 | 14.3 | 16.2 | 15.7 | 18.7 | 16.5 | 16.0 |
| Total users | 36.1 | 39.5 | 43.7 | 45.0 | 48.0 | 49.2 | 50.7 |
| Served beer but did not drink it | 8.2 | 11.6 | 8.9 | 10.5 | 11.2 | 14.0 | 13.0 |
| Total served | 44.3 | 51.1 | 52.6 | 55.5 | 59.2 | 63.2 | 63.7 |
| Total population | 100.0 | 100.0 | 100.0 | 100.0 | 100.0 | 100.0 | 100.0 |

*Assume that these hypothetical percentages are for a population of males ages 35–49.
†Heavy: 15 or more glasses in the past week. Medium: 5 to 14 glasses. Light: 1 to 4 glasses.

prove at all effective, the users of the data would have to be able to formulate their own requests at their own office sites, rather than expect a technical intermediary to be present to instruct them how to formulate their requests. Second, if it turned out to be too difficult for the user to operate the system, the system simply would not be used, regardless of its technical or theoretical capabilities.

On the basis of a goal of simplicity in what the user must do, the system leads the user through the typing of all information needed in specifying the desired report. For instance, in specifying a cross-tabulation such as that in Fig. 42, the user provides four types of information:

Description of the report itself (title, stubs, headers, need for row percentages, etc.).

Definition of the population the user desires to scan.

Specification of the portions of the population that fall in the categories defined by rows of the report.

Specification of the portions of the population that fall in the categories defined by columns in the report.

A typical row or column specification might be a statement such as the following.

MIDINC MEN: MEN.AND.INC 10–15000;

Each line consists of a stub or header (which precedes the colon) and a Boolean specification of the characteristics of people in the column or row being specified. In the example above, the stub suggests middle income men (MIDINC MEN) and is defined as having the properties from the database of being male (this is obviously just yes or no) and having an income in the range $10,000–$15,000 (another item directly obtainable from the original survey).

The specification of a population is fully as general as the specification of a row or a column. The only difference is that results for each population are printed in separate reports. Since the report title is assumed to describe the population, no stub or header is associated with this kind of item.

In general, any specification can be an arbitrary Boolean condition on any constituents in the database. In addition, the user is able to refer to an item in the database in any one of three different language forms:

Mnemonic name (for example, MEN).

An @ name, which relates to the form in which the data item is encoded by the original questionnaire (for example, @01091 represents a 1 punch in column 9 of card 1 of the original survey, and this happens to be where the answer to the question "Male?" is located).

A # quantity, which refers directly to the way the data item is actually stored in the database (#1 is block 1 of the system's data storage, #2 is block 2, etc.).

Almost all users make their requests in mnemonic or @ form, but system operations personnel often find it useful to be able to refer to the actual structure of data by # for system reliability checking and maintenance.

### B.  The Available Applications

IMS offers ten different products that are relevant to various aspects of the media selection task. Of these, only four important ones will be discussed here.

### 1.  Cross-Tabulation

Cross-tabulation is used to gain an understanding of the target population and its habits or demographics. The sample cross-tabulation in Fig. 42 might have been used to help understand the beer consumption habits of readers of the magazines listed across the top of the report. In order to specify that this cross-tabulation was required, a user would start by describing the target population and then specify the headings and stubs for the rows and columns. Although this type of report can provide useful insights into the habits of a target population, it is limited in that either mental or mechanical transformation is required before the report can influence media-selection decisions.

### 2.  Market Segmentation Analysis by Means of AID

One of the characteristics of many markets is segmentation into a series of submarkets that have unique combinations of characteristics. These combinations can be viewed as interactions among the characteristics, which produce results above and beyond those produced by the same characteristics in isolation. To help system users study market segmentation and the effects of interactions, IMS acquired the use of AID, a program for Automatic Interaction Detection.[2] This program creates successive splits of multivariate database. From all possible splits, the next split chosen is the one that explains the largest proportion of the remaining unexplained variance in a criterion function. For example, consider the analysis of a target population consisting of 1000 men about each of whom available data include age, salary, beer consumption, cigarette consumption, and type of occupation. The variable being analyzed is consumption of pizza, which is viewed as either high or low. An AID run might produce the equivalent of Fig. 43 as a representation of the relationship between these characteristics and the consumption of pizza. The splits in the figure are strictly binary, although this need not be so. The partial analysis in Fig. 43 might indicate to a marketer of pizza that high beer consumers aged 18–29 could be a very good target population for a media campaign, whereas low beer consumers with high salaries would not be. (This assumes that pizza consumption is not a major determinant of beer consumption.) The marketer would design his media campaign accordingly. AID is better than cross-tabbing for the analysis of market segments because the combined effects of characteristics, rather than the characteristics taken independently, are often needed to explain consumer behavior. Cross-tabs are useful for observing the characteristics independently, but AID goes further toward the understanding of their interactions.

### 3.  Reach and Frequency Analysis

Reach and frequency analysis is a method for evaluating the potential effectiveness of a planned media campaign. Reach and frequency are characteristics of a given

---

[2]This program is described by Sonquist and Morgan (1964).

*FIGURE 43     An Example of the Analysis of Interactions*

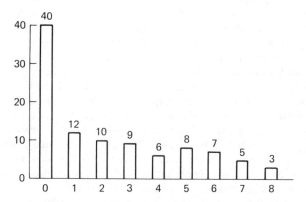

```
                              ┌──────────┬─────────────────────────────┐
                              │1,000 MEN │ 600 High pizza consumption   │
                              │          │ 400 Low pizza consumption    │
                              └──────────┴─────────────────────────────┘
            ┌──────────────────────┴──────────────────────┐
    ┌───────────────┐                              ┌───────────────┐
    │  HIGH BEER    │                              │  LOW BEER     │
    │   350 High    │                              │   250 High    │
    │   200 Low     │                              │   200 Low     │
    └───────────────┘                              └───────────────┘
   ┌──────┴──────┐                              ┌──────┴──────┐
┌───────────┐ ┌───────────┐              ┌─────────────┐ ┌─────────────┐
│ AGE 18-29 │ │ AGE 30-44 │              │ HIGH SALARY │ │ LOW SALARY  │
│ 210 High  │ │ 140 High  │              │  90 High    │ │ 160 High    │
│ 100 Low   │ │ 100 Low   │              │ 120 Low     │ │  80 Low     │
└───────────┘ └───────────┘              └─────────────┘ └─────────────┘
```

media schedule and a target population. The *reach* of a media schedule is the number of people who looked at any of the magazines in a media schedule. The *frequency* relates to a breakdown of the target population in terms of subgroups based on the number of exposures to the media in the campaign. For example, consider a media campaign consisting of four ads in *Time* and four in *Newsweek* intended to influence a target population of 100 people. The distribution of the population in terms of the number of issues read that contained these insertions might be as shown in Fig. 44. The reach of this campaign is $100 - 40 = 60$. The number of "gross impressions" (i.e., the number of ads that may have been seen) is

$$0 \times 40 + 1 \times 12 + 2 \times 10 + \ldots + 8 \times 3 = 224.$$

This gives an average frequency of $224/100 = 2.24$.

*FIGURE 44*

Since reach and frequency analysis provides a way of evaluating the potential effectiveness of a planned media campaign, it goes a step further than cross-tabulation as a tool in allocating advertising dollars. In fact, the input to such an analysis is a cross-tabulation of the media habits and product usage habits of the target population. The output is the reach and frequency analysis, which can be extended to include a cost-effectiveness ranking of various media.

Reach and frequency analysis is useful, but it has limitations. There is a great deal of disagreement as to the proper mix of reach and frequency. For instance, consider two media campaigns, A and B, which put one insertion into each of 24 magazines and four insertions into each of six magazines, respectively. Campaign A has a reach of 94 percent and an average frequency of 1.9, and B has an 89 percent reach and an average frequency of 2.7. Obviously, there is a trade-off between reach and frequency, which must be resolved by the person making the media-scheduling decision.

Another question concerns the weighting that should be given to various points along the frequency distribution. Some advertising experts give no weight to people who see 0–3 insertions. The feeling among these experts is that four or more insertions must be seen before the message will be absorbed. Further, some believe that media should be weighted on the basis of different levels of recall that appear to exist for different magazines. The reason for such a recall differential is that some magazines tend to be read much more carefully and thoroughly than others.

## 4.  Optimization

Given a target population and an advertising budget, the objective of this program is to select a media schedule that maximizes any linear combination of net reach and gross impressions. Alternatively, it can minimize cost, subject to a net reach goal. The program includes the consideration of media discounts and the ability to handle multiple target groups and to weight them according to their market potential. Currently in development are capabilities to handle average frequency constraints and to produce optimal or near-optimal schedules for objective functions other than linear combinations of reach and gross impressions.

This optimization is sold on a two-part basis. The first part, called STEP-1, uses a strategy of incremental hill climbing. In other words, it produces a schedule by the sequential choice of additional insertions that are marginally most cost-effective in terms of the objective. For instance, at a certain point in developing the initial schedule, the program will choose between the marginal benefit of a third insertion in *Newsweek* and a seventh insertion in *Reader's Digest* or a first insertion in *New Yorker*. When the total budget has been used, STEP-1 terminates.

The second part, called the MASTER optimization, uses a branch and bound technique to backtrack through the various choices that were made by STEP-1. At each branch (choice) of the decision tree, it searches for other choices that may lead toward "global optimality," in spite of the fact that the initial choice was consistent with the most efficient local increment. The initial stepwise generation process never removes an insertion once it is included. Rather, it simply adds the marginally best insertion at each step. The branch and bound process makes it possible to replace insertions chosen earlier. For a large optimization, this process could go on indefinitely. To avoid this, it is halted after a fixed amount of computer time.

Optimization is sold as a guide rather than as an end-all. Maximizing some combination of reach and frequency with budget constraints is only one of the objectives of a media campaign. Other objectives include the type of image that is to be projected and possible attempts to go after new market segments. For instance, a campaign with a 90 percent reach may be preferred to an equally costly campaign with a 92 percent reach if the first campaign emphasizes magazines with a particularly desirable editorial content. However, it is considered desirable to know how much reach and frequency are being sacrificed for these other factors whenever a decision of this type is made.

### C.  The Evolution of the IMS Products

An interview with the president of IMS began with the question, "How did IMS evolve?" He answered "The first thing is that it was the wrong product. When we went into this, our concept was that our users wanted us to cross-tabulate syndicated media research data like Simmons data. We found out that what they really wanted us to do (in large part) was a specific form of cross-tab which would serve as input to subsequent (reach and frequency and cost-effectiveness) analysis. It turned out that the subsequent analyses were the bread and butter of the business.

"This happened because our original approach was to develop a product in cooperation with an initial large client which provided financial support. This client wanted the ability to do cross-tabs, which they would transcribe later for use as input to their own internal reach and frequency system. When we went to other potential clients, they liked the cross-tabs but said that what they really wanted was reach and frequency analysis. It took the better part of four months to develop a basic capability to meet these needs."

Customers using the reach and frequency analysis were often observed attempting to perform a rough heuristic optimization of a schedule according to some relatively simple budget constraints. The two designers developed a way to use a branch and bound technique to perform this optimization automatically. Before producing a completed product, they surveyed the customers to ascertain whether such a procedure would be used. The survey indicated clearly that optimization would *not* be a viable product. In spite of this, the optimization procedure was programmed and made available. It has proved to be a widely used tool.

## III.  THE USES OF THE IMS SYSTEM

IMS views its business as the answering of media and marketing questions of a repetitive and semistandardized nature by means of time-shared computation. In order to understand the use of its products, one must consider a number of contexts, such as the objectives of the user groups, the level and responsibilities of the actual users of the system, and the importance of the interactive aspects of the system.

### A.  The Objectives of User Groups

As stated earlier, three distinct groups of people are interested in the allocation of advertising dollars to media: advertisers, media representatives, and agencies. These groups have different objectives for the allocation, however. The advertisers want to allocate their advertising dollars in a cost-effective way in the hope that advertising will have a positive net impact on their business. The media people want to persuade advertisers and agencies to allocate advertising dollars to their magazines or TV programs. The agencies want to do a good job of allocating advertising dollars in order that they will be retained by the advertisers. Each group attempts to use IMS to further its own objectives. For clarity, we will discuss the users in the order of increasing use of IMS products.

### 1. *Advertisers*

Advertisers use IMS for identification of their target markets, but they are not at present major users of the IMS media systems for a number of reasons. First is the fact that cross-tabulation is not a particularly good tool for identifying target markets. It provides some information about simple correlations between two attributes, but it can't help in understanding the interaction between multiple attributes across a population. The program for Automatic Interaction Detection (AID) was obtained recently in order to help attract more advertisers as IMS customers.

Another relevant fact is that advertisers typically have a market research department rather than a media research department. The brand managers and the people in the market research department are interested in market identification, usage patterns, and so on, but may not be especially interested in the readership of any one magazine. Consistent with this emphasis, they often prefer to focus their efforts on questions within their industry and to delegate media-related decisions to agencies, which have expertise in that area. This general attitude is reinforced by the fact that each company using the Simmons database must pay a substantial sum for it before being permitted to ask IMS to machine it. Since agencies have paid for access to that database and are familiar with it, advertisers often consider it unnecessary for them to incur both the monetary and time-related human costs of accessing that database directly.

A third factor is the nature of the data available through IMS and, sometimes, its inconsistency with industry data. IMS products reference Simmons and Simmons-like data and other data related to local television market analysis. As with much media research data, this is not the kind of data needed by industry market research departments. (This is not a criticism of the data per se, since it is designed primarily to meet the needs of media planning rather than of general marketing analysis.) In addition, many advertisers feel that Simmons data does not contain enough detail to be useful for their marketing decisions. For example, a men's apparel manufacturer would want a breakdown of usage by brands of slacks, but Simmons data contains only the purchase of slacks in general. Marketers of seasonal products find Simmons data inadequate because the data released is annual rather than seasonal. Furthermore, industry market data is generated on the basis of a wide range of measurement assumptions and with various periodicities, such as bimonthly; quarterly; on 4, 4, 5 week schedules; and so on. When the measurement assumptions and periodicity of data conflict with those of data from external sources, such as IMS, people in industry find it difficult to assimilate all the data into a unified and cogent viewpoint. As a result, they tend to disregard data that is not consistent with industry standards.

A general direction in attracting advertisers is the development of capabilities that meet the needs of advertisers more directly. Advertisers frequently use numeric (rather than binary) panel data and product tracking data. Such data is hierarchical in nature and has the characteristic of being updated infrequently. Several years of thinking have gone into work on a data management scheme that uses internal directories in an efficient manner to expedite the retrieval of existing data and the appending of new data. Using this capability, advertisers may be able to reconcile the existing inconsistencies of geography and periodicity between their data and the databases IMS maintains. When these capabilities are fully operational and their implications are fully known, advertisers may increase their use of IMS products.

## 2. Agencies

Agencies use IMS as a planning tool in answering such questions as: How should we design advertising campaigns? What are the appropriate definitions of our market segments? Will we get our messages across to our market segments? What is an appropriate mix of print and television? What kind of performance can we expect from a given network or magazine buy? How satisfactory is a given schedule in terms of cost-effectiveness (based on some combination of audience reach or total impressions per unit cost)?

The IMS applications mentioned earlier can be used in answering those questions. Cross-tabulation and AID are used for market identification. Reach and frequency analysis is used to measure the potential impact of a given media schedule on a target population. By including the costs of insertions in various media, the reach and frequency analysis can be extended to a cost-effectiveness analysis. Given a criterion such as maximizing some combination of reach and frequency within a given budget or minimizing cost while achieving a certain reach, the optimization program can generate media schedules that more or less satisfy the criterion. Thus IMS provides the agencies with answers to many of their important questions about media scheduling.

Advertising agencies are of course involved with many other activities, such as looking for potential business, marketing their own services, creating copy, and so on. IMS helps them directly in the media-scheduling task, but it can also provide peripheral aid in the other areas. An example is the preparation of "switch presentations." Occasionally, certain agencies learn that a given brand handled by a competitor has been weak in an otherwise favorable product segment. The agency prepares a presentation arguing that they can do the job better than their competitor. In the course of the presentation, a reach and frequency analysis or optimization can provide a convincing quantitative argument to supplement or enhance other, more qualitative arguments about copy quality, tactics, and so on. One example was a case in which a reputedly "creative" agency had implemented for a major hardgoods manufacturer a media campaign that had a total reach of 64 percent. A competitive agency found that this was 12 percent below the reach of a campaign that was generated by the optimization. This fact was used as part of a switch presentation, which argued that although qualitative considerations (e.g., editorial content) could legitimately lead to media campaigns that were several points below the numerical optimum, the advertiser should certainly be aware that the campaign designed by its current agency was 12 points below optimum. Within six months, that advertiser switched agencies.

## 3. Media

Magazines constitute the largest portion of IMS's customer base. They use IMS in two ways. Most important to them is the competitive use of IMS information and analyses in acquiring new advertising business and in maintaining existing business. In addition, they often run off reports requested specifically by advertisers or agencies.

The latter usage is quite routine. Basically, it is a matter of buyers asking sellers to provide information in the hope of gaining business. Occasionally, a given advertiser will ask three or four magazines to run a similar series of reports. In some cases, magazines find it advantageous to interpret the request for an analysis in such a way that the analysis turns out favorably. By comparing the analyses that are submitted, the advertiser can gain a greater understanding of the desirability of his options in terms of target population and campaign design.

The self-initiated use of IMS reports by magazines is often quite competitive. In attempting to sell advertising pages to a particular advertiser or agency, one magazine will say "If you use us, you will get 3 percent more coverage in your media campaign." Another will reply, "Yes, but we're cheaper." A third will argue that although the target market is men in general, their magazine is particularly strong among men 18–29 with high salaries and an interest in sports.

Thus some of the use of IMS reports is explained by the fact that there does not exist a totally proven algorithm by which advertisers can "optimize with respect to their advertising expenditures." In order to develop such an algorithm, it would be necessary to have precise knowledge of the impact of advertising on sales, the recall of advertising as a function of advertising quality and number of exposures, the persuasiveness of any given advertising insertion, the attractiveness of particular types of appeals to various market segments, etc. None of these factors are known with certainty.

Prior to the existence of Simmons-like data and IMS-like retrieval capabilities, it was quite difficult to develop any kind of quantitative basis for advertising decisions. Fundamentally the decision was either qualitative or based on cost per unit of circulation. With the advent of these additional capabilities, it is now possible to design media campaigns with an underlying quantitative rationale based on the industry's standard concepts of target markets, reach and frequency, and cost-effectiveness. The competitive use of these concepts contributes to the movement toward the quantitative. Instead of relying solely on personal relationships, past advertising, and qualitative arguments, magazines vying for the same advertising pages are forced to produce quantitative justifications as part of their sales effort.

From the viewpoint of the advertiser or agency, the competitive use of IMS reports is a source of information and insight that may be helpful in optimizing the design of media campaigns. From the viewpoint of the magazine, the optimization problem is on a different level. The magazine's goal in using IMS is to find and present to the advertiser an objective function (including a target population) optimized by a media schedule that includes that magazine. The problem is to find a persuasive and advantageous objective function and target market, rather than to optimize a given objective function over a rigidly specified population. This is one of the areas in which the on-line character of IMS is sometimes important. With slow turnaround, it would be difficult to do a reasonably efficient job of searching for a favorable sales pitch. Of course, this kind of activity can go just so far, since usable results must be persuasive and sensible.

Still, there is always the possibility that the data will be stretched or misused, either out of ignorance or in a particularly aggressive sales effort. In order to minimize the possibility of such misuse, the reports include automatically generated asterisk patterns and footnotes whenever samples become too small and whenever the original Simmons data is adjusted in any way. Excessively small samples sometimes occur when a restricted target population is broken down further. Inferences based on such a sample tend to have a high probability of error. It is possible to use small samples, but the user should certainly be aware that the results may go awry.

The original Simmons data can be adjusted for a number of reasons. For instance, it may be appropriate to adjust the readership of a rapidly growing magazine such as *Penthouse* or *Intellectual Digest* upward by a percentage depending on the average circulation during the most recent Simmons study versus the circulation at the time of the analysis. The impact of ads in magazines with small page sizes is sometimes discounted. The editorial content of some magazines is considered particularly favorable or unfavorable for certain purposes or target populations. Accordingly, their readerships may receive an additional subjective weighting. Much of the weighting activity occurs in agencies in an attempt to introduce subjective factors into the quantitative analysis. Magazines tend to be reluctant to indulge in weighting, because tampering with the original data may appear somewhat suspicious. At minimum, the magazine would have to explain any adjustments very carefully. This would not be a problem for an agency, since its task is to decide on a campaign rather than to influence someone else's media decision.

The optimization program is used by some magazines. The sales pitch is very simple: "Here is a numerically optimal media campaign. Please note that the computer has chosen us as part of this campaign after evaluating 20,000 (or 10,000 or 40,000) schedules." This type of approach must be used advisedly if the magazine occasionally fails to appear on optimized schedules. Using the optimization for a presentation is tantamount to saying to an agency or advertiser that that is how the magazine wishes to be judged.

A problem for some magazines in using IMS reports for aggressive marketing of advertising pages is that the salesmen are often quite unsophisticated about the types of quantitative analysis that are available. As a result, even a well-reasoned analysis can go flat when it is being presented to the potential buyer.

### B. The Human Aspects of System Usage

Whatever the objectives of the advertiser, agency, or magazine using IMS, someone must decide exactly what is needed and must express the request to the computer. The level and responsibility of the person who actually types at the terminal vary widely. About 50 percent of the time, it is someone with no decision-making prerogatives, who is told by a superior exactly which cross-tabs or reach and frequency analyses are to be run. A typical request might be: "Run these three schedules against these three databases or target markets. Give me a cost-efficiency for each one. Do a cost-ranking on the publications, and give me a STEP-1 schedule construction analysis against the first target market." The user logs on, types the specifications for the reports, and returns the reports to the superior. This type of user is often a very junior researcher rather than a clerk or typist since people without training may not understand enough about the analysis to operate the terminal effectively.

Another 35 percent of the users are empowered to make a limited range of substantive decisions. When they see numbers that look particularly good or unusual, they can try to pursue that path on their own. Up to 15 percent of the users are full project directors. The smaller the magazine or agency, the more likely it is that a managerial individual will work directly with the system, principally because there isn't a large amount of staff help available. Major users of IMS may turn out 20 to 30 reports a day. In such companies, people with decision-making responsibility simply don't have the time to type at the terminal. Thus the decision to use IMS is made by managers, whereas the nitty-gritty of using the system is often left to more junior personnel.

In addition to the range of responsibility among the users, there is also a wide range in terms of substantive knowledge and understanding of the computer system. A secretary may know how to type inputs to the system but may not understand the intricacies of the advertising business. A project manager may know what is wanted but may be extremely uncomfortable at a terminal. Sometimes a potential user who is weak in both spheres knows only that there is a problem to which IMS may be relevant.

IMS has chosen a business strategy that recognizes the wide range of users and user needs. This strategy is reflected in a high level of customer service and support. In the words of the president of IMS, "This isn't a time-sharing business. We don't sell these specialized products the way others sell commercial time-sharing. We are not selling connect time, storage, and CPU usage. Rather, we are selling answers to media and marketing questions of a repetitive and semistandardized nature. The users must be able to turn to us as knowledgeable experts, not computer specialists. Consulting (concerning both the workings of the system and its application to substantive problems) is part of the product and something we expect our clients to ask us for. People are an integral part of the IMS system."

User assistance begins with a two-day training session for new users. Typically, one or two persons will run the system in each company, unless it is large or does quite a lot of media research. For most new users , the idea of coding a report is new and requires some practice. For some, the form and significance of the database require detailed explanation. The most difficult task is to understand the code books that describe the content and format of the databases. A minor but observable phenomenon is that the mechanics of logging onto the time-sharing system and then calling the IMS programs are sometimes mysterious to new users. Part of the problem is that they don't really know when they are talking to the time-sharing system's supervisory program and when they are talking to an IMS application program. This is particularly true when they make major typing errors that go unnoticed until it is too late to recover gracefully.

In general, users are not good typists, although this problem tends to be minor. Typing seems to become burdensome only in the specification of large crosstabs involving 20 or 30 rows and columns. Considerable frustration results when the time-sharing system or phone lines go down, or when the user makes a nonrecoverable typing mistake while specifying a large report. Fortunately, technical reliability is good, and IMS programs are forgiving of typing errors that are detected immediately. However, these programs can't anticipate all the possible ways in which unnoticed user errors can be compounded. As a result, users are urged to phone IMS whenever they get lost or confused while specifying a report. Since the report specifications are built up as files that are stored on a disk attached to a DEC-10, it is often possible for someone at IMS to modify files containing erroneous report specifications that the user cannot correct (e.g., accidentally typed break characters, incorrect commands on previous steps, etc.).[3]

A member of the IMS staff whose main job was user support and education stated that phone calls from clients broke down as follows: clarification of coding and logic errors, 25 percent; correction of user typing errors, 20 percent; taking orders for reports from users who don't have a terminal, 25 percent; and general inquiries and other help, 30 percent. With the exception of large users, particularly certain magazines, clients tend not to have enough time to learn the IMS system efficiently enough to solve everything on their own. People who use the system once a week need more help than people who use it once a day. Still, the staff member's feeling was that most users don't have a great deal of trouble with the system, because they have two phones and are smart enough to call IMS when they have trouble.

Users have the option of typing requests at their own terminals or asking IMS personnel to produce the reports for them. For convenience and speed, frequent users of IMS products prefer to use the terminals. In most instances, the complexity of the required analysis determines whether the system is used with or without consultation. Before embarking on a difficult or unusual analysis, even experienced or expert users will call to discuss the validity of the procedure. Furthermore, since really large jobs take a lot of time and tend to be error-prone, users often request that IMS personnel either do these jobs for them or check their coding before the run.

## C.  The Importance of Industrywide Concepts and Standards

One of the original developers of the system stated that IMS had been successful for two basic reasons. One was technical and managerial expertise. The second was the fact that its major customers knew about Simmons data before IMS existed and had experience in trying to apply this data to repetitive problems. When approached by IMS sales personnel, therefore, they realized they would not have to invest a lot of time and effort in understanding the concepts behind the system and the ways in which the system might help them. Instead of having to sell both problem and solution, IMS had to sell only the technical or other advantages of using its answering system rather than some other answering system for this restricted class of repetitive questions.

One implication of this familiarity and acceptance was a simplified design process for the developers of IMS software. The industry had grown to accept certain numbers that were computed in certain ways and certain analyses that were run with those numbers. For this reason, the tasks of identifying and collecting relevant information, finding measures, designing systems, etc., were greatly simplified. The business opportunity for IMS was basically one of developing better ways to deliver the existing types of analysis. Developing new types of analysis—e.g., optimization and an improved type of reach and frequency—were secondary considerations originally.

Another implication is that knowledgeable users seldom have serious difficulty in defining exactly what they want. The kinds of reports that IMS produces are

---

[3]The files containing report specifications can be accessed and modified by IBM personnel using the TECO text-editing language.

in essence the standardized information requirements of the user community. In settings where the information requirements are not standard to a user community, a common problem in using computers effectively is to specify exactly what the manager or user wants.

A final implication is that the question of who does the typing—a clerk or a manager—is a false question. In each case, the manager or decisionmaker is the one who wants the information and who does the planning (and who decides to purchase the services of IMS and its competitors). IMS has chosen to provide active support for both the problem formulation and the clerical input phases of system use for customers with various levels of expertise. Thus less knowledgeable customers will be able to use IMS, sophisticated customers will receive help with sophisticated analysis, and all customers can count on help with clerical functions.

### D. The Importance of Being On-Line

IMS provides an on-line capability for answering semistandard media and marketing questions. Providing on-line service is important for four reasons: speed and convenience, the ability to monitor results and test alternatives, personnel development, and privacy.

#### 1. Speed and Convenience

Speed and convenience appear to be important aspects of the IMS facilities. Clients want fast response. In the words of one IMS staff member, "Being on-line per se isn't the main point. If the reports came fast, but by carrier pigeon, that would be good enough. But 20 minutes might not be fast enough. People get spoiled very easily. They expect a system to be there always, to give rapid response, to crash rarely, and so on. If you fail on any of these, people don't think they're getting what they should be getting." The general opinion was that next-day service would result in a major loss of business.

#### 2. Monitoring Results and Testing Alternatives

Being on-line means that the user gets results back quickly. This has two implications. The first is that most coding and logic errors can be found almost immediately. The user doesn't have to wait until the next day or next week to discover that the aim should have been a slightly different target population or form of analysis. Thus it is possible to correct errors without having to reconstruct what the user (or the user's boss) was thinking about and why the analysis was important.

It is possible to test alternatives by telling a junior researcher to run a prespecified series of reports that cover the apparent range of alternatives. If the reports that come back indicate that other alternatives should be tested, the junior researcher can be instructed accordingly. The on-line nature of the system will help the researcher debug the coding but won't affect the actual consideration of alternatives.

The on-line nature of IMS is more important when a person with greater decision-making prerogative uses it to explore potential target markets or to develop a quantitative rationale for a sales presentation. The user can then start with a general goal and can try to attain that goal by means of an adaptive search. This is a relatively atypical use of IMS, but it does occur occasionally.

3. *Personnel Development*

One reason clients want to use IMS as an on-line system is that they want their staff to know what is going on. If a manager calls IMS to order a given run, the staff doesn't learn anything. By using an on-line terminal, junior people learn about the Simmons data and about the types of analysis that are available through IMS. As a result, the client organizations can develop greater knowledge and expertise in their personnel.

4. *Privacy*

Customers sometimes don't want to publicize what they are doing. If they do the reports themselves, using the on-line capabilities of IMS, there will be no leakage.

## IV. THE TECHNICAL IMPLEMENTATION

The previous sections concerned the content and use of IMS products. This final section brings an additional perspective by discussing some of the technical aspects of the development of IMS.

### A. The Initial Idea

In 1969, as a result of conversations concerning the advertising industry, the current president of IMS decided to form the company that would become IMS. He felt that the application of sophisticated on-line technologies to the standard problems of media selection constituted a fine business opportunity. He enlisted the aid of two colleagues who were exceptionally competent programming experts. After months of effort, he also persuaded an existing company to provide monetary support for a feasibility study to test his assumptions about the technical requirements of the system he envisioned. The feasibility study was performed in the summer of 1969 with favorable results.

### B. Technical Issues

In light of the favorable results, the development of a prototype system was authorized by the financial backers. The two programming experts were to design the prototype and get it running as quickly as was possible.

Early discussions among the three principals made it clear that IMS did not want to become involved in the direct management of computer operations. This decision was based on the following considerations.

1.  The substantial amount of capital that would be required even to lease an appropriately large computer

2.  The necessity of hiring and managing an operations staff

3.  The headaches involved in operating a computer installation

4.  The availability of a large number of existing time-sharing computer services

The decision was made to seek a supplier of time-sharing services who would permit (and encourage) a "piggy-backing" operation, whereby IMS customers would use a computer provided by the time-sharing service and software provided by IMS. A survey of existing time-sharing services was undertaken. The criteria used for evaluating services offered by the various suppliers included the following.

1.  Price (charges for terminal time, CPU, storage, and peripherals)

2.  Protection capabilities

3.  Support of terminals

4.  Financial stability

5.  Availability of both higher level language and assembly language

6.  System development tools (debugging languages, diagnostics, etc.)

7.  System availability

8.  System reliability

9.  Storage capacity

10.  Communications

The vendor chosen offered a DEC-10 computer with both Fortran IV and the assembly language MACRO. At this point, it was necessary to consider whether to proceed and implement in Fortran or in MACRO. The factors arguing for Fortran were its ease of reading and writing and its self-documentation properties. On the other side, MACRO was much more flexible (i.e., more of the machine features could be used), and some MACRO code was clearly going to be necessary. Both implementers (the third principal was to be in charge of business operations) felt they would much rather defer this decision. However, since a target date for completion of the first running system was only a couple of months away, delays to collect further information could not be tolerated. They therefore decided to commit themselves to an implementation program that involved as much Fortran as possible, using MACRO only to perform functions that could not be handled effectively in the higher-level language.

They also agreed to divide the task of developing expertise in using the new (at least to them) time-sharing system. One assumed the task of learning the Fortran system and its supporting software. The other would concentrate on the machine itself and MACRO. In particular, he would be responsible for learning the intricacies of using the standard input/output control system. Since the implementers had worked on several projects before, each felt confident that he could count on the expertise of the other. It was clear that eventually both would have to learn all aspects of the system's operation. Nonetheless, by dividing the problem, each could become an active source of information for the other and could thus cut down on the time required to find out about obscure aspects of the system's operation.

In the design and implementation of IMS, great care was taken to avoid predicating any of the programs on features that were available only on the time-sharing system supplied by the vendor. Rather, the only facilities used were those that were part of the normal DEC-10 time-sharing system and were therefore common to virtually all DEC-10 time-sharing systems in general use. The value of this approach became apparent when technical problems forced the vendor to curtail service to unacceptable levels. The response by IMS was simply to move to another vendor. The move was accomplished with relatively little pain because the IMS software was highly compatible with that of the new vendor.

Implementation of the system was divided into three distinct components: (1) development of a user language; (2) development of a program organization and strategy; and (3) development of a strategy for storing the rather large quantity of data in the Simmons database.

The user language has already been discussed. The question of program organization was important for two reasons. First, since computer time would be a major component in the cost of delivering information to the consumer, it was necessary to develop a program organization strategy for keeping costs to a reasonable minimum. Second, the implementers recognized that if the system was successful, it would necessarily grow and change over time. It was thus necessary to develop an organization strategy flexible enough to allow the system to grow substantially without incurring the costs of rewriting a large part of it. The details of program organization could be the topic of a case study in themselves. The basic point here is that the issue was considered very important and was addressed carefully. Decisions about storage strategy were also important. Early in the design process, a commitment was made to deliver any report that could logically be constructed from the data in the database. This commitment necessitated the maintenance of the entire database in disaggregated form and made it impossible to reduce the large quantity of data in storage simply by aggregating over some of the dimensions. It would therefore be fruitful to try to compact the data as much as possible without losing any. To some extent, it is necessary in such circumstances to face a trade-off between computation costs and storage costs, since any compaction scheme usually involves incurring costs both for the compaction of the data and for later expansion. In this case, however, the implementers felt that most of the data expansion could be performed by the computer while other data were being retrieved, thus minimizing the net effect on computer costs.

It is also significant that the data delivered by the data supplier are organized by question within the respondent. Thus, all data about respondent 1 appear in the first "card" of the database, all data about respondent 2 in the second "card," etc. Answering questions in an on-line system with the data stored in this form would be very expensive both in time and money, since any request for retrieval would involve scanning through the entire database. For instance, a cross-tabulation involving all male adults would require a search through every "card" in the database to determine whether that respondent was a male adult and should therefore be included. This type of inefficient search was avoided by a process called database inversion, whereby the data are reorganized, in this case by question rather than by respondent. In other words, for every question in the database, a list is maintained of all consumers with a "1." To find the number of consumers who read *Newsweek* and are heavy beer drinkers, it is necessary only to compare the list of *Newsweek* readers with the list of heavy beer drinkers. This inversion process proved to be a cost-effective trade-off. To answer any specific question using the inverted file, it is necessary only to access those parts of the database that refer to that question, thus allowing a great saving in both elapsed time and money. Costs are incurred by inverting the data file into one organized by respondent within question, but since it is necessary to perform this function only once each year when the new data are collected, this cost can be amortized over all the retrievals performed during the year.

With these issues resolved, it seemed logical to divide the systems effort into two distinct parts. The first was the development of an interactive system that would carry on a dialogue with the user, retrieve requested information, and print the desired reports. The second part of the system (the so-called periodic system) would be run only when it was necessary to build a new database from basic data. This part of the system would also have the responsibility of allowing the operations personnel to develop new directories through which the users could access the information. It was necessary to introduce several levels of directories in order to provide flexibility in the user language, as well as to adapt the system to minor modifications in the sample from year to year. (For example, questions are often added or deleted, or the responses to the questions are recorded in different places in the basic data set.) Later, a third part of the system was developed, namely, that associated with such auxiliary functions as customer billing and the capability of estimating the cost of a given run prior to actually making it.

In the early stages of system implementation, the designers decided to maintain a system log that recorded the occurrence of major system operations (e.g., input/output operations, major calculations, etc.). Information written into this log file consists of such quantities as job identification, time of day, elapsed amount of computer time, cost up to this point in the calculation, and indication of what activity is going on at this time. This information proved to be immensely useful during the debugging of the system. When errors arose and crashes occurred, it was possible to look at the log to discover the most recent major activity of the system and thus get a good notion of the cause of the difficulties. By the addition of a few extra logging commands, it was possible to bill customers directly from the system log file. Thus the auxiliary program written to enable the system to produce customer bills could perform its function by merely scanning the system log file.

Perhaps most important of all, by inspecting and summarizing the system log, operations personnel could easily locate those parts of the overall system that were incurring the largest costs. These high-cost stages of the process were obvious places to look for ways to reduce costs. For example, there was always the option of attempting to optimize the actual referencing of the disk during data retrieval, but the log showed that the referencing of the disk was not a very substantial cost element in the system. As a result, this aspect of system operation has not been reworked to reduce costs. On the other hand, the portion of the system devoted to tabulating the final report proved to be a major cost component. By focusing efforts in this area, the designers were able to achieve cost reductions in excess of 70 percent. Thus the decision to include a system log proved to be tremendously important to the overall computational efficiency of the process.

## C.  Implications of the Design Methodology: A Managerial View

In retrospect, the president of IMS has mixed feelings about the way the IMS systems developed. He feels that the system was built in a rather unstructured way, which worked in this particular situation, but which would not be a generally acceptable way of implementing most systems. His comments can be paraphrased in the following way.

The two system designers worked remarkably well together. Their ability to communicate with one another was quite important in reducing many of the problems of systems design and implementation. They had worked together before and had a common set of design philosophies in many areas. They had great confidence in each other and could settle differences quickly. Because they also had a tremendous amount of ability, they could take more risks than others.

Their approach was quite unstructured. There was no prior system specification or design document. Basically, they started with some design strategies and tried to implement those strategies. They tried to isolate the major problems and to produce a viable, running tool. In seven weeks they produced something that turned out to be a robust implementation. We are still able to use major pieces of what they did, although we have gone back and redone much of it in order to make it more general. For 99 percent of the systems community, it would have been impossible to do what they did in that length of time. (Other commitments restricted the length of time they could spend on the system.)

Unfortunately, a lot of long-term problems came bundled in with the short-term returns. What we got after those seven amazing weeks was a viable and running but undocumented and nonunderstandable tool. We have an organization of talented humans, not talented superhumans. There are costs of implementing a system the way we did, and those costs burden you for a long time afterward.

The lack of documentation in the original system was a serious problem. The designers were not simplistic programmers. They were elegant, insightful programmers. Elegant, insightful code is extremely difficult to figure out. We have spent the better part of two and a half years trying to get under control the things they did in the beginning. That's expensive. But it doesn't demean what they did—that was absolutely remarkable.

The president of IMS went on to explain that for several years the original designers were occasionally called in on a consulting basis to help in developing new applications that required special skill and insight. The relationship was still quite good. The designers were involved in academic careers, and it was never assumed that they would devote a great deal of time to the day-to-day affairs of IMS after the prototype was working.

With the development of a full-time, in-house system staff, the consulting arrangement was no longer necessary, particularly since the head of the staff was reluctant to work with the original designers because of his lack of control. He was the person responsible for the system, yet he couldn't have control over people who work in such an unstructured way. Currently, documentation and other aspects of the system are well under control, with in-house people in charge of all aspects of the system. During the development process described above, the original designers developed methods of on-line documentation in order to prevent recurrence of the problems mentioned here. However, their methods were not adopted by the in-house systems staff, who found that more "traditional" methods sufficed.

The vice president of IMS noted a problem that developed after the initial implementation: "We started with a simple system (disregarding lack of documentation and complex programming), and it grew into a monster. People kept adding this bell and that whistle. Our marketing people kept going to our systems people and saying they needed this or that for some special client.

"We weren't aware we were building such a monster. What happened was that the naive user began to have difficulty using our system because he had to answer 88 questions just to get out one number. We have since gone back and revised many of our user I/O routines to have a quick and easy way of generating simple reports. The more sophisticated users can use the more complete versions of the programs."

### Questions for the Reader

1. At the beginning of the case, it was stated that the "system" was actually a combination of a database and a series of analysis programs. Was this a "system"? Was it more or less of a system than the systems described in previous cases?

2. Why was the development of this system technically challenging? Describe the principal technical challenges in the earlier cases and compare the challenges. Were they basically similar or did they concern quite different issues?

3. It has been said that the key issues in the computer area are primarily behavioral rather than technical. Discuss this statement in the light of this case and previous cases.

4. What type of data is used in this system? Compare the data in this system with the data in the other cases in terms of source, accuracy, timeliness, etc.

5. If this system was designed to support analysis related to advertising decisions, why was it used least by advertisers?

6. How was the technical implementation in this case different from that in other cases? Was it reasonable to allow the technical implementation to proceed as it did?

# THE GREAT NORTHERN BANK: A SYSTEM FOR BUDGETING, PLANNING, AND CONTROL

CASE SIX

## I. INTRODUCTION

This case study concerns an on-line system for planning, budgeting, and control at the Great Northern Bank. The system was originally conceived in late 1969 by the head of the Administration and Control Department as a budgeting and control tool within the bank's Computer Services Division. He called it Budget Information System, or BIS. When this case was completed (summer, 1974), the system was still called BIS, even though it had been expanded to include long-range planning, profit and loss consolidations, and various other applications. The case begins with a brief explanation of the organizational setting and an overview of the history of the system. Next is a section on the operation of BIS, the functions it serves, and the ways it is used. The final section provides additional perspectives on the history, acceptance, use, and future development of BIS.

## II. SETTING AND BACKGROUND

### A. The Setting

The Great Northern Bank is one of the leading banks in a large city. Its basic organizational structure is illustrated in Fig. 45. There are five line divisions, an operating group, and a corporate staff function. The Automated Customer Services Division was originally part of the Computer Services Division in the operating group, but the two have been split. For purposes of this case, it is important to note that there is a Corporate Comptroller's Division, which communicates with the other line and staff divisions through division comptrollers assigned to the division, rather than to the corporate comptroller.

The bank's line divisions are as follows:

1. *Investment and Financial Planning* is responsible for determining the financial investment plan for the bank.

2. *Mutual Funds* serves as a custodian of mutual funds and performs related services.

3. *Commercial Banking* is concerned with major loans to companies and with a wide variety of other retail services, such as checking and savings accounts, Master Charge, personal loans, safe-deposit boxes, and so on.

4. *Personal Trust* provides a variety of services concerned with creating and maintaining trusts.

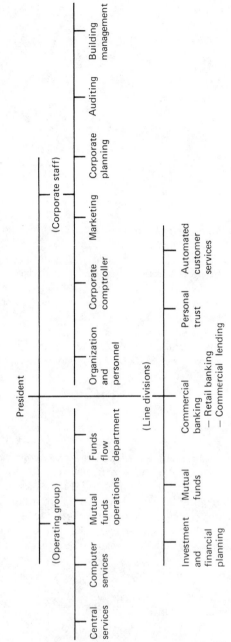

FIGURE 45   Organization Chart of the Great Northern Bank

5. *Automated Customer Services* markets computer software services to other financial institutions.

The Computer Services Division is organized as shown in Fig. 46. The departments and functions of the division are as follows:

1. *Operations* operates and controls the daily activities of the computer facility and handles related activities, such as keypunching.

2. *Planning and Development* performs analysis, design, and maintenance of various computer-based systems in the bank's divisions. These are primarily transaction-oriented systems.

3. *Administration and Control*

    *a)* *Internal Account Managers* serve as a link between the Computer Services Division and the other user divisions in operational troubleshooting and maintenance and in the development of computer-based systems.

    b) The *Comptroller* performs the financial accounting, billing, and budgeting for the Computer Services Division.

    c) *Management Science* applies the principles of management science in solving a wide range of problems in various divisions. The computer-based systems that are developed here tend to be for analysis, planning, and management control, rather than for transaction processing.

*FIGURE 46 The Computer Services Division*

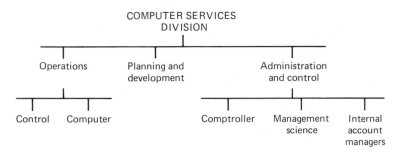

## B. Overview of the History of BIS

The idea of developing BIS was conceived in late 1969 by Mr. Ronald Hansen, who at that time was head of the Administration and Control Department within the Computer Services Division. The original purpose of BIS was to serve as a tool for planning and control in the Computer Services Division. Mr. Hansen was supported by top managers of the bank, who felt it was important to get a good handle on computer expenses and budgets.

Because of its limited scope and cost, the original project required only the approval of the head of the Computer Services Division. It was first operative during the spring of 1970, with Mr. Hansen and the comptroller of the Computer Services Division as the main users of the system. As Mr. Hansen gained experience with the use of BIS, he came to realize that its basic concepts might be applicable to bankwide budgeting and planning.

The first step in a major marketing and educational effort was to persuade several other divisions to use BIS. The first new division to come on board was Automated Customer Services, whose comptroller was a close friend of the comptroller of the Computer Services Division. Next, the comptroller of Commercial Banking began to use BIS. At this point, the bank's president was convinced that BIS could be useful on a bankwide basis. With his backing, a proposal for a bankwide implementation of BIS for budgeting, planning, and performance evaluation went through the bank's project-priority reporting system. On the basis of an analysis done by the Comptroller's Division, which would become an important user of the expanded version of BIS, the top management of the bank approved the proposal. By 1974, much of the expanded BIS (plus P and L consolidation) was operational, although final details were still being tailored to the various users' needs.

Mr. Hansen, who had been transferred in the interim to an area with line responsibility, felt that the main challenge in the development of the system involved questions of internal politics, marketing, and education. He felt that BIS had been the beneficiary of strong support from top management. Without that support, he doubted whether BIS would have progressed as far as it had. He also said that his main disappointment with BIS was the length of time it took to get the thing going.

Much of the development and implementation of BIS has been the responsibility of Mr. Clive Ferguson, who is head of Management Science and has a background similar to Mr. Hansen's. One of Mr. Ferguson's main activities in this area has been an ongoing process of trying to get more people in more divisions to understand and use BIS. Part of his strategy for accomplishing this goal was to reduce out-of-pocket costs of running BIS by transferring it from the external time-sharing system to the in-house computer system when this became feasible technically because of an upgrading of the in-house computer. The changeover utilized IBM's VM/CMS software on the new 370/158, plus MVT batch processing under the VM monitor.

Mr. Ferguson feels that a key to the success of BIS is the evolutionary and modular approach that was taken initially and has been maintained. Conceptually, the database and its maintenance are separated from the applications programs. Therefore, new parts of the database and new applications can be added with relative ease. While under the aegis of the bankwide BIS approval, individual modifications to BIS are justified on an incremental basis on their own merit. This is possible because of the modular way in which BIS is constructed.

Mr. Ferguson agrees with Mr. Hansen's view that systems of this sort are almost necessarily in a continuous state of evolution. Their corollary to this is that when such a system stops changing, people are no longer really using it or thinking about it.

## III.  THE OPERATION AND USE OF BIS

What is called BIS currently entails a series of separate applications, including performance evaluation (controlling to budgets) with an emphasis on staff and operating divisions, bankwide planning, P and L statement analysis (control from a line division's viewpoint), and a number of special applications. This section will briefly discuss the technical aspects of BIS but will concentrate on its applications.

## A. The BIS Database

The BIS database consists of 50-word records designed for use in a budgeting and planning context. These records are organized by cost center and by transaction code within cost center. Each record has four words of identifier information, the two above and two others that provide additional identification. The remaining 46 words include the following information.

Five-year actual history (5YA)

Last year's actual by month (MALY)

This year's actual by month (MATY)

This year's revised budget by month (MBTY)

Current long-range plan (LRP)

Figure 47 illustrates the layout of a typical record in the BIS database in early 1973. Last year's actual total can be obtained by summing the monthly totals. After the new long-range plan is accepted, the new plan replaces the old plan.

*FIGURE 47   A Typical Record in the BIS Database in Early 1973*

|  | Cost center | | Transaction code | | Numeric type | | Alpha type |
|---|---|---|---|---|---|---|---|
| 5YA | 1967 | 1968 | 1969 | 1970 | 1971 | | |
| MALY | (1972) J | F | M | A | M | J | |
| | J | A | S | O | N | D | |
| MATY | (1973) J | F | M | A | M | J | |
| | J | A | S | O | N | D | |
| MBTY | (1973) J | F | M | A | M | J | |
| | J | A | S | O | N | D | |
| LRP | 1973 | 1974 | 1975 | 1976 | 1977 | | |

Within cost center, there are five transaction types:

1. Direct expenses, broken down further by expense class, e.g., telephone, public relations, stationery.

2. Indirect expenses, i.e., allocation of overhead to the charged cost center, broken down by charging division.

3. For charging cost centers, an allocation of expenses on a 100 percent basis by charged cost center.

4. Charges for the data processing services of the Computer Services Division.

5. Miscellaneous data, such as transaction volumes, incomes, and personnel by grade.

Thus the basic budgeting and planning activity of the bank takes place at the cost center level. Naturally, cost center data can be aggregated in planning or evaluating the performance of such larger units as product lines, profit centers, departments, and divisions. In order to produce P and L's, it was necessary to augment the BIS database with income data by profit center and then to allocate expense data by cost center to the appropriate profit centers and functions or sub-functions. Considerable effort went into the specification of this process.

The budget and long-range plan figures are entered on-line to individual planning files by the cost center manager and/or the division comptroller. The "actual" figures in the database are updated by standard monthly update runs. The information is obtained from other accounting systems within the bank. This procedure is consistent with the BIS philosophy of tying together systems rather than replacing them.

Access to the database is controlled by means of a user ID, which must be typed while "logging in." Each user is given full access only to the data within that user's jurisdiction. Thus a cost center manager may access only records affecting that cost center, whereas a division comptroller has access to all records affecting that division. In the future, it may be possible to compare data across cost centers and divisions for certain data types. This might be done by means of a data extractor program, which, given certain security constraints, would develop a file that could be manipulated by means of the inquiry capabilities of BIS. Currently, security is not considered a major issue. Given the nontechnical nature of the system users and the relatively routine nature of the data on BIS, the simple password scheme is considered adequate.

## B.  The Hardware

BIS had to be developed through an external time-sharing vendor, because the bank's computer facility did not have time-sharing capabilities. At one point, the bank changed time-sharing vendors in order to take advantage of virtual memory and other features that were available from a second vendor with an IBM 360/67. At that time, some of the BIS application programs (which are in Fortran) were rewritten to take advantage of these additional facilities and to make them compatible with the bank's IBM hardware and software. In order to decrease out-of-pocket costs of running BIS, it was brought in-house under VM/CMS.

Users accessed BIS by means of video display terminals or printing terminals. A user working at a video terminal could get hard copy of reports by means of a command that created a file for printing on a terminal. Although this hard copy was adequate for some purposes, producing lengthy reports at a terminal was awkward and costly. For this reason, and because the terminals produced reports that didn't look as good as line-printer output and couldn't be copied clearly, lengthy reports were printed off-line. While BIS was being used through the time-sharing vendor, it was necessary to perform such off-line printing at the time-sharing vendor's local printer and then to send the report to the bank by taxicab. At that time, therefore, using off-line facilities in this way resulted in both convenience and a cost savings because of the reduced charge for connect time.

## C.  BIS Applications

As stated earlier, BIS is used for a number of different applications, which are considered parts of an entity called BIS for a number of reasons. The first is historical. In its current form BIS is an outgrowth of the original budgeting system developed by Mr. Hansen in 1970. The second reason is that a single database architecture consisting of the 50-word records described earlier serves all applications. Third, BIS applications and inquiry routines are written in the form of interlocking subroutines. Often-repeated procedures are performed by general subroutines that may be called by any BIS program. A series of BIS applications will be described in turn.

1.   *Interactive Exception Reporting*

Interactive exception reporting is a performance evaluation function whereby a cost center manager or division comptroller prepares a *customized* monthly variance report comparing actual with budgeted performance by cost center or centers. This may be done in either interactive or noninteractive mode. This interactive exception reporting feature is also available in the planning package discussed in the next section. Performance for each data type (direct expenses, indirect expenses, incomes, and personnel) may be evaluated. When the performance evaluation function is invoked, the user is able to tailor the report by means of a number of choices that are presented. For instance, the user can title the report, specify the transaction types to be considered, and specify whether the output should be at a terminal or a printer. It is possible to perform computations (additions, percentages, etc.), create forecasts using a linear regression function, retrieve selected data, print comments, and prepare graphs. Most important for exception reporting, the user can state both dollar and percentage criteria for what constitutes an exception. By doing so, the user can eliminate from the report those expense items that are within budget and do not require additional attention.

The main users of the interactive exception reporting features are the comptrollers of the Computer Services and Commercial Banking Divisions. Since these are large divisions with many cost centers, tight budgetary control is significant. Both comptrollers feel that BIS is an important aid in budgetary control. An explanation of their use of it follows.

On or after the eighth business day of each month, the BIS database is updated with direct expenses (by type within cost center) for the previous month. All of this data is obtained from the Responsibility Accounting System (RAS), a previously developed transaction-oriented expense accounting system, which captures and displays all transactions within each expense class for each cost center. The comptroller specifies dollar and percentage criteria for the BIS exception report. He scans the exceptions on-line, annotating them with any comments deemed appropriate. Next, the report goes to the cost center manager, who attempts to justify any variances the comptroller did not understand. In explaining these variances, the cost center manager often refers to the detailed batch report generated monthly by RAS (e.g., whereas BIS will state that the month's expense for stationery was $2,000, RAS will have this information broken down by transaction). Later, the cost center manager returns the annotated report to the comptroller and discusses the significance of any variances that may indicate problems.

Thus BIS is designed as a tool for facilitating communication between comptrollers and cost center managers. Instead of being forced to thumb through the transaction-by-transaction detail of the RAS batch reports, the comptroller can allow BIS to select for his attention only those expense classes in each cost center that merit his attention. The cost center manager, who should have a close fix on the detailed expenses, can then refer to RAS output to explain what happened wherever it isn't apparent.

Although exception reports can be generated in batch mode, the on-line nature of BIS permits the customizing and annotation of these reports. The cost center manager knows that the exception report contains only variances that really require some explanation. In addition, the process of customizing exception reports means that both comptrollers and cost center managers will have given some thought to the exceptions prior to their meeting, thus facilitating communication.

In the Comptroller's Division and in some of the line divisions, comptrollers currently prefer to use RAS for budgetary control. RAS is thoroughly debugged and well understood, and it has been used for five years. The comptrollers in these divisions are generally satisfied with RAS and see no overwhelming reason to start using terminals to do something they can do adequately without terminals. Some feel that the necessary investment of time and effort in learning this aspect of BIS simply isn't warranted.

The key issue here is apparently the amount of effort that is required in controlling to budgets. In a large division with many cost centers, BIS facilitates this process. In smaller divisions, where control of expenses is not a difficult problem, BIS does not have as much to offer.

The implicit counterargument from Management Science is that BIS offers greater capabilities than RAS. All the comptrollers get with RAS is one large monthly batch report with a lot of extraneous information, i.e., a great deal of detail about expense classes that are within budget tolerances and require no action. With BIS they would get whatever report they wanted, including only the desired transaction types and only those expense classes that are outside tolerances. Furthermore, it would be possible to do trend analysis and other kinds of relevant computations with the capabilities in BIS. As stated repeatedly by the people interviewed, a major internal marketing effort will be necessary if BIS is to be used more extensively for this purpose.

A member of the Comptroller's Division felt that if the people in the Comptroller's Division started to use BIS for their monthly monitoring of budgetary performance in the divisions, the division comptrollers might feel a need to use BIS. That is, when they met with people from the Corporate Comptroller's Division who were using BIS, they would expect to see BIS reports and might feel obligated to come armed with their own BIS reports. This individual actually doubted that the Comptroller's Division would use BIS for this purpose, because it was generally felt that RAS summary reports were adequate.

The same individual felt that including budgeted incomes in BIS in addition to expenses might increase its potential usefulness. Historically, the bank has been quite tight on the expense side but not so precise on the income side. If BIS could aid in the analysis of incomes, it might find greater use. This fact is recognized by the Management Science Department. One of the next extensions of BIS will be the inclusion of budgeted incomes in its database.


2. *Interactive Planning Tools*

Interactive planning tools are a series of programs that are available for developing both the long-range plan and the yearly budget. There are two types of functions.

The first is Planner, which provides a status report by expense type (with a selective exception reporting feature) for the manager to review before entering the interactive planning mode. This report consists of two sections: a standard format section, which may be produced without interaction, and a customized section, generated in interactive mode for exception testing and analysis by means of standard analysis routines. The second type of function, Projection, leads managers through each data item that must be included in their long-range plans or annual budgets. It allows them to experiment with various projections for any item and to perform revisions in order to help them arrive at plans that are appropriate. The program relieves managers of clerical work and allows them to spend more time thinking about alternatives. BIS utility programs summarize and print the plans in a standard report format.

In order to understand the ways BIS is used for planning, one must have a familiarity with the bank's planning process. The process changes from year to year, but generally goes as follows: Bank managers attend an annual planned-growth conference in May. At the conference, they work out the kinds of strategies and programs they want to pursue over the five-year planning horizon. Last year, most of the "major new ventures" had been worked out prior to the conference and were revised as a result of the conference. In the previous year, most of the new ventures were generated as a result of the conference. The financial implications of the long-range plan are developed fully after the conference (i.e., by mid-July). Around September, the budget for the next year is firmed up. Historically, this process of generating and firming up the budget has required a great deal of clerical work on three levels. First, the cost center manager has to develop a one-year budget and five-year plan that seems adequate. In the past, cost center managers have found this task highly distasteful, particularly since it involved extensions of payroll taxes and other items that applied differently to employees of different grades, to part-time vs. full-time employees, and to overtime vs. regular time. Next, the division comptroller must consolidate the cost center tabulations to produce a one-year budget and five-year plan for the division. Whenever the total budget seems too high, iteration and pruning of cost center budgets are required. Each iteration requires more clerical work. Finally, the Corporate Comptroller's Division consolidates all budgets to produce an overall financial plan for the bank. Once again, consultations between the division comptrollers and the Corporate Comptroller's Division result in revisions of the division budgets and yet more paperwork on all three levels. In addition to the work required of clerks and accountants, a painful typing effort was required of secretaries, who were fine at typing letters but not particularly good at typing numbers in columns.

It is generally felt that BIS has played a valuable role in reducing the clerical work at all levels. BIS aids the cost center managers and division comptrollers in preparing a budget by providing listings for each expense class of last year's actuals, this year's budgeted, year-to-year actuals, and projected actuals for the remainder of the year. This helps the cost center manager reconstruct the thinking of last year and helps to produce a new budget, which incorporates both the history and the new considerations that have become relevant. BIS allows the user to generate new plans that differ from previous ones by percentages or fixed amounts. This streamlines the clerical process of producing a plan and allows the user to consider several alternative plans before deciding which one to submit. Particularly important is the automatic calculation of estimated expenditures for taxes, office space, insurance, and so on. The cost center manager merely states the number of people of each grade and the number of square feet; BIS produces the dollar amounts.

The consolidation of divisional plans is now done automatically. The Comptroller's Division can now look at both individual budgets and the overall bank budget and five-year plan without expending a considerable effort on manual consolidations. As a result of using BIS, the Comptroller's Division spent nothing on overtime in preparing the bankwide budget. Previously, a significant amount was budgeted and used. This year, no overtime is budgeted for that purpose.

In 1974, BIS allowed the Comptroller's Division to correct a faulty budgeting assumption that had affected each division and cost center. The error was introduced when a new member of the staff budgeted pay increases as though they were all effective on January 1. In fact, the salary review process is spread across the year. The action necessary to correct the error was to reduce budgeted salary increases by one-half. With the cooperation of several members of the Comptroller's Division and several people from Management Science, the change was accomplished in an hour.

By expediting the production of budgets and long-range plans, BIS frees time formerly needed for clerical functions and allows the comptrollers on both levels to consider more alternatives and thus to do more analysis. The assumption is that these improvements in the planning process will lead to "better" plans. Whether "better" plans are being produced is not known with certainty, but it is clear that tighter and more consistent plans are developed, given the assumptions on which the plans are based. The plans are tighter because the calculations are more accurate and because the growth of the plan can be tracked from year to year. The plans are more consistent because it is possible to make comparisons across divisions or cost centers and thereby to spot discrepancies.

Although BIS has received considerable acceptance in this area, it has met varying degrees of resistance in some divisions. One problem is that some division comptrollers simply didn't like to use terminals. After experience with the time savings afforded by BIS, the comptrollers who found BIS most useful became more enthusiastic.

A more basic problem than reluctance to use computer terminals is that generating plans is an important and time-consuming operation mainly in the larger divisions, such as Computer Services, Commercial Banking, and Mutual Funds. In the smaller divisions, the problem BIS attacks is not an important one, and consequently BIS is not considered especially helpful. An example is the Investment and Financial Planning Division, which has only 42 people, one of whom serves as a part-time comptroller. Unlike the large, high-volume, transaction-oriented divisions, which must control expenses involving many hundreds of employees, this division has no major problem with planning. Fully half the people in the division are salaried professionals performing economic and financial analysis. Since an on-line computer system is not needed for control of expenses in this area, the part-time comptroller tends to consider BIS an imposition rather than an aid. Initially, instead of merely spending an hour or so filling out a spread sheet, he was forced to input his budget to BIS so that it could be included in the bankwide budget. In spite of the fact that a clerk can now enter the division's budget directly from a spread sheet, and although the comptroller understands that BIS is quite useful in the larger divisions, he still resents having to spend time using it, not to speak of the time spent learning to use it. Furthermore, the division has to pay for using it.

*3. Profit and Loss Statements*

The newest application in BIS is the quarterly preparation of P and L statements. Formerly these statements were prepared by hand by cost analysts in the Comptroller's Division. It was a cumbersome clerical process involving the allocation of expense categories from cost centers to profit centers, product lines, and products throughout the bank. In order to program the allocation process, a major effort was required in defining the relationships between particular cost centers and profit centers and in capturing and allocating incomes. This computerized P and L consolidation process is currently in the implementation stage. When it is ready, transfers will be made automatically by the computer rather than by hand. The cost analysts will spend more of their time analyzing the P and L statements rather than simply preparing them.

A Comptroller's Division cost analyst who was involved in this implementation process was extremely enthusiastic about BIS. The computer was now doing awkward consolidations that he had done previously using pencil and calculator. He could now spend more time working as a cost analyst instead of as a high-priced clerk.

Initially, that cost analyst and others in his department had been apprehensive about the introduction of BIS. After initial training, he became more enthusiastic as he started to realize how much time and effort it would save. At that point, he discerned a fairly even split among colleagues who were either "for" or "against" the computer. Fear of replacement was an important component of the feelings of those in the latter group. In his words, people in that group began to cite "any little problems" that would come up as a reason why the computer was not appropriate. For instance, they made much of the fact that the computer always seemed to go down during demonstrations. The opinions of some of those individuals changed when it became apparent that BIS would become a useful tool and would not take away their jobs.

The out-of-pocket cost of using BIS for quarterly P and L consolidations may be a problem. One manager said that a meeting had been scheduled at which this matter would be discussed. As mentioned earlier, one strategy for reducing out-of-pocket expenses was to bring BIS in-house as soon as was feasible. Since this has now been accomplished, there is hope that the implementation process may run more smoothly.

*4. Free-Form Inquiry, Analysis, and Report Preparation*

In effect, the free-form inquiry, analysis, and report preparation application is a report generator. It is a group of small BIS applications that allow users to structure their own reports based on information available in the database. They can specify the data they want to examine, the computations and logical operations they want to perform, and the output desired. The available functions include compute, display, forecast (using regression), graph, query, print, revision, list, store, and so on.

The initial idea was that the planning and budgeting application programs would provide standard uses of BIS, whereas the inquiry capabilities would allow users to generate other reports they might want on an ad hoc basis. Ideally, they would be able to do so without the help of a programmer.

To date, BIS has been used mostly for standard budgeting and planning applications. Except as subroutines called by application programs within BIS, the inquiry and report generation capabilities have received only minimal use. Most of this use was by the comptrollers of Computer Services and Commercial Banking, who occasionally performed trend analysis by means of these capabilities. Both felt that inquiry had significant long-range potential and regretted that they didn't have enough time to make greater use of it. They felt that it was a way to get a better fix on the overall expense picture, and they hoped they would be able to allocate more time to its use.

The day-to-day time pressure of routine work is only one explanation of the minimal use of the inquiry capabilities to date. Another is that extensive training in using these functions has not yet been provided. Further, many users are still in the process of gaining facility with the standard aspects of BIS. They are quite happy to wait until they are confident with the basics before proceeding to more advanced uses. A third point made by one of those interviewed is that many who are not computer professionals lack motivation and interest regarding "imaginative" or "original" uses of BIS (or other computer systems). So long as BIS applications save time and help them directly with their problems, they will use the system. However, expecting them to design their own reports on an ad hoc basis may be unrealistic. In general, it appears that the inquiry functions will continue receiving minimal use until it can be demonstrated that potential users can employ them for accomplishing genuinely significant results.

### 5. Sophisticated Management Aids

An area that has not received much attention is sophisticated aids to management. In internal education flyers that were circulated, this area was mentioned as one in which BIS might have potential for growth. According to these flyers, relevant techniques might include linear programming, model building, and probabilistic analysis. Models might be used in the preparation of long-range plans that managers could fine-tune. These models or analytic techniques would be used in conjunction with BIS but might include non-BIS data or programs.

To date, some modeling efforts have been undertaken, but primarily not as part of BIS. Mr. Hansen feels that BIS developments along these lines may be more limited than he initially anticipated, because the types of financial and accounting data that are maintained on BIS are not the kinds of data that would tend to be useful in modeling efforts.

## IV.  PERSPECTIVES ON BIS: PAST, CURRENT, AND FUTURE

### A.  Past

Like many other on-line systems, BIS has evolved over time. It was originally conceived by Mr. Hansen as a planning and control system for the Computer Services Division. After its successful use was demonstrated in that division, comptrollers in two other divisions began to use it. During that period, the database was expanding continually in terms of data included and cost centers covered. As a result of discussions with the bank president and other top managers, a favorable decision was returned on a proposal for a bankwide implementation of BIS for budgeting, planning, and P and L analysis. The bankwide implementation would require that all budgets and actual expenses and income figures be included in BIS. Only then could bankwide consolidations be performed automatically.

Although the entry of budgets is required of all comptrollers and/or cost center managers, the use of BIS is by no means obligatory. The comptrollers of several larger divisions find BIS extremely helpful in developing budgets and in controlling to those budgets, whereas comptrollers of several small divisions merely enter their budgets into BIS but make no real use of the system.

As in most systems involving large numbers of people, politics, marketing, education, learning time, and fear of displacement have appeared as considerations at various times. Politics became particularly important at the time of the decision to go bankwide. Without strong support from the top, BIS would not have developed as far as it has. The opposite side of this issue is that some of the people who were affected in one way or another by BIS were not and still are not particularly enthusiastic about its usefulness. Some of these individuals were satisfied with existing batch systems, such as RAS, and were not pleased about the prospect of learning to do things by means of computer terminals. Some felt they were being forced to act as clerks rather than as managers or analysts.

Almost everyone interviewed stated explicitly that marketing and educational efforts on the part of the Management Science Department have been quite important and should continue to be important. One interesting aspect was the wide variation in people's estimates of how long it would take to learn to use BIS effectively. The two comptrollers who had used BIS most extensively stated that their cost center managers could learn to use it in two or three terminal sessions. Other individuals stated that learning to use BIS took "a long time" and required a burdensome amount of training. Naturally, this variation depended on the number and type of applications that were being taught and on the interest and ability of the individual. In retrospect, it was rather like the question of whether a glass is half-full or half-empty, with enthusiastic individuals coming out on the half-full side.

The same phenomenon applied to comments on the reliability of time-sharing in general. A cost analyst, who occasionally lost a full hour of work when the system went down, would not let this disturb him, because BIS usually helped him accomplish in an hour tasks that had previously required a full day. At the same time, he noted that those who were against the expansion of BIS into their areas of work seemed never to forget that the computer went down during a demo (apparently it happened several times).

Given the existence of top management support, Mr. Hansen felt that the main problems in developing BIS were mechanical rather than political. As always happens in systems involving a great deal of data from various sources, painstaking effort went into defining data items, resolving accounting and budgeting inconsistencies among cost centers and divisions, and obtaining clean data. Occasionally, the resolution of inconsistencies in order to develop a workable overall system required that individuals change some of the ways they had been doing things. Needless to say, some were not pleased.

## B.  Current

BIS appears to have had a significant impact on the process of planning and control to budgets in several of the divisions of the bank.

1.  From the viewpoint of cost center managers, it removes much of the drudgery from the process of developing long-range plans and annual budgets.

2.  By decreasing the time and effort required to generate plans, it allows cost center managers to think about their plans a bit more, to consider alternatives, and to spend more time on profitable work, such as selling and talking to customers.

3.  BIS facilitates the review of proposed plans and of monthly cost center performance. By eliminating much of the clerical paperwork and displaying relevant information on clear, well-designed forms, it aids in communication between comptrollers and cost center managers.

4.  BIS standardizes forms and procedures, thus facilitating the consolidation and interpretation of bankwide budgets and performance.

5.  BIS eliminates the need for a great deal of typing that secretaries were once forced to do.

The impact of BIS on P and L consolidations will probably run parallel to the impact noted above for the earlier applications.

As stated earlier, it is not known with certainty whether the use of BIS resulted in "better" plans or tighter control. The effects listed above are in terms of process, not in terms of what constitutes a good plan or an effective control system. The obvious problem is that it is extremely difficult (if at all possible) to measure the quality of a given plan or of a control system. Thus all that can be said at this point is that BIS has clearly improved the process and, by doing so, has probably improved the outcome at least a little.

The on-line nature of BIS appears to be convenient but not entirely essential for the planning and performance evaluation functions. If necessary, it would probably be possible to redesign BIS to perform many of its most helpful functions on the basis of coding sheets that could be filled out by cost center managers or comptrollers and keyed in by clerks. However, some advantages would be lost. People would not be able to consider alternative plans as easily. Iterations of the budgeting process would take more time—a serious consequence in the light of the time pressure and deadlines under which planning and budgeting are performed. Coding and typing errors would become more of a problem because they would not become apparent until the next day, thus causing further delays. The inquiry capabilities could not be used effectively. Thus the on-line nature of BIS makes it easier and more convenient to use, but it is not intrinsic to the basic tasks at hand.

Several steps have been taken to alleviate some of the problems related to the use of time-sharing by BIS. Secondary budgeting and performance evaluation applications have been developed whereby comptrollers and cost center managers who are not interested in exploiting the on-line nature of BIS can have a clerk enter their data from coding sheets. In addition, a user-invoked "insurance option" has been created. When this option is used, temporary work areas are stored on disk at specified intervals. If the computer goes down, the user loses only several minutes of work, not an hour. (Previously, this could happen if the system went down just before the completion of the budget for a given cost center.) Since charges for disk I/O can be substantial, the user has the responsibility of specifying how often the temporary work area is stored.

## C.  Future

The current work on BIS has two main thrusts. One is the completion of the implementation of existing applications. This includes the further implementation of P and L consolidations and possibly some additional tailoring of the planning applications to the needs of specific users. The other is a continuing effort to persuade more people to use BIS. The premise of this effort is that BIS currently contains many capabilities that should be useful to people who don't know about them or who aren't using them for various reasons; through an educational effort, it may be possible to persuade these people that they should give BIS a chance.

### Questions for the Reader

1.  Why are budgeting, planning, and control important? Is it possible to estimate the value of an improved budgetary control process?

2.  How does BIS improve the budgetary control process? Is it possible to estimate the value of BIS?

3.  How could BIS be expanded? Is anything missing in terms of data? After reviewing the taxonomy of decision support systems in Chapter 2, describe other approaches for supporting budgetary decision making that might be tried.

4.  Who was Mr. Hansen's client (that is, the president or the comptrollers) in this case? Who were the principal clients for systems developers in the other cases?

5.  The need to "sell the system" was noted several times. Compare the efforts to sell the system in this case and in the other cases.

6.  Is it important that BIS be on-line? Compare it with the systems in other cases with regard to the significance of on-line access.

# THE COST OF LIVING COUNCIL: DECISION SUPPORT IN A REGULATORY SETTING

## CASE SEVEN

### I. INTRODUCTION

Acting under the power granted him by the Economic Stabilization Act of 1970, and in response to varied economic pressures, President Nixon initiated a phased Economic Stabilization Program on August 15, 1971. As outlined by the President in his address to the nation, the goals of this program were to stabilize the economy, to reduce inflation, to minimize unemployment, to improve the competitive position of the United States in world trade, to protect the purchasing power of the dollar, and to increase the rate of economic expansion. In order the help accomplish these goals, a regulatory agency called the Cost of Living Council (CLC) was established to regulate wages and prices. This case study traces the history of a computer system utilized by the Pay Board, the branch of the CLC that regulated wage increases.

The history of the Economic Stabilization Program is fascinating from many viewpoints—economic, political, organizational, to name a few. Note that the focus of this study is the development and use of a particular computer system that evolved over the course of two years. Details concerning other aspects of the overall history are presented to give context and meaning to the discussion of this system.

Exhibit 1 presents a brief overview of the four phases of the Economic Stabilization Program. Phase I was basically a holding action to prevent further deterioration of the economic situation before workable ongoing controls could be instituted. Phase II imposed governmental controls over wage and price increases. Phase III loosened the controls over most industries and relied instead on governmental monitoring and voluntary compliance to guidelines. Phase IV returned to more active controls over price increases.

This case study is based on interviews conducted during June and December 1973, i.e., during Phases III and IV. Much of the information presented here is a distillation of the recollections and then current concerns of staff members of the Cost of Living Council. Since the history of the Pay Board system is complicated, this case begins by describing what in retrospect was the problem faced by system designers at the Pay Board as they planned for Phase II. Simply stated, the problem was to create a computer system that would help the Pay Board accomplish its goals in Phase II. Following the introduction of many of the main issues, the remainder of the case describes the development and use of this system at the Pay Board during Phases II and III. An appendix describes extensions of the system at the Price Commission during Phase IV.

---

**Exhibit 1:  Overview of the Economic Stabilization Program**

*Phase I* (August 15, 1971–November 13, 1971)

A 90-day wage and price freeze was established. A tax revision package was proposed, which included the repeal of the auto excise tax, a 10 percent surcharge on imports, and negotiations leading to revaluation of world currencies. The Cost of Living Council was created to provide policy guidance. The goals of Phase I were to cause an immediate 90-day halt to wage and price increases, to restore confidence in the economy by changing the expectations of the American people about inflation, and to provide the necessary time to develop a plan for the following phase.

*Phase II* (November 13, 1971–January 11, 1973)

The Cost of Living Council was directed to establish policy, administer the program, determine program coverage, and direct compliance. The Price Commission and Pay Board were created to review price and pay increases, respectively. Other advisory committees were created. The Internal Revenue Service was designated as the enforcement arm of the program. The goals of Phase II were to reduce the rate of inflation to 2–3 percent by the end of 1972, to avoid inhibiting a more vigorous economic expansion, to keep the bureaucracy small, to administer a flexible and equitable system, and to reduce inflationary expectations.

*Phase III* (January 11, 1973–June 14, 1973)

Phase II requirements for prior approval of changes in wages and prices were eliminated, except in the food, health services, and construction industries, which remained subject to mandatory controls. Although premised on voluntary compliance, the program retained authority to reimpose specific controls where

---

## II. THE PROBLEM: DESIGNING A COMPUTER SYSTEM FOR THE PAY BOARD IN PHASE II

For the purpose of explaining the development of the Phase II computer system at the Pay Board, it would be very useful to have detailed documentation of the original goals and plans of the implementers of the first version of that system. No such documentation exists, however. What does exist is a series of recollections about what happened. The present section sets the stage by describing the organizational setting, the regulatory goals, and a series of alternative computer system goals that were apparently considered by the initial developers of the Pay Board system. Upon finishing this section, the reader should stop to consider the alternatives: Which are most important? Which seem most feasible? In this setting, where should the primary efforts be focused?

### A.  The Setting

The Cost of Living Council was established for policy guidance during Phase I. For Phase II, it was given responsibility for the establishment of policy, the administration of the regulatory program, the determination of program coverage, and the

actions occurred that were unreasonably inconsistent with the standards and goals of the program. Much of the federal control machinery was to be eliminated. This included the Price Commission, the Pay Board, and several advisory committees. The performance of companies was monitored through reviewing reports, spot checks and audits of firm records, and the use of government and trade data.

*Phase III½* (June 14, 1973–August 12, 1973)

A freeze on all retail prices, including those of food, was established for up to 60 days. Rents, wages, interest, and dividends remained within current Phase III controls. The prices paid to the producers of raw agricultural products were not frozen. The purpose of this action was to stop current inflation, which was running at an annual rate of more than 9 percent, and to provide time for the formulation of the policies and controls under which Phase IV would operate.

*Phase IV* (August 12, 1973–April 30, 1974)

Phase IV reinstituted controls but was tailored for the eventual decontrolling of the economy through increased supplies and productivity. The key features of Phase IV included:

A sector-by-sector approach with controls tailored around particular economic conditions in each sector.

More flexible exceptions policy to permit relief in cases of real hardship or to permit necessary supply increases.

Establishment of a senior committee of governmental officials to hear appeals and to continually assess the exceptions and exemptions policy.

On April 30, 1974, the Economic Stabilization Act expired, thereby terminating authority for wage and price controls.

direction of compliance. The CLC was directly responsible to the president of the United States.

General guidelines for the Phase II program were established. Inflation was to be reduced to an annual average rate of 2–3 percent by the end of 1972. While inflation was being reduced, care was to be given to maintaining a low level of unemployment that would not inhibit economic growth. A key issue was to make the system both flexible and equitable while keeping the bureaucracy small. It was hoped that a well-administered system could achieve not only a reduced rate of inflation but also a reduced public expectation of inflation as well.

The Pay Board and Price Commission were created by executive order on October 15, 1971, to be responsible for the review of pay and price increases, respectively. The Internal Revenue Service was designated as the enforcement arm of the program. All three agencies reported directly to the Cost of Living Council. Several other advisory committees were created to support the Pay Board and Price Commission. These included the Rent Board, the Construction Industry Stabilization Committee, and the Federal Mediation and Conciliation Service. The internal government relationship between these agencies and their external relationship with industry and labor are depicted in Fig. 48.

Figure 49 describes the organization of the Pay Board. The chairman reported to the Cost of Living Council. The Pay Board itself was a policy-making group that

*FIGURE 48    Organization of Phase II Price and Wage Regulation*

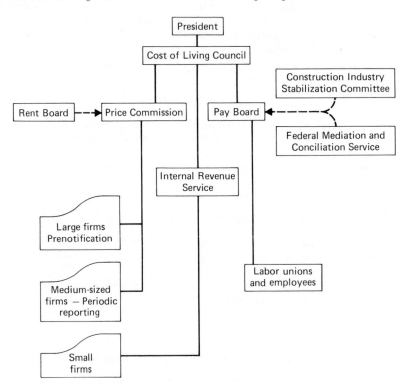

originally consisted of fifteen members, five each representing labor, management, and public interests. After some of the labor members left, the Pay Board shrank to seven. The staff operation consisted of three main branches, whose purposes were data and computer operations, economic analysis, and case analysis. The Operations Control group was responsible for maintaining the data and computer programs used to expedite processing of wage increase requests. The Office of the Chief Economist performed economic analyses that were primarily concerned with economic policies or with particular cases or industries. The Case Management and Analysis group had the responsibility of adjudicating requests for wage increases.

## B.  Framework for Adherence to the CLC Program

A 5–6 percent per year maximum increase in overall wages and prices was established. Requests for increases were to be adjudicated by comparisons with wages or prices during a recent base period. This general rule was subject to modification based on an evaluation of the impact of each individual case on the economy as a whole and the above-mentioned desire for equitability across different types of industry. The concept of varying degrees of economic impact from case to case led the CLC to establish varying degrees of monitoring and controls on the basis of the

FIGURE 49    Organization of the Pay Board

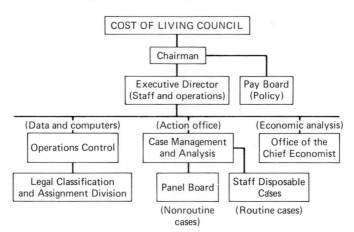

size of the firm or labor unit desiring an increase. Figure 50 depicts the relationship between size and type of procedure required.

FIGURE 50    Type of Regulation by Size of Unit

|  | **Price Commission** | **Pay Board** |
|---|---|---|
| Prenotification | 1300 firms<br>More than $100 M in sales<br>45% of U.S. sales | 500 labor units<br>More than 5000 workers<br>10% of U.S. labor force |
| Reporting | 1100 firms<br>$50–100 M in sales<br>5% of U.S. sales | 4000 labor units<br>1000–5000 workers<br>7% of U.S. labor force |
| IRS monitoring | 10 M firms<br>Less than $50 M in sales<br>50% of U.S. sales | 10 M labor units<br>Less than 1000 workers<br>83% of U.S. labor force |

Figure 50 indicates that firms representing 50 percent of total U.S. sales and labor units constituting 17 percent of the total U.S. labor force were required to furnish data to the Price Commission and Pay Board, respectively. Requirements included both historical accounting data on costs and revenues and periodic submissions providing the current status of these items. In addition, 1300 firms and 500 labor units were required to file detailed prenotification forms when price or wage increases were desired. These prenotifications were formal requests for increases, which might be granted, modified, or denied by the appropriate branch of the CLC. Information requested in prenotification form PB-3 is listed in Exhibit 2.

**Exhibit 2: Outline of Information Collected on Prenotification form PB-3**

*General Information*

Identification and address of employer and union

Industrial classification code and principal product, activity, or service

Number of employees on payroll

Location of employment

Type of adjustment

Cross-reference to previous prenotifications

*Identification of Base and Control Year*

Beginning and ending dates of base payroll period, i.e., the most recent pay period prior to the control year

Explanation of why this base period might not be representative

Beginning and ending dates of control year, i.e., the year to which the prenotification applies

*Straight-Time Hourly Rates and Hours*

Total payroll expenditures (at straight-time rates) during base period

Total work hours paid for during base period

Average straight-time hourly rate

Planned control year adjustments in straight-time hourly rates (i.e., increases in hourly pay); for each adjustment, the date of the adjustment and the dollar amount

*Employee Benefit Expenditures in Base Year and Control Year*

Base year hourly expenditures for shift differentials, overtime, vacations, holidays, sick leave, unemployment benefits, etc.

Planned control year hourly expenditures in the same categories

Base year hourly expenditures for qualified types of life insurance, group health insurance, accident benefits, annuities or funded pensions, etc.

Planned control year expenditures in the same categories

*Computation of Percent Increase*

Base compensation rate: sum of average straight-time hourly rate and average hourly rate for benefits

Control year adjustments: sum of changes in average straight-time hourly rate and average hourly rate for benefits between base year and control year

Percentage change from base year to control year

Additional supporting calculations and explanations of exceptions

## C. Case Processing at the Pay Board

The Pay Board had up to 30 days to act on prenotifications, which were grouped into three action categories.

1.    Cases within guidelines: cases involving less than a 5.5 percent adjustment; cases declared tandem or within the precedent of a previous ruling; and cases involving deferred adjustments of less than 7 percent. No adjudication was necessary for these cases, although the accuracy of the submitted calculations had to be checked.

2.    Staff-disposable cases: cases that could be adjudicated by the Case Management and Analysis group. These cases usually involved adjustments between 5.5 percent and 7 percent.

3.    Cases for the Panel Board: cases of particular importance due to their size or their impact through tandem cases; all appealed cases.

The first step in obtaining permission to increase wages and salaries was the submission by the employer of a PB-3 form to the Pay Board. As outlined in Exhibit 2, the form requested detailed information concerning the proposed wage adjustment in addition to identifying information concerning the employer and the union. Each case to be acted on by the Pay Board was placed in one of three action classes, as noted above.

When a prenotification arrived at the Pay Board, it went through the following processing steps.

Initial screening: New cases were identified as such and were logged in.

Information analysis and classification: New cases were reviewed to determine whether sufficient information was available to take action. Cases were routed to appropriate processing locations. Requests within guidelines were granted automatically. Other requests went through the remaining adjudication steps.

Labor cost accounting: A labor economist verified the consistency and accuracy of the calculations on the PB-3 form. Although these calculations were routine, the interpretation of any particular company's submission often required a substantial amount of intelligence and thought. Occasionally it was necessary to phone the company to clarify the assumptions underlying the calculations that were submitted.

Legal analysis and adjudication: This was the action step, the point at which a staff lawyer decided whether the requested increase should be granted or modified.

Typing

Review and signature

In the course of the analysis and adjudication process, it was sometimes necessary to obtain aid from the offices of the general counsel or the chief economist or direction from the executive director or the Panel Board chairman. Further action on a given case often had to await the completion of these legal, economic, or policy-oriented analyses.

The goal of case processing was speedy and equitable adjudication. Rapid turnaround was important for an obvious reason: Workers did not appreciate waiting for their increases (even though the settlements were retroactive to the appropriate date).

Arriving at an equitable settlement involved a number of considerations. There was no question about cases that were within the 5.5 percent guidelines. Those requests over 5.5 percent had to be considered both on their merits and on their impact. Even a small case could have an important impact because of the political necessity that the rulings be reasonably consistent. If similar groups received different rulings for similar requests, the system would simply blow up. The consistency notion was complicated by the fact that it had a number of dimensions. Ideally, a given case should be consistent with prior rulings concerning that company, that union, that geographical region, that industry, and tandem industries. The importance of these considerations varied from case to case. A settlement on nurses' pay in Mississippi might have no effect whatsoever on nurses' pay in New York, whereas a steel industry case involving only a small number of employees in California might have implications for steel cases across the country. Furthermore, historical tandem relationships between industries could imply that a 7 percent allowance in one industry should result in a 7 percent increase in a tandem industry.

## D.  Computer Support for the Pay Board

From the outset, it seemed likely that computerized support might help the Pay Board attain its primary goals:

Speedy and equitable adjudication of cases

Adjudication consistent with the need to control the economy

Adjudication without creating a huge bureaucracy

Computerized support in attaining these goals seemed possible in a number of areas:

Management of information

Access to information concerning other cases

Automatic case processing

Control of the case workload of the Pay Board

Administrative reporting

Development of an economic information system

Each of these possible application areas will be described in turn.

### 1.  Management of Case Information

Three different types of information were directly relevant to each case:

1.   Current information concerning the case itself, e.g., company name, desired increase, justification, etc. This constituted the information provided in the prenotification.

2.   Historical information concerning the firm or labor unit submitting the prenotification; background information concerning the industry in general. This was primarily accounting information and aggregated industry sector information.

3.   Information additions made during case processing leading to the final decision. In some instances, a great deal of additional information was required in the course of adjudication. Typically, the companies replied by mail, sending a variety of company documents and other explanatory information.

The main concern was the linking of all three types of data together in a manageable and accessible form.

### 2. *Access to Information Concerning Other Cases*

One of the principal goals of the Pay Board was the equitable adjudication of cases. This required that each case be settled in a manner reasonably consistent with previous settlements in related cases. It seemed possible that historical information concerning past settlements could be maintained in a form that made it accessible to lawyers and economists who were adjudicating new cases. An important constraint on any such application was that it had to be easy for a lawyer or economist who was not a computer programmer to use.

### 3. *Automatic Case Processing*

Motivated by the necessity of limiting the size of the regulatory bureaucracy, management was interested in the degree to which case processing could be automated. Since there were certain guidelines below which a requested increase was automatically granted, it might be possible to process these decisions automatically through the computer system. On the other hand, differences in accounting methods and labor unit terminologies might make any degree of automatic case processing infeasible.

### 4. *Control of the Case Workload of the Pay Board*

It was clear that a large number of cases would be flowing through the Pay Board. It seemed possible that a computer system could be used as a workload control mechanism to monitor and expedite the flow of cases through the case processing procedures. Given the large volume of cases that would be processed, a good tracking system might be useful in preventing cases from being lost or delayed unreasonably.

### 5. *Administrative Reporting*

It seemed likely that at least some administrative reporting would be required. Such reporting might concern cases in the adjudication process, past settlements, or other information about the progress of the Economic Stabilization Program and its impact on the U.S. economy. To say the least, the required content, format, detail, and periodicity of these reports were not immediately obvious. Another question was whether the reports would be generated automatically or generated on request and custom-tailored to each administrator's needs.

### 6. Development of an Economic Information System

One unique characteristic of the Cost of Living Council was its ability to extract normally confidential financial information from private industry. The original Defense Production Act gave the CLC the authority to gather any information deemed necessary. The implication of this information-gathering authority was that the potential existed for accumulating an up-to-date "snapshot" of the entire economy. Until that time, the most up-to-date and complete information of this type had been gathered and made available through the Commerce Department. Such data tended to be old by the time it became available.

Although not a necessity for the performance of the CLC's immediate responsibilities, it might be possible to create a large database reflecting the current state of the entire U.S. economy. Information relevant to the case processing needs of the Pay Board and Price Commission might be only a subset of the database. Other applications of this data, such as econometric modeling and forecasting, might be possible. Given the massive data-gathering effort necessary for the CLC, it might be logical to aim toward a large-scale system with greater capabilities than those dictated by the immediate short-run processing needs of the Cost of Living Council.

Regardless of which applications were to be included in the system for supporting case processing, several additional factors merited consideration.

1.  Although some information needs could be specified to a first approximation on the basis of an initial understanding of the adjudicating procedure, it was inevitable that forms, procedures, and responsibilities would change. Thus it was important that the computer system have enough flexibility to accommodate such changes without causing disruptions, delays, or inaccuracies.

2.  If adjudication was to be somewhat dependent on the data in a computer system, it was important to develop mechanisms for monitoring the accuracy of data entry, policing the system, and guaranteeing the integrity of the data. If the system users had reason to doubt the validity of the data, the system would simply break down, and it would be ignored.

3.  It was necessary that the system be capable of providing the lawyers, economists, and other users with the information they needed in a manageable format. It might be desirable that these nonprogrammer users be able to interface directly with the computer, thus eliminating the use of a computer specialist as a buffer.

### Questions for the Reader

If you were the head of Operations Control and were looking forward to the beginning of Phase II, what would you try to do? Which of the possible areas would you attack first, and how would you proceed? In thinking about any particular system, try to be clear about the issues raised by the following questions.

What data will be included?

How will the data enter the system?

Who will use the system and in what manner?

Who will be responsible for the system?

How will the system help the Pay Board attain its goals?

What could possibly go wrong with the system?

## III. THE PHASE II SYSTEM AT THE PAY BOARD

This section describes the development and use of the Phase II computer system at the Pay Board. It starts by discussing difficulties that were encountered by the Pay Board as it began to adjudicate cases. Next, it describes organizational and technical changes that resolved many of the initial problems. The computerized support for the improved case processing system is described. Finally, some of the lessons from this effort are discussed.

### A. Difficulties Encountered by the Initial Pay Board System

#### 1. Start-Up

When the Pay Board was first set up in October 1971, it seemed apparent that some kind of computer support would be necessary, although the form that the support would take was not at all obvious. Computer experts from the Department of Defense and other established agencies were lent to the Pay Board to help it get off the ground. Initially there was little continuity in either personnel or management, with some individuals "drafted" from other agencies for 30 or 60 days of work and then returning to their original assignments.

The original head of Operations Control was an articulate and intelligent man, who was viewed (in retrospect) as primarily a technical expert. The general feeling among the people interviewed was that, although technically competent, he was not user-oriented and did not really understand the job that the lawyers had to do. In particular, he did not appreciate the fact that virtually none of the lawyer/adjudicators had any background in using computers. As a result, the system that was designed did not meet the needs of the Pay Board. Although the details are no longer clear, there were apparently problems on two levels: first, the organization of case processing itself, and second, the excessive complexity of the computer system.

#### 2. The Initial Organization of Case Processing

In late 1971 and early 1972, cases were processed under a sequential station-to-station approach.[1] The steps in case processing were as follows:

Receipt in the mail room

Identification as a case

---

[1]This section is largely based on a preliminary draft of McNamar (1973).

Confirmation and classification in an information analysis section

Review for completeness of information

Entry of case tracking data into the computer system

Data and arithmetic review in a labor cost–accounting section

Analysis and adjudication in a legal section

Typing of decisions in a typing pool

Review of the entire package

Signing and mailing

Assembly-line approaches such as this one are common throughout both the public and the private sectors. Task specialization and easier training and supervision of employees are typically cited as the primary advantages of such methods. Unfortunately, assembly-line methods also tend to create jobs that are highly fragmented and limited in scope. A common complaint is that workers encouraged to concentrate on details fail to appreciate the relationship between the details and the "big picture."

McNamar (1973) reports that the first four months of case processing at the Pay Board encountered serious difficulties. No one held complete responsibility for the processing of any particular case. People who performed processing steps felt only custodial responsibility for the paperwork crossing their desks. It was difficult to assess individual performance. Since few individuals appreciated what was done in other sections, lack of respect for the quality of work performed elsewhere in the processing chain also became a problem. Furthermore, a "yo-yo" effect developed whereby cases were returned to previous sections or to the applicant when insufficient information was present for the current step. This led to delays and continual rereading of cases at each station. Finally, a single unusual case could keep a large number of easy cases sitting in an in-box for several days. By mid-March 1972, the delays in case processing had become critical; fewer than 10 percent of cases were completed within 30 days.

### 3. Problems in the Initial Computer System

The details of the initial computer system are no longer clear. Apparently it attempted to keep track of both the cases themselves and the documents submitted by companies to support their requests. Documents received document control numbers and were cross-referenced to cases, which also had numbers. Since the documents relevant to a given case tended to be spread about in several locations, a significant effort was sometimes necessary to collect all the documents that were relevant to a particular step in the adjudication process. To expedite this effort, document locations were maintained in an on-line file.

Cases could be in any of about 60 different stations, which in combination constituted the status of the case and its location. Each time a case went through only the subset of the 60 stations that was relevant to it, a large amount of effort was required just to keep the file up to date. The 60 different stations were apparently "overdefined." In one extreme instance, a single person could be five different stations with respect to the processing of a given case. Further, it was often difficult to decide exactly what station a case was in, since the lawyers found some of the station definitions ambiguous. This was only part of a growing problem with inconsistent use and interpretation of information on the system.

Another problem was that the system had many loopholes. There were a number of ways a case could enter the processing stream. In some instances, an analyst received a case, assigned a case number, and began processing, even though the case had not formally entered the system. This resulted in discrepancies in the database and delays in processing.

In summary, the computer system became more of a hindrance than an aid, its main failure being in the area of human engineering. Although there was a logic to its notion of tight control over both documents and cases, the realization of this approach was a computer system so complicated that it became a burden to the lawyers who were its potential users. They rejected it. The data in the system became worse as the backlog of cases grew.

## B.  Organizational and Technical Changes

In April 1972, help was obtained in the form of a management consultant and his deputy, both of whom had been working in other agencies. After some preliminary analysis, the management consultant convinced the executive director and the director of CMA that he could design and implement a system that would work. He was appointed the new head of Operations Control and given a chance to straighten things out.

When he took the job, he and his deputy had a fairly good idea of what had to be done technically in terms of systems design. At the beginning of his tenure, he made a special point of trying to convince the lawyers who would use the system that he really understood their jobs, that he was a "good guy," that he was all for them, and that he also had enough technical expertise and intelligence to solve the problems that had been plaguing the operation.

To solve the organizational problems in case processing, the entire operation was overhauled. The assembly-line method of case processing was replaced by an interdependent work-group concept. Each work group consisted of a lawyer (adjudicator), a labor cost accountant, an information analyst, and a secretary. The adjudicator had complete management responsibility and decision-making authority for a specific set of cases. Cases now remained under the team's control, and much of the inefficiency of the assembly-line approach was eliminated.

To support the new organization, a new computer system was built on two fundamental principles: simplicity and the integrity of the database. The basis of the move toward simplicity was the replacement of the 60 stations of the original system by two clearly stated coordinates, the location of a case and its status. Possible locations included one of 11 teams, the Panel Board, the executive director, the screening desk, and so on. The possible statuses of a case included actionable, nonactionable, awaiting decision, awaiting legal ruling or interpretation, awaiting economic analysis, closed, withdrawn, or denied. By giving the location and status separately, the new system avoided the ambiguity of the old system. Now cases could be tracked in a simpler and more intuitive fashion. The attempt to track all documents was abandoned as useless, particularly with the development of the team concept, which allowed individuals to keep track of cases assigned to them.

In addition to the changing of the codes, the elimination of document numbers, and the restructuring of the organization, a full-scale audit was conducted to help formalize the changeover. Each active case was noted and categorized as to status and location. The computer system was modified to flag any attempt to move a case that had not been included in the audit. Thus cases that were temporarily misplaced or otherwise inactive and unaccounted for could not reenter the flow without being spotted. Manual counts prior to the audit had shown 2300 active cases. The audit showed 2800. Over the next two or three weeks, several hundred cases "trickled out of the woodwork." The audit had two major results that contributed to the overall improvements: increased accuracy and currency for the data in the system and increased credibility for the new system and its implementers.

The changes in the processing method and in the computer system proved to be quite successful. In addition to improving morale, it led to the following dramatic productivity increases.

With virtually no increase in staff, the rate of case completions increased from 131 per week to 204 per week within three months and 312 per week within six months.

Average turnaround time decreased from 81 days for cases submitted in February to 15 days for cases submitted in October.

The percentage of cases completed within 60 days increased from 28 percent in March to 71 percent in July.

## C. Operation of the Computer System

### 1. Purpose and Design Philosophy

The computer system that was developed served three purposes.

Tracking the flow of cases through the case processing pipelines.

Providing the adjudicating information relevant to the decisions on individual cases.

Automating some of the processing of those cases that were within guidelines.

The integrity of the database was promoted by separating functions between the action office, Case Management and Analysis (CMA), and the systems and procedures office, Operations Control. Contrasted with CMA, which was responsible for analyzing and adjudicating wage adjustment requests, Operations Control came to consider themselves advocates of the database. It was their charter to get the original PB-3 data onto the system accurately, to capture all relevant location and status data as the case was processed, and to ensure that all data were present at case closing time. The head of Operations Control felt that by maintaining particularly stringent standards on the accuracy and consistency of the data as the case entered and left the system, he could ensure that the database would be accurate enough to be useful. He felt that this "front-end–back-end" concept was one of the main reasons for the success of the system. Further, he felt that one of his key functions was to maintain a centralized office that would be a focal point for establishing rules, definitions, and standards for what all data fields and numbers meant. This centralization was in response to early difficulties due to inconsistencies in use and interpretation of information. The head of Operations Control felt that such inconsistencies were a problem in most systems that failed and he was determined to prevent the recurrence of that problem during his tenure. In his words: "Not one number got changed, not one new coding structure was generated, not one (standard) report got put out that I didn't sign off on to say that the definitions were correct and agreed upon by all parties. When the numbers came out, there were standard definitions that these numbers applied to."

The computer system continued to evolve over the duration of its existence. When the database became accurate in the late summer of 1972, system usage as both a management control tool and an operational tool increased greatly. At one point, it became apparent that a large number of cases within guidelines were being submitted. Since the policy was to grant all such requests, these were good candidates for the kind of automatic processing discussed in Section II D above. The data entry process was modified to check the figures on these submissions automatically and to "turn them around at the front door" before their sheer number caused things to bog down. By the late fall of 1972, the system was working smoothly in all three of its functions and could be modified with confidence as new requirements appeared. The director of CMA felt that certain technical aspects of the system could have been improved at that point, but that the system generally provided most of the information needed.

## 2. Some Details Concerning the System

### THE COMPUTER

The computer that was used was a more or less dedicated PDP-10, which was maintained by a time-sharing vendor. After a period of operating on a charge-per-report basis, it was decided to obtain a fixed-charge contract for the use of the computer. All computerized activities of both the Pay Board and the Price Board were then subsumed under the contract. (Those activities included a number of applications not reported here.)

### THE DATA

The system was based on two master files, one of open cases and one of closed cases. The master files were organized by case number. Each record consisted of approximately 70 fields, containing such information as the following.

Address and identifying information about the company and union

Category (within guidelines; staff-disposable; for the Panel Board)

Types of adjustment requested (one or more): retroactive, tandem, catch-up, cost-of-living, merit, deferred, stock option, executive compensation, incentive plan, bonus plan, etc.

Current case status: actionable, nonactionable, awaiting decision, awaiting legal interpretation, awaiting economic analysis, closed, withdrawn, or denied

Current case location (one of 11 teams): Panel Board, Board chairman, executive director, legal counsel, etc.

Case location history: where the case had been

Percent adjustment requested and granted

Dollar breakdowns of various types of benefits

Initially information about each case was entered directly from its PB-3 form. After each stage in processing, case location and status fields were updated. At case closing, the dollar breakdowns of the allowed adjustment were entered, and the case went to the closed file.

### DATA ENTRY

The "system" encompassed data entry, standard reports, and ad hoc reports. The initial PB-3 data were keyed in on a CRT terminal. The data entry process was controlled by means of a Fortran program. The program displayed a form to be filled in and automatically moved a cursor to the next data field to be entered. Most data fields were tested for obvious errors. The consistency of numerical data on the PB-3 form was automatically checked. Earlier, a trained labor economist had had to perform these calculations. Now an economist still had to interpret them in many cases but did not have to do as much repetitious programmable work with a calculator.

### WORKLOAD CONTROL

Workload control reports were generated from the master files on a weekly or daily basis. These reports were used by the director of CMA as a basic management control tool. Figure 51 contains a sample report for Team K. The purpose of this report was to help monitor the flow of cases through the case analysis process and to isolate bottlenecks. The actionable vs. nonactionable distinction in Fig. 51 refers to the fact that some cases could not be processed further until Team K received a response from some outside source. In addition to team inventory reports, the workload control system included other types of reports. Aging reports triggered expediting action on particular cases by highlighting cases that had been delayed. Average turnaround time reports helped in monitoring the learning curve that was in effect. To the extent possible, the director avoided intervention and encouraged the teams to use these reports to control their own progress.

Although this system provided information in controlling the flow of cases through the pipeline, it could not provide information about whether the cases were being adjudicated in accordance with any substantive standards. One idea considered was to compare the percentage adjustments granted by the different teams. This idea was discarded because the greater part of any differences could be explained in terms of differences in the types of cases that were assigned to the various teams. The only real way to check the quality of adjudication would have required either a careful legal audit of randomly chosen decisions or a comparison of duplicate adjudications for the same cases. Since there was a high degree of confidence in the competence of the teams and in the head of the Staff-Disposable group, these measures seemed unnecessary, if not wasteful of resources, and possibly contrary to good interpersonal relations.

FIGURE 51    Typical Team Inventory Report

| Team K          Date 10-19-72 | Panel Board | Staff-Disposable | Within Guidelines | Total |
|---|---|---|---|---|
| Total beginning inventory | 2 | 5 | 211 | 218 |
|    Actionable | 2 | 4 | 146 | 152 |
|    Nonactionable | 0 | 1 | 65 | 66 |
| Nonactionable cases becoming actionable | 0 | 0 | 23 | 23 |
| Actionable cases becoming nonactionable | 0 | 0 | 2 | 2 |
| Total cases received | 0 | 0 | 85 | 85 |
|    Opened | 0 | 0 | 78 | 78 |
|    Appeals/reconsiderations | 0 | 0 | 7 | 7 |
|    Transferred to other teams | 0 | 0 | 0 | 0 |
| Total cases completed | 0 | 1 | 119 | 120 |
|    Withdrawn | 0 | 0 | 0 | 0 |
|    Closed | 0 | 0 | 94 | 94 |
|    Deleted | 0 | 1 | 20 | 21 |
|    Transferred to other teams | 0 | 0 | 4 | 4 |
|    Awaiting decision transmittal | 0 | 0 | 1 | 1 |
| Total remaining inventory | 2 | 3 | 178 | 183 |
|    Actionable | 2 | 3 | 147 | 152 |
|    Nonactionable | 0 | 0 | 31 | 31 |
| Summary of weekly performance | | | | |
|    Total cases closed this week | 0 | 0 | 94 | 94 |
|    Total cases closed last week | 0 | 0 | 80 | 80 |
|    Net change in actionable inventory | 0 | − 1 | 1 | 0 |
|    Net change in nonactionable inventory | 0 | − 1 | − 34 | − 35 |
|    Net change in total inventory | 0 | − 2 | − 33 | − 35 |

AD HOC REPORTS

Ad hoc reports were valuable for clarifying some of the equity and consistency issues that arose in adjudication. For example, the adjudicator of the California steel case mentioned earlier might want to obtain details of previous steel industry cases, such as average adjustment, rationales used most frequently, percentage breakdowns of dollar benefits, and so on. The adjudicator might want to know about all previous heavy industry cases in California, as well as whether other steel cases were in process.

The capability of obtaining these types of information was provided by means of a data-retrieval language called Oliver, which is embedded in Fortran. By means of Oliver, it was quite easy to perform a conditional selection of appropriate records and then to calculate averages, sums, and so on, using dummy variables where necessary. These reports were generated in a more or less on-line mode. The person wanting the report either programmed it or asked someone else to do so. The response was quite fast, and the report could be used immediately to aid in the adjudication process.

Figure 52 contains a sample ad hoc report. This report selects those cases of a particular type (field 300 = 2) which originated in Michigan (field 7 = MI). It counts these cases and prints the total number of employees involved (sum of fields 59) and the average of the percent increase sought (average of fields 77).

*FIGURE 52   A Sample Oliver Program*

The user types:
```
S IF F300 = "2" AND F7 = "MI"
FINAL IS $COUNT, "TOTAL NO OF CASES", $SUM, $SUM(F59),$AVG(F77) (6,3)
*END
```
The system responds:

    47   TOTAL NO OF CASES       15862       9.618

Most of the people interviewed were relatively enthusiastic about this capability, although the form of the usage varied. Some people made it a practice of programming their own reports. Others felt that programming was not their job and directed their assistants to obtain the reports that were needed. The head of Operations Control felt that an important component of the success of the overall system was the shared feeling that much relevant data was available on the system and that it could be obtained easily and quickly (regardless of who did the actual programming).

The on-line nature of the retrieval capability was useful but not essential. In general, the users apparently thought of themselves as needing to obtain some information that they could define explicitly in advance rather than needing to interact with a database in the course of an adaptive search or optimization process. The only mentioned example of the latter was an episode during which an administrator spent an hour at a terminal trying various forms of similar reports in order to provide one of his superiors with a single management control report that appeared as favorable as was possible within the constraints of truthfulness.

In summary, the Pay Board's computer system was based on a carefully controlled data entry process, which maintained two on-line master files organized by case number. The system had three main purposes. It was used as a management control tool for generating reports on workload changes, turnaround time, and case aging. It was used to support the adjudication process by means of an on-line report generation capability. Finally, it expedited the processing of cases by checking the consistency of the calculations submitted by the companies.

## D. In Retrospect

In a discussion of the history of the system, the first comments of the director of CMA were aimed at three factors that in his estimation contributed to the success of the system.

1.  The activities engaged in were regulatory in nature. They consisted mainly of taking a set of regulations and applying them to a factual situation, a case that moved through various stages.

2.  The men who were concerned with hardware and programming were very conscious of design aspects and user orientation. They were careful to involve the users in the design process.

3.  This was a new, young organization with unsettled ways of doing things. As a result, it was possible to mold people in a very facile way.

Thus it was easy to get the system off the ground. A learning curve was operating to their advantage. This factor was not understood originally, but it seemed important in retrospect.

A technical characteristic of Oliver turned out to be quite valuable in this environment. With the definite evolutionary philosophy of the system, it was often necessary to add new fields to the files and to change some of the processing routines. The head of Operations Control noted that the use of Oliver provided a genuine and unexpected bonus in this area. He found that with Oliver it was quite easy to restructure files and to change data and get running in two days. That kind of flexibility was particularly significant in a dynamic organization like the Pay Board, where major changes seemed to occur every other week.

It is interesting that the people interviewed would not have gone on-line originally had it been their decision at that point. In the interim, most of them, ranging from the management consultant to a lawyer-administrator who had been "anti-computer," became much more enthusiastic about on-line capabilities. The head of Operations Control was particularly impressed with the "psychology" of on-line system usage that arose. It was almost as though the computer was another member of the staff who happened to have a large memory. People who had never known anything about computers confidently walked up to a terminal to program a report. Originally, the computer staff helped them with their programming, but as they gained experience, many of them saw that they could program the requests themselves and stopped bothering the computer staff members. On the other hand, one economist almost never used the computer himself, feeling that his job was economics rather than programming. He always asked someone else to obtain the reports he needed.

In spite of his enthusiasm for on-line systems, the head of Operations Control was quick to note that the Pay Board system did not have to be on-line. The workload control reports were effectively batch reports. The data entry and automatic costing operations probably could have been done about as well by means of a programmable terminal rather than on-line. It probably would have been adequate to do the ad hoc reports overnight on request. Nevertheless, the history of the system favored the on-line approach. The designers of the first system seemed to assume that was the only way to go. When the designers of the current system arrived in April of 1972, they found an existing on-line capability, which they felt they could use effectively. Instead of pondering the batch vs. on-line issue, they proceeded to do what they viewed as the most important task—to produce a workable system that would help get the case processing going at an acceptable level. After that time, they were concerned primarily with substantive Pay Board issues and saw no particular reason to restrict a system that was working.

The two basic ideas of the computer system revision, simplicity and control of the database by means of the front-end-bank-end concept, worked quite well, although they were not greeted with equal enthusiasm. In particular, operational managers were not uniformly happy about having someone else control their database. They weren't always impressed by the argument that databases tend to become degraded in systems where different people use the same information for different purposes and interpret the numbers differently, depending on their office's point of view. To paraphrase the head of Operations Control, "The bulk of the people who will interface a database, particularly if they are not computer-oriented by nature, won't understand it, won't want to understand it, and don't care if it's wrong." A parallel complaint was raised by a lawyer who had been in charge of the Staff-Disposable teams. He could not understand why some of the people he dealt with could not understand the concept of a system and the fact that things that they did in their areas often affected other people through the medium of the database. The head of Operations Control concluded that the main reason for the success of the system was not the on-line capabilities but the stringent back-end–front-end control of the database that he fought for and enforced.

## IV.  PHASES III AND IV AT THE PAY BOARD

On January 11, 1973, Phase III began. Under Phase III, restraints on wage increases became voluntary in most industries, with food, health services, and construction as exceptions. For this reason, the CMA group lost most of its regulatory power. The case processing system described earlier simply ceased to function.

Organizationally, the situation was highly ambiguous. The future function of the Pay Board apparatus was unclear. Morale dropped. Along with many others, the Phase II director of CMA waited for a new assignment. The head of Operations Control was shifted to a similar post at the Price Board. In the words of one observer:

> "Initially Phase III psychology was that this wasn't a program anymore. Now it was just a Mickey Mouse operation. . . . It took staff a long time to give a damn. One of the problems was that when a case came in the door, it often wasn't clear what to do with it, and whether it should sit in a drawer or whether it should be acted upon."

The new managers of Phase III at the Pay Board were not interviewed. In the opinion of several Phase II managers, the new managers were not as interested in computers as the Phase II managers had been. As a result, the system began to atrophy. The system was not modified to suit the slightly different needs of Phase III. Furthermore, the careful control of the database loosened considerably.

As case loads in the food, health services, and construction industries began to increase, the lawyer who had previously been in charge of the Staff-Disposable teams started to work to maintain the overall integrity of the database. His idea was to maintain the front end and the back end without the middle. The opinion of the former head of Operations Control was that the database was once again in reasonable shape by June 1973.

With the onset of Phase III$\frac{1}{2}$, the future of the Pay Board was once again up in the air. In the meantime, some thought was being given to how the system might be improved. The general feeling was that the system structure was sound but that additional data should be provided. For instance, data fields should be provided for the case numbers of tandem cases. Also, the sections of the law that were cited in each judgment should be in the file in order to provide a feeling for the relative distribution of the types of exceptions that were being granted. The next major change might be to store the wage adjustment breakdowns within companies. Formerly only the weighted average of percentage adjustments had been kept on the master file. Since a given bargaining unit or company could easily have ten or more different wage structures, true wage comparability could not be guaranteed unless the wage rates and adjustments for each job classification were in the file. With this information available, it would be possible to compare across job classifications within region. Mechanically, it was not clear how this change should be implemented.

The real problem, of course, was that the future requirements for the system were not known. Particularly difficult was the fact that top-level policy changes are often decided independent of operational considerations, yet they require operational support. When asked for some comments as to guidelines for the future (in a June 1973 interview), the Phase II director of CMA said that he would endeavor to be simple, would not undertake projects that required more than three months for complete implementation, and would continually try to be aware of all thinking about what might happen next. He felt that one of the inputs to the consideration of options for Phase IV should certainly be an assessment of current computer capabilities and the capabilities required for the various options. Of course, it was doubtful whether such an assessment would occur.

At the time of our final interviews (December 1973), Phase IV was in place. Because of the influx of cases from many small food establishments, the active case inventory was up to about 4000 from approximately 2500 near the end of Phase II. Another change was that the 5.5 percent figure was now genuinely a guideline, with some settlements coming in below that figure. The computer database was also expanded a bit to include cross-references among tandem cases and the identifier numbers of the specific regulations that applied to the decisions. The system operated basically as it had operated during Phase II. On April 30, 1974, the Economic Stabilization Act expired, thereby terminating authority for wage and price controls.

## APPENDIX: PHASE IV AT THE PRICE BOARD

As Phase III commenced, a number of procedural changes and personnel transfers occurred. The Pay Board and Price Commission were reorganized as separate Pay Board and Price Board divisions of the Cost of Living Council. With this reorganization, the head of Operations Control at the Pay Board during Phase II was transferred along with his deputy to the Systems and Procedures group of the reformed Price Board. This Appendix describes the way their experience with the Phase II Pay Board system helped them in their new assignment.

At the time of the initial interviews, the Price Board Systems and Procedures group was starting to gear up for Phase IV under the leadership of the former head of Operations Control for the Pay Board. Although the Price Board's charter for Phase IV was not yet clear, it was nonetheless possible to prepare for certain likely responsibilities. First of all, the Phase IV computer system would strive for database integrity, using the same concept that was successful at the Pay Board during Phase II. This would include a very rigorous front-end screening to ensure that the input forms met the regulations. If a form passed this screening, it would then go to a data entry station, where it would be keyed into an on-line file. The system would contain three files: (1) base profit and profit and cost variation; (2) line and product line detail; and (3) case tracking information. The analyst would decide to accept, reject, or challenge each quarterly report and each prenotification. Exactly what would happen in each of these cases was not yet known. One problem that had arisen under Phase II was that submissions from firms had occasionally employed varying interpretations of certain regulations. That would of course have to be corrected if the new system was to work well.

Finally, it was not even clear how the Price Board analysts would use the new system. File folders would be available for each firm. The analysts might prefer to use these as their source of information, particularly since they would contain supporting documents from the companies and accounting firms that would not be maintained on-line.

The period of speculation ended on July 26, 1973, when the Phase IV procedures were published. The procedures specified that much of the monitoring and case analysis was to be done in decentralized fashion by 29 IRS offices and eight regional offices. The implication was that by August 12 a computer network to support this decentralized processing would have to be up and running. Initially the system would provide for tracking and analysis of two main types of submissions, prenotifications and exceptions/reconsiderations. There were some added complications. Certain categories of submissions were to be processed by the CLC, thus requiring that separate systems and procedures be established for the IRS and CLC. Furthermore, the adjudication criteria were somewhat more complex. Price increases were to be granted or disallowed on the basis of the projected maintenance of certain profit margins. The rulings would be on a firm-by-firm basis rather than on industrywide criteria. These factors expanded information requirements. On top of that, the Systems and Procedures group had less than three weeks to complete the job!

The first step was to get organized. The following tasks were identified.

1.  Negotiation and execution of contracts with the three vendors who would provide communications, computer terminals, and the computer itself

2.  Installation of telephone lines and data sets linking the remote IRS work stations to the central computers

3.  Installation of the display terminals and printers in all work locations

4.  Development of foreground/background data entry screens for the two initial types of forms

5.  Development of initial tracking and workload status reports

6.  Development of two procedural manuals, one for data terminal operators and one for work flow control

7.  Training of personnel of both the IRS and the CLC, including both data terminal operators and people responsible for workload control

It was necessary that the computer system be fully operational in less than three weeks in order that the IRS and CLC personnel could have hands-on experience with the actual system at their own facilities prior to start-up.

The man who was put in charge of technical procurement and installation felt that he had received outstanding response and cooperation from the vendors. An important factor was that they appreciated the national significance of having the system running on time. As a result, the terminal vendor doubled production for two weeks, the communications arrangements were installed with exceptional dispatch, and all hardware details were tested and debugged on time.

Since the Systems and Procedures staff had been working with Oliver and Fortran for more than a year, the programming of two data entry screens for the terminals (in Fortran) and of a number of work-load control reports (in Oliver) could also be accomplished on time without difficulty.

The biggest potential problem was training people. Unlike the CLC people, who were quite familiar with the idea of case processing and the accompanying terminology and consistency requirements, the people in the IRS field offices had never been involved in this kind of adjudication process. Furthermore, most of them had never used a computer terminal. And in two and a half weeks, the IRS offices would have to begin processing cases.

The first step was to document a set of procedures telling people exactly what to do under all normal circumstances. This was not a trivial task, because the Phase IV procedures required that IRS personnel be able to recognize, process, and control 11 different Phase IV documents. Doing so would involve a combination of manual and computerized screening and control techniques of some sophistication.

The next step was initial training in Washington. At least one person came from each office. Part of the training involved definitions of terms and procedures and the use of the procedure manual. Another part involved familiarization with the computer terminals. To make the learning task easier, the initial contact with terminals took the form of playing computerized football and other games. When the basics of terminal use were understood and the people were no longer scared of the black box, the training went ahead to the use of the case-handling procedures on test data.

It was anticipated that this initial training would not be adequate for ensuring that people would remember everything. It was likely that individuals would forget how to turn on the terminals or how to control the display screen cursors or what to do if a submission did not conform to the proper format. Therefore every IRS office was given a CLC telephone number with strong encouragement to call whenever there was a question or when something went wrong.

In addition, an error correction group was set up. Every morning, this group received a listing of every transaction from the previous day. They inspected the listings carefully. When they found errors, they called the appropriate people to tell them what they had done wrong and why it was an error. After the first two weeks, errors on data entry dropped substantially. When the first 30-day processing deadline arrived, errors rose and then fell again as people straightened out the case-closing procedure.

During the initial period, CLC teams were sent to several major IRS district offices to help them set up procedures. It was anticipated that those districts would have the largest volume of submissions. Therefore the "bugs" in the system would be exposed earliest in those locations. In addition, it was likely that those offices would receive most of the erroneous submissions. The teams were able to catalogue a number of system bugs and generic errors, on the part of both the companies and the case-processing personnel. The bugs were corrected. Warnings about those errors and appropriate recovery procedures were circulated.

Given the experience from Phase II with regard to controlling the database and work flow, such careful attention to training and error correction was thought to be absolutely essential. The main goal was the uniform processing of cases and the avoidance of ad hoc and ultimately inconsistent solutions to the individual case-handling problems that arose. People in the field offices came to understand the logical separation between their decentralized decision-making authority and the overall necessity of consistent record keeping and procedures across the system.

After the initial break-in period, the Phase IV computer system grew significantly. In comparison with the first Phase II workload control reports, this initial system produced about 25 different management reports based on the processing of two forms. By the end of 1973, a large number of subsystems had emerged and produced about 150 management reports.

Many of the reports were circulated in a weekly 44-page publication, the *General Management Review Bulletin,* which began with an executive summary of occurrences of the previous week and cumulative Phase IV actions in various industries. Other data presented included detailed tabular summaries of prenotification decisions, exceptions and exemptions, and compliance with Phase IV rules. The bulletin gave CLC administrators an up-to-date picture of the workings of the Cost of Living Council. Used in conjunction with specific case-processing goals, the bulletin became a standard management tool. In addition, it served a major public relations function by helping Cost of Living Council administrators answer frequent external inquiries concerning the efficiency of processing procedures, the nature of settlements, and the cumulative impact of settlements in various areas. Thus, given the experience at the Pay Board during Phase II, it had been possible to upgrade the Price Commission's work-load control system in less than a year into a system that played a major role in both case processing and the overall administration of the Cost of Living Council.

### Questions for the Reader

1. How did the organizational setting in this case differ from that of previous cases? In what ways was the organizational setting an advantage or a disadvantage?

2. What are some possible guidelines for computer-based systems in organizations that are changing rapidly? What are the advantages and possible disadvantages of each guideline?

3. Compare the implementation process in this case with that in the other cases. If the initial difficulties in this case could have been avoided, what kind of implementation process might have helped to avoid them?

4. Compare the principal decision-making task in this case with that in other cases. Does this type of decision making have special informational needs that other types of decision making do not have?

5. How was the computer system used as a lever in bringing about organizational change in the early stages of Phase II? Were the DSSs in other cases used to promote organizational change? If so, how?

6. The head of Operations Control concluded that the main reason for the success of the system was the stringent controls he enforced. Did controls such as these occur in other cases?

7. At the end of the appendix, it is noted that a management review bulletin served a major public relations function during Phase IV. To what extent did decision support systems in other cases serve this type of role?

# AAIMS: AN ANALYTIC INFORMATION MANAGEMENT SYSTEM

## CASE EIGHT

## I. INTRODUCTION

AAIMS, An Analytical Information Management System, is an APL-based software package for data analysis and report generation. It is an outgrowth of an econometric modeling effort begun in 1970 by Richard Klaas and Charles Weiss of the Corporate Planning and Operations Research Departments of American Airlines under the direction of Joe D. Kingsley, Director of Systems Planning. During the four years of its existence, AAIMS has grown continually, both in terms of its scope and capabilities and in terms of its usage in American Airlines and elsewhere. In the fall of 1974, AAIMS was being marketed through APL Services, Inc., an external time-sharing vendor with customers across the country.

The case study begins with a discussion of the capabilities of AAIMS in terms of its orientation, command language, and database. The second section discusses the development of AAIMS and some of the ways it has been used by a wide range of individuals within American Airlines. The final section puts the use, strengths, and limitations of AAIMS into better perspective. The case draws on two earlier descriptions of AAIMS (Klaas, 1972, and Taplin, 1973). A more recent description of the system is also available (Klaas, 1977).

## II. WHAT IS AAIMS?

In American Airlines, a large number of clerks and analysts spend much of their time developing answers to such questions as the following.

> How does this series of monthly actual performance figures compare with another series of monthly budgeted figures?

> How does the trend in our monthly load factor on important routes compare with the trends experienced by other airlines?

> Is there a relationship over time between these two performance variables?

> How does our monthly performance in this area compare with what we have done in recent years?

AAIMS consists of a standard database and a collection of functions for data retrieval and manipulation and report generation. It is especially useful in minimizing the clerical work required in answering questions such as those above. It is designed for use by either programmers or nonprogrammers. In order to accommodate nonprogrammers, the command structure attempts to be as similar to English as is feasible.

## A. Time Series Orientation

Each of the questions above involves "time series" data. AAIMS is designed specifically for the retrieval and manipulation of this type of data. A times series is a set of numbers that represent the values of an activity at consecutive points in time. For example, the collection of 24 numbers representing the sales volume of a product monthly from January 1970 through December 1971 is an example of a time series. Conversely, the collection of 24 numbers representing the sales volume of 24 products in the month of December 1971 does not constitute a time series.

Time series orientation is an extremely important feature of AAIMS. Herein lie both a strength and a limitation of this system. Many tasks, such as budgeting, planning, and environmental scanning, are or can be deeply involved with the manipulation of time series. For tasks of this type, AAIMS can be extremely useful in facilitating data analysis and report generation. AAIMS is not useful, however, if the data is not of this type or if the task calls for calculations other than the manipulation of existing time series. It is also significant that AAIMS is basically a data retrieval system rather than a modeling system. For example, AAIMS would not be especially useful in the development of a simulation model, although it might be helpful in formatting and reporting any time series outputs of such a model.

## B. Data

Two types of data are accessed through AAIMS: standard data that are obtained automatically from transaction-oriented systems and user databases that are set up for use in special projects.

### 1. Standard Data

The airline industry is unusual in that the available standard data includes fairly detailed quarterly (sometimes monthly) operating data for all major airlines. This data is required by the Civil Aeronautics Board, the government agency that regulates the industry. It is submitted monthly or quarterly on CAB Form 41 and is made available to all airlines.

The total database of Form 41 data is quite extensive. It includes traffic, capacity, operating statistics, revenue, expense, and balance sheet data. The data are broken down along the following six dimensions.

Airline (e.g., American, United, TWA) *Trans World Airlines.*

Marketing entity (e.g., domestic, Latin American, Pacific)

Function (e.g., flight, maintenance)

Account (e.g., fuel, pilots)

Aircraft (e.g., Boeing 747, DC-10)

Time (e.g., first quarter 1974, second quarter 1974)

FIGURE 53

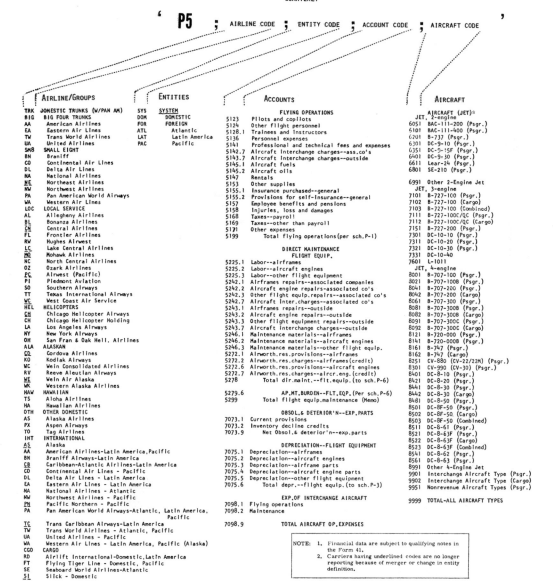

A ☂AIMS FORM 41

SCHEDULE **P5** --DIRECTORY OF NAMES

AIRCRAFT OPERATING EXPENSES
QUARTERLY

' **P5** ; AIRLINE CODE ; ENTITY CODE ; ACCOUNT CODE ; AIRCRAFT CODE '

### AIRLINE/GROUPS

| | |
|---|---|
| TRK | DOMESTIC TRUNKS (W/PAN AM) |
| BIG | BIG FOUR TRUNKS |
| AA | American Airlines |
| EA | Eastern Air Lines |
| TW | Trans World Airlines |
| UA | United Airlines |
| SM8 | SMALL EIGHT |
| BN | Braniff |
| CO | Continental Air Lines |
| DL | Delta Air Lines |
| NA | National Airlines |
| NE | Northeast Airlines |
| NW | Northwest Airlines |
| PA | Pan American World Airways |
| WA | Western Air Lines |
| LOC | LOCAL SERVICE |
| AL | Allegheny Airlines |
| BL | Bonanza Airlines |
| CN | Central Airlines |
| FL | Frontier Airlines |
| RW | Hughes Airwest |
| LC | Lake Central Airlines |
| MO | Mohawk Airlines |
| NC | North Central Airlines |
| OZ | Ozark Airlines |
| PC | Airwest (Pacific) |
| PI | Piedmont Aviation |
| SO | Southern Airways |
| TT | Texas International Airways |
| WC | West Coast Air Service |
| HEL | HELICOPTERS |
| CH | Chicago Helicopter Airways |
| CH | Chicago Helicopter Holding |
| LA | Los Angeles Airways |
| NY | New York Airways |
| OH | San Fran & Oak Hell. Airlines |
| ALA | ALASKAN |
| CO | Cordova Airlines |
| KO | Kodiak Airways |
| WC | Wein Consolidated Airlines |
| RV | Reeve Aleutian Airways |
| WE | Wein Air Alaska |
| WK | Western Alaska Airlines |
| HAW | HAWAIIAN |
| TS | Aloha Airlines |
| HA | Hawaiian Airlines |
| OTH | OTHER DOMESTIC |
| AS | Alaska Airlines |
| PX | Aspen Airways |
| TO | Tag Airlines |
| INT | INTERNATIONAL |
| AS | Alaska |
| AA | American Airlines-Latin America,Pacific |
| BN | Braniff Airways-Latin America |
| CB | Caribbean-Atlantic Airlines-Latin America |
| CO | Continental Air Lines - Pacific |
| DL | Delta Air Lines - Latin America |
| EA | Eastern Air Lines - Latin America |
| NA | National Airlines - Atlantic |
| NW | Northwest Airlines - Pacific |
| PN | Pacific Northern - Pacific |
| PA | Pan American World Airways-Atlantic, Latin America, Pacific |
| TC | Trans Caribbean Airways-Latin America |
| TW | Trans World Airlines - Atlantic, Pacific |
| UA | United Airlines - Pacific |
| WA | Western Air Lines - Latin America, Pacific (Alaska) |
| CGO | CARGO |
| RD | Airlift International-Domestic,Latin America |
| FT | Flying Tiger Line - Domestic, Pacific |
| SE | Seaboard World Airlines-Atlantic |
| SI | Slick - Domestic |

### ENTITIES

| | |
|---|---|
| SYS | SYSTEM |
| DOM | DOMESTIC |
| FOR | FOREIGN |
| ATL | Atlantic |
| LAT | Latin America |
| PAC | Pacific |

### ACCOUNTS

**FLYING OPERATIONS**

| | |
|---|---|
| 5123 | Pilots and copilots |
| 5124 | Other flight personnel |
| 5128.1 | Trainees and instructors |
| 5136 | Personnel expenses |
| 5141 | Professional and technical fees and expenses |
| 5142.7 | Aircraft interchange charges--ass.co's |
| 5143.7 | Aircraft interchange charges--outside |
| 5145.1 | Aircraft fuels |
| 5145.2 | Aircraft oils |
| 5147 | Rentals |
| 5153 | Other supplies |
| 5155.1 | Insurance purchased--general |
| 5155.2 | Provisions for self-insurance--general |
| 5157 | Employee benefits and pensions |
| 5158 | Injuries, loss and damages |
| 5168 | Taxes--payroll |
| 5169 | Taxes--other than payroll |
| 5171 | Other expenses |
| 5199 | Total flying operations(per sch.P-1) |

**DIRECT MAINTENANCE**
**FLIGHT EQUIP.**

| | |
|---|---|
| 5225.1 | Labor--airframes |
| 5225.2 | Labor--aircraft engines |
| 5225.3 | Labor--other flight equipment |
| 5242.1 | Airframes repairs--associated companies |
| 5242.2 | Aircraft engine repairs-associated co's |
| 5242.3 | Other flight equip.repairs--associated co's |
| 5242.7 | Aircraft inter.charges--associated co's |
| 5243.1 | Airframes repairs--outside |
| 5243.2 | Aircraft engine repairs--outside |
| 5243.3 | Other flight equipment repairs--outside |
| 5243.7 | Aircraft interchange charges--outside |
| 5246.1 | Maintenance materials--airframes |
| 5246.2 | Maintenance materials--aircraft engines |
| 5246.3 | Maintenance materials--other flight equip. |
| 5272.1 | Airworth.res.provisions--airframes |
| 5272.2 | Airworth.res.charges--airframes(credit) |
| 5272.6 | Airworth.res.provisions--aircraft engines |
| 5272.7 | Airworth.res.charges--aircr.eng.(credit) |
| 5278 | Total dir.maint.--flt.equip.(to sch.P-6) |
| 5279.6 | AP.MT.BURDEN--FLT.EQP.(Per sch.P-6) |
| 5299 | Total flight equip.maintenance (Memo) |

**OBSOL.& DETERIOR'N--EXP.PARTS**

| | |
|---|---|
| 7073.1 | Current provisions |
| 7073.2 | Inventory decline credits |
| 7073.9 | Net Obsol.& deterior'n--exp.parts |

**DEPRECIATION--FLIGHT EQUIPMENT**

| | |
|---|---|
| 7075.1 | Depreciation--airframes |
| 7075.2 | Depreciation--aircraft engines |
| 7075.3 | Depreciation--airframe parts |
| 7075.4 | Depreciation--aircraft engine parts |
| 7075.5 | Depreciation--other flight equipment |
| 7075.6 | Total depr.--flight equip.(to sch.P-3) |

**EXP.OF INTERCHANGE AIRCRAFT**

| | |
|---|---|
| 7098.1 | Flying operations |
| 7098.2 | Maintenance |
| 7098.9 | TOTAL AIRCRAFT OP.EXPENSES |

### AIRCRAFT

| | |
|---|---|
| | AIRCRAFT (JET)☆ |
| | JET, 2-engine |
| 6051 | BAC-111-200 (Psgr.) |
| 6101 | BAC-111-400 (Psgr.) |
| 6201 | B-737 (Psgr.) |
| 6301 | DC-9-10 (Psgr.) |
| 6351 | DC-9-15F (Psgr.) |
| 6401 | DC-9-30 (Psgr.) |
| 6611 | Lear-24 (Psgr.) |
| 6801 | SE-210 (Psgr.) |
| 6991 | Other 2-Engine Jet |
| | JET, 3-engine |
| 7101 | B-727-100 (Psgr.) |
| 7102 | B-727-100 (Cargo) |
| 7103 | B-727-100 (Combined) |
| 7111 | B-727-100C/QC (Psgr.) |
| 7112 | B-727-100C/QC (Cargo) |
| 7151 | B-727-200 (Psgr.) |
| 7301 | DC-10-10 (Psgr.) |
| 7311 | DC-10-20 (Psgr.) |
| 7321 | DC-10-30 (Psgr.) |
| 7331 | DC-10-40 |
| 7601 | L-1011 |
| | JET, 4-engine |
| 8001 | B-707-100 (Psgr.) |
| 3021 | B-707-100B (Psgr.) |
| 8041 | B-707-200 (Psgr.) |
| 8042 | B-707-200 (Cargo) |
| 8061 | B-707-300 (Psgr.) |
| 8081 | B-707-300B (Psgr.) |
| 8082 | B-707-300B (Cargo) |
| 8091 | B-707-300C (Psgr.) |
| 8092 | B-707-300C (Cargo) |
| 8121 | B-720-000 (Psgr.) |
| 8141 | B-720-000B (Psgr.) |
| 8161 | B-747 (Psgr.) |
| 8162 | B-747 (Cargo) |
| 8251 | CV-880 (CV-22/22M) (Psgr.) |
| 8301 | CV-990 (CV-30) (Psgr.) |
| 8401 | DC-8-10 (Psgr.) |
| 8421 | DC-8-20 (Psgr.) |
| 8441 | DC-8-30 (Psgr.) |
| 8442 | DC-8-30 (Cargo) |
| 8481 | DC-8-50 (Psgr.) |
| 8501 | DC-8F-50 (Psgr.) |
| 8502 | DC-8F-50 (Cargo) |
| 8503 | DC-8F-50 (Combined) |
| 8511 | DC-8-61 (Psgr.) |
| 8521 | DC-8-63F (Psgr.) |
| 8522 | DC-8-63F (Cargo) |
| 8523 | DC-8-63F (Combined) |
| 8541 | DC-8-62 (Psgr.) |
| 8561 | DC-8-63 (Psgr.) |
| 8991 | Other 4-Engine Jet |
| 9901 | Interchange Aircraft Type (Psgr.) |
| 9902 | Interchange Aircraft Type (Cargo) |
| 9951 | Nonrevenue Aircraft Types (Psgr.) |
| 9999 | TOTAL-ALL AIRCRAFT TYPES |

NOTE: 1. Financial data are subject to qualifying notes in the Form 41.
2. Carriers having underlined codes are no longer reporting because of merger or change in entity definition.

*All propeller aircraft codes are listed on the back.

American Airlines, Inc.
November, 1974

Figure 53 illustrates the degree of detail in the database by listing just the entries under the heading "Aircraft Operating Expenses."

The decision was made early to maintain all data on-line.[1] It was clear that some parts of the data would be quite useful, and other parts would be relatively useless. However, the designers felt that it was cheaper to put all the data on-line than to try to do an analysis of all information needs across the company. Furthermore, maintaining only part of the Form 41 data might have resulted in a recurring cost of introducing time series that had been excluded originally but became relevant later. That decision has since proved worthwhile in that the database is now being offered commercially, with customers located across the country in banking, consulting, manufacturing, and transportation.

In addition to the industrywide data, the standard database also includes companywide data extracted monthly from Flight Traffic Statistics, a module of the American Airlines Sabre System. In total, the standard database includes general economic indicators plus data concerning the operations of American Airlines and of other airlines (to a lesser extent). A breakdown of this database is presented in Fig. 54.

FIGURE 54    AAIMS Database

|  | Airline | Marketing Entity | Function | Account | Aircraft Type | Time |
|---|---|---|---|---|---|---|
| Traffic | X | X |  |  | X | Daily |
| Revenue | X | X |  | X |  | Quarterly |
| Expenses | X |  |  | X | X | Quarterly |
| Balance sheet | X |  |  | X | X | Quarterly |
| Headcount | X |  | X |  |  | Quarterly |

2.  User Databases

The nonstandard user databases are developed by users, often in conjunction with the Information Science Department. Given the time series orientation of AAIMS, a user database consists of a set of time series that the user or a secretary must enter or that is extracted from other systems.

Entering a new time series is quite simple. The user types the following statement.

INPUT 'data file name'

The computer will then ask for certain characteristics of the time series that must be known before it can store or retrieve the series as an AAIMS data file. Characteristics include the following.

*Periodicity:*    Daily, weekly, monthly, quarterly, or yearly.

*First date:*    When the time series starts.

---

[1]According to Richard Klaas (1977), the database contained 150,000 times series in early 1977.

*Data type (sum or average):* Sums can be averaged. Averages and percentages cannot be averaged meaningfully in general. This specification prevents some errors due to careless use of data.

*Units:* Whether the units are tens, hundreds, millions, etc.

*Storage allocation:* The storage allocation for any time series is classified as either standard or high according to its maximum storage requirements:

| Periodicity | Storage | |
|---|---|---|
| | *Standard* | *High* |
| Daily | 14 months | 19 months |
| Weekly | 2 years | 5 years |
| Monthly | 12 years | 24 years |
| Quarterly | 11 years | 23 years |
| Yearly | 10 years | 25 years |

*The data:* Typed consecutively with a space after each value and a carriage return at the end of each line of data.

*Source, comments, etc.*

With this information about a time series, the computer can automatically perform a great deal of the clerical work necessary for report generation. For example, if a data series named SALES has been entered, typing DISPLAY 'SALES' results in a formatted report with months on the horizontal axis and years on the vertical axis. Since starting points, periodicity, data type, units, and so on, are stored in a directory, a number of simple rules can be applied automatically in ensuring that time series are aligned, compared, and reported in a manner that is at least superficially consistent. The result is expedited report generation and avoidance of many careless errors.

Note that the data entry protocol is sufficiently simple that someone with minimal training can enter a user's time series directly. As will be noted later, some secretaries have become proficient in the use of the data analysis commands.

### C. Command Language

The AAIMS command language is a series of functions sufficiently powerful to cover a wide range of data retrieval and analysis tasks. Figure 55 contains examples of AAIMS commands and the resulting reports. Along with many other examples, these appear in the AAIMS User's Guide. Note that these examples are all based on the assumption that the time series SALES, PRICE, and EMPLOYEES exist in the user's AAIMS database. If they had not been entered specifically as AAIMS files, they could not be referenced by AAIMS subroutines.

Except for number 14, the examples in Fig. 55 appear in the form of ad hoc requests for information. AAIMS also contains facilities sufficient for the generation of standard reports having the complexity of balance sheets, budget reports, etc. In addition to simple manipulation operators of the sort represented in the examples,

*FIGURE 55*

**① DISPLAY 'SALES'**
A×AIMS
3/03/72

| YEAR | JAN | FEB | MAR | APR | | NOV | DEC | TOTAL | AVERAGE |
|------|-----|-----|-----|-----|---|-----|-----|-------|---------|
| 1968 | 13200 | 13480 | 13650 | 13960 | | 18410 | 18520 | 188790 | 15732.5 |
| 1969 | 18550 | 18550 | 18610 | 18630 | | 19750 | 19820 | 227680 | 18973.3 |
| 1970 | 19860 | 19910 | 19940 | 20030 | | 20570 | 20610 | 243130 | 20260.8 |
| 1971 | 20640 | 20850 | 20850 | 21090 | | 20850 | 20640 | 252140 | 21011.7 |
| 1972 | 20610 | | | | | | | ******** | ********* |

**② DISPLAY 'PRICE'**
A×AIMS
3/03/72

| YEAR | JAN | FEB | MAR | APR | | NOV | DEC | TOTAL | AVERAGE |
|------|-----|-----|-----|-----|---|-----|-----|-------|---------|
| 1968 | 49.95 | 49.95 | 49.95 | 49.95 | | 49.95 | 49.95 | 599.40 | 49.950 |
| 1969 | 49.95 | 49.95 | 49.95 | 55.00 | | 55.00 | 55.00 | 644.85 | 53.737 |
| 1970 | 55.00 | 55.00 | 55.00 | 55.00 | | 55.00 | 55.00 | 660.00 | 55.000 |
| 1971 | 69.95 | 69.95 | 69.95 | 69.95. | | 69.95 | 69.95 | 839.40 | 69.950 |
| 1972 | 69.95 | | | | | | | ******** | ********* |

**③ DISPLAY ('SALES' TIMES 'PRICE' FROM 1 68 THRU 12 68)**
A×AIMS
3/03/72

| YEAR | JAN | FEB | MAR | APR | | NOV | DEC | TOTAL | AVERAGE |
|------|-----|-----|-----|-----|---|-----|-----|-------|---------|
| 1968 | 659340 | 673326 | 681817 | 697302 | | 919579 | 925074 | 9430060 | 785838.4 |

**④ DISPLAY ('SALES' DIVIDED BY 'SALES' AT 1 68)**
-A×AIMS
3/06/72

| YEAR | JAN | FEB | MAR | APR | | NOV | DEC | TOTAL | AVERAGE |
|------|-----|-----|-----|-----|---|-----|-----|-------|---------|
| 1968 | 1.000 | 1.021 | 1.034 | 1.058 | | 1.395 | 1.403 | 14.302 | 1.1919 |
| 1969 | 1.405 | 1.405 | 1.410 | 1.411 | | 1.496 | 1.502 | 17.248 | 1.4374 |
| 1970 | 1.505 | 1.508 | 1.511 | 1.517 | | 1.558 | 1.561 | 18.419 | 1.5349 |
| 1971 | 1.564 | 1.580 | 1.580 | 1.598 | | 1.580 | 1.564 | 19.102 | 1.5918 |
| 1972 | 1.561 | | | | | | | ******** | ********* |

**⑤ DISPLAY (YEARLY RATIO 'SALES')**
A×AIMS
3/13/72

| YEAR | JAN | FEB | MAR | APR | | NOV | DEC | TOTAL | AVERAGE |
|------|-----|-----|-----|-----|---|-----|-----|-------|---------|
| 1969 | 1.405 | 1.376 | 1.363 | 1.335 | | 1.073 | 1.070 | 14.704 | 1.2253 |
| 1970 | 1.071 | 1.073 | 1.071 | 1.075 | | 1.042 | 1.040 | 12.818 | 1.0682 |
| 1971 | 1.039 | 1.047 | 1.046 | 1.053 | | 1.014 | 1.001 | 12.447 | 1.0372 |
| 1972 | 0.999 | | | | | | | ******** | ********* |

*FIGURE 55 (continued)*

**⑥.** *DISPLAY (PERIODIC RATIO 'SALES')*
A*AIMS
3/13/72

| YEAR | JAN | FEB | MAR | APR | | NOV | DEC | TOTAL | AVERAGE |
|------|------|------|------|------|--|------|------|---------|----------|
| 1968 | | 1.021 | 1.013 | 1.023 | | 1.005 | 1.006 | ******** | ******** |
| 1969 | 1.002 | 1.000 | 1.003 | 1.001 | | 1.006 | 1.004 | 12.068 | 1.0057 |
| 1970 | 1.002 | 1.003 | 1.002 | 1.005 | | 1.001 | 1.002 | 12.039 | 1.0033 |
| 1971 | 1.001 | 1.010 | 1.000 | 1.012 | | 1.000 | 0.990 | 12.002 | 1.0002 |
| 1972 | 0.999 | | | | | | | ******** | ******** |

**⑦.** *DISPLAY (YEARLY CHANGE 'SALES')*
A*AIMS
3/14/72

| YEAR | JAN | FEB | MAR | APR | | NOV | DEC | TOTAL | AVERAGE |
|------|------|------|------|------|--|------|------|--------|----------|
| 1969 | 5350 | 5070 | 4960 | 4670 | | 1340 | 1300 | 38890 | 3240.8 |
| 1970 | 1310 | 1360 | 1330 | 1400 | | 820 | 790 | 15450 | 1287.5 |
| 1971 | 780 | 940 | 910 | 1060 | | 280 | 30 | 9010 | 750.8 |
| 1972 | ‾30 | | | | | | | ******** | ******** |

**⑧.** *DISPLAY (PERIODIC CHANGE 'SALES')*
A*AIMS
3/14/72

| YEAR | JAN | FEB | MAR | APR | | NOV | DEC | TOTAL | AVERAGE |
|------|------|------|------|------|--|------|------|--------|----------|
| 1968 | | 280 | 170 | 310 | | 90 | 110 | ******** | ******** |
| 1969 | 30 | 0 | 60 | 20 | | 120 | 70 | 1300 | 108.3 |
| 1970 | 40 | 50 | 30 | 90 | | ‐0 | ‐40 | 790 | 65.8 |
| 1971 | ‾30 | 210 | 0 | 240 | | 0 | ‾210 | 30 | 2.5 |
| 1972 | ‾30 | | | | | | | ******** | ******** |

**⑨.** *DISPLAY (CUMULATIVE 'SALES' FROM 1 69 THRU 12 69)*
A*AIMS
3/15/72

| YEAR | JAN | FEB | MAR | APR | | NOV | DEC | TOTAL | AVERAGE |
|------|-------|-------|-------|-------|--|--------|--------|---------|-----------|
| 1969 | 18550 | 37100 | 55710 | 74340 | | 207860 | 227680 | 1462510 | 121875.8 |

**⑩.** *DISPLAY (QUARTERLY AVERAGE ('SALES'DIVIDED BY'EMPLOYEES'))*
A*AIMS
3/09/72

| YEAR | 1ST | 2ND | 3RD | 4TH | TOTAL | AVERAGE |
|------|-------|-------|-------|-------|--------|---------|
| 1969 | 6.215 | 5.909 | 5.833 | 5.910 | 23.868 | 5.9669 |
| 1970 | 5.758 | 5.774 | 5.734 | 5.724 | 22.990 | 5.7476 |
| 1971 | 5.711 | 5.784 | 5.748 | 5.591 | 22.834 | 5.7084 |

**⑪.** *DISPLAY (('SALES' TIMES 'PRICE')MINUS ('SALES' TIMES 'COST'))*
A*AIMS
3/06/72

| YEAR | JAN | FEB | MAR | APR | | NOV | DEC | TOTAL | AVERAGE |
|------|--------|--------|--------|--------|--|--------|--------|---------|-----------|
| 1968 | 257400 | 262860 | 266175 | 272220 | | 346108 | 315396 | 3574362 | 297863.5 |
| 1969 | 315906 | 315906 | 316928 | 411350 | | 386112 | 387481 | 4547765 | 378980.4 |
| 1970 | 388263 | 389240 | 380854 | 382573 | | 364089 | 364797 | 4517815 | 376484.6 |
| 1971 | 673896 | 680752 | 680752 | 688588 | | 633840 | 627456 | 7900383 | 658365.3 |
| 1972 | 626544 | | | | | | | ******** | ******** |

FIGURE 55 (continued)

⑫    *TABLE ('SALES' FROM 1 69 THRU 12 69) AND('SALES' FROM 1 70 THRU 12 70)*

```
JAN 1970      18550        19860
FEB 1970      18550        19910
MAR 1970      18610        19940
APR 1970      18630        20030
MAY 1970      18690        20160
JUN 1970      18690        20190
JUL 1970      18820        20280
AUG 1970      18850        20510
SEP 1970      19090        20520
OCT 1970      19630        20550
NOV 1970      19750        20570
DEC 1970      19820        20610
A*AIMS    3/06/72
```

⑬    *DISPLAY 'SALES' AND 'PRICE' AND 'COST' AND     ☐*
☐:
     *'EMPLOYEES' FROM 1 69 THRU 6 70*
     A*AIMS
     3/06/72

| YEAR | JAN | FEB | MAR | APR | | NOV | DEC | TOTAL | AVERAGE |
|------|-----|-----|-----|-----|--|-----|-----|-------|---------|
| 1969 | 18550 | 18550 | 18610 | 18630 | | 19750 | 19820 | 227680 | 18973.3 |
| | 49.95 | 49.95 | 49.95 | 55.00 | | 55.00 | 55.00 | 644.85 | 53.737 |
| | 32.92 | 32.92 | 32.92 | 32.92 | | 35.45 | 35.45 | 405.16 | 33.763 |
| | 2936 | 2964 | 3066 | 3095 | | 3348 | 3377 | 38195 | 3182.9 |
| 1970 | 19860 | 19910 | 19940 | 20030 | | | | ******** | ******** |
| | 55.00 | 55.00 | 55.00 | 55.00 | | | | ******** | ******** |
| | 35.45 | 35.45 | 35.90 | 35.90 | | | | ******** | ******** |
| | 3444 | 3460 | 3466 | 3473 | | | | ******** | ******** |

```
⑭    ∇REPORT1
[1]   USE ('SALES') DATED 1 71 THRU 12 71
[2]   USE 'EMPLOYEES'
[3]   USE (COL 1) TIMES 'PRICE'
[4]   USE (COL 1) TIMES 'COST'
[5]   USE (COL 3) MINUS (COL 4)
[6]   TITLE '    SALES    HD-CNT   REVENUE   EXPENSE    PROFIT'
[7]   DECIMALS 0
[8]   TABLE ABOVE ∇

      REPORT1

               SALES   HD-CNT   REVENUE   EXPENSE   PROFIT
JAN 1971       20640    3618    1443768   769872    673896
FEB 1971       20850    3645    1458457   777705    680752
MAR 1971       20850    3652    1458457   777705    680752
APR 1971       21090    3661    1475245   786657    688588
MAY 1971       21160    3671    1480142   789268    690874
JUN 1971       21480    3686    1502526   849534    652992
JUL 1971       21480    3691    1502526   849534    652992
AUG 1971       21160    3697    1480142   836878    643264
SEP 1971       21090    3700    1475245   834109    641136
OCT 1971       20850    3710    1458457   824617    633840
NOV 1971       20850    3714    1458457   824617    633840
DEC 1971       20640    3727    1443768   816312    627456
A*AIMS    3/14/72
```

AAIMS has such analytical capabilities as graphing, regression, correlation, and so on. A full listing of the available operators is presented in Fig. 56.

## D.  AAIMS and APL

AAIMS is implemented in APL. That is, user commands in AAIMS are actually functions written in APL. The first word of each command identifies the function, and succeeding words serve as function arguments. Instead of using symbols as APL does, AAIMS presents itself to the user as a limited vocabulary of nouns, which refer to data and verbs and adverbs that specify the operations to be performed on the data. The central notion is that APL has great potential for easy manipulation and report generation with certain types of data, but that it is not palatable to non-programmers (or to many programmers, for that matter). The AAIMS command language was developed in order to permit the use of APL capabilities by nonprogrammers who could not or would not learn APL (as a matter of taste, training, or ability).

In effect, AAIMS is a disguised subset of APL. The goal in developing AAIMS was to provide a broad set of operators that could satisfy certain typical requirements of report generation and data manipulation. The advantage of AAIMS is that it greatly facilitates the generation of many typical reports. It does so by fully exploiting the ability of APL to handle vectors in performing such operations as the termwise multiplication of two series. AAIMS supplements the capabilities inherent in APL by keeping track of details, such as the starting time and periodicity of series, the proper alignment of series in reports, the generation of monthly headings, and so on.

A clear limitation of a set of subroutines such as AAIMS is its finiteness. A user who wants to do something for which AAIMS subroutines do not suffice will be forced to use APL or to ask someone else for help. Equally clear is the fact that the AAIMS functions were designed to span most of the typical requirements of data analysis and report generation. Unsophisticated users rarely want to do fancy things and certainly appreciate the simplicity of the AAIMS commands. On the other hand, programmers and information analysts often employ a mix of AAIMS and APL. They prefer to use AAIMS wherever possible because it allows them to obtain reports with very little programming. Where AAIMS does not suffice, they specify the desired processing in APL.

## III.  THE DEVELOPMENT AND USE OF AAIMS

### A.  Development

The development of AAIMS has been described in the papers cited earlier. Most of this section is based on those papers.

In the spring of 1970, under the direction of Joe D. Kingsley, Director of Systems Planning, Richard Klaas of the Corporate Planning Department and Charles Weiss of the Operations Research Department began work on an econometric modeling system to be used by the Corporate Planning Department. Since the model was to be used for forecasting and for reporting forecasting results, it was given a time series orientation. This was the major design decision.

Both operational and analytical requirements evolved. There were three operational requirements. The system had to be (1) easy to use, with the command

*FIGURE 56    AAIMS Commands*

| Analysis | Activate | Expression |
|---|---|---|
| | )LOAD <library number> AAIMS | |
| Display a series | | DISPLAY series |
| Display a series from a date thru most current | | DISPLAY series FROM date |
| Display a series for an interval. | | DISPLAY series FROM date THRU date |
| Determine value at a certain date | | series AT date |
| Determine periodicity, start and end dates, maximum and minimum values of a series | | RANGE series |
| Input a data series (temporary) | | series ← TEMPINPUT |

CALCULATIONS                                          Single Expressions
```
     Multiply a series by a series                      series TIMES series
     Multiply a series by a constant                    constant TIMES series
     Divide a series by a series                        series DIVIDED BY series
     Divide a constant by a series                      constant DIVIDED BY series
     Add a series to a series                           series PLUS series
     Add a constant to a series                         constant PLUS series
     Subtract a series from a series                    series MINUS series
     Subtract a series from a constant                  constant MINUS series
     Year-over-year ratios                              YEARLY RATIO series
     Period-over-preceding period ratios                PERIODIC  RATIO series
     Year-over-52 weeks prior ratios--daily, weekly     SPECIAL RATIO series
     Year-to-year changes (differences)                 YEARLY CHANGE series
     Period-to-preceding period changes (differences)   PERIODIC CHANGE series
     Year-to-52 weeks prior changes--daily, weekly      SPECIAL CHANGE series
     Calculate an 'n' term centered moving average      n MOVAVG series
     Calculate an average by exponential smoothing      α EXSMOOTH series
     Calculate centered moving annual totals            CENTERED   MOVTOTAL series
     Calculate year ending totals                       YEAREND MOVTOTAL series
     Calculate cumulative values to date                CUMULATIVE series
     Convert a series to natural logarithms             LN series
     Convert a logarithm series to a decimal series     ANTILN series
     Disregard positive or negative signs               ABSOLUTE series
     Indicate a series leading 'n' periods              n LEAD series
     Indicate a series lagging 'n' periods              n LAG series
     Generate series representing 'time'                TIME series
     Combine forecasts and actuals into one series      forecast series WITH series
     Convert a monthly flow series to quarterly         QUARTERLY series
     Convert a monthly balance series to quarterly      QUARTERLY AVERAGE series
     Convert a monthly (quarterly) flow series to yearly    YEARLY series
     Convert a monthly (quarterly) balance series to yearly YEARLY AVERAGE series
```

REPORTS
```
     Help for designing a display                       DISPLAY LAYOUT
     Help for designing a table                         TABLE LAYOUT
     Refer to previously computed series in LAYOUT      (COL n)
                                        Multiple Expressions
     Display multiple series (line format)              DISPLAY series AND series AND series
     Table multiple series (column format)              TABLE series AND series AND series
     Specify the dates for a report                     DISPLAY(series)AND(series)AND(series)DATED date THRU date
     Establish report titles for 'n' series             TITLE n
     Specify 'n' decimal places                         DECIMALS n
     Specify decimal places for each series             DECIMALS n1 n2 n3 ...
```

PLOTS
```
                                        )COPY <library number> PLOT
     Help for designing plot                            PLOT LAYOUT
     Plot series or multiple series over time           PLOT series AND series AND series
     Plot scatter diagram                               PLOT series VS series
```

STATISTICS
```
                                        )COPY <library number> STATISTICS
     Calculate simple correlation matrix                CORRELATE series AND series AND series
     Calculate mean, variance, range, etc.              DESCRIBE series
     Calculate single or multiple regression            dependent REGRESSION series AND series
     Estimate (forecast) from regression results        series ← ESTIMATED series AND series
```

DATAMGMT
```
                                        )LOAD <library number> DATAMGMT
     Input a new series into the Data Base              INPUT 'data file name'
     Update an existing series                          UPDATE 'data file name'
     Correct an erroneous value                         CORRECT 'data file name'
     Insert or delete values in a series                ALTER 'data file name'
     List portion of items in Data Base Index           INDEX item number THRU item number
     Rename a series                                    'old data file name' RENAME 'new data file name'
     Remove the series just entered                     CANCEL 'data file name'
     Determine number of series in Data Base            SIZE
     Find where in Index a series is located            FIND 'data file name'
```

COMMAND DEFINITION
```
                                        )CLEAR
     Begin definition                               ∇ name
     Specify first column (line)                [1] USE (single expression) DATED date THRU date
     Specify subsequent columns (lines)         [x] USE ...
     Specify report title                       [y] TITLE ' title goes here '
     Specify output format                      [z] TABLE ABOVE
     End definition                             [ ] ∇
     Save the Command Definition    )SAVE <workspace name>
```

structure minimizing computer terminology and maximizing business terminology; (2) interactive, with prompting if needed, but able to accept commands directly; and (3) capable of routine as well as ad hoc use.

The analytical requirements stated that the system should include trend analysis (moving averages and period-over-period ratios), statistical analysis (correlation, regression, descriptive statistics), and graphic analysis (time series plots and scatter plots). An additional requirement was that the analytical capabilities be extendable just as the database would be.

Guided by these requirements, analysis and programming began. The first routines developed were the output functions that formatted data, functions that calculated moving averages and period-to-period ratios, and functions that provided database establishment and maintenance. Within the first month of development, AAIMS was capable of performing many of the tasks frequently done on an electronic calculator. From that point on, new functions were written and old ones revised, both to perform the tasks for which AAIMS was being used and to satisfy the original requirements.

According to Joe Kingsley, Director of Systems Planning, valuable results were being produced in less than one month. In addition, the system's ability to adapt quickly to new needs and its reliable production of daily reports improved its reputation. As new projects made new demands on the system, Klaas and Weiss were often able to develop new functions that satisfied those demands.

As Klaas (1972) points out, the analysis and programming of AAIMS were done simultaneously from the start. Also, no one had written a complete set of design specifications. This strictly incremental approach is contrary to the way most transaction-oriented systems are developed. However, it worked well for this data retrieval system, which was being developed for a small number of initial users, who began receiving benefits almost immediately.

Klaas reports that the impact of APL on AAIMS must not be underrated. AAIMS could not have been developed easily in any other language. APL's facilities for handling vectors is the basis for all the manipulative and analytic capabilities of AAIMS. Furthermore, APL contributed to the economics of the development process. Since the AAIMS functions were being implemented in a higher-level language, programming was expedited greatly. Furthermore, the interactive nature of APL allowed new functions to be tested and debugged immediately.

## B. First Major Use

Although AAIMS had been useful for clerical and analytical work in the Corporate Planning Department, it did not receive recognition among higher management until it was used for the analysis of a proposed merger. In the preparation of arguments for that merger, AAIMS was used in producing a handbook of historical information and forecasts. This handbook was used by the American Airlines lawyers and the Civil Aeronautics Board.

The data in the handbook was necessarily of a public nature. Most of it was financial and operating statistics from the annual reports for the previous 10 years. (The CAB Form 41 data was not part of AAIMS at that time.) The information that was developed included more than 100 tables and ratios concerning American Airlines by itself, the potential partner by itself, the proposed merged entity, and other major airlines. Since the potential partner had few routes overlapping those of

American, complicated calculations of estimates of route shrinkage, etc., were not necessary.

The vice president of Corporate Planning played a major role in developing the initial portfolio. Later, additional numbers were produced by the Corporate Planning staff in response to requests from a member of the team in Washington. These reports were produced in New York and sent to Washington by the next morning. Near the end of the negotiations, a corporate planning analyst was sent to Washington along with a terminal in order to produce reports immediately. At one point, the chairman of the Board and several other top managers spent several hours in a session around a computer terminal. They started with a general idea of what they wanted to say but no specific way of saying it. By experimenting with various displays and ratios, they found new and interesting avenues they could pursue in developing their arguments.

Today top managers are not as involved in the use of AAIMS as they were at that time. The vice president of Corporate Planning, who was active in the merger analysis, has taken another assignment. His successor did not learn to use AAIMS directly but was an enthusiastic proponent of AAIMS. He saw it not as a tool for himself but, rather, as a tool for his department's analysts that would help them do their work in an efficient manner.

## C.  Ongoing Use

For several years, the Corporate Planning Department was one of the main users of AAIMS. In addition to using AAIMS in developing one-year and five-year plans, its managers and analysts used AAIMS in producing ad hoc reports for many types of special analysis. According to Joe Kingsley, the throughput of the department increased 50 percent over the course of three years of AAIMS usage in spite of a reduction in staff from 30 to 17. Formerly the department had six clerks whose main job was posting data from computer printouts. Typical of the reports they worked on were month-over-month comparisons, load factor calculations, and so on. In 1973, the department had few managers and analysts and no clerks. The needed data was loaded into AAIMS from magnetic tapes; the reports were generated by means of AAIMS.

Currently AAIMS is used to varying extents in a number of departments of American Airlines. This usage can be broken down into standard reports and ad hoc reports. The ad hoc reports follow no particular pattern other than that they tend to be the work of the more sophisticated and quantitatively oriented users of AAIMS. The standard reports are usually programmed for the users by people in the Information Science Department. These reports often replace and improve on previously clerical efforts in the areas of budgeting, cost control, operations analysis, and financial analysis. Some of the standard reports use the AAIMS database; the data for other reports comes from private user databases.

Four examples of AAIMS applications follow.

### 1.  Budget Consolidation

A budget consolidation for one department was programmed in a combination of AAIMS and APL. The combination was necessary because AAIMS could not produce reports in the format that was desired for this budgeting application. The reports were monthly budgets of 57 items for 55 cities. Formerly all consolidations and resulting reports were done by hand (with calculators). Doing these consolidations automatically has resulted in an important saving in clerical time and effort. Much of this type of work has been performed by people whose title is "analyst." This type of AAIMS application frees them from the strictly clerical aspect of their jobs and allows them to do more analysis.

### 2. Revenue Yield Analysis

One of the standard ways of analyzing recent revenue performance is to break down all changes by source. Volume changes can be due to changes in a number of factors, such as industry volume, market share, average length per haul, and so on. For a given volume level, the revenue can be affected by such factors as the distribution of traffic between first class and coach.

AAIMS was used for programming a standard form of revenue yield analysis. By exploiting AAIMS capabilities to report comparisons of actual vs. budgeted, actual vs. a year ago, and actual vs. the preceding period, it was possible to expedite a highly iterative effort that was required in developing a series of formulas and analysis procedures that were not well understood in advance. Because it was possible to change the program very easily, it was relatively painless to proceed by generating some initial variance reports, thinking about the usefulness and clarity of particular variances reported, and then improving the formulas and reporting schemes. When this application has become routine, it will probably be either converted to a batch system or reprogrammed in APL to reduce its operating costs.

### 3. Ad Hoc Reporting

A director of market planning in the Freight Department felt that AAIMS was extremely useful in satisfying his needs for ad hoc access to historical and current air freight market data concerning trade volume, capacities, and so on. Prior to the development of AAIMS, it seemed to take months to get the reports he needed, even if the raw data was readily available. With the AAIMS database and retrieval capabilities, he had come to expect one-day turnaround in obtaining the information he wanted. He himself never used AAIMS directly but, rather, directed a programmer to generate the reports needed.

The programmer stated that she used AAIMS only when the required data resided in an AAIMS database. Under other circumstances, she used APL because it took her less time to specify the reports she wanted.

This leads to several important points. The first is that the director of market planning didn't really care whether the AAIMS language or APL per se was used to generate his reports. His only concern was that he could get the information he wanted quickly and in a usable format. When he thought of AAIMS, he was thinking not of a programming language as such but, rather, of an overall capability to produce reports effectively. From the programmer's viewpoint, the AAIMS language was helpful only when the data was provided through an AAIMS database.

The programmer tended to develop two different types of reports. One type usually involved the manipulation and printing of monthly time series data. For these reports, AAIMS was especially useful in formatting the outputs. The other type of report usually involved a considerable amount of manipulation but printed only yearly breakdowns in small tables. For these reports, APL sufficed. Typically, these tables were retyped by a secretary before being sent to the person requesting the information.

### 4. Corporate Performance Indicators

Producing performance indicators was a temporary application that has been superseded. It is interesting because the personnel involved were nonprogrammers.

A monthly report of corporate performance indicators was produced for use by the president and other senior officers. This report consisted of approximately 100 graphs and tables that compared the performance of American Airlines with that of its major competitors. It contained a large number of ratios, moving averages, and so on, many of which were derived from the CAB Form 41 data in the AAIMS database.

The man in charge of this effort has the title Supervisor of Management Information Systems. He was a nonprogrammer whose main function over the years had been the noncomputerized reporting and analysis of various types of data. Although he had great difficulty learning to use a computer terminal, he persevered and learned to use AAIMS. (He later tried to learn APL but dropped out of a training class very quickly because he didn't understand what was happening.)

His secretary used AAIMS to obtain the monthly updates to the corporate performance indicators. She felt that AAIMS was essential for the generation of this information. Without it, she would have had to spend most of her time calculating ratios, moving averages, etc., by hand. Although she was still learning how to use some of the features of AAIMS, she knew enough to be able to generate the numbers she needed. The key to this kind of use of a data retrieval system is that the data must be available in the database and that the performance indicators must be defined in advance.

### D. The Diffusion Process

The further development and diffusion of AAIMS has been delegated to the AAIMS subgroup of the Information Science Department (which also contains Operations Research and Scientific Programming). The activities of this group include education, consulting, and programming. Their educational efforts are primarily directed to classes in the use of AAIMS and APL. Their consulting activities include aid in defining problems, in deciding whether AAIMS is appropriate, and in mastering the mechanics of using AAIMS. They also program applications of a repetitive nature. The manager of this group stated that they are not actively seeking new users at this time because they are quite busy helping people who have come to them on their own initiative.

The use of AAIMS is always voluntary. Thus, a soft sell technique can be employed to inform potential users of its capabilities. The main proponents of AAIMS feel that it has a lot to offer, and they want people throughout American Airlines to know it is available. Once potential users know that AAIMS exists, it is up to them to decide whether to pursue its potential benefits. If they do choose to use AAIMS, they will have to pay for the computer time they use.

Proponents of AAIMS mentioned several factors that tend to retard the diffusion of AAIMS across the company. The main factor is a combination of fear and a desire to do things as they have been done in the past. The manager of the AAIMS group felt that some people are more daring and others less so with regard to their use of terminals. Some people are willing to experiment, and others are "scared to death" of the thought of using a computer directly. These people are particularly unhappy when things go wrong and they are confronted with error diagnostics and the like.

As mentioned earlier, the supervisor in charge of performance indicator reporting had a difficult time learning to use a terminal and never managed to learn APL. After he had learned to use AAIMS and become convinced of its value, he recommended it to several of his friends in an operations analysis group. He added, however, that they "wouldn't get close to AAIMS," even though he offered to sit at a terminal with them to help them learn to use it.

Another factor retarding the diffusion of AAIMS is that some potential users would rather do things by hand than have a machine do them automatically. Typically, these people have been with the company 15 to 20 years and have been classified as analysts during much of that time. Many of these individuals honestly feel that they get a better intuitive grasp of what is going on when they do the calculations by hand.

## IV. PERSPECTIVES

### A. Users

AAIMS has been used directly by a wide range of individuals in American Airlines. By title, these people have included over the years a vice president, a number of directors and managers, many programmers and analysts, and several secretaries.

One of the proponents of AAIMS was especially proud of the fact that it is sufficiently helpful and easy to use for someone with the rank of vice president to have become proficient in its use. He felt that AAIMS was a powerful counterexample to what he viewed as the standard approach to executive use of computers, namely, avoidance. He pointed out that IBM had been sufficiently impressed with the use of AAIMS by executives to have mentioned AAIMS explicitly in one of its sales brochures entitled "A Personal Information Machine." The brochure said that AAIMS gives executives the ability to analyze data and design reports "relevant to their organization in almost any way they choose, with virtually no programming experience or training." It cited as an example a vice president who took a terminal home with him over the Easter holidays in order to study potential impacts of the recession that was then in force.

Although it is impressive that a vice president desired to use AAIMS directly on certain occasions, on balance it may be more important that AAIMS has been useful for ongoing work by people in lower organizational positions. The report of performance indicators mentioned earlier is a case in point. Here, an individual who could not understand APL was able to use AAIMS to produce needed reports. Later, his secretary was able to generate these reports while she was learning to use other features of AAIMS. If a large amount of genuinely important data is available online, this kind of retrieval capability could be of value in many business environments.

Taken on balance, however, both the use by the vice president and the use by the secretary were unusual. As its use has settled down, AAIMS has typically become a tool of programmers rather than nonprogrammers. Its effectiveness has generally taken the form of allowing programmers to be more efficient in the utilization of their own time.

## B. Strong Points and Limitations

Like any other data retrieval system, AAIMS has a number of strong points and a number of limitations. Whether such a system would be useful in any particular business environment would depend on the balance between the strong points and limitations *as they apply in that environment.*

The strong points of AAIMS include the following. Some apply only to this setting, but others are general.

1. AAIMS is simple to learn and use. Thus a wide range of people within a corporation can use it.

2. AAIMS can be used on various levels of sophistication. A person can obtain simple results with only a very basic knowledge. More sophisticated users can produce more complex results. People who know APL and AAIMS can intermix them, using APL for any parts of the computation or report generation that cannot be accomplished in AAIMS.

3. AAIMS is interactive. Thus users get immediate response. They can discover all syntax errors and most logic errors immediately. When they don't know exactly what they want, they can try various reports in an effort to discover interesting paths to pursue.

4. AAIMS makes good use of what the computer "knows." It uses these facts to align time series in reports, to print titles, to keep track of units, and so on. The user does not have to specify redundant information, and the results are easier programming and fewer errors.

5. AAIMS can be used for either ad hoc or routine standard reports.

6. AAIMS is embedded in APL. Thus it is possible to intermix AAIMS and APL commands whenever AAIMS does not suffice. In addition, it is possible to define new AAIMS commands by means of the APL function definition protocol.

7. The time series orientation of AAIMS is powerful for most business reporting. A great deal of business analysis requires series of numbers over time.

8. In American Airlines, a considerable amount of clerical effort went into generating reports and consolidations that are easily described and programmed. It was an environment in which a software package for data manipulation and report generation had many apparent uses.

9. A great deal of useful data was readily available. If the CAB Form 41 data had not been considered of value, AAIMS might not have had the impact it has had and might not have gained so much attention. Since this information was available, it was possible to do a considerable amount of analytic work without lengthy preliminary research concerning the development of systems for creating and maintaining the relevant data.

The limitations of AAIMS include the following. Again, some apply only to this setting, but others are general.

1. AAIMS is a finite set of APL functions. Although users can extend it by writing new functions, most of them won't do so.

2. AAIMS has a very strong time series orientation. If a user wants to do something that does not involve the manipulation of time series, AAIMS simply has no relevance.

3. The use of AAIMS for modeling applications is limited. In order to evaluate strategies, etc., it is often necessary to use formal models. Thus AAIMS is relevant only if the crux of the problem is the manipulation of existing raw data and simple report generation. AAIMS can answer "what if" questions of the form "How will the bottom line look if I replace this series of numbers with some other series of numbers in a consolidation?" It cannot answer "what if" questions of the form "What if I change these parameters of this model?" or "What if the underlying structural model or assumptions change?"

4. Report formatting in AAIMS is relatively limited. All reports in AAIMS must contain time as one dimension. There is no way to use asterisks or other symbols to flag exceptions on budget and cost control reports. Reports with subtotals require some APL. Since many potential users want to continue with the formats they have always used on their reports, it is often necessary to program reports in a combination of APL and AAIMS. Therefore, although AAIMS can be quite useful in expediting the programming of many reports, by itself it is not adequate for some kinds of reports.

5. A data retrieval and manipulation package is valuable only if a large amount of data is available. In many other settings (such as non-regulated industries), the development and maintenance of a large and genuinely valuable database would probably require a major systems-design effort.

6. AAIMS is expensive for cross-sectional rather than longitudinal reports. Reports concerning a given item in each of 20 time series are much more expensive (and more awkward to specify) than reports concerning 20 items in one time series.

7. The AAIMS functions occupy approximately half of a 48K APL "workspace." Therefore the annoying "workspace full" diagnostic appears more frequently in large jobs that combine AAIMS with APL.

8. AAIMS can reference only time series that exist in an AAIMS database and therefore have special header records.

9. As in APL, the question of what to do with missing values is important.

★    ★    ★

Can any company use AAIMS? As noted earlier, the usefulness of such a system in any particular business environment depends on the balance between its strong points and limitations as they apply in that environment. In American Airlines, a large and useful database of time series data was readily available. A great deal of effort went into the clerical preparation of reports concerning this data and other data. In such an environment, AAIMS has had an important impact. Had the standard database been less useful or relevant, AAIMS probably would not have achieved as much visibility as it has achieved to date, but it might still have been useful in expediting the programming of standard reports in APL.

In other regulated industries and in companies such as brokerage houses with high needs for data manipulation and report generation, AAIMS can also be quite valuable. In companies where a large and relevant time series database does not exist, AAIMS will not be so valuable.

### Questions for the Reader

1. Would a system similar to AAIMS have been useful in supporting decisions described in the other case studies? If so, describe the system and the data it would contain.

2. Comment on the following assertion: "AAIMS is more a programming language or report generator than it is a decision support system."

3. Compare AAIMS to the systems described in the other cases. Is AAIMS more structured or less structured than the other systems? Is a typical AAIMS application more structured or less structured than a typical application of the other systems?

4. Compare the implementation of AAIMS with the implementations of systems in the other case studies. Who was the client? Who was the user? What were the main stages in the implementation effort?

5. On the basis of the data provided, was AAIMS successful? What data would be needed to perform a careful study of its true impact?

# REFERENCES

Ackoff, R. L. "Management Misinformation Systems." *Management Science*, vol. 14, no. 4, pp. B147–156, Dec. 1967.

Allison, G. T. *The Essence of Decision*. Boston: Little, Brown, 1971.

Anthony, R. N. *Planning and Control Systems: A Framework for Analysis*. Cambridge, Mass.: Harvard University Graduate School of Business Administration, 1965.

Argyris, C. "Resistance to Rational Management Systems." *Innovation*, no. 10, pp. 28–34, Nov. 1970.

_____. "Management Information Systems: The Challenge to Rationality and Emotionality." *Management Science*, vol. 17, no. 6, pp. B275–292, 1971.

Bardach, E. *The Implementation Game: What Happens When a Bill Becomes Law*. Cambridge, Mass.: M.I.T., 1977.

Bariff, M. L., and E. J. Lusk. "Cognitive and Personality Tests for the Design of Management Information Systems." *Management Science*, vol. 23, no. 8, pp. 820–829, April 1977.

Bean, A. S., et al. "Structural and Behavioral Correlates of the Implementation of Formal OR/MS Projects: Success and Failure in U.S. Business Organizations." In R. Schultz and D. Slevin (eds.), *Implementing Operations Research/Management Science*, pp. 77–132. New York: American Elsevier, 1975.

Bennis, W., K. Benne, and R. Chin (eds.). *The Planning of Change*. New York: Holt, Rinehart, and Winston, 1969.

Boehm, B. "Software and Its Impact: A Quantitative Assessment." *Datamation*, pp. 48–59, May 1973.

Brooks, F. P. "The Mythical Man-Month." *Datamation*, pp. 44–52, Dec. 1974.

_____. *The Mythical Man-Month*. Reading, Mass.: Addison-Wesley, 1975.

Burlingame, J. "Information Technology and Decentralization." *Harvard Business Review*, vol. 39, no. 6, pp. 121–125, 1961.

Canning, R. "APL and Decision Support Systems." *EDP Analyzer*, vol. 14, no. 5, May 1976.

Cardenas, A. F. "Technology for Automatic Program Generation of Application Programs—A Pragmatic View." *MIS Quarterly*, pp. 49–72, Sept. 1977.

Carlisle, J. "Interaction between Conceptual Complexity and Environmental Complexity in Man-Computer Interactive Problem Solving." Unpublished Ph.D. dissertation, Yale University, 1974.

Carlson, E. D. "Evaluating the Impact of Information Systems." *Management Datamatics,* vol. 3, pp. 57–68, April 1974.

———— (ed.). "Proceedings of a Conference on Decision Support Systems." *Database,* vol. 8, no. 3, Winter 1977.

Carlson, E. D., et al. "The Design and Evaluation of an Interactive Geo-Data and Display System." In *Info Processing '74,* pp. 1057–1061. Amsterdam: North Holland, 1974.

Carter, N. "The Executive and the Terminal." *Proceedings, Seventh Annual Conference for the Society for Management Information Systems.* Management Information Systems Research Center, University of Minnesota, July 1976.

Chambers, J. "Total versus Modular Information Systems: Empirical Experience in Finance and Personnel." In R. Smith (ed.), *Management Information Systems in the 1970s.* Center for Business and Economic Research, Kent State University, 1970.

Chin, R., and K. Benne. "General Strategies for Effecting Changes in Human Systems." In W. Bennis, K. Benne, and R. Chin (eds.), *The Planning of Change,* pp. 32–59. New York: Holt, Rinehart, and Winston, 1969.

Churchman, C. W., and A. H. Schainblatt. "The Researcher and the Manager: A Dialectic of Implementation." *Management Science,* vol. 11, no. 4, pp. B69–87, Feb. 1965.

Date, C. J. *An Introduction to Database Systems.* Reading, Mass.: Addison-Wesley, 1976.

Dearden, J. "Myth of Real Time Management Information." *Harvard Business Review,* pp. 123–131, May–June 1966.

Derthick, M. *New Towns In-Town: Why a Federal Program Failed.* Washington: Urban Institute, 1972.

Dickson, G., and J. Simmons. "The Behavioral Side of MIS." *Business Horizons,* pp. 59–71, Aug. 1970.

Doktor, R. H., and W. F. Hamilton. "Cognitive Style and the Acceptance of Management Science Recommendations." *Management Science,* vol. 19, no. 8, pp. 884–894, April 1973.

Downs, A. "A Realistic Look at the Final Payoffs from Urban Data Systems." *Public Administration Review,* vol. 27, pp. 204–209, Sept. 1967.

Drake, J. *The Administration of Transportation Modeling Projects.* Lexington, Mass.: D.C. Heath, 1973.

Driver, M. J., and T. J. Mock. "Human Information Processing, Decision Style Theory, and Accounting Information Systems." *The Accounting Review,* vol. 50, no. 3, July 1975.

Forrester, J. W. *Urban Dynamics.* Cambridge, Mass.: M.I.T. Press, 1969.

Garrity, J. "Top Management and Computer Profits." *Harvard Business Review,* vol. 41, no. 4, pp. 6–12, 1963.

ᵃGerrity, T. P., Jr. "The Design of Man-Machine Decision Systems." Ph.D. dissertation, M.I.T., 1970.

_____. "The Design of Man-Machine Decision Systems: An Application to Port-
folio Management." *Sloan Management Review*, vol. 12, no. 2, pp. 59–75,
Winter 1971.

Gibson, C. F., and R. L. Nolan. "Managing the Four Stages of EDP Growth."
*Harvard Business Review*, vol. 52, no. 1, pp. 76–88, Jan–Feb. 1974.

Gilman, L., and A. J. Rose. *APL/360—An Interactive Approach.* New York: Wiley,
1970.

Ginzberg, M. J. Unpublished Notes on Interviews of Portfolio Managers. Sloan
School of Management, M.I.T., 1973.

_____. "A Process Approach to Management Science Implementation." Ph.D. dis-
sertation, M.I.T., 1975.

_____. "A Study of the Implementation Process." Paper presented at Implementa-
tion II: An International Conference on the Implementation of Management
Science in Social Organizations, University of Pittsburgh, 1976.

Gorry, G. A., and M. S. Scott Morton. "A Framework for Management Information Systems." *Sloan Management Review*, vol. 13, no. 1, pp. 55–70, 1971.

Grayson, C. J. "Management Science and Business Practice." *Harvard Business
Review*, vol. 51, no. 4, pp. 41–48, July 1973.

Gregory, R., and R. Van Horn. *Automatic Data Processing Systems*, 2nd edition.
Belmont, Cal.: Wadsworth, 1963.

Hamilton, W. F., and M. A. Moses. "A Computer-Based Corporate Planning
System." *Management Science*, vol. 21, no. 2, pp. 148–159, Oct. 1974.

Hammond, J. S., III. "The Roles of the Manager and Management Scientists in Successful Implementation." *Sloan Management Review*, vol. 15, no. 2, pp. 1–24,
Winter 1974 (a).

_____. "Do's and Don't's of Computer Models for Planning." *Harvard Business
Review*, vol. 52, no. 2, pp. 110–125, 1974 (b).

Haseman, W. D., and A. B. Whinston. *Introduction to Data Management.* Home-
wood, Ill.: Irwin, 1977.

Heany, D. G. "Is TIMS Talking to Itself?" *Management Science*, vol. 12, no. 4,
pp. B146–155, Dec. 1965.

Hodges, D. A. "Microelectronic Memories." *Scientific American*, vol. 237, no. 3,
pp. 130–145, 1977.

Holten, W. C. "The Large Scale Integration of Microelectronic Circuits." *Scientific
American*, vol. 237, no. 3, pp. 82–99, 1977.

Huysmans, J. H. B. M. "The Effectiveness of the Cognitive Style Constraint in
Implementing Operations Research Proposals." *Management Science*, vol. 17,
no. 1, pp. 92–104, Sept. 1970.

Iverson, K. E. *A Programming Language.* New York: Wiley, 1962.

Johnson, J. "The Implementation of Computer Assisted Underwriting." *Interfaces*,
vol. 6, no. 2, pp. 2–13, Feb. 1976.

Keen, P. G. W. "Implementation: A Brief Position Paper." In P. G. W. Keen (ed.), *Proceedings of a Conference on the Implementation of Computer-Based Decision Aids.* Center for Information Systems Research, M.I.T., 1975 (a).

––––––. "Computer-Based Decision Aids: The Evaluation Problem." *Sloan Management Review,* vol. 16, no. 3, pp. 17–29, 1975 (b).

––––––. "Interactive Computer Systems for Managers: A Modest Proposal." *Sloan Management Review,* vol. 18, no. 1, pp. 1–17, Fall 1976.

Keen, P. G. W., and E. M. Gerson. "The Politics of Software Development." *Datamation,* vol. 23, no. 11, pp. 80–84, Nov. 1977.

* Keen, P. G. W., and M. S. Scott Morton. *Decision Support Systems: An Organizational Perspective.* Reading, Mass.: Addison-Wesley, 1978.

King, J. L., and E. L. Schrems. "Cost Benefit Analysis in Information Systems Development and Operation." *Computing Surveys,* vol. 10, no. 1, pp. 19–34, March 1978.

* Klaas, R. "AAIMS for Planning." Unpublished paper presented before the ORSA-TIMS-AIIE National Meeting, Atlantic City, N.J., Nov. 9, 1972..

––––––. "DSS for Airline Management." *Database,* vol. 8, no. 3, pp. 3–8, Winter 1977.

Kling, R. "The Organizational Context of User-Centered Software Designs." *MIS Quarterly,* pp. 41–52, Dec. 1977.

Knight, K. E. "Changes in Computer Performance." *Datamation,* pp. 40–54, Sept. 1966.

––––––. "Evolving Computer Performance 1963–1967." *Datamation,* pp. 31–35, Jan. 1968.

Kolb, D. A., and A. L. Frohman. "An Organization Development Approach to Consulting." *Sloan Management Review,* vol. 12, no. 1, pp. 51–65, Fall 1970.

Kroenke, D. *Database Processing.* Chicago: Science Research Associates, 1977.

Larreche, J. C. "Managers and Marketing Models: A Search for a Better Match." Ph.D. dissertation, Stanford Business School, 1974.

Laudon, K. *Computers and Bureaucratic Reform.* New York: Wiley, 1974.

Lavin, M. "Conclusions from the First Time Allocations Questionnaire." Unpublished Internal Memorandum of the M.I.T. Project on the Impact of Conversational Computer Systems, January 24, 1972.

Leavitt, H. J., and T. L. Whisler. "Management in the 1980's." *Harvard Business Review,* vol. 36, no. 6, pp. 41–48, 1958.

Lewin, K. "Group Decision and Social Change." In T. M. Newcomb and E. L. Hartley (eds.), *Readings in Social Psychology.* New York: Holt, 1952.

Licklider, J. C. R. "Man-Computer Symbiosis." *IRE Transactions on Human Factors in Electronics,* HFE 1, pp. 4–11, 1960.

Little, J. D. C. "Brandaid, an On-Line Marketing Mix Model, Part 2: Implementation, Calibration, and Case Study." *Operations Research.* vol. 23, no. 4, pp. 656–673, 1975.

Lorange, P., and V. Norman. "Portfolio Planning in Bulk Shipping Companies." In P. Lorange and V. Norman (eds.), *Shipping Management.* Bergen, Norway: Institute for Shipping Research, 1973.

Markowitz, H. M. *Portfolio Selection: Efficient Diversification of Investments.* New York: Wiley, 1959.

Martin, J. *Principles of Database Management.* Englewood Cliffs, N.J.: Prentice-Hall, 1976.

McKenney, J. L., and P. G. W. Keen. "How Managers' Minds Work." *Harvard Business Review,* vol. 52, no. 3, pp. 79–90, May–June 1974.

McNamar, R. "White Collar Enrichment: The Pay Board Experience." *Public Administration Review,* vol. 33, no. 6, pp. 563–568, Nov.–Dec. 1973.

Meadows, D. H. et al. *The Limits to Growth.* New York: Universe Books, 1972.

Mintzberg, H. "Managerial Work: Analysis from Observation." *Management Science,* vol. 18, no. 2, pp. B97–B110, 1971.

_____. *The Nature of Managerial Work.* New York: Harper and Row, 1973.

Montgomery, D. B. "The Outlook for MIS." *Journal of Advertising Research,* vol. 13, no. 3, pp. 5–11, 1973.

Montgomery, D. B., and G. L. Urban. "Marketing Decision Information Systems: An Emerging View." *Journal of Marketing Research,* vol. 7, pp. 226–234, 1970.

Myers, C. (ed.). *The Impact of Computers on Management.* Cambridge, Mass.: M.I.T. Press, 1967.

Ness, D. N., and C. Sprague. "An Interactive Media Decision Support System." *Sloan Management Review,* vol. 14, no. 1, pp. 51–61, Fall 1972.

_____. "Interactive Market Systems A, B, and C." Sloan School of Management, M.I.T., 1972.

Ness, D. N., C. Sprague, and G. A. Moulton. "On the Implementation of Sophisticated Interactive Systems." Sloan School of Management Working Paper 506–71, M.I.T., 1971.

Nolan, R. L. "Managing the Computer Resource: A Stage Hypothesis." *Communications of the ACM,* vol. 16, no. 7, pp. 399–405, July 1973.

Noyce, R. N. "Microelectronics." *Scientific American,* vol. 237, no. 3, pp. 62–69, 1977.

Parkinson, C. N. *Parkinson's Law.* Boston: Houghton Mifflin, 1957.

Powers, R. F., and G. W. Dickson. "MIS Project Management: Myths, Opinions, and Reality." *California Management Review,* vol. 15, no. 3, pp. 147–156, Spring 1973.

Pressman, J. L., and A. Wildavsky. *Implementation.* Berkeley: University of California Press, 1973.

Radnor, M., et al. "Integration and Utilization of Management Science Activities in Organizations." *Operational Research Quarterly,* vol. 19, no. 2, pp. 117–141, June 1968.

Radnor, M., et al. "Implementation in Operations Research and R & D in Government and Business Organization." *Operations Research,* vol. 18, no. 6, pp. 967–991, Nov.–Dec. 1970.

Reisman, A., and C. de Kluyver. "Strategies for Implementing Systems Studies." In R. Schultz and D. Slevin (eds.), *Implementing Operations Research/Management Science,* pp. 291–309. New York: American Elsevier, 1975.

Roberts, E. B. "Strategies for Effective Implementation of Complex Corporate Models." *Interfaces,* vol. 8, no. 1, part 1, pp. 26–33, Nov. 1977.

Rubenstein, A. H., et al. "Some Organizational Factors Relating to the Effectiveness of Management Science Groups in Industry." *Management Science,* vol. 13, no. 8, pp. B508–518, 1967.

Schein, E. H. "Management Development as a Process of Influence." *Industrial Management Review,* vol. 2, no. 2, pp. 59–77, Spring 1961.

Schultz, R., and D. Slevin (eds.). *Implementing Operations Research/Management Science.* New York: American Elsevier, 1975.

Scott Morton, M. S. "Interactive Visual Display Systems and Management Problem Solving." *Industrial Management Review,* pp. 69–81, Fall 1967.

_____. *Management Decision Systems: Support for Decision Making.* Cambridge, Mass.: Harvard University Graduate School of Business Administration, 1971.

_____. "Decision Support Systems—The Design Process." Sloan School of Management Working Paper 686–73, M.I.T., 1973.

Sharpe, W. F. *Portfolio Theory and Capital Markets.* New York: McGraw-Hill, 1970.

Simon, H. A. *The New Science of Management Decision.* New York: Harper and Row, 1960.

Solomon, M. B. "Economies of Scale and the IBM/360." *Communications of the ACM,* vol. 9, no. 6, pp. 435–440, June 1966.

Sonquist, J., and J. Morgan. *The Detection of Interaction Effects.* Monograph 35, Survey Research Center, Institute for Social Research, University of Michigan, 1964.

Sprague, R. *Information Utilities.* Englewood Cliffs, N.J.: Prentice-Hall, 1969.

Sprowls, R. C. *Management Data Bases.* Santa Barbara, Cal.: Wiley Hamilton, 1976.

Stabell, C. B. "Individual Differences in Managerial Decision Making Processes: A Study of Conversational Computer Usage." Ph.D. dissertation, M.I.T., 1974.

Stewart, R. *How Computers Affect Management.* Cambridge, Mass.: M.I.T. Press, 1971.

Taplin, J. "AAIMS: American Airlines Answers the What Ifs." *Infosystems,* pp. 40–41, Feb. 1973.

Terman, L. M. "The Role of Microelectronics in Data Processing." *Scientific American,* vol. 237, no. 3, 1977.

Tsichritizis, D. C., and F. H. Lochovsky. *Data Base Management Systems.* New York: Academic Press, 1977.

Turn, R. *Computers in the 1980's.* New York: Columbia Univ. Press, 1974.

Urban, G. L., and R. Karash. "Evolutionary Model Building." *Journal of Marketing Research,* vol. 8, pp. 62–66, 1971.

Wagner, H. M. "The ABC's of OR." *Operations Research,* vol. 19, no. 6, pp. 1259–1281, Oct. 1971.

Wiederhold, G. *Database Design.* New York: McGraw-Hill, 1977.

Withington, F. G. "Future Computer Technology." *Data Base,* vol. 7, no. 4, pp. 7–14, Spring 1976.

Wolverton, R. W. "The Cost of Developing Large-Scale Software." *IEEE Transactions on Computers*, vol. C–23, no. 6, pp. 615–636, June 1974.

Zand, D. E., and R. E. Sorenson. "Theory of Change and the Effective Use of Management Science." *Administrative Science Quarterly*, vol. 20, no. 4, pp. 532–545, Dec. 1975.

# INDEX